The New Famines

The recent famines in Ethiopia, Southern Africa and Niger have propelled the issue of famine back into the public arena for the first time since 1984. Once again, famine is becoming a priority not only for developing countries but also for the international community.

The New Famines explores the paradox of the persistence of famine in the contemporary world, by examining the changing nature of famine in the face of globalization and shifting geo-political forces and alliances. This book provides fresh conceptual frameworks and analytical tools for understanding contemporary famines, through the introduction of new concepts such as 'hidden famines', 'new variant famines' and 'post-modern famines'.

Individual contributions carefully examine a range of recent famines including those in Ethiopia, Sudan, Malawi, Madagascar, Iraq and North Korea, as well as food crises which have been averted in Bosnia and India, while also actively engaging with the most relevant theories. Major theoretical frameworks which have previously been applied to analyse famines, such as the 'democracy ends famine' argument, Sen's 'entitlement approach' and the 'complex political emergency' framework, are empirically challenged. This volume also examines the politics of famine response and famine relief as part of a global humanitarian system, in which famines compete for resources, as well as exploring new developments in famine prevention.

Stephen Devereux is a Fellow at the Institute of Development Studies.

Routledge studies in development economics

The New Famines

Why famines persist in an era of globalization

Edited by Stephen Devereux

Routledge
Taylor & Francis Group

LONDON AND NEW YORK

First published 2007
by Routledge
2 Park Square, Milton Park, Abingdon, Oxon OX14 4RN

Simultaneously published in the USA and Canada
by Routledge
270 Madison Ave, New York, NY 10016

Routledge is an imprint of the Taylor & Francis Group, an informa business

© 2007 selection and editorial matter, Stephen Devereux; individual
chapters, the contributors

Typeset in Baskerville by Wearset Ltd, Boldon, Tyne and Wear
Printed and bound in Great Britain by TJI Digital, Padstow, Cornwall

British Library Cataloguing in Publication Data
A catalogue record for this book is available from the British Library

Library of Congress Cataloging in Publication Data
A catalog record for this book has been requested

ISBN10: 0-415-36347-0 (hbk)
ISBN10: 0-203-01442-1 (ebk)

ISBN13: 978-0-415-36347-1 (hbk)
ISBN13: 978-0-203-01442-4 (ebk)

Contents

Figures

Tables

Boxes

Contributors

Dan Banik is Associate Professor at the Centre for Development and the Environment, University of Oslo, where he teaches graduate courses on poverty and development. In his doctoral work, he studied the role of democracy and public action in preventing starvation deaths in drought-prone districts of India. Dan has recently edited a textbook for graduate students, *Poverty, Politics and Development: interdisciplinary perspectives* (Fagbokforlaget, 2006) and is the author of *Starvation and India's Democracy* (Routledge, forthcoming 2007).

Luka Biong Deng is currently a Chief Economic Advisor to the Government of Southern Sudan and a Senior Economist with the World Bank in Southern Sudan. His PhD research at IDS, University of Sussex focused on dynamics of vulnerability and poverty during civil war. As a visiting fellow at IDS, he wrote a discussion paper titled 'Famine in Sudan: causes, preparedness and response'. He has published articles on conflict, poverty, famine, peace and constitution in various journals including the *IDS Bulletin, Oxford Journal on Forced Migration* and *Journal of Civil Wars*. His previous experience includes peace negotiations, civil wars, constitution, poverty and complex political emergencies.

Stephen Devereux is a Fellow in the Vulnerability and Poverty Reduction Team at the Institute of Development Studies, Sussex. He is the author of *Theories of Famine* (Harvester Wheatsheaf, 1993) and co-editor with Simon Maxwell of *Food Security in Africa* (ITDG, 2001). Following the food crisis in Malawi in 2002/03 he was appointed Specialist Advisor to the UK's House of Commons International Development Committee for its *Inquiry into the Humanitarian Crisis in Southern Africa*. More recently, he has led large research studies on vulnerability and food insecurity in highland Ethiopia, pastoralist Ethiopia and rural Malawi.

Jenny Edkins is Professor of International Politics at the University of Wales Aberystwyth, where she teaches on famine and genocide, postcolonial politics and poststructuralism. She is author of *Trauma and the Memory of Politics* (Cambridge University Press, 2003), *Whose Hunger?*

Concepts and Famine, Practices of Aid (Minnesota University Press, 2000) and *Poststructuralism and International Relations: bringing the political back in* (Lynne Rienner, 1999) and editor, with Véronique Pin-Fat and Michael J. Shapiro, of *Sovereign Lies: power in global politics* (Routledge, 2004) and with Nalini Persram and Véronique Pin-Fat of *Sovereignty and Subjectivity* (Lynne Rienner, 1999).

Michel Garenne has a PhD in demography (University of Pennsylvania, USA). For about ten years, he directed a series of field research on health and nutrition in Niakhar, Senegal. He taught demography at the Harvard School of Public Health for five years. Since 1994, he has been based in Paris and directs research projects on various demographic and public health issues in Africa, with focus on political and economic crises, demographic trends, new health challenges, and emerging diseases, e.g. HIV/AIDS. He serves as a scientific advisor for the Agincourt field site in South Africa.

Haris Gazdar is a director of the Collective for Social Science Research, Karachi. His work on Iraq was done as part of humanitarian fact-finding missions to the country in 1991 and 1996. He trained as an economist at the London School of Economics, and works on poverty, social policy, political economy, migration, conflict and urban governance. He has taught economics at Sussex University, worked as an associate at the Asia Research Centre of the London School Economics, and has been a visiting fellow at the United Nations Institute for Disarmament Research in Geneva and the Delhi School of Economics.

Paul Howe is a Policy Advisor for the United Nations World Food Programme. Among other responsibilities, he was the lead author and team leader for the inaugural edition of the *World Hunger Series*, WFP's flagship publication. He has previously worked with other humanitarian agencies and conducted field research on famine in southern Sudan. He holds a doctorate from the Institute of Development Studies at the University of Sussex.

Sue Lautze is the owner/director of The Livelihoods Program, a disaster management consulting business. A Fulbright Scholar, she is also pursuing a DPhil in Development Studies at Oxford University and is studying the livelihoods systems of Ugandan army soldiers and their families in northern Uganda. From 1997 to 2005, she was Director of the Livelihoods Initiatives Program at the Feinstein International Famine Centre at Tufts University. Prior to joining Tufts, Sue Lautze lived and worked in the People's Republic of China and Sudan for the UN World Food Programme and the United States Agency for International Development, respectively.

Daniel Maxwell is Associate Professor of International Nutrition at Tufts

University in Medford Massachusetts and Research Director of Food Security and Livelihoods in Complex Emergencies, at the Feinstein International Famine Center. Prior to joining the faculty at Tufts in July 2006, he was the Deputy Regional Director for CARE International in Eastern and Central Africa. His recent research has focused on food security, chronic vulnerability, famine, and humanitarian response in complex emergencies. He is the co-author, with Chris Barrett of Cornell University, of the recent book, *Food Aid After Fifty Years: Recasting its Role.*

Marcus Noland is a Senior Fellow at the Institute for International Economics. His book, *Avoiding the Apocalypse: The Future of the Two Koreas*, won the prestigious Ohira Memorial Prize. He is co-author, with Stephan Haggard, of the report, *Hunger and Human Rights: The Politics of Famine in North Korea*, which has been published in both English and Korean. Another book he has written is, *Famine in North Korea: Markets, Aid, and Reform*, which is also co-authored with Stephan Haggard and with a preface by Nobel laureate Amartya Sen, is forthcoming from Columbia University Press in English and from Maekyung Publishing in Korean.

Ian Scoones is a Professorial Fellow with the Knowledge, Technology and Society Team at the Institute of Development Studies, Sussex. He is an agricultural ecologist by training and has worked particularly on institutional and policy issues surrounding agriculture, food security and livelihoods, particularly in Africa. He coordinates the Future Agricultures Consortium (www.future-agricultures.org) which aims to generate policy dialogue on agricultural change through work in east and southern Africa. His recent books include *Science and Citizens: Globalisation and the Challenge of Engagement* (Zed, 2005); and *Science, Agriculture and the Politics of Policy: The Case of Biotechnology in India* (Orient Longman, 2006).

Zoltan Tiba recently finished his PhD in Economics at the School of Oriental and African Studies in London. His research focused on the causes and consequences of the Malawi famine of 2002 and analysed the impact of the emergency food aid programme in a remote village in Southern Malawi. Previously he was a research fellow at the Institute for World Economics of the Hungarian Academy of Sciences. He currently works for the UN World Food Programme in Rome.

Alex de Waal is a Fellow of the Global Equity Initiative at Harvard and Program Director at the Social Science Research Council. Since receiving his DPhil from Oxford University, Alex has written several books on famine, human rights, conflict and the HIV/AIDS epidemic in Africa, including *Famine Crimes: Politics and the Disaster Relief Industry in Africa* (James Currey, 1997) and *AIDS and Power: Why There is No Political Crisis*

– *Yet* (Zed Books, 2006). He served as Associate Director of Africa Watch from 1990–1992; was a founder and director of African Rights and Chairman of Mines Advisory Group 1993–1998, and is a director of Justice Africa.

Fiona Watson is an international public nutritionist who has worked extensively in food crises. Her initial experience was in Africa including a two-year period from 1990–1992, working in Mozambique during the latter part of the war. Since then, she has largely been employed as a consultant and worked with UN, NGO, Red Cross and government agencies in Africa, the Middle East and Eastern Europe. Fiona's field experience has frequently been in war situations including Bosnia and Kosovo, the Gaza Strip, Liberia and Sierra Leone. Fiona is a partner in NutritionWorks, an international public nutrition resource group.

Acknowledgements

This book originated in a conference titled 'Ending Famine in the 21st Century', and a workshop titled 'Operational Definitions of Famine', both held at the Institute of Development Studies (IDS) at the University of Sussex. Some chapters are expanded versions of papers presented at the conference, which were published in an IDS Bulletin titled 'The 'New Famines'' in October 2002. Conference and workshop participants who contributed to the thinking reflected in this book include: Edward Clay, Carlo del Ninno, Tim Dyson, Mike Fitz, Alyson Froud, Paul Harvey, Sharon Harvey, Julius Holt, Robin Jackson, Noriatsu Matsui, Nick Maunder, Marie McGrath, Celestine Nyamu-Musembi, Cormac Ó Gráda, Kay Sharp, Jonathan Steele, Jeremy Swift, Maloes van der Sande, Tony Vaux, William Whelan and Girum Zeleke.

Paul Howe and Luka Deng, both DPhil students at IDS at the time, conceptualized the 'Ending Famine in the 21st Century' project with me and contributed to planning the conference and workshop. Milasoa Cherel-Robson, Wing Lam and Colette Solomon provided expert comments on specific chapters, and Colette Solomon copy-edited several drafts. I am especially indebted to Jenny Edwards, who has provided invaluable inputs to this project from start to finish, from organizing the conference, to meticulous proof-reading and reference tracking, to compiling the book's index.

The publisher and editor are grateful to the following publishers for permission to reprint articles:

Devereux, S. (2001) 'Sen's Entitlement Approach: Critiques and counter-critiques', *Oxford Development Studies*, 29(3): 245–63. Reprinted with permission of Taylor & Francis Ltd.

Howe, P. and Devereux, S. (2004) 'Famine Intensity and Magnitude Scales: a proposal for an instrumental definition of famine', *Disasters*, 28(4): 353–72. Reprinted with permission of Blackwell Publishing.

Abbreviations

AAH	Action Against Hunger
AATF	African Agricultural Technology Foundation
ACC/SCN	Administrative Committee on Coordination/ Subcommittee on Nutrition of the United Nations
ADLI	Agricultural Development-Led Industrialization
ADMARC	Agricultural Development and Marketing Corporation
AFORD	Alliance for Democracy
ARNC	AIDS Related National Crisis
ART	Anti-Retroviral Treatment
ARV	Anti-Retroviral
BBC	British Broadcasting Corporation
BCSR	*Bureau de Commercialisation et de Stabilisation du Riz* (Madagascar)
BJP	Bharatiya Janata Party
BMI	Body Mass Index
BPL	Below Poverty Line
Bt	*Bacillus thuringensis*
CAP	(UN) Consolidated Appeal Process
CASI	Campaign Against Sanctions on Iraq
CCJP	Catholic Commission for Justice and Peace
CED	Chronic Energy Deficiency
CGIAR	Consultative Group on International Agricultural Research
CISANET	Civil Society Agriculture Network
CMDT	Compagnie Malienne des Textiles
CMR	Crude Mortality Rate
CNN	Cable News Network
CPE	Complex Political Emergency
CPIM	Communist Party of India, Marxist
DANIDA	Danish International Development Agency
DFID	Department for International Development (UK)
DHS	Demographic and Health Surveys
DMZ	Demilitarized Zone

DPAP	Drought-Prone Areas Programme
DPPC	Disaster Prevention and Preparedness Commission
DPRK	Democratic People's Republic of Korea
DRC	Democratic Republic of Congo
ECHO	European Commission for Humanitarian Aid
EDR	Effective Dependency Ratio
EFSN	European Food Security Network
EFSR	Emergency Food Security Reserve (Ethiopia)
EPRDF	Ethiopian People's Revolutionary Democratic Front
EWS	Early Warning System
FAD	Food Availability Decline
FANR	Food, Agriculture and Natural Resources
FAO	Food and Agriculture Organization
FAOSTAT	FAO Statistical Databases
FASAZ	Farming Systems Association of Zambia
FEWS NET	Famine Early Warning System Network
FSAU	Food Security Assessment Unit
FSRP	Fertilizer Subsidy Removal Programme
GAM	Global Acute Malnutrition
GDP	Gross Domestic Product
GIEWS	Global Information and Early Warning System
GM	Genetically Modified
GNP-PPP	Gross National Product expressed in Parity Purchasing Power
GoE	Government of Ethiopia
GoM	Government of Malawi
GTZ	*Deutsche Gesellschaft für Technische Zusammenarbeit*
HIPC	Heavily Indebted Poor Country
HIV/AIDS	Human Immunodeficiency Virus/Acquired Immune Deficiency Virus
HTF	Hunger Task Force
IAS	Indian Administrative Service
ICC	International Criminal Court
ICDS	Integrated Child Development Services
ICG	International Crisis Group
ICRC	International Committee of the Red Cross
ICTY	International Criminal Tribunal for the former Yugoslavia
IFPRI	International Food Policy Research Institute
IGWG	Intergovernmental Working Group (on the Right to Food)
IHS	Integrated Household Survey
IMF	International Monetary Fund
IRIN	Integrated Regional Information Networks
KINU	Korea Institute for National Unification

LSMS	Living Standards Measurement Survey
MAS	Marker Assisted Selection
MCP	Malawi Congress Party
MDGs	Millennium Development Goals
MEJN	Malawi Economic Justice Network
MGF	Malagasy Francs
MT	Metric Tonne
NAIDS	Nutritionally Acquired Immune Deficiency Syndrome
NATO	North Atlantic Treaty Organization
NCHS	National Centre for Health Statistics
NFRA	National Food Reserve Agency
NGOs	Non-Governmental Organizations
NSS	National Sample Survey
NVF	New Variant Famine
OCHA	(United Nations) Office for the Coordination of Humanitarian Affairs
OECD	Organization for Economic Co-operation and Development
OFDA	Office for Foreign Disaster Assistance
OFF	Oil-for-Food
OLS	Operation Lifeline Sudan
PDS	Public Distribution System
PRSP	Poverty Reduction Strategy Paper
PTMTC	Prevention of Mother to Child Transmission of AIDS
R & D	Research and Development
RDA	Recommended Daily Amount
RNIS	(United Nations) Refugee Nutrition Information System
RR	Risk Ratio
RRC	Relief and Rehabilitation Commission
SACA	Smallholder Agricultural Credit Association
SADC	Southern African Development Community
SAfAIDS	Southern Africa HIV and AIDS Information and Dissemination Service
SAHIMS	Southern Africa Humanitarian Information Network
SAP	Structural Adjustment Policies
SC	Scheduled Caste
SCF	Save the Children Fund
SG 2000	Sasakawa-Global 2000 Programme
SGR	Strategic Grain Reserve
SLF	Sustainable Livelihoods Framework
SME	Small and Medium-Sized Enterprise
SNNPR	Southern Nations, Nationalities and People's Region
SPLM	Sudanese People's Liberation Movement
SRRA	Sudanese Relief and Rehabilitation Association
ST	Scheduled Tribe

TB	Tuberculosis
TMS	Tropical Manioc Selection
TPLF	Tigrayan People's Liberation Front
U5MR	Under-Five Mortality Rate
UDF	United Democratic Front (Malawi)
UK	United Kingdom
UN	United Nations
UNAIDS	Joint United Nations Programme on HIV/AIDS
UNDP	United Nations Development Programme
UNHCR	United Nations High Commission for Refugees
UNHRC	United Nations Human Rights Commission
UNICEF	United Nations Children's Fund
UNSCN	United Nations Standing Committee on Nutrition
US	United States
USAID	United States Agency for International Development
USD	United States Dollars
VAC	Vulnerability Assessment Committee
WFP	World Food Programme
WHO	World Health Organization

1 Introduction

From 'old famines' to 'new famines'

Stephen Devereux

Introduction

This book explores the paradox of the persistence of famine in the contemporary world. In an era of global food surpluses, high-technology early warning systems and a sophisticated international humanitarian relief system, how is it possible that more than one million people have died in famines since the world declared 'never again' after Ethiopia 1984? Answering this question requires looking beyond technical factors, towards political explanations. In the past, attempts to understand famines focused on the causes and consequences of food production decline, or, more recently, disrupted access to food. Famines were conceptualized as a disruption of the food system, and analysed in terms of 'supply failure' or 'demand failure'. These technical explanations are often a large part of the story, but they are not enough. Contemporary famines are either caused deliberately (acts of commission) or they are not prevented when they could and should have been (acts of omission). Many recent famines are associated with catastrophic governance failures or collapses of the social order, such as conflict. Even when a livelihood shock such as drought triggers a food shortage, it is the failure of local, national and international response that allows the food shortage to evolve into a famine.

Contributions to this book challenge received wisdom about famine in several ways. First, contrary to popular perception that famines have receded into history, recent food crises in east Africa (Ethiopia, Sudan), southern Africa (Malawi) and west Africa (Niger) have propelled famine back into public consciousness, and famine prevention is once again of great concern to policymakers. This book provides comprehensive analyses of half a dozen major famines that have occurred since the mid-1980s, in Africa (Ethiopia, Madagascar, Malawi, Sudan) and Asia (Iraq, North Korea), as well as one averted famine in Europe (Bosnia).

Second, several contributors engage critically with established theoretical frameworks for famine analysis, including Sen's 'entitlement approach' (the dominant approach of the 1980s) and 'complex political emergencies' (the dominant approach explaining 'conflict famines' of the 1990s). The recent crisis in southern Africa occurred in countries that are neither at war nor dictatorships, but are peaceful democracies. Does this subvert the theory that 'democracy ends famine', does it point to failed democratic transitions, or does it support the argument by Banik (Chapter 13) that a disaggregated analysis of democracy is needed in each context?

Third, the case-study famines discussed in this book identify several contributory causes of the 'new famines' that were not factors in famines of the past. These include HIV/AIDS, flawed processes of political liberalization and economic reform, problematic government–donor relations, and international sanctions. Fourth, this book presents new conceptual frameworks and analytical tools for understanding contemporary famines. It introduces concepts like 'new variant famine', 'post-modern' famine, 'famine scales' and 'priority regimes'.

Finally, some contributors explore new thinking on famine prevention. Traditional 'solutions' were technical or technocratic – Green Revolution crops, population control, early warning systems – and these ideas persist, for instance in biotechnology debates, or the Government of Ethiopia's resettlement programme. Both these issues are also highly politicised (can GM crops be pro-poor? Is resettlement of farmers voluntary or coercive?), but current thinking is increasingly focused on the politics of famine prevention – building accountability through democratization, the development of 'social contracts' between governments and citizens, and strengthening the 'right to food' in international law, including the criminalization of famine.

This Introduction sets the context for the chapters that follow. It starts with an overview of 'old famine' trajectories and theories. This is followed by a review of the origins of 'new famine' thinking, beginning with first-generation theories that focused on failures of food supplies (exemplified by Malthusianism); identifying a paradigm shift in the 1980s, to failures of access to food (initiated by Sen's entitlement approach); and arguing for a new paradigm shift, to failures of accountability and response. Three implications of 'new famine' thinking are explored: reinterpretation of historical famines; responsibility for famine causation; and accountability for famine prevention. The evolution of famine thinking is seen as analogous to failures of production-based, market-based and transfer-based entitlements to food. Next, the fourteen contributed chapters to this book are introduced. This chapter concludes with a brief discussion about possible trajectories of future famines.

The 'old famines'

Trajectories of famine

Before the twentieth century, most famines were triggered by natural disasters – droughts, floods, extreme cold, locusts, crop blight, livestock disease – or by conflict, which destroyed the subsistence basis of agrarian communities, leaving them with insufficient food for survival. These triggers operated in contexts where local economies were weak (limited storage capacity, undiversified livelihoods, poor transport and communications, fragmented markets), and political will and capacity to intervene were lacking (no central government or international donors to provide food aid). Although pre-capitalist societies have been praised for their egalitarian ethos and mutual support systems, which buffered vulnerable community members through 'moral economy' redistributive mechanisms (Watts 1983), their limited resources left them unable to cope with the consequences of severe livelihood shocks, such that local harvest failures or devastating wars led inexorably to localised subsistence crises. Even today, the combination of 'poverty plus livelihood shocks' captures much of the structural vulnerability to famine that persists, especially in sub-Saharan Africa. Conversely, poverty reduction plus improved risk management – not least, publicly provided social protection – largely explains the eradication of famine from Europe and most of Asia. Even in Africa, however, the national and international contexts within which local livelihood shocks occur have changed to such an extent that explanations based on a simple linear progression from food shortage to famine are no longer sufficient, either empirically or theoretically.

In the early decades of the twentieth century, rapid developments in transport networks and communications infrastructure integrated rural communities into wider political economies, reducing their vulnerability to harvest failure (Iliffe 1987). In previously isolated areas such as northwest China, the eastern Soviet Union and rural India, the construction of railroads allowed food to be transported more efficiently between surplus and deficit regions, and enabled governments and private traders to respond more promptly to emerging food crises (Mallory 1926; Dando 1980).[1] In Africa, the development of railway and road networks was slower than in Europe and Asia, and instrumentally organized around the extraction of agricultural and mineral wealth. Even today, parts of highland Ethiopia and southern Sudan cannot be reached by motor vehicle, and 'remoteness' is recognized as contributing to the persistence of chronic poverty and food insecurity (Bird *et al.* 2002).

Despite the successes of infrastructure development in reducing 'environmental vulnerability' factors, 'political vulnerability' persisted in many countries of Asia, Europe and sub-Saharan Africa, as states acquired increasing power to implement destructive agricultural and economic policies. The Soviet famines of the 1920s to 1940s, China's 'Great Leap Forward' famine of 1958–1962, the Ethiopian famine of 1984 and North Korea's famine of the 1990s were largely attributable to the malevolent or incompetent exercise of state power by authoritarian and unaccountable regimes, which collectivized agriculture, extracted grain quotas from peasants, banned trade and were unresponsive to signals of food crisis. In cases such as Stalin's genocidal policies against the Ukraine in the 1930s, famine conditions were deliberately constructed by the state. The last famines in Europe (to date) occurred as recently as the Second World War, when sieges were applied against Leningrad, Warsaw and the Netherlands.

In both Africa and South Asia, the part played by the state in contributing to famine creation or prevention was complicated by the ambiguous role of colonial administrations. In some cases (e.g. Namibia and Tanzania), starvation was used to crush initial resistance to colonial rule. In India, the 'Famine Codes' were established by the British in the 1880s, after up to ten million Indians had died in a terrible famine in 1876–1879. The British saw famine prevention as helping to legitimize their rule, and this was the first institutionalized 'famine early warning system' (Drèze 1990). Nonetheless, another catastrophic famine in the 1890s claimed even more Indian lives (Davis 2001), and colonial India was to suffer a final famine in Bengal as late as 1943. All of these tragedies can be attributed, to varying extents, to the indifference or callousness of the colonial administration.

Since colonialism was associated with intensified exports of agricultural produce and mineral resources from Asia and Africa to global markets, this period also accelerated the integration of previously isolated communities into the global economy, which had mixed consequences for poverty and food security. Marxist writers of the 1970s argued that the penetration of capitalism into subsistence-oriented economies (the commodification of food and expansion of cash cropping) heightened the vulnerability of peasants to natural disasters and economic shocks. The 1970s Sahelian famine was blamed on the expansion of groundnut cultivation during the colonial period, as farmers in West Africa switched out of food production and encroached onto pastoralist grazing land (Meillassoux 1974; Franke and Chasin 1980). With hindsight, this increased vulnerability appears to have been transitional, and the economic benefits of incorporation into regional and global markets have generally outweighed the risks. On the other hand, contemporary processes of globalization are creating new sources of vulnerability (e.g. commodity price collapses) and the marginalization of certain regions from the global economy – with sub-Saharan Africa again being especially at risk.

After independence, historically famine-prone countries took one of two routes. Some, like India, continued to make progress in reducing famine vulnerability, partly by strengthening political accountability for famine prevention, partly through Green Revolution improvements in crop production. Following the British administration's failure to prevent the Bengal famine in 1943, the Government of India successfully prevented several potential famines, and although a major famine struck Bangladesh in 1974, soon after independence, later famine threats – in 1984, 1988 and 1998 – were successfully contained (del Ninno *et al.* 2002). There has been no major famine in south Asia since 1975, an outstanding achievement given the history of this region. On the other hand, malnutrition and hunger-related deaths remain unacceptably high in much of south Asia and Africa, even in countries where mass-mortality famines appear to have been consigned to history. As Iliffe (1987: 81) observed for sub-Saharan Africa, 'capitalist scarcity replaced pre-capitalist famine'.

In contrast to Asia's success in virtually eradicating 'famines that kill' during the twentieth century, in many African countries independence was associated with increased political instability and the emergence of famines where militarization, counter-insurgency and civil war played major roles. These countries saw a rise in political vulnerability and a radical shift in the nature of famine. After a lengthy period of low famine incidence between the 1920s and 1950s, military dictatorships replaced colonial administrations in much of Africa, conflicts over the post-colonial settlement developed, and a new era of war-triggered famines began, the first significant case being Biafra in the 1960s – a region of Nigeria which had not previously been vulnerable to famine, and has not been so since. During the 1980s and 1990s a number of African countries that were not historically famine-prone suffered conflict-triggered food crises (Angola, Mozambique, Liberia, Sierra Leone, Uganda), while others that had been susceptible to drought-triggered famines experienced 'complex emergencies' (Ethiopia, Somalia, Sudan) in which the roles of drought and insecurity were inextricably interconnected. This lethal combination of political instability, conflict and drought has contributed to the persistence of famine in the Horn of Africa to the present day.

Theories of famine

Theoretical explanations of famine tend to share two limitations: they focus on either a single trigger factor (e.g. drought, market failure or war) or a single underlying vulnerability factor (e.g. population growth or HIV/AIDS), and they reflect the disciplinary specialization of their advocates (e.g. geography, economics or politics).[2] The two best-known theories of famine are both single-factor explanations: Malthusianism and the 'entitlement approach'.

The most famous theory of famine was conceived over 200 years ago, by an English priest. In his *Essay on the Principle of Population* (1798; see 1976 edition), Thomas Malthus argued that human populations could not increase indefinitely in a world of limited natural resources – famine would eventually intervene to regulate population growth and balance the demand for food with food supplies. Malthusianism has been extremely influential, and is responsible for the environmental determinism that underpins contemporary resource scarcity debates, but as a theory of famine it has several limitations. Malthus developed his theory in England, before the Industrial Revolution moved most Europeans out of vulnerable agriculture into cities, before advances in transport and communications allowed food to be shipped around the world to meet deficits, and before scientific advances in agricultural research dramatically increased crop yields. Malthus also failed to foresee the demographic transition when populations stabilize at zero growth: the world's population is projected to stabilize during the twenty-first century, well within global food production capacity. Neo-Malthusianism does retain some relevance in explaining demographic vulnerability – high dependency ratios in poor households (exacerbated by HIV/AIDS), and population pressure in areas such as the Ethiopian highlands – but as one vulnerability factor, not as a theory of famine causation.

The most influential book about famine since Malthus is Amartya Sen's *Poverty and Famines* (1981), which introduced the concept of 'entitlement to food'. Sen pointed out that people can acquire food legally from several sources – production, trade, labour, gifts or transfers – and he demonstrated that famine is not primarily about food availability or harvest failures at the regional or national level, but about failures of access to food at the individual or household level. Paradoxically, farmers who produce food are often most vulnerable to famine, because their entitlement to food derives from a single source (production) which is dependent on unreliable rainfall. Sen also demonstrated that many famines have occurred with no aggregate decline in food availability, but because of 'exchange entitlement decline' faced by specific vulnerable groups. In Bangladesh in 1974, rapid food price inflation caused by expectations of harvest failure made food unaffordable for market-dependent landless labourers, because wealthy people and traders hoarded rice in anticipation of a shortage. The artificial scarcity that followed resulted in 1.5 million deaths – even though there was more food in the country than in the year before the famine. The entitlement approach explains famines that are caused by poverty and market failures very well, and it can accurately identify who is most at risk in such contexts. The approach is less able to explain famines that are triggered by government policies, war or failures of the international relief system, because it is essentially a theory about the economics of famine processes.

The multi-dimensional nature of famine has been recognized at least since Mallory's classic study, *China: Land of Famine* (1926), which included chapters on 'economic', 'natural', 'political' and 'social' causes of famine.[3] More recently, von Braun et al. (1998: 8) presented a flowchart that relates causal determinants in various domains, including institutional and policy failures, poverty and climate shocks, and population pressure. Nonetheless, even recent theories of famine – such as 'complex political emergencies' (conflict) and 'new variant famine' (HIV/AIDS) remain narrowly preoccupied with single causal factors. This raises the question of whether a phenomenon as complex as famine can adequately be explained by a single theoretical approach, or whether different analytical frameworks should be invoked to explain different famines, depending on the configuration of causal factors in each case.

The 'new famines'

Two features are distinctive about 'new famine' thinking. The first is a focus on politics as central to explanations of famine causation, and the second is an analytical focus on failures to prevent famine, rather than on the triggers of food shortage or disrupted access to food.

Several recent contributions to famine-theorising emphasize the role of political factors. These include: the absence of democracy and 'anti-famine political contracts'; 'complex political emergencies'; 'priority regimes'; and failures of international response. Although the recognition that famines are political is hardly an original insight – it has been a truism throughout history that famines affect countries and populations that are politically marginalized as well as economically impoverished – these ideas all share a growing preoccupation with *accountability* for famine creation and famine prevention. These arguments also challenge outdated 'natural disaster' and demographic theories, which explain famines in terms of inadequate food production, and currently dominant economic theories, which analyse famines in terms of poverty and market failure. Again, these triggers and vulnerability factors may tell part of the narrative of a famine process, but contemporary famines are, ultimately, political failures or political successes.

Politics is central to 'new famine' thinking in at least four distinct respects. First, famines are related to political regimes. Most twentieth-century famines occurred under authoritarian, unaccountable regimes – colonial administrations, military dictatorships, one-party states – or during wartime. It is no coincidence that five of the worst famines of the century took place in Stalin's Soviet Union, Mao's China, Pol Pot's Cambodia, Mengistu's Ethiopia and Kim Jong-il's North Korea. Conversely, according to Amartya Sen (1999: 178), 'there has never been a famine in a functioning multiparty democracy'. Complementing his entitlement approach, Sen argued that several features of democracy protect citizens against famine. These include a vigilant media and campaigning civil society to publicize emerging food crises, and free and fair multi-party elections, which ensure the state's accountability to its citizens – any elected government that fails to prevent a famine can be dismissed by the electorate. Alex de Waal (1997) extends this idea to argue that India's success in averting famines since independence in 1947 is largely due to an 'anti-famine political contract', against which the public, the media and opposition politicians can hold the government to account. Conversely, the persistence of famine in countries where democratic institutions are absent or weakly embedded – as is still typical of much of Africa (van de Walle 2001) – might be explained in terms of an absence of such an implicit contract.

Second, recent famines are often connected with conflict, but in more complicated ways than in historical conflict-famines. In the 1990s, the phrase 'complex political emergencies' was coined to characterize the relationship between the 'new wars' and famine. Wars disrupt all components of a food system – agricultural production and food stores, trade routes and aid flows – but in complex emergencies starvation is not only a by-product; it is also often an intended consequence of conflict. Two key insights that challenge 'old famine' thinking are that complex emergencies produce beneficiaries as well as victims (Keen 1994), and that asset ownership does not necessarily provide buffers against livelihood shocks, but can increase vulnerability to famine as wealthier people are targeted during counter-insurgency attacks (Duffield 2001; Deng, Chapter 11, this volume).

Third, the factors that create famine have become 'globalized' to an unprecedented extent. Several 'new famines' have followed directly from the exercise of economic and political leverage by powerful countries and global institutions against weak and vulnerable countries, ostensibly with benign or virtuous intentions – to 'correct' bad government policies or to undermine a dictator. Two famines analysed in this volume – in Madagascar and Malawi – followed radical economic reform processes that were imposed on these countries via donor conditionalities, and which had the unintended effect of undermining the livelihoods of poorer population groups. A more dramatic instance of political leverage creating famine conditions was the 'sanctions famine' in Iraq in the 1990s (Gazdar, Chapter 6, this volume). All three crises were associated with breakdowns of coordinated mechanisms for pooling food security risks, and the erosion of public institutions such as grain reserves and marketing parastatals that had been mandated to stabilize food prices and supplies.

A fourth political factor in contemporary famines is the role of the 'international social safety net' (Noland, Chaper 9, this volume) in famine prevention. The emergence since the Second World War of the global humanitarian industry has played a significant role in reducing famine deaths across the world. Regrettably, the rapidly increasing technical, logistical and institutional capacity to prevent famine has not been accompanied by a corresponding strengthening of accountability. Instead, there is a 'black hole of unaccountability' at the heart of the international relief system (Devereux *et al.* 2002), with national governments, international donors and NGOs indulging in mutual recriminations whenever emergency food aid is not delivered in time.

Political tensions between aid donors and national governments have played a role in failing to prevent many famines, and food aid has frequently been used as a political weapon. During the 1974 famine in Bangladesh the United States withheld food aid because Bangladesh was trading with Cuba, and ten years later the United States delayed sending food aid to Ethiopia in an attempt to undermine the Marxist Derg regime. Howe (Chapter 15, this volume) would explain these famines as by-products of 'priority regimes' that privileged other policy goals above famine prevention. More recently, donors failed to respond to a drought-triggered famine in southern Ethiopia in 1999–2000 because the drought coincided with a border war between Ethiopia and Eritrea that created a climate of mistrust between the government and its donor partners (Lautze and Maxwell, Chapter 10, this volume). A similar deterioration in government–donor relations, triggered by allegations of government corruption, was largely to blame for the failure of humanitarian response in Malawi in 2001–2002 (Devereux and Tiba, Chapter 7, this volume).

Paradigm shifts

The intellectual progression from 'old famine' to 'new famine' thinking requires two paradigm shifts: from famines as failures of food availability, to failures of access to food, to failures of accountability and response. Until Sen introduced the entitlement approach, famine theorists were preoccupied with explaining failures of food supply. 'Food availability decline' (FAD) theories focused on demographic processes (e.g. Malthusian predictions that famine will occur when population exceeds an area's 'carrying capacity'), environmental processes (desertification, soil fertility decline) and climatic shocks (droughts, floods, *El Niño* events). One implication of this way of thinking (challenged by Scoones, Chaper 14, this volume) is that the solutions to food insecurity and famine lie in pursuing food production self-sufficiency by raising crop yields through biotechnology (Green Revolution and GM crops).

The 'old famine' theories have several limitations.

- They depersonalize and depoliticize famines, attributing causality to 'acts of God'
- They explain only disrupted *availability* of food (e.g. crop failure), but pay little attention to failures of *access* to food, or to failures of *response* to food shortage
- They do not explain why some people are more vulnerable than others, because they do not understand famine as a socially differentiated process with political dimensions
- They explain only one component of famine (production shocks), failing to recognize famine as a simultaneous or sequential failure of *all* components of a food system.

In the early 1980s, famine thinking went through its first paradigm shift in almost two centuries. By elaborating the entitlement approach, Sen shifted the focus of famine analysis from failures of food *supply* to failures in *access* to food. Inevitably, this shifted the focus of analysis from food production systems to the relationship between people and food. Instead of asking: 'Is there enough food to feed everybody?', the question was turned around: 'Does everybody have enough food?' Failures of access to food can be explained either by poverty – lack of purchasing power, which is why 'entitlement failure' is a demand-side approach – or by failures of markets. Both these explanations fall broadly in the realm of economic analysis.

The entitlement approach provided analysts with a powerful tool for disaggregating the impacts of food shortages on different groups of people, and for explaining famines that occur with no food shortage at all. However, the approach was unable to explain famines that are triggered by gross violations of entitlements, as is typical of conflict, and famines that are consequences of catastrophic government policies or failures of humanitarian relief. As Edkins (Chaper 3, this volume) argues, Sen 'did not consider the possibility that famines could be a *product* of the social or economic system rather than its *failure*'. Explaining these scenarios required new approaches, such as 'complex political emergencies', and an explicit recognition that famines are essentially political phenomena rather than natural disasters or economic crises.

The time is right for a second paradigm shift in famine thinking: from failures of *access* to failures of *response*. In the twenty-first century, it is not shocks to a food system, but failures to respond to such shocks, that need to be explained. The critical question is no longer: 'What caused the food shortage?' (drought, poverty, market failure, war?), but 'Why did the food shortage become a famine?' or – more politically – 'Who allowed the famine to happen?' or even 'Who made it happen?' (government, militia, aid agencies?). The conceptual shift required is from asking '*What* caused the famine?' to asking '*Who* caused the famine?'

Two types of capacity are needed to prevent famine: technical and political. Technical capacity includes surplus food, timely information, logistics and management expertise. Thanks to subsidised over-production of grain in Europe and North America, institutionalized famine early warning systems, and an efficient international shipping and delivery infrastructure, the technical capacity required to prevent a localized food shortage becoming a famine has been well established since approximately the mid-twentieth century. Political capacity implies political will, which can be created at the national level through democratic accountability and an 'anti-famine contract' between governments and citizens, and at the international level by a humanitarian relief industry that is mandated to save lives and prevent starvation. Famines that have occurred since they became technically preventable have been political failures – or successes, in cases of malevolent intent. Recent famines discussed in this book have occurred either in contexts of civil war (Ethiopia, Sudan), under unaccountable dictatorships (North Korea), following flawed democratic transitions and imposed economic reforms (Madagascar, Malawi) or because of the application of international sanctions (Iraq). In all of these cases, the national and international humanitarian response was either absent or fatally delayed, invariably for political rather than logistical reasons.

Summing up the argument so far, 'new famine' thinking differs from past thinking in several respects:

- Whereas past famines were understood as 'acts of God' (natural disasters, population growth), contemporary famines are understood to be 'acts of man' (they are caused by human action or inaction)
- Even when production and market failures occur, famines are not inevitable until transfers also fail
- The 'new famines' are *political* because they are almost always *preventable*.

Evolution of 'new famine' thinking

The evolution of thinking on the causes of famine can be illustrated as a sequence of 'entitlement failures' (Figure 1.1). For a famine to occur in farming communities – given that smallholders are often most vulnerable to famine – all legal sources of food have to fail: production-based entitlements, trade- and labour-based entitlements (which can be conflated to 'market-based' entitlements) and transfer-based entitlements. As noted above, the first generation of famine theories focused on explaining failures of food production to meet subsistence needs ('food availability decline'). The first paradigm shift switched the focus of analytical attention to the inability of people to acquire food, especially through commodity and labour markets, because of poverty and market failures. In Gazdar's terminology (Chapter 6, this volume), this is a shift from 'pre-modern' to 'modern' famines.

Our critique of these approaches, apart from their apolitical nature, is that they do not explain why a production shock or disrupted access to food is not compensated by transfers of food (or cash to buy food). 'Food availability decline' theories only explain food shortages. If poverty and market failures result in food price rises and collapsing asset prices (or 'exchange entitlement decline'), the food shortage will develop into a food crisis. Even at this stage of the famine process, mass mortality can still be prevented – if humanitarian assistance is delivered in time. In other words, explaining the famine must explain not only food shortages and market failures, but also failures of public action. These failures – or successes, in cases of malevolent intent – constitute what Gazdar labels 'post-modern' famines.

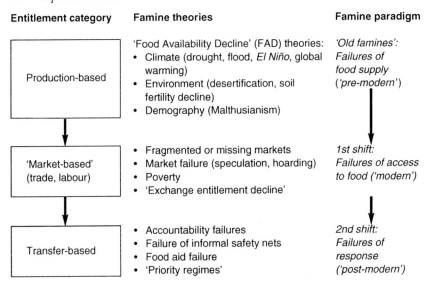

Entitlement category	Famine theories	Famine paradigm
Production-based	'Food Availability Decline' (FAD) theories: • Climate (drought, flood, *El Niño*, global warming) • Environment (desertification, soil fertility decline) • Demography (Malthusianism)	*'Old famines':* *Failures of* *food supply* *('pre-modern')*
'Market-based' (trade, labour)	• Fragmented or missing markets • Market failure (speculation, hoarding) • Poverty • 'Exchange entitlement decline'	*1st shift:* *Failures of access* *to food ('modern')*
Transfer-based	• Accountability failures • Failure of informal safety nets • Food aid failure • 'Priority regimes'	*2nd shift:* *Failures of* *response* *('post-modern')*

Figure 1.1 Evolution of famine thinking.

Missing from Figure 1.1 are 'conflict famines' and 'complex political emergencies', as well as 'new variant famines'. Although these frameworks are quite specific in the causal triggers and vulnerability factors they identify, the impacts of conflict and HIV/AIDS cut across all sources of entitlement to food, so it would be inappropriate to allocate these theories or hypotheses to a single entitlement category or 'famine paradigm'. Food crises triggered by war or complex emergency disrupt food *production* (farmers are displaced, conscripted, disabled or killed; crops and granaries are destroyed; livestock are raided or slaughtered), food *marketing* (trade routes are disrupted; markets are bombed) and food *transfers* (aid agencies are banned; food convoys are attacked; conflict zones become inaccessible). Similarly, rather than offering a generic theory of famine causation, the 'new variant famine' hypothesis asserts that HIV/AIDS 'exacerbates existing social and economic problems [and] changes the pattern of vulnerability to famine' (de Waal, Chapter 5, this volume). For instance, HIV/AIDS intensifies food insecurity by reducing household labour power, undermining food production and raising dependency ratios, it erodes household and community coping capacities and it compromises government capacity by weakening public services.

Implications of 'new famine' thinking

A number of implications follow from a paradigm shift that understands famines as caused by response failures rather than (or as well as) by failures of food supply and access. Three of these implications are considered here. The first is that past famines might be amenable to reinterpretation, the second is that individuals and institutions must take responsibility for contemporary famines, and the third is that there is an urgent need to introduce enforceable mechanisms of accountability for famine prevention.

'Old famine' thinking continues to dominate contemporary understandings of famine causation, long after it should have been superseded by more nuanced analyses. The 1984 famine in Ethiopia, for instance, was simplistically represented by the media and many academics as a 'Biblical' drought famine,[4] when in fact it had elements of 'entitlement failure' and 'complex emergency', being caused as much by civil war, government policies such as agricultural collectivization, trade restrictions and forced resettlement, failures of accountability and failures of humanitarian relief. 'Old thinking' has persisted in accounts of this famine, despite several analyses which convincingly exposed its political nature as the product of a dictatorial regime that grossly violated basic human rights (Clay and Holcombe 1985; de Waal 1997). More recent food crises in Ethiopia and in Malawi have similarly been attributed to drought and Malthusian population pressure. Contributions to this book highlight the central roles of domestic politics and the international community in creating or failing to prevent famine conditions in both these countries, and in Iraq, Madagascar, North Korea and Sudan. For example, as Deng reveals (Chapter 11, this volume) the intersecting interests of the Sudanese Government and foreign oil companies in extracting oil from south Sudan prolonged the civil war and contributed to famines in the 1980s and 1990s.

The assertion that contemporary famines are mainly attributable to human action or inaction – are 'man-made' crises rather than natural disasters – begs the question: are the new famines more political than the old famines, or are we simply recognizing the centrality of political factors more than before? It is arguable that 'new famine' thinking applies equally to historical as to contemporary famines. Mike Davis, in his 'political ecology' analysis of *Late Victorian Holocausts* (2001), demonstrates that the causes of nineteenth-century famines in India, China and Brazil were political as much as environmental – being triggered by a lethal combination of *El Niño* droughts and the forcible incorporation of peasantries across the newly constructed 'Third World' into the global economy during the era of colonial imperialism. It follows that the conceptualization of famines as failures of political accountability could be retrospectively applied to many or perhaps most famines, going back not just decades but centuries.

The second implication relates to identifying who is responsible for causing famines, or at least allowing them to happen. The twin themes of responsibility for famine causation and accountability for famine prevention run throughout this book. Several contributors argue that contemporary famines are almost always avoidable, and that most recent famines could either have been prevented or (drawing on the insight from 'complex emergencies' theorists, that famines produce beneficiaries as well as victims) were deliberately allowed to happen.

The third implication follows logically from the second. If famines are preventable social and political phenomena, rather than unavoidable natural disasters, then social and political actors and institutions should be held accountable for allowing famines to happen. 'Failures of response' introduces the parallel concept of 'failures of accountability', and it is in this sense that contemporary famines are 'political' in different ways than in the past. Accountability for famine prevention can now be attributed and (theoretically) enforced in a world of nation states, the humanitarian relief industry and international law. National governments bear the ultimate responsibility for protecting their citizens against famine and upholding their right to food and freedom from starvation. Where governments lack the capacity to uphold these rights, part of this responsibility is delegated to the international community, which has the capacity and a mandate for famine prevention – but does not bear ultimate responsibility. The 'right to food' is enshrined in international declarations and covenants, but is not yet directly enforceable in international law (Edkins, Chaper 3, this volume). If the technical capacity to eradicate famine, achieved within the past fifty years, is to be realized in practice during the twenty-first century, further progress in these arenas must be prioritized.

Overview of chapters

The contributions to this book are clustered into theoretical chapters and case-study chapters. This Introduction is followed by four chapters that address theoretical issues in famine thinking. Chapter 2 revisits the unresolved question of how to define 'famine', and proposes a new definition. Chapter 3 equates famine with genocide, and argues for the criminalization of 'mass starvations' in international law. Chapter 4 critically reviews the contribution of Sen's 'entitlement approach' to famine theorizing, while Chapter 5 locates the role of HIV and AIDS in contemporary famines in a theoretical framework – the 'new variant famine' hypothesis.

Chapters 6–12 present seven case studies of recent famines or 'near famines'. Four of these occurred in sub-Saharan Africa. Ethiopia, Malawi and Sudan all experienced mass mortality famines within the first few years of the twenty-first century, while Madagascar suffered a famine in the mid-1980s that was only recently 'discovered' by demographers. The two most recent famines in Asia did not occur in India, Bangladesh or China (all historical 'lands of famine') but in Iraq – the 'sanctions famine' of the early 1990s – and North Korea – the 'totalitarian famine' of the late 1990s. Our final case study comes from Europe, and considers how Bosnia narrowly averted a famine during its war in the early 1990s.

The concluding three chapters consider the claims of democracy, biotechnology and 'priority regimes' for reducing vulnerability to famine. Chapter 13 combines an assessment of Sen's assertion that 'democracy ends famine' with an exploration of the reasons for India's success in eradicating famines since independence, and the limitations of that success. Chapter 14 asks whether a 'pro-poor biotechnology' is politically as well as technically feasible. Finally, Chapter 15 argues that famines persist because of skewed 'priority regimes' that either create famine conditions, intentionally or unintentionally, or fail to prioritize famine prevention. As with most contributions to this book, these three chapters share a conviction that the key to eradicating famine is more likely to be found in the realm of politics than that of technology.

Chapter by chapter review

Controversy has surrounded the application of the term 'famine' to several recent food crises. Nonetheless, the debate about whether a precise definition of famine is needed at all is as vigorous and long-running as the debate over actual definitions itself. In Chapter 2, Paul Howe and Stephen Devereux argue that achieving international consensus on a definition of famine is crucial for both operational clarity (improved famine response) and political accountability (for famine prevention). An 'instrumental definition' is proposed, based on two complementary scales. The 'intensity scale' monitors the severity of famine conditions by combining outcome indicators (anthropometry and mortality rates) and food security descriptors (food prices, coping strategy adoption). Agreed thresholds for key indicators will identify when conditions have deteriorated from 'food secure' to 'food crisis' and ultimately to 'famine'. The 'magnitude scale' quantifies the human cost of famine in terms of excess mortality, and is designed for *ex post* comparison and assessment, with greater accountability being applied to famines of greater magnitude (proportionate accountability). Formidable technical and political challenges need to be overcome if the 'famine scales' are to be adopted by the international humanitarian community – not least because of the diffusion of responsibility for famine prevention among an array of local, national and global actors – but clarifying these lines of political accountability is as important an objective of this proposal as is achieving consensus on a technical definition.

In Chapter 3, Jenny Edkins sets out a powerful case that underpins one of the main arguments of 'new famine' thinking: 'nothing 'causes' famines: people commit the crime of mass starvation'. Edkins challenges the dominant view of famine as a breakdown or failure of food systems that is amenable to 'technologized responses', arguing that such responses are not only incapable of responding adequately to the politics of mass starvations, but are themselves implicated in politics. Famines are not events defined by economic relationships between people and commodities, as famine theorists often imply, but are political processes involving relationships between people. She insists that famines are crimes against humanity requiring a political analysis (asking not just who are the victims, but who benefits from famine?) and politicized responses (including attributing responsibility and enforcing accountability under international law). Different degrees of 'faminogenic behaviours' should incur proportionate sanctions: while government incapacity or incompetence might not give sufficient cause for criminalization, 'recklessness' or intentionality certainly should. Edkins concludes by suggesting that the word 'famine' itself should be replaced by the phrase 'mass starvations', 'faminogenic behaviours' or 'famine crimes', to shift conceptualizations of famine away from benign notions of 'breakdown' or 'failure' and towards a recognition that contemporary famines are 'perpetrated' and have more in common with genocides than with natural disasters.

A quarter of a century after the publication of *Poverty and Famines* in 1981, Amartya Sen's 'entitlement approach' remains the dominant intellectually coherent 'theory' of famine. In Chapter 4, Stephen Devereux argues that its importance has been overshadowed by ongoing controversy, which derives from confusion between two seminal contributions that *Poverty and Famines* made to famine literature: providing a robust *general* analytical framework for examining all famines (the 'entitlement approach'), and advancing a new theory of famine causation – that *certain* famines are characterized by declines in access to food for specific population groups, irrespective of food availability at aggregate level ('exchange entitlement failure'). The chapter then examines four limitations of the approach, as acknowledged by Sen: 'choosing to starve' (protecting assets rather than converting them into food), disease- rather than starvation-driven famine mortality, ambiguities in entitlement specification due to 'fuzzy' property rights, and 'extra-legal entitlement transfers'. This fourth limitation comes closest to recognizing that many contemporary famines are politically constructed, being characterized by violations of entitlements – such as deliberate starvation, asset seizures or non-delivery of food aid. Nonetheless, as a framework for understanding the 'new famines', the entitlement approach is conceptually and analytically weakened by its methodological individualism and by its privileging of economic aspects of famine to the virtual exclusion of social and political determinants.

The contribution of HIV/AIDS to poverty and food insecurity in Africa has been recognized since the 1980s, but only recently have attempts been made to theorize the epidemic's role in famine causation. In Chapter 5, Alex de Waal elaborates the 'new variant famine' (NVF) hypothesis, which explains how HIV/AIDS raises vulnerability to famine by creating new categories of poor and vulnerable people and undermining individual resilience and institutional capacity to cope with additional shocks such as drought: 'the trajectory of destitution when a famine occurs is sharper, and recovery is slower'. At the national level, HIV/AIDS also erodes public services and institutions of governance. Importantly, de Waal emphasizes that the NVF hypothesis is not a new theory of famine – it 'supplements rather than displaces other explanations'. HIV/AIDS exacerbates existing social, economic and political pathologies, and rising HIV-prevalence is one major difference between an averted famine in southern Africa in 1991–1992 and the famine that occurred in the region in 2001–2002. De Waal also shows how famine and HIV/AIDS mutually reinforce and complement each other. Not only does HIV/AIDS elevate vulnerability to famine, but outcomes of famine processes, such as destitution, migration and social dislocation, are also risk factors for HIV transmission. Moreover, whereas famine kills the very young and the very old, AIDS disproportionately kills adults of reproductive age. Between them, HIV/AIDS and famine threaten to devastate many African countries in the coming decades.

There is some debate over whether the humanitarian emergency that followed the imposition of sanctions against Iraq in 1990 should be labelled a 'famine'. Sceptics have argued that the problems were associated with a breakdown of public health rather than food systems, while another objection is that the crisis unfolded over many years – there is no epidemiological evidence of a sharp 'spike' in mortality over a few months, as is typical of most famines (see, for instance, the mortality patterns in the Madagascar and Malawi famines). In Chapter 6, Haris Gazdar defines Iraq's protracted crisis during the 1990s as a 'post-modern' famine – one that occurred in a relatively affluent society with strong institutions and functioning markets. This is in contrast to both 'pre-modern' famines, which are triggered mainly by production collapses and occur in weakly integrated subsistence-oriented agrarian societies, and 'modern' famines, which follow sudden 'exchange entitlement' declines and are related to market failures. Post-modern famines are explicitly political in nature, and can occur even in sophisticated economies with functioning social welfare systems, when macro-shocks such as sanctions or war send these economies 'into freefall'. Gazdar speculates that the famine in Iraq, which was created by the malevolent exercise of global political leverage against a pariah state, has given us a 'gruesome glimpse' of the 'post-modern' form that many twenty-first century famines might take. Gazdar's terminology also provides a useful typology for 'old' famines ('pre-modern' famines or 'food availability crises') and 'new' famines (or 'capabilities failures'), with 'modern' famines (or 'food entitlement failures'), like Sen's entitlement approach itself, falling between the two.

The Malawi famine of 2001–2002 appears to conform to 'old famine' characteristics, but on closer scrutiny displays a number of 'new famine' elements. In Chapter 7, Stephen Devereux and Zoltan Tiba present four survey-based estimates of famine-related mortality, which fall in the range

46,000 to 85,000, refuting claims that no mass mortality famine occurred in Malawi in 2001–2002. The famine process was triggered by a 'food availability decline', following erratic weather during the farming season. The resulting food gap was underestimated because cassava production estimates had been exaggerated for several years. 'Exchange entitlement failure' followed as food prices rose to unprecedented levels, and asset prices and labour markets collapsed. A humanitarian response failure turned the food shortage into a famine. These proximate factors were compounded by political actions (or inactions) – such as the government's delayed declaration of an emergency, and its misappropriation of the Strategic Grain Reserve – that constructed and perpetuated famine conditions, and are attributed here to a 'controlling institution' acting opportunistically for political and economic gain. Underlying vulnerability factors included deepening rural poverty and rising HIV/AIDS prevalence which eroded asset buffers and informal social support systems; an economic liberalization trajectory since the 1980s that had systematically undermined the capacity of Malawian smallholders to maintain sustainable livelihoods; and a political transition in the mid-1990s that marginalized large segments of the population.

The Madagascar famine of 1985–1986 is atypical in several respects. It occurred in an urban area in peacetime, most deaths were caused by outright starvation rather than infectious diseases, and it was a 'hidden famine' that was discovered through retrospective demographic analysis. In Chapter 8, Michel Garenne locates the causes of this famine in radical shifts in economic policies adopted after independence from France in 1960. During the 1970s the government followed Marxist policies with support from the Soviet Union, China and North Korea, but these policies only delivered dramatic economic decline. In the early 1980s, the government switched its political orientation from East to West and implemented structural adjustment policies in order to access credits and grants from the IMF and World Bank. Food security policies such as rice price stabilization were phased out as rice marketing was liberalized. One consequence was an exceptional rise in rice prices, peaking in the second half of 1985, which coincided with the famine period. Garenne concludes that 'the combination of adverse economic policies together with extensive poverty was the main immediate cause for the famine'. Since rice production was lower in many years both before and after the famine, food availability decline is an inadequate causal explanation. Rather, the market-dependent urban poor suffered from 'exchange entitlement failure' as prices rose to unaffordable levels due to market failure (speculation by private traders), and compounded by institutional failure (inability of the government to intervene to stabilize prices or supplies).

North Korea experienced a famine in the late 1990s that resulted in 600,000 to one million deaths, or 3–5 per cent of the pre-famine population. In Chapter 9, Marcus Noland argues that North Korea shares many features of earlier twentieth-century famines in totalitarian states (e.g. the Soviet Union and China), but that 'the increasing centrality of internal institutional changes and involvement of external actors in the post-Cold War context of globalization simultaneously situates it in the contemporary milieu of 'post-modern' famine'. Noland locates the origins of the famine in the partition of the Korean peninsula after the Second World War, when most Korean industries were located in the North, with the South being the breadbasket. North Korea established a heavily militarized, centrally planned economy: agriculture was collectivized and markets were suppressed. However, an ideology of self-reliance concealed a growing dependence on Soviet and Chinese support, which was exposed following the withdrawal of Soviet aid and collapse of trade in the late 1980s, precipitating an economic crisis. Catastrophic floods in 1995 and 1996 exacerbated the agricultural crisis in North Korea and created famine conditions that the government had inadequate capacity or political will to alleviate. The resulting famine is explained as the outcome of several decades of social engineering, economic mismanagement, militarization and political isolationism.

In Chapter 10, Sue Lautze and Dan Maxwell argue that famines in Ethiopia are perceived differently inside the country and by outsiders. Within Ethiopia, famines have historically constituted 'a significant threat to state power', contributing in recent decades to the violent overthrow of both Haile Selassie and the Derg regime. Outsiders have consistently perceived famines as food production shocks triggered by erratic rainfall, and have paid little attention to either the politics of famine or the underlying livelihoods crisis that reproduces famine. While the search for technical solutions continues (improved early warning systems and safety net programmes by the donors, resettlement of farmers by the government), the persistence of 'interlocking vulnerabilities' (demographic processes, environmental constraints, health crises, policy failures, political marginalization of vulnerable populations) means that food crises can at best be contained, but not eradicated. A humanitarian crisis in 2002–2003 was effectively contained, while an earlier crisis in 1999–2000 was not. Significantly, Lautze and Maxwell locate the reasons for this differential success in political rather than technical factors, such as the location of each crisis (in politically peripheral and conflict-affected pastoralist regions in 1999–2000, but in politically favoured highland areas in 2002–2003); and the coincidence of the 1999–2000 emergency with the Ethio-Eritrea war (which soured relations between the government and donors at a critical time). As long as those with a mandate for reducing famine vulnerability in Ethiopia continue to conceptualize the problem in 'old famine' terms (i.e. famines are caused by drought, population pressure and poverty), critical 'new famine' aspects (such as problematic government–donor relations, high levels of insecurity and conflict in peripheral regions, and weak democratic institutions with only partial accountability) will continue to be unrecognized, and famines will persist in Ethiopia.

South Sudan suffered several major famines during the two decades of its second civil war between 1983 and 2004, and the 'complex emergencies' approach was developed largely as a response to this evidence from the Horn of Africa of powerful causal linkages between civil conflict and famine. In Chapter 11, Luka Biong Deng broadens this analysis beyond the domestic level by locating Sudan's recurrent famines in relation to historical processes such as the British colonial legacy, and to contemporary processes of globalization. Deng also demonstrates that conflict can raise vulnerability of wealthier households – whose livestock are targeted by counter-insurgents – contradicting the predictions of the 'asset-vulnerability framework' and the 'entitlement approach', that households with more assets are necessarily better buffered against livelihood shocks. This 'curse of assets' also affects south Sudan as a region, since the civil conflict has been largely driven by a struggle for control over lucrative oilfields, in which the Government of Sudan and transnational corporations are profoundly implicated. By carefully examining the evolution of Sudan's political economy from the colonial period to the present, and by deepening the analysis of political tensions between north and south Sudan beyond simplistic explanations based on ethnic and religious hostility, Deng reveals that the roots of subsistence crises in south Sudan cannot be internalized but must be contextualized within global economic and geopolitical interests. Given this causal complexity, Deng calls on global actors – including international relief and development agencies – to acknowledge their role in contributing to famine vulnerability in Sudan and, rather than simply providing food aid, to take action to address these underlying causes.

In Chapter 12, Fiona Watson asks why no famine struck the besieged areas of Bosnia during the war of 1992–1995 – despite the precedent of several European siege famines earlier in the century – and finds that the population was effectively buffered against livelihood shocks by favourable pre-crisis economic, demographic and health conditions, and by a generous and effective humanitarian response. Before the war, Bosnians enjoyed a relatively affluent standard of living, the economy was sound and infrastructure was well developed. Health services were good, and most Bosnians were immunized and well-nourished: obesity was more prevalent than undernutrition. By contrast, Africans vulnerable to famine tend to be poor, nutritionally stressed and exposed to infectious diseases – diarrhoea, malaria, AIDS – that lower their resistance to hunger. They live in low-income economies with limited access to health services and weak institutional response capacity. Bosnia's averted famine is a salutary reminder of the importance of the economic, demographic and health contexts within which famine threats emerge. The Bosnian case also raises questions about the international response to famine threats. Watson concludes that 'food aid requirements were over-estimated in Bosnia', and that the diversion of food aid from developing countries to Bosnia and other East European countries provided some protection for conflict-affected Bosnians against starvation. This finding raises questions about the relative prioritization that the international community attaches to humanitarian needs in different parts of the world.

Amartya Sen has famously claimed that famines do not occur in democracies, and that India's successful prevention of famine since independence in 1947 is due primarily to its free press and democratic political structures. In Chapter 13, Dan Banik broadly endorses Sen's insights, but he critiques the record of democratic institutions in India in combating less sensational manifestations of hunger. To the extent that an anti-famine 'political contract' exists between the government and citizens, it operates to prevent high-profile famines – because failure to do so would incur high political costs – rather than to eradicate low-profile 'silent hunger'. The 'political triggers' of an independent media and active opposition parties are conspicuously absent with regard to chronic malnutrition and non-famine starvation deaths. This argument is explored in a comparison of two Indian districts – Kalahandi in Orissa, and Purulia in neighbouring West Bengal. Tribal-dominated and drought-prone Kalahandi has achieved notoriety as the 'starvation capital' of India, but, despite being equally drought-prone and with comparable poverty levels, no starvation deaths have been reported in Purulia. Banik provides an explanation for these contrasting outcomes in contrasting political climates. Orissa is politically volatile with a demotivated district administration and a heavily politicized press, whereas West Bengal has a stable government, an effective decentralized bureaucracy and an independent press, all sharing the consensus that 'starvation deaths' are politically and socially unacceptable. Banik's analysis highlights the need to move beyond generalizations about the relationship between democracy and famine prevention, towards a disaggregated analysis of how democracy operates in specific local contexts.

A key message of this book is that the persistence of famine is not a technical problem amenable to technical solutions, but a failure of policies and politics that requires a political economy analysis and political solutions. This is well illustrated by the 'biotech debate'. For those who believe that famine is primarily a problem of inadequate food supplies or 'food availability decline', the promise of biotechnological innovations in agriculture is seductive, and a new Green Revolution is advocated as the solution to Africa's chronic food insecurity and vulnerability to famine. In Chapter 14, Ian Scoones questions whether the GM storyline – 'food supply is the problem, biotechnology is the solution' – can be the simple panacea that its proponents believe. Scoones critiques the neo-Malthusian underpinnings of the GM lobby, and its 'silence' on economic and political issues of food access and distribution. He argues that the problems of food insecurity in Africa are only partly related to low-yielding varieties and declining soil fertility, and are largely related to drought, conflict, political instability and policy failures – none of which are amenable to 'technological fixes' like improved seeds. He also questions whether a 'pro-poor biotechnology' is possible, given the powerful commercial interests that are represented in the lucrative agri-food sector. Whether science can deliver appropriate seeds that meet the priority needs of poor farmers is only part of the problem. Getting these seeds to these farmers equitably and affordably is another challenge altogether – one which requires radical political choices as well as substantial public investment.

In the concluding chapter, Paul Howe explains the 'paradox of persistence' of famine in a globalizing world by introducing the concept of 'priority regimes', which he defines as 'the sets of concerns that are privileged in the decision-making and actions of institutions and individuals'. Howe critiques famine-theorizing for its tendency to externalize, isolate and 'negativize' the famine process, thereby ignoring the range of actors involved other than 'victims', the relationship between famines and other policy priorities, and the interaction of positive and negative processes in creating or preventing famines. Howe argues that understanding why famines persist requires drawing on insights from the 'new wars', policy processes, participation and rights literatures. Priority regimes have spatial, temporal and effectual dimensions – they apply to defined geographic areas or populations, for particular periods of time, and have positive as well as negative effects. Whereas earlier theorists attributed famines to 'undirected occurrences' (such as drought or market failures), contemporary famines must be seen as the product of 'undirected occurrences' and 'directed' priority regimes or (where no external trigger is involved) as the intentional or unintended by-product of priority regimes. Eradicating famine requires shifting the priority regimes of governments and the international community, and empowering individuals and communities so that their priorities are better reflected in the priority regimes of those whose decisions ultimately determine their vulnerability to famine.

Conclusion: the future of famine

Contemporary famines are less widespread and less severe than historical famines – fewer countries are vulnerable to famine, and fewer people die during famines, than in the past. This is a partial success story. But famines have not yet been eradicated, and there are reasons to believe that they will persist for many years. Recent famines have been exacerbated by a number of new vulnerability factors – externally imposed policies of economic liberalization, flawed processes of political democratization, rising prevalence of HIV/AIDS, problematic relationships between national governments and international aid donors, the 'new wars'.

Contemporary famines are also more complex than ever before, because there are more ways of both causing and preventing them. When a famine happens, all sources of food fail or are deliberately disrupted, at the same time or in sequence – food production, food markets and food aid – as well as the 'coping strategies' that people deploy to survive livelihood shocks. In the past, the causes of and responses to famine were localized; now they are globalized. All contemporary famines are fundamentally political, in the sense that political decisions contribute either to creating famine conditions or to failure to intervene to prevent famine. Recognizing that political responsibility can be assigned whenever a famine occurs is a fundamental shift in famine thinking, away from previous theories that attributed famine to natural disasters, demographic processes or the impersonal logic of market forces.

Recent food crises discussed in this book suggest at least three likely trajectories for future famines. First, war and famine have been inextricably linked for millennia, and are likely to remain so. In 'complex political emergencies' and the 'new wars', the interests of national and international actors work against – rather than in support of – the interests of vulnerable populations. Governments, militia groups, the arms trade, multinational corporations and international financial institutions all collude in the extraction of mineral resources and agricultural produce from poor countries. Famine conditions can be created in these contexts as a by-product of civil insecurity, with food production, asset ownership, markets and trade, and humanitarian interventions all being inadvertently disrupted or deliberately undermined. In certain cases famine is a malevolent policy goal, successfully achieved.

Second, in 'post-modern' famines, powerful members of the international community may choose to exercise their political leverage and apply economic sanctions against pariah states, inflicting extreme hardship on affected populations. The destruction of public services and institutions – health, water and sanitation facilities, social security systems – can also follow military intervention, in extreme cases (such as Iraq) bringing famine conditions to previously well-functioning and seemingly food-secure societies. Given current trends towards global political polarization, economic inequality and military imbalances, this type of famine looks increasingly plausible, and a growing number of countries may be vulnerable to having 'post-modern' famines inflicted on them.

Finally, in 'response failure' famines, neither national governments nor international donors assume full responsibility for upholding the right to food, in contexts of acute and rising vulnerability among large segments of the population. In many countries, especially in sub-Saharan Africa, several trends and processes have pushed farmers closer to the edge of survival, raising their vulnerability to even the smallest livelihood shocks. These include demographic pressures and environmental stress, increasingly erratic rainfall in economies dominated by rain-fed agriculture (possibly a consequence of climate change), HIV/AIDS (Malawi, in particular, displayed elements of 'new variant famine' in 2001–2002), economic liberalization policies (which removed several pillars of food security without replacing them) and governance failures (countries like Ethiopia and Malawi are fledgling democracies whose governments are not yet fully accountable to their citizens). In these economically weak and politically marginalized countries, sluggish donor responses to recent food crises suggest that the international community is pursuing different 'priority regimes' than famine prevention. The 2001–2002 famine in Malawi is paradigmatic of these 'new famines', being characterized by most of these new vulnerability factors and sequential entitlement failures.

Common to all the scenarios sketched above is an absence of political accountability. Political will to prevent famine needs to be constructed at both national and international levels. At the level of nation states, democratic institutions must be strengthened and deepened, ideally through domestic pressure from citizens and civil society activism. At the global level, the right to adequate food is enshrined in the Universal Declaration of Human Rights of 1948 and the International Covenant on Economic, Social and Cultural Rights of 1966. Little progress has been made in enforcing this right under international law, despite commitments made by governments and international organizations at the World Food Conference in 1974 and the World Food Summit in 1996, and the adoption in 2004 of 'Voluntary Guidelines on the Right to Food'. Until an enforceable 'anti-famine contract' is established at both national and global levels, famines will continue to be tolerated, when they should already have been consigned to history.

Notes

1   In northern China, 9–13 million people died during a protracted drought in the 1870s. In the early 1920s, 'almost analogous climatic conditions obtained throughout the same territory' (Mallory 1926: 30), but famine mortality was contained to half a million, as a consequence of improved communications and the construction of 6,000 miles of railway in the interim, which facilitated prompt relief intervention. Similarly, in India, according to an early twentieth-century edition of the *Imperial Gazetteer*: 'Railways have revolutionized relief. The final horror of famine, an absolute dearth of food, is not known' (quoted in Becker 1996: 14).

2   It is no coincidence that William Dando, a geographer, wrote *The Geography of Famine* (1980), Amartya Sen, a liberal economist, focused on the links between *Poverty and Famines* (1981), Martin Ravallion, a World Bank economist, argues for market failure in *Markets and Famines* (1987), and Alex de Waal, a human rights activist, blames governments and the international community in *Famine Crimes* (1997).

3   According to Mallory, *economic causes* of famine in China included poverty ('the cost of living'), underproduction of food ('antiquated agricultural methods' and soil fertility decline), population growth ('overcrowding'), unemployment and underemployment ('surplus labour'), lack of access to credit, poor com-

munications and 'inefficient transportation methods'. *Natural causes* included deforestation, drought, flood and locusts. *Political causes* included 'civil strife', weak government, 'abolition of public granaries' in 1912, 'heavy taxation' of farmers, neglect of famine prevention measures, and 'excess troops' who 'live off the country'. *Social causes* included the 'high birth rate in China' (partly due to 'early marriage' and motivated by parents seeing children as 'old-age insurance'), 'waste due to ceremonies and feasts' (which contemporary development academics might gloss as 'investment in social capital') and 'conservatism of the people' (which later development economists would reinterpret as 'risk aversion').

4 See, for instance, Dyson and Ó Gráda (2002: 15): 'Famine in the classical sense of widespread hunger and starvation, steeply rising mortality and, perhaps above all, social breakdown, is a relatively rare event today. Perhaps the last such episode – of famine in an almost biblical sense – occurred in Ethiopia in 1984–1985.'

References

Becker, J. (1996) *Hungry Ghosts: China's Secret Famine*, London: John Murray.

Bird, K., Hulme, D., Moore, K. and Shepherd, A. (2002) 'Chronic poverty and remote rural areas', *CPRC Working Paper*, 13, Manchester: IDPM, University of Manchester.

Clay, J. and Holcombe, B. (1985) *Politics and the Ethiopian Famine, 1984–1985*, Cambridge, MA: Cultural Survival.

Dando, W. (1980) *The Geography of Famine*, London: Edward Arnold.

Davis, M. (2001) *Late Victorian Holocausts: El Niño Famines and the Making of the Third World*, London: Verso.

del Ninno, C., Dorosh, P. and Islam, N. (2002) 'Reducing vulnerability to natural disasters: lessons from the 1998 floods in Bangladesh', *IDS Bulletin*, 33(4): 98–107.

de Waal, A. (1997) *Famine Crimes: Politics and the Disaster Relief Industry in Africa*, Oxford: James Currey.

Devereux, S., Howe, P. and Deng, L. (2002) 'Introduction: the "new famines"', *IDS Bulletin*, 33(4): 1–11.

Drèze, J. (1990) 'Famine prevention in India', in J. Drèze and A. Sen (eds), *The Political Economy of Hunger, Volume II: Famine Prevention*, Oxford: Clarendon Press, Ch. 1.

Duffield, M. (2001) *Global Governance and the New Wars: The Merging of Development and Security*, London: Zed Books.

Dyson, T. and Ó Gráda, C. (2002) 'Introduction', in Dyson, T. and Ó Gráda, C. (eds), *Famine Demography: Perspectives from the Past and Present*, Oxford: Oxford University Press.

Franke, R. and Chasin, B. (1980) *Seeds of Famine*, Montclair: Allanheld and Osmun.

Iliffe, J. (1987) *The African Poor: A History*, Cambridge: Cambridge University Press.

Keen, D. (1994) *The Benefits of Famine: A Political Economy of Famine and Relief in Southwestern Sudan, 1983–1989*, Princeton, NJ: Princeton University Press.

Mallory, W. (1926) *China: Land of Famine*. New York, NY: American Geographical Society.

Malthus, T. (1798, 1976 edn) *An Essay on the Principle of Population*, New York, NY: W. W. Norton.

Meillassoux, C. (1974) 'Development or exploitation: is the Sahel famine good business?', *Review of African Political Economy*, 1: 27–33.

Ravallion, M. (1987) *Markets and Famines*, Oxford: Oxford University Press.

Sen, A. (1981) *Poverty and Famines: An Essay on Entitlement and Deprivation*, Oxford: Clarendon Press.

Sen, A. (1999) *Development As Freedom*, Oxford: Oxford University Press.

van de Walle, N. (2001) *African Economies and the Politics of Permanent Crisis, 1979–1999*, Cambridge: Cambridge University Press.

von Braun, J., Teklu, T. and Webb, P. (1998) *Famine in Africa: Causes, Responses, and Prevention*, Baltimore, MA: Johns Hopkins University Press.

Watts, M. (1983) *Silent Violence: Food, Famine and Peasantry in Northern Nigeria*. Berkeley, CA: University of California Press.

2 Famine scales

Towards an instrumental definition of 'famine'

Paul Howe and Stephen Devereux

Introduction[1]

Considerable controversy has surrounded the application of the term 'famine' to several recent humanitarian emergencies, including many discussed in this book: Iraq (1990s), Sudan (1998), Ethiopia (1999–2000, 2002–2003), and Malawi (2002).[2] Both before and during these crises, observers failed to agree on how serious the situation was, or how serious it was likely to get. For example, while most stakeholders concur, in retrospect, that a famine took place in southern Sudan in 1998, in the early months of that year there was no consensus about whether or not a famine was developing (see Box 2.1). The debate reflected both genuine confusion over whether – and precisely when – the situation merited the designation of 'famine', as well as pragmatic and political concerns about the implications of declaring a famine for the complex agendas of different stakeholders (Howe 2002).

In the case of Ethiopia in 1999–2000, a vigorous debate about whether a famine had occurred continued long after the crisis had ended. International organizations such as the USAID and WFP claimed to have 'averted' a famine in the Somali region in the early months of 2000.[3] A WFP spokesperson argued that: 'this was a very serious food crisis and because of the response, didn't slide over into famine ... we should save that term for those very severe, severe situations. Otherwise, we are debasing the coinage' (IDS 2002). The contentious issue here was that of scale: because the emergency was confined to a single region, the 'F-word' was considered too strong a term. However, a retrospective mortality study suggested that far from preventing famine, aid organizations had responded late and exacerbated the crisis by drawing people into relief camps – where communicable diseases such as measles spread rapidly, contributing to an estimated 19,900 deaths in Gode zone alone (Salama *et al.* 2001: 568). Writing two years after the crisis, Dan Maxwell (2002: 53) concludes:

> There is still a major controversy over whether the Ethiopia crisis of 1999–2000 should be labelled a 'famine' or not, in light of the

Box 2.1. Famine or no famine? Sudan 1998

> With the present level of humanitarian intervention in the region, it is imminent that thousands of women, children and elderly people will simply starve to death within the coming weeks because of inadequate food intake and poor health services.
>
>   Sudanese Relief and Rehabilitation Association, March 1998
>
> There is no famine in Sudan yet, nor need there be one.
>
>   'Hope in Hell', *The Times*, leader, April 1998
>
> The people of Bahr al Ghazal are facing a crisis, but not yet a famine.
>
>   Mike Aaronson, Save the Children Fund (UK), *Financial Times*, May 1998
>
> The latest UN estimate says up to 1.2 million people now face starvation in the south of the country – many more than previously thought. The dramatic increase has prompted the World Food Programme to call for an unprecedented relief operation to target those most at risk in several areas it describes as 'famine zones'
>
>   'UN declares famine in Sudan', BBC, June 1998

emotive and political connotations of the word. In the author's view – given the number of people affected, the damage to livelihoods and human development, and the loss of human life – there is no question about whether Ethiopia 1999–2000 was a famine. But the continued controversy over this issue points to the need for a broadly accepted operational definition of famine.

Far from being merely a semantic issue, these controversies have important implications for famine response and accountability. Operationally, lack of consensus on a definition has contributed to delayed interventions and inequitable distribution of resources among areas of need. In the periods leading up to and during a crisis, disagreements over terminology and concepts have made it difficult for observers – governments, donors, NGOs, the media – to identify whether a famine is occurring, or is likely to occur, creating uncertainty about the appropriate nature, timing and scale of response. Recent studies have also questioned whether, in the absence of universal benchmarks or criteria, aid is given 'according to need' (Darcy and Hofmann 2003), or is determined more by non-humanitarian considerations, such as donor country interests in any given situation (Olsen *et al.* 2002). Watson (2002), for example, has shown how a disproportionate amount of aid went to the Kosovo crisis in 1998 at the time of the famine in southern Sudan, suggesting that the European crisis held greater priority for Western donor nations.

Politically, the absence of an agreed definition has made it difficult to hold stakeholders accountable, where appropriate. As demonstrated by the recent cases of Sudan, Ethiopia and Malawi, famine is a highly emotive term that has the potential not only to galvanize relief, but also to incite calls for accountability. Governments and agencies with notional responsibility for famine prevention have often exploited the ambiguities in the term to contest whether a famine has occurred, thereby evading even limited accountability for their actions – or inaction. Following the Sudan famine of 1998, when an estimated 70,000 people died (Deng 1999), accountability essentially took the 'soft' form of internal agency evaluations and lesson-learning workshops. To those who argue for the 'criminalization of mass starvation' (Edkins 2002), the main purpose of the definitional exercise is to uphold the right to food, and to enforce accountability when that basic human right is violated.[4] So the search for an internationally accepted definition of famine is not merely a technocratic or instrumentalist concern – it also has political significance.

Recognizing the often fatal consequences of failing to resolve the ambiguities in current understandings of famine, this chapter proposes a new approach. The next section reviews previous attempts to define famine, and explores their limitations in terms of addressing the two instrumental concerns of response and accountability. The third section outlines and motivates our proposal for defining famine, based on 'intensity and magnitude scales'. The final section concludes.

Alternative approaches to defining 'famine'

The literature contains several distinct approaches to defining famine.[5] These include theoretical definitions, early warning systems, 'coping strategies' and nutrition surveillance. This section briefly examines each of these in turn.

Theoretical definitions

Although numerous academic and dictionary definitions of famine have been proposed, most are ambiguous or descriptive, and lack the clarity that an operationally useful definition requires. Consider this succinct statement, from the journal *Science* in 1975 (Mayer, 1975: 572):

> In statistical terms, [famine] can be defined as a severe shortage of food accompanied by a significant increase in the local or regional death rate.

Despite its apparent ('statistical') precision, this definition offers no quantifiable criteria for 'severe', 'significant' and 'local or regional', and it therefore provides no practical basis for either triggering interventions or enforcing accountability.

Also, by focusing on food shortage as the immediate cause, and on excess mortality as the defining outcome, this definition falls into the 'famine as natural disaster' category and thus represents only one particular perspective on the nature of famine. During the 1980s, this view was challenged by writers who saw famine instead as a 'social process' (Rangasami 1985) and as a 'community crisis' (Currey and Hugo 1984).[6] The debate over whether famine should be conceptualized as a 'process' or an 'event' is evident by contrasting Mayer's definition with Walker's (1989: 6):

> Famine is a socio-economic process which causes the accelerated destitution of the most vulnerable, marginal and least powerful groups in a community, to a point where they can no longer, as a group, maintain a sustainable livelihood. Ultimately, the process leads to the inability of the individual to acquire sufficient food to sustain life.

One source of divergence between the 'event' and 'process' views relates to the temporal dimension. While Sen (1981: 47) writes of people being 'plunged into starvation', Walker describes a more extended 'socio-economic process' leading to 'accelerated destitution' and – 'ultimately' – death. Rangasami (1993) takes this thinking further, and identifies a three-phase 'famine process': 'dearth', or incipient famine; 'famishment', or maturing famine; and full-blown 'famine'. Rangasami also suggests that indices of 'dearth', 'famishment' and 'famine' need to be devised, and she argues that 'appropriate indices of distress should be taken from the perceptions of victims . . .: and made 'operational'' (Floud 1993: 6). It is well established, for instance, that people who experience famine identify different degrees of food crisis, and that they perceive famines as being as much about social breakdown, loss of livelihoods and disease as about hunger and death (de Waal 1989).

While these definitions offer important insights – for instance, on the perspectives of famine-affected populations – and provide the academic grounding for the development of any instrumental definition, their imprecision and conflicting theoretical stances limit their usefulness for practical purposes. As Sen (1981: 40) acknowledges, most definitions merely provide 'a pithy description' of what happens during famines, rather than 'helping us to do the diagnosis – the traditional function of a definition'. 'Helping us to do the diagnosis' is one of our objectives in constructing the famine scales.

Early warning systems

A pragmatic approach to defining famine emerged from the practical requirements of efforts to prevent famines, and to implement timely and appropriate relief responses. Rather than attempting to express the essence of famine in a sentence or a paragraph, common characteristics or correlates of famine are monitored to indicate whether a famine is either imminent or occurring. An early example of this approach was the Indian Famine Codes. Developed in the 1880s by the British colonial regime, the Famine Codes were an attempt to codify administrative responses to food crises, partly as a policy response to a sequence of famines in several Indian states between 1860 and 1877, and partly as a political effort to shore up the legitimacy of British rule (Brennan 1984; Drèze 1990).

The Famine Codes distinguished between three levels of food stress – 'near-scarcity', 'scarcity' and 'famine' – but individual states adopted their own definitions of these terms. Generally, 'scarcity' was defined as 'prevailing want of food or other necessaries', while 'famine' was 'the aggravation of conditions of scarcity into a state of extreme scarcity' (Singh 1993: 149). Scarcity was identified by: three successive years of crop failure; crop yields of 4–6 *annas* (compared to a normal yield of 12 *annas*); and large populations in distress. The declaration of famine was based on additional criteria, including food price rises above the 'scarcity rate' (defined as 40 per cent above the 'normal price'), signs of increased migration, and the extent of mortality. The Punjab Famine Code, for instance, stated that: 'Imminence of death is the sole criterion for declaration of a famine' (Singh 1993: 150).

As de Waal (1989: 19) notes: 'the notion of famine as mass starvation was current, and the Famine Codes were devised with the restricted objective of preventing starvation deaths'. In this limited sense, the Codes have been acknowledged as an effective famine prevention instrument (Bhatia 1963; Drèze 1990). However, the Codes – and their post-colonial successor, the Scarcity Manuals – have been less successful in terms of eradicating widespread hunger from India, or in preventing loss of livelihoods. The Madras Code of 1905, for instance, asserted that: 'though the State is bound to protect the people from starvation in times of distress, it is no part of its duty to maintain them at their normal level of comfort or to insure them against all suffering' (cited in de Waal 1997: 14). This reflects the narrow definition of 'famine as an event' that is implicit within the Famine Codes, which had pragmatic as well as conceptual rationales: while the colonial administration recognized the political risks and the financial costs (in terms of provision of famine relief) of failing to prevent famines, they felt no moral obligation to institute social welfare programmes for poor Indians in non-emergency contexts. Singh (1993) also critiques the subjective nature of many criteria, arguing that more precise quantification would make them less amenable to manipulation by claimants, relief lobbies and the government.

The Famine Codes were the historical antecedent for a range of early warning systems relying on food security indicators that were developed following the mid-1980s famines in sub-Saharan Africa (Walker 1989; Buchanan-Smith and Davies 1995). Several agencies, including FAO, FEWS NET, Oxfam and Save the Children (UK), have devised their own systems (see Darcy and Hofmann 2003, for an analysis of their differences), but most are not based on a cogent definition of famine. One of the most successful is the Turkana District Early Warning System, which was designed for famine prevention in pastoralist areas of northern Kenya, but is explicitly based on the Indian Famine Codes. Context-specific food security indicators are monitored, such as rainfall; market prices and availability of cereals, livestock production, purchases and sales, rangeland condition and trends, ecological changes, and enrolment on food-for-work projects (Swift 1989). Regular monitoring of these indicators allows analysts to assess whether the current situation qualifies as a potential or actual food crisis. Three levels of crisis are identified – alarm, alert and emergency – each associated with a pre-planned set of 'off-the-shelf' responses.[7]

In his work on famine early warning systems, Cuny (1999: 37) distinguished between 'Indicators of Vulnerability', 'Indicators of Imminent Crisis' and 'Indicators of Famine'. An innovative application of Cuny's system was devised by the World Food Programme in Ethiopia in 2002 (Kerren Hedlund, pers. comm.). Drawing on a range of primary data and secondary sources, drought-affected areas were ranked by the number of 'pre-famine indicators'[8] observed (the highest was nine out of fourteen, in the pastoral lowlands). This information was complemented with anthropometric data, where available (e.g. 'Malnutrition rates of crisis proportions over 15 per cent in Afar'), to reach judgements about the severity of the food situation and its likely evolution in the coming months (e.g. 'The situation is expected to deteriorate rapidly unless food aid is provided on time').

Another contemporary application of an 'indicator-based' early warning system is the food security classification scheme devised for Somalia by the Food Security Assessment Unit (FSAU). Four levels are identified: 'Non-alert' ('near normal conditions'); 'Alert' ('requires close monitoring'); 'Livelihood Crisis' ('requires urgent livelihood support interventions'); and 'Humanitarian Emergency' ('requires urgent humanitarian assistance'). Two indicators of Livelihood Crisis are '>10 per cent global acute malnutrition (GAM)' and 'large-scale migration'. Two indicators of Humanitarian Emergency are '>20 per cent GAM' and 'large-scale destitution' (FSAU 2004: 2). As will be seen, this approach resonates with the combination of anthropometric indicators and food security descriptors that will form our 'intensity scale' for famine.

'Coping strategies'

The 1980s and 1990s saw a proliferation of case studies documenting the behavioural responses of populations affected by food crisis (cf. Watts 1983; Davies 1996). Generalizable patterns and sequences in the adoption of 'coping strategies' were identified (Corbett 1988), which led some analysts to suggest that these could be used as indicators of intensifying famine conditions.[9] Walker (1989: 49–50), for example, describes four 'stages' in the famine process. Stage (a) includes strategies for overcoming 'normal seasonal stress', such as rationing food, or diversifying income. If food stress is prolonged, increasingly irreversible strategies are employed in Stage (b) – such as selling breeding livestock, or mortgaging land – 'which trade short-term gain for long-term problems'. Stage (c) is characterized by dependence on external support (e.g. food aid), while if all these coping mechanisms fail, the terminal Stage (d) of starvation and death will follow. Walker (1989: 50) remarks:

> The essential difference between stage (a) and stage (b) strategies is that those in the second stage directly undermine the basis of the victim's means of survival ... [T]hey sacrifice future security for present survival. If one wished to mark the true beginnings of famine, as opposed to seasonal food shortage, this might be the appropriate place.

An important insight from the coping strategies literature is that famines threaten livelihoods as well as lives, and that effective famine prevention requires early intervention to protect livelihoods, rather than mandating famine relief just to 'save lives'. However, these coping sequences have some practical limitations. First, they are not universal but context-specific, and therefore require detailed assessment and modification in each affected area. This undermines their potential for providing generalizable famine descriptors. Second, isolating the 'stages' from each other is not as simple as it appears. Davies (1996) demonstrates the complexities of distinguishing 'coping' from 'adaptive' strategies, while Devereux (1993a) argues that coping strategies are not neatly sequenced but are often adopted in parallel.

More recently, the Coping Strategies Index has been devised as a tool for monitoring four categories of household adjustments to food stress: dietary change, rationing, short-term increases in food availability, and reducing household numbers to feed (CARE/WFP 2003). The authors accept the need to develop context-specific indicators and cut-offs for these generic coping strategies, and they avoid the terminology of 'famine stages', arguing simply that changes in the number of strategies adopted, or in the intensity of their adoption, can indicate a deteriorating or improving food security situation over time. So the Coping Strategies

Index is both a 'concurrent indicator' and a 'leading indicator' of famine, since it provides indications about both current food security status and impending food crises. These insights will prove useful for the development of our famine intensity scale.

Nutritional surveillance

If the context-specificity of coping strategies limits their instrumental value in terms of defining famine, a major advantage of nutritional surveillance lies in the fact that it provides universally comparable indicators of nutritional outcomes. Table 2.1 lists some of the definitions and benchmarks suggested by the United Nations Refugee Nutrition Information System (RNIS) and included by WFP in its *Food and Nutrition Handbook* (WFP 2000).

While these indicators and benchmarks are useful for differentiating between levels of humanitarian crises, they too have significant limitations in terms of predicting or defining famine. First, there are no generally

Table 2.1 RNIS definitions and benchmarks for interpreting nutritional data

Indicator	Definition interpretation	Benchmark for guidance in
Wasting	Less than –2 SDs, or sometimes 80% weight-for-height, usually in children aged 6–59 months	5–10% usual in African populations in non-drought periods >20% 'undoubtedly high and indicating a serious situation' >40% 'a severe crisis'
Oedema	Clinical sign of kwashiorkor	'any prevalence detected is cause for concern'
Crude mortality rate (CMR)	The number of deaths per 10,000 of the population within a specific time period	1/10,000 per day 'serious situation' >2/10,000 per day 'emergency out of control'
Under-five mortality rate (U5MR)	The number of deaths among children under five years of age within a specific time period	2/10,000 per day 'serious situation' 4/10,000 per day 'emergency out of control'

Source: WFP (2000: 39).

Notes
SD = Standard deviation from the reference norm. Weight-for-height is a measure of malnutrition based on the ratio of the actual weight of an individual to his/her height and comparing that ratio to the one expected for a well-nourished person of a reference population with similar height. The benchmark percentages for wasting refer to the percentage of children between six and fifty-nine months experiencing wasting in the population from which the sample was drawn. Oedema is a condition resulting from severe malnutrition whose symptoms include swelling of limbs.

accepted criteria of what rates of malnutrition or mortality indicate specifically that a famine has started. Even within the humanitarian community, some nutritionists and epidemiologists favoured a crude mortality rate (CMR) of one or more deaths daily per 10,000 people as the cut-off to define 'the emergency phase of a complex humanitarian emergency' (Spiegel *et al.* 2002: 1927), rather than the two deaths per 10,000 proposed by the RNIS. Salama *et al.* (2001) also favour a CMR cut-off of 1/10,000 per day to determine that a famine occurred in Ethiopia in 1999–2000.

Second, most nutritional indicators refer to children aged between six and fifty-nine months. As the Sphere Project (2004) points out, there are no agreed definitions and thresholds for moderate and severe malnutrition among older population groups: children over five years old, adolescents, working-age adults and elderly people. Yet, as Davis (1996: 868) argues, 'children over 5 and adults are disproportionately more affected by exposure to emergency risks than are younger children'. In households facing food stress, adults often reduce their consumption to ensure that their children are adequately fed. During famines, therefore, child malnutrition might be a 'trailing indicator' that may not manifest itself until well after adult nutrition status has deteriorated significantly.

A third difficulty is that the relationship between nutritional status and food crisis is complex and ambiguous. On the one hand, malnutrition outcomes can be the result of other factors besides inadequate food intake, such as disease, an unsanitary public health environment or poor childcare practices (Young 2001). This makes the interpretation of nutritional indicators problematic. In particular, it suggests that high rates of malnutrition should not be taken as indicative of famine conditions in the absence of complementary food security information (Chastre and le Jeune 2001). On the other hand, because it can be a late or 'trailing' indicator of food insecurity, low rates of malnutrition may mask a developing famine process: severe erosion of livelihoods and exhaustion of coping strategies.

Intensity and magnitude scales

For purposes of operational clarity – specifically, timelier and more equitable responses to famine threats – as well as greater accountability for famine prevention, we propose the adoption of famine intensity and magnitude scales. In this context, 'intensity' refers to the severity of a crisis at a point in time, which varies from place to place over its duration; while 'magnitude' refers to the aggregate impact of the crisis on affected populations. The scales aim to apply the understanding of famine contained in theoretical definitions, together with the empirical insights of the early warning and coping strategies literatures, to the diagnosis and classification of actual cases, and thereby to introduce a degree of rigour to what has hitherto been left vague and 'intuitive'. While our proposal draws on insights and indicators from various strands of literature reviewed above, the famine scales differ from previous models, such as the Indian Famine Codes and the Turkana District early warning system, in several respects.

First, the scales are intended to provide generalizable criteria for identifying famines so that situations across the globe can be compared (while at the same time recognizing that each food crisis is grounded in a specific context) by selecting locally appropriate food security indicators which capture the complex experiences of famine-affected populations, to complement standardized anthropometric cut-offs. Second, by disaggregating two distinct dimensions of famines – their intensity and their magnitude[10] – the scales capture a greater complexity of famine impacts than other approaches and definitions. Third, by moving away from a binary declaration of 'famine' or 'no famine' to a graduated approach based on impact levels, the scales offer the prospect of a more nuanced and operationally useful diagnosis of a range of food insecurity situations, which should eliminate the terminological debates that have caused fatal delays in several recent food crises.

Intensity scale

One feature that has confounded the adoption of appropriate criteria for identifying a famine is that humanitarian crises are dynamic and constantly evolving. Famines affect the same and different areas to different degrees at different times, which makes it problematic to apply a single label to the entire phenomenon. It is common, for instance, to speak of a famine as having an 'epicentre', suggesting that its impacts are concentrated in some areas more than in others.[11] The intensity parameter recognizes that famines do not have a uniform effect over an entire population area.[12]

A system of intensity levels can be used to identify the severity of conditions in a given area and to make comparisons with the situation in other areas, or in the same location at other times. An intensity level can be assigned to the population area using a combination of anthropometric and mortality indicators, as well as food security descriptors.[13] The anthropometric and mortality indicators provide cut-offs for each level that can be compared across situations. The food security descriptors capture the dynamic, self-reinforcing changes in the livelihood system associated with increasing degrees of food insecurity and famine, and can be adapted to specific circumstances (e.g. drought or conflict) and diverse contexts (see Howe and Devereux (2004), for an application of the famine scales to cropping *versus* pastoralist areas of Ethiopia). The anthropometric/mortality indicators and food security descriptors can be thought of as registering the effects of a crisis on the 'lives' and 'livelihoods', respectively, of the affected population (see Table 2.2).

Since there are two sets of criteria (anthropometric/mortality and food security), it is important to decide which should be given more weight in determining the intensity level for a given crisis. The assignment of weights might be made on the following basis:

- *Optimal*: both anthropometric/mortality and food security criteria point to a certain level
- *Sufficient*: anthropometric/mortality indicators on their own point to a certain level, and the affected population indicates that the onset of the crisis was predominantly about food[14]
- *Strongly suggestive, but not confirmatory*: food security descriptors on their own point to a certain level.

This system recognizes the information constraints facing decision-makers operating during humanitarian crises, by allowing all available information to be considered while assigning different confidence ratings to different data sources. For example, the geographical pattern of a food crisis in a given country could be mapped on the basis of information obtained from various sources, such as ongoing nutritional surveillance or one-off nutrition surveys, food security monitoring and 'rapid food security assessments'. The map could be colour-coded to represent different intensity levels or different 'confidence levels' (e.g. high intensity at the epicentre of the food crisis, but low confidence where this intensity level is assigned solely on the basis of food security descriptors such as high food prices and collapsing markets, without anthropometric confirmation).

An unresolved issue is the appropriate unit of analysis for determining the intensity level. Clearly, a nutritional assessment in a refugee camp or a village at the epicentre of a food crisis will find higher malnutrition rates than will an assessment over an entire district or region. This issue becomes particularly pertinent in the context of declarations of famine – there is a danger that actors will choose the unit of analysis to suit their interests in either declaring or not declaring a crisis a famine. There is no obvious resolution to this, except to note that the intensity and magnitude scales are designed to be used in combination (see below).

Although these designations may only be known for certain areas and be subject to constant revision and updating, they do convey important operational information. First, they offer clear guidelines for assessing food insecurity conditions in specific places at specific times, and for identifying both the start and end of a famine. Once an area reaches 'level 3' conditions, a famine can be said to be occurring among the local population, while the famine would 'officially' be over when all affected areas return to 'level 2' conditions or lower for a continuous period of, say, six months (to ensure that the improvement is not just temporary).[15]

Second, the intensity levels provide support to famine early warning systems that are linked directly to response. Concerned stakeholders could monitor trends carefully in areas that have received a 'level 1' or

Table 2.2 Intensity scale

Levels[a]	Phrase designation	'Lives': malnutrition and mortality indicators	'Livelihoods': food security descriptors[b]
0	Food security conditions	CMR <0.2 *and* wasting $<2.3\%$ strategies	Social system is cohesive; prices are stable; negligible adoption of coping
1	Food insecurity conditions	CMR ≥ 0.2 but $<5/10{,}000$ per day *and/or* wasting ≥ 2.3 but $<10\%$	Social system remains cohesive; price instability and seasonal shortage of key items; reversible 'adaptive strategies' are employed
2	Food crisis conditions	CMR ≥ 0.5 but $<1/10{,}000$ per day *and/or* wasting ≥ 10 but $<20\%$ and/or prevalence of oedema	Social system significantly stressed but remains largely cohesive; dramatic rise in price of food and other basic items; adaptive mechanisms start to fail; increase in irreversible coping strategies
3	Famine conditions	CMR ≥ 1 but $<5/10{,}000$ per day *and/or* wasting $\geq 20\%$ but $<40\%$ and/or prevalence of oedema	Clear signs of social breakdown appear; markets begin to close or collapse; coping strategies are exhausted and survival strategies are adopted; affected population identify food as the dominant problem in the onset of the crisis
4	Severe famine conditions	CMR $>5=$ but $<15/10{,}000$ per day *and/or* wasting $\geq 40\%$ and/or prevalence of oedema	Widespread social breakdown; markets are closed or inaccessible to affected population; survival strategies are widespread; affected population identify food as the dominant problem in the onset of this crisis
5	Extreme famine conditions	CMR $\geq 15/10{,}000$ per day	Complete social breakdown; widespread mortality; affected population identify food as the dominant problem in the onset of the crisis

Notes

CMR = Crude Mortality Rate

Wasting: Proportion of child population (six months to five years old) who are below 80 per cent of the median weight-for-height or below −2 Z-score weight-for-height (cf. NCHS 1977)

a The idea of using a system of levels was originally suggested to the authors by Hamish Young of UNICEF.

b These food security descriptors are examples of the types of experiences that may be associated with each intensity level, but not all of them have to be present in every situation that is given that intensity designation.

'level 2' designation, making recommendations for interventions appropriate to that level of food insecurity, while striving to prevent progression to higher levels. (Of course, moving from 'level 0' to 'level 1', or from 'level 1' to 'level 2', does not imply that further deterioration is inevitable: circumstances could improve with no external assistance.) This system does not wholly remove the uncertainty involved in making early warning predictions – because data are always unreliable or incomplete, and the trajectory of any humanitarian crisis is always unpredictable to some extent – but it does indicate more precisely which category of food insecurity, food crisis or famine is being observed.

Third, the introduction of a food security descriptor that refers to the affected population's interpretation of the role of food provides a way to distinguish between famines and other humanitarian crises. Fourth, a harmonized set of terms should facilitate better coordinated response and advocacy efforts, by ensuring a consistent and widely accepted language for declarations by governments and humanitarian agencies.

Fifth, the famine scales can contribute to more equitable distribution of aid resources, both within and across crises. Within a country, the intensity scale provides a differentiation between circumstances in various locations. Designation and mapping allow stakeholders to prioritize their resource allocations among different areas and, in combination with early warning indicators of trends, to design a coherent overall strategy for response. The scales also provide a standard for making comparisons across countries. During the crises in Kosovo and southern Sudan in 1998, the intensity scale would have shown that, in terms of both intensity and magnitude, the situation in southern Sudan was more serious than that in Kosovo. Although the adoption of the famine scales is unlikely to bring about a realignment of donor interests, the scales do provide a vocabulary and an analytical basis for making a more forceful argument for equity in aid allocations.

Magnitude scale

Over time, the areas and populations affected by famine and food insecurity will change – expanding and contracting in size, increasing and decreasing in intensity. It is only in retrospect that a complete assessment of the full magnitude of a crisis can be made. Given the practical difficulty of measuring all the impacts of a humanitarian crisis – including its macroeconomic, socio-cultural, psychological and other consequences – 'magnitude' refers here to the scale of human suffering caused by the entire crisis, as proxied by excess mortality. A graduated scale can be used to make crude estimates of the magnitude of a famine while it is ongoing, as well as to classify famines *ex post* (see Table 2.3).

Note that mortality in the 'magnitude scale' begins at 0 rather than 1, because our criteria for famine conditions in the 'intensity scale' include malnutrition rates that need not imply deaths, and because a rise in the

Table 2.3 Magnitude scale

Category	Phrase designation	Mortality range
A	Minor famine	0–999
B	Moderate famine	1,000–9,999
C	Major famine	10,000–99,999
D	Great famine	100,000–999,999
E	Catastrophic famine	1,000,000 and over

CMR is not a prerequisite for a declaration of 'level 3' famine. This decision speaks to a long-running debate in the famine literature, as to whether famines are, by definition, characterized by excess mortality. On the one hand, since death is the most tragic human consequence of famine, quantifying the aggregate impact of a famine by the number of deaths it causes seems logical, and provides a basis for comparison across famines. On the other hand, allowing a 'minor famine' to be declared even if no deaths have occurred endorses the view that famines are complex processes that are characterized by hunger and destitution, but not necessarily by death, and rejects the reductionist position that famine equates to 'mass death by starvation'.[16]

Using intensity and magnitude scales together

The intensity and magnitude scales are designed to be complementary. Any intensity level of 3 or above will register as a famine on the magnitude scale, even if it occurs in a very localized area, and even if no deaths are recorded (this would be a 'Category A' famine). However, the converse does not necessarily apply: not every situation that involves excess mortality is a famine. 'Level 2: food crisis conditions' may result in mortality, but the crisis associated with these deaths will not be classified as a 'famine' unless the intensity of conditions reaches 'level 3' or above in at least one assessment area. (However, as long as one population area experiences famine conditions, the deaths from other areas associated with the crisis should be included in the total mortality figures to determine the magnitude, even if the intensity only reaches 'level 1' or 'level 2' in those places.)

Using these scales, it is possible to make more precise differentiations among crises and to suggest proportionate assignments of responsibility under different circumstances. For instance, a small population area may experience 'level 4: severe famine conditions', but the crisis, because it involves a limited population, will register as a 'minor famine'. The scales allow concerned stakeholders to acknowledge the intensity of the crisis in that area, but at the same time to distinguish the magnitude of this localized crisis from those that involve larger and more widespread popula-

Table 2.4 Examples of magnitude classifications

Famine (year)	Estimated mortality	Magnitude classification	Phrase designation
Sudan (1998)	70,000	Category C	Major famine
Ethiopia (2000)	6,070	Category B	Moderate famine
Malawi (2002)	300–500	Category A	Minor famine

Sources: For Sudan, Deng (1999); for Ethiopia, Salama *et al.* (2001), most conservative estimate based solely on Gode District without extrapolation; for Malawi, Devereux (2002). Note that Devereux and Tiba (this volume) have subsequently produced higher mortality estimates for the Malawi famine.

tions. Greater *accountability* would be expected for famines of greater magnitude.

To illustrate the use of these scales, we now return briefly to the three cases mentioned at the start of this paper. The crises in Sudan (1998), Ethiopia (2000) and Malawi (2002) would all be recognized as famines, but they would be categorized differentially by the magnitude scale, according to their respective mortalities (Table 2.4).

Within each of these crises, the intensity level, as measured by CMRs, varied from place to place (see Table 2.5). In southern Sudan (1998), Ajiep Village experienced 'level 5: Extreme famine conditions', while Rumbek Town suffered 'level 3: Famine conditions'. Similar distinctions could be made among sites in Ethiopia and Malawi. The evidence from southern Malawi reveals that this was a highly localized famine, with Salima being one of the worst affected districts, while Mchinji and other districts registered 'food insecurity' but not 'famine' conditions.

Table 2.5 Examples of intensity classifications

Famine (year)	Location	CMR	Intensity classification	Phrase designation
Sudan (1998)	Ajiep Village	26/10,000 per day	Level 5	Extreme famine conditions
	Rumbek Town	3.7/10,000 per day	Level 3	Famine conditions
Ethiopia (2000)	Gode District	3.2/10,000 per day	Level 3	Famine conditions
Malawi (2002)	Salima District	1.23/10,000 per day	Level 3	Famine conditions
	Mchinji District	0.21/10,000 per day	Level 1	Food insecurity conditions

Sources: For Ajiep and Rumbek, Sudan, UNSCN (1999); for Gode District, Ethiopia, Salama *et al.* (2001); for Salima and Mchinji Districts, Malawi, King (2002). These figures are 'snapshots' and do not reflect the trends in each of these locations.

Combining the scales, we can say in hindsight that southern Sudan (1998) was a 'Category C: Major famine' with intensity levels varying between 3 and 5. At the time of the crisis, stakeholders would have identified the 'level 5' and 'level 3' conditions in Ajiep Village and Rumbek Town, respectively, and could have declared a 'famine'. They might also have projected that the magnitude of the crisis would qualify it as a 'Category C: Major famine', and that without further intervention, it could become a 'Category D: Great famine'.

Even though Ethiopia (2000) registered in retrospect as a 'Category B: Moderate famine', conditions in Gode District were similar to those experienced in parts of southern Sudan, which became a 'Category C: Major famine'. However, in Ethiopia the intensity levels affected a smaller population for a shorter period of time, and in other areas of southern Sudan intensity levels were much higher. It would be appropriate to demand greater accountability in the case of Sudan, since the magnitude of the famine was greater: many more people lost their lives.

The discussion in this section has focused on acute food crises, as opposed to chronic food insecurity. There are other situations where high rates of malnutrition and mortality persist for long periods of time, but do not achieve general recognition as 'famines'. Examples include Iraq under UN sanctions throughout the 1990s (Gazdar 2002), and Somalia over the last several years. Prendiville (2003) makes the point that humanitarian intervention in southern Africa in 2002 was triggered by malnutrition rates in one area rising from 2.5 to 5 per cent. In the same year, a routine nutrition survey in southern Somalia recorded 13 per cent malnutrition, but no special interventions were recommended as this figure 'was (tragically) within the range regularly seen in Somalia' (Prendiville 2003: 6). What distinguishes Malawi in 2002 from Somalia at the same time is not the absolute level of malnutrition observed, but its level relative to what is considered 'normal' or 'acceptable' in the local context.

Somalia in the early 2000s would not qualify as a famine on our famine scales. Why not? Because famines are synergistic crises, associated with rapidly rising anthropometric and/or mortality indicators *and* corresponding degrees of economic and community stress, as indicated by the food security or 'livelihoods' descriptors. A famine is an accelerated process of rising individual malnutrition, household destitution and social breakdown. For a famine to occur, there has to be a rapid deterioration in food security indicators – a rise from one level to the next on our intensity scale – in a short time period. Some writers have even argued that famines are qualitatively different from other forms of extreme food insecurity – as different, say, as freezing water is from ice (Rivers *et al.* 1976).

The danger of this approach is the 'normalization' of conditions of extreme food insecurity or 'quiet emergencies' (cf. Bradbury 2000). One way to avoid this is to use the famine scales to apply different labels to situations like Iraq or Somalia, which are characterized by persistently poor food security outcomes but no discrete famine 'event'. Specifically, a 'chronic famine' might be defined as a population area that experiences intensity levels (in anthropometric terms) that remain persistently between '2: food crisis conditions' and '3: famine conditions' over a minimum period of, say, three years. A 'chronic food crisis' might be defined as a population area where intensity levels fluctuate between '1: food insecurity conditions' and '2: food crisis conditions' over a similar period of time.

Implications for accountability

The famine scales have significant implications for accountability. During a crisis, the scales provide a basis for exerting pressure on responsible actors to intervene. After the crisis, the scales offer a basis for assigning proportionate accountability. This might also have a galvanizing effect: if stakeholders realize that an internationally agreed definition has been adopted that could be used to assign culpability, they should take greater efforts to prevent famines from occurring.

Proportionate accountability is an important principle in the context of assigning liability for famine. Proportionality relates not only to number of deaths on the magnitude scale, but also to intent. Devereux (1993b) draws a distinction between acts of commission (deliberate attempts to create famine conditions) and acts of omission (failing to intervene to prevent famine). When famine is used as a weapon of war or genocide, the perpetrators could, in theory, be put on trial at the International Criminal Court (ICC) for crimes against humanity (Edkins 2002). Relevant cases might include the actions of the Derg Government before the Ethiopian famine of 1984, and the actions of the Government of Sudan and the rebel leader Kerubino Bol before the famine in southern Sudan in 1998 (Keen 1999).

Acts of omission describe cases where governments or donors fail to respond appropriately and in good time to prevent food crises from developing into famines, despite having the power to do so. When governments pursue policies that inadvertently create famine conditions, or donors withhold food aid for political reasons – both these allegations were made about the 'moderate famine' in Ethiopia in 2000 and the 'minor famine' in Malawi in 2002 – the culpability may not be as great as when famines are malevolently engineered, but some sanction should surely follow: the dismissal of negligent government and donor officials, for instance. On the other hand, it is important to ensure that strengthening accountability for famine prevention does not create perverse incentives, such that governments and humanitarian agencies devote disproportionate resources and energy to ensuring simply that threshold malnutrition and mortality rates on the famine scales are not crossed. Ideally, policymakers will recognize that the best way to reduce the risk of famine is to tackle its underlying causes, which implies implementing a broader range of policies that protect and promote long-term livelihoods, as well as establishing effective safety nets.

An instrumental definition is only one tool to help achieve accountability. There remains an urgent need to establish global accountability structures for protecting the right to food and ensuring freedom from famine. Two problems with current structures include the diffusion of responsibility among a range of national and international actors – which has created a 'black hole' of unaccountability (IDS 2002) – and the absence of direct lines of accountability to affected populations. Addressing the first issue requires a clear designation of responsibilities among relevant actors in each country (what are the specific famine prevention roles in Ethiopia, Sudan, Malawi and elsewhere of the national government, international donors, NGOs and other actors?). One possibility would be to construct an 'accountability matrix' as a way of identifying the various functions involved in famine prevention and assigning responsibility for each function to named institutions. Devising and applying an accountability matrix would have four steps:

1   Recognizing the various roles played by a range of mandated stakeholders – government, major donors, operational agencies (e.g. WFP), international NGOs, local NGOs, early warning systems (e.g. FEWS NET) – in attempting to ensure that famines do not occur in a given country;
2   Assigning direct responsibility for each specific function (e.g. providing food security information, delivering food aid) to specified stakeholders;
3   After a famine occurs, examining which stakeholders failed to meet their responsibilities (e.g. inappropriate government policies, inaccurate information or late delivery of food aid);
4   Holding these stakeholders to account, by imposing appropriate sanctions.

Addressing the second issue – the absence of direct lines of accountability – requires establishing mechanisms for affected populations to voice their concerns and ensure a response. Ideally, this would be achieved by building 'anti-famine political contracts' (de Waal 1997) between governments and citizens. Another option is for national human rights institutions or food security activists, where they exist, to include campaigning for the 'right to food' in their mandates and activities (IGWG 2003: 11). Alternatively, since many governments are unable to ensure food security and have ceded partial responsibility for this to the international community, a global 'food security ombudsperson' might need to be appointed (Howe 2003). This is, of course, a second-best option that reflects the failure of national-level accountability, but until national governments are able to ensure food security as a basic citizenship right, a mechanism that recognizes the right of all 'global citizens' to freedom from famine is perhaps an appropriate interim solution.

Conclusion

The intensity and magnitude scales outlined in this chapter address several longstanding ambiguities in theoretical definitions and practitioner understandings of 'famine', and attempt to contribute to the purposes of better informed and more effective anti-famine interventions, as well as greater accountability. By drawing on the strengths of previous approaches, and recognizing the complexities and uniqueness of each crisis, the famine scales aim to provide a means of defining and categorizing food crises in a way that is rigorous, disaggregated but comparable across diverse contexts, and useful to stakeholders responsible for famine prediction and prevention.

The famine scales are not intended to replace early warning systems; rather, they complement each other, and both should be components of any 'humanitarian information system' (Maxwell and Watkins 2003). While the famine scales register the intensity and magnitude of food crises, early warning systems predict potential movements up or down the scales. Used together, the scales should provide more precision in using (or not using) the term 'famine'. Importantly, the famine scales lower the threshold of famine definitions currently used by donors and UN agencies. They also provide a framework for focusing more policy attention on famine prevention and less on famine response, through building consensus among stakeholders while ensuring accountability.

However, we do not underestimate the conceptual, methodological and political difficulties of translating the famine scales into reality. Most fundamentally, any definition of famine, especially one that selects a range of indicators and sets thresholds, will have an element of arbitrariness. Several authors (cf. Edkins 2000; Howe 2002) have questioned the possibility of arriving at a single incontestable definition of famine that corresponds to the 'truth'. It follows that any definition represents a choice and is therefore more political than technical: rather than being 'found', a definition of famine must be 'agreed'.

Notes

1 The authors thank, without implication, participants in an 'Operational Definitions of Famine' workshop at IDS Sussex on 14 March 2003, participants in the USAID 'Famine Forum' in Washington, DC on 24–25 March 2004, and individuals who have commented on earlier drafts, including Alex de Waal, Beth Dunford, Frances Mason, Nick Maunder, Dan Maxwell, John Seaman, Phil Steffen and Tim Shortley.
2 On the debate over the use of the term 'famine' in Sudan (1998), see Deng

1999 and Howe 2002; for the case of Ethiopia (1999/2000) see Salama *et al.* 2001 and Maxwell 2002; on Ethiopia (2002–2003) see Lautze *et al.* 2003; on Malawi (2002) see Devereux 2002.

3 'Despite an extended drought and conflict in the Horn of Africa, famine was averted this summer, largely as a result of USAID activities that provided early warning and prompt delivery of food aid to the region. Catherine Bertini, head of the UN World Food programme, declared September 20 that early action "helped us to avert a famine in the Horn of Africa", which had threatened more than 16 million people' (Anderson 2000: 1).

4 Ongoing efforts to reach intergovernmental consensus on the 'right to food' would benefit greatly from global agreement on key terms, including 'famine'. Interestingly, the draft 'Voluntary Guidelines to Support the Progressive Real-ization of the Right to Adequate Food in the Context of National Food Secur-ity' (IGWG 2003) includes two 'Guidelines' on 'Emergencies' and two on 'International Food Aid', but makes no reference at all to famine.

5 For reviews of this extensive literature, see *inter alia* Sen 1981; de Waal 1989; Devereux 1993b.

6 Currey and Hugo's (1984: 1) full definition is: 'Famine is a community crisis; a syndrome with webs of causation through which communities lose their ability to support marginal members who consequently either migrate in families because of lack of access to food, or die of starvation or starvation related disease'.

7 CARE (2003) has adopted a similar system of 'states' for its work in chronically vulnerable areas.

8 These were derived from Cuny's 'indicators of imminent crisis', which included: prolonged drought; rise in price ratio of staple grain to prevailing wages; increase in sales of livestock and decrease in average sale price; increase in deaths among livestock; consumption of famine foods (Cuny 1999: 37).

9 Though related, the coping strategies literature is distinct from the early warning literature. While many early warning systems have drawn on studies of coping strategies, they monitor a range of food availability and access indic-ators that are not coping strategies. Conversely, coping strategies provide more than early warning information, since they also tell us about the impact of livelihood crises.

10 A similar distinction is made in earthquake measurement (cf. www.seismo.unr.edu; wwwneic.cr.usgs.gov; www.zephyrus.demon.co.uk). This section has also drawn on scales used for hurricanes (cf. www.nhc.noaa.gov) and tornadoes (cf. www.tornadoproject.com).

11 Seaman and Holt (1980), for instance, identified 'waves' or 'ripples' of food price rises during the course of a food crisis, with scarcity conditions at the epi-centre gradually pushing up prices at the periphery.

12 The 'population area' refers to the geographic location inhabited by the affected population.

13 Both the anthropometric indicators and the food security descriptors are illus-trative at this point. For the intensity scales to generate widespread support from agencies involved in emergency response, the anthropometric/mortality cut-off points and food security descriptors may need to be discussed in more detail by technical specialists and experts, including affected populations.

14 Without the qualifying food security descriptor, elevated anthropometric and mortality data might reflect a health crisis (e.g. an epidemic) rather than a food crisis.

15 Continuous monitoring and application of the intensity scale could also help to prevent what Dyson and Ó Gráda (2002: 13) have labelled 'bang-bang famines' – the fact that 'food crises often come in pairs'.

16 Similarly, de Waal (2000: 7) identifies 'three degrees of famine severity', the first being 'Famines involving primarily hunger and destitution', while only second- and third-degree famines are characterized by 'elevated rates of mortality'. (Third-degree famines also involve 'severe social dislocation and collapse'.)

References

Anderson, J. (2000) 'Preventing famine', *Front Lines*, August/September. Washington, DC: USAID.

Bhatia, B. (1963) *Famines in India*, London: Asia Publishing House.

Bradbury, M. (2000) 'Normalizing the crisis in Africa', *Journal of Humanitarian Assistance* (available at www.jha.ac/articles/a043.htm, accessed 3 June 2003).

Brennan, L. (1984) 'The development of the Indian Famine Codes: personalities, politics, and policies', in B. Currey and G. Hugo (eds), *Famine as a Geographical Phenomenon*, Dordrecht: Reidel Publishing.

British Broadcasting Corporation (BBC) (1998) 'UN declares famine in Sudan', BBC News Online Network, (available at www.news.bbc.co.uk, accessed 11 June 2003).

Buchanan-Smith, M. and Davies, S. (1995) *Famine Early Warning and Response: The Missing Link*, London: Intermediate Technology Publications.

CARE (2003) *Managing Risk, Improving Livelihoods: Program Guidelines for Conditions of Chronic Vulnerability*, Nairobi: CARE Eastern/Central Africa Regional Management Unit.

CARE/WFP (2003) *The Coping Strategies Index: Field Methods Manual*, Nairobi: CARE and WFP.

Chastre, C. and Le Jeune, S. (2001) 'Strengthening analysis of the nutrition situation through linking food security and nutrition information: pitfalls and potentials', *Field Exchange*, 13: 8–9.

Corbett, J. (1988) 'Famine and household coping strategies', *World Development*, 16(9): 1009–112.

Cuny, F. (1999) *Famine, Conflict, and Response: A Basic Guide*, West Hartford, CT: Kumarian Press.

Currey, B. and Hugo, G. (eds) (1984) *Famine as a Geographical Phenomenon*, Dordrecht: Reidel Publishing.

Darcy, J. and Hofmann, C. A. (2003) 'According to need? Needs assessment and decision-making in the humanitarian sector', *HPG Report* 15, London: Overseas Development Institute.

Davies, S. (1996) *Adaptable Livelihoods: Coping with Food Insecurity in the Malian Sahel*, London: Macmillan Press.

Davis, A. (1996) 'Targeting the vulnerable in emergency situations: who is vulnerable?', *Lancet*, 348: 868–71.

Deng, L. B. (1999) 'Famine in the Sudan: causes, preparedness, and response', *IDS Discussion Paper* 369, Brighton: Institute of Development Studies.

Devereux, S. (1993a) 'Goats before ploughs: dilemmas of household response sequencing during food shortages', *IDS Bulletin*, 24(4): 52–9.

Devereux, S. (1993b) *Theories of Famine*, London: Harvester Wheatsheaf.

Devereux, S. (2002) 'The Malawi famine of 2002', *IDS Bulletin*, 33(4): 70–8.

de Waal, A. (1989) *Famine That Kills: Darfur, Sudan, 1984–1985*, Oxford: Clarendon Press.

de Waal, A. (1997) *Famine Crimes: Politics and the Disaster Relief Industry in Africa*, Oxford: James Currey.

de Waal, A. (2000) 'Democratic political process and the fight against famine', *IDS Working Paper* 107, Brighton: Institute of Development Studies.

Drèze, J. (1990) 'Famine prevention in India', in J. Drèze and A. Sen (eds), *The Political Economy of Hunger, Volume II: Famine Prevention*, Oxford: Clarendon Press.

Dyson, T. and Ó Gráda, C. (2002) *Famine Demography*, Oxford: Oxford University Press.

Edkins, J. (2000) *Whose Hunger? Concepts of Famine, Practices of Aid*, London: University of Minnesota Press.

Edkins, J. (2002) 'Mass starvation and the limitations of famine theorising', *IDS Bulletin*, 33(4): 12–18.

Floud, J. (1993) 'Famine and society: a report of the proceedings', in J. Floud and A. Rangasami (eds), *Famine and Society*, New Delhi: Indian Law Institute.

Food Security Assessment Unit (FSAU) (2004) *Monthly Food Security Report: Somalia, February 2004*, Nairobi: FSAU.

Gazdar, H. (2002) 'Pre-modern, modern, and post-modern famine in Iraq', *IDS Bulletin*, 33(4): 63–9.

Howe, P. (2002) 'Reconsidering "famine"', *IDS Bulletin*, 33(4): 19–27.

Howe, P. (2003) 'Contesting "famine": a study of conceptual ambiguities and their implications for response and accountability in Southern Sudan, 1998', PhD thesis, Brighton: Institute of Development Studies.

Howe, P. and Devereux, S. (2004) 'Famine intensity and magnitude scales: applying the famine scales in Ethiopia' (mimeo), Brighton: Institute of Development Studies.

Institute of Development Studies (IDS) (2002) *Learning the Lessons? Famine in Ethiopia, 1999–2000* (video), London: Rockhopper Productions.

Intergovernmental Working Group on the Right to Food (IGWG) (2003) *Voluntary Guidelines to Support the Progressive Realisation of the Right to Adequate Food in the Context of National Food Security (draft for consideration at the Second Session of the IGWG)*, Rome: IGWG Bureau.

Keen, D. (1999) 'Making famine in Sudan', *Field Exchange*, 6: 6–7.

King, S. (2002) 'Malawi food shortage: how did it happen and how could it have been prevented?', *Field Exchange*, 16: 21–2.

Lautze, S., Aklilu, Y., Raven-Roberts, A., Young, H., Kebede, G. and Leaning, J. (2003) 'Risk and vulnerability in Ethiopia: learning from the past, responding to the present, preparing for the future', Report for the US Agency for International Development, Medford: Feinstein Famine Center, Tufts University.

Maxwell, D. (2002) 'Why do famines persist? A brief review of Ethiopia 1999–2000', *IDS Bulletin*, 33(4): 48–54.

Maxwell, D. and Watkins, B. (2003) 'Humanitarian information systems and emergencies in the Greater Horn of Africa: logical components and logical linkages', *Disasters*, 27(1): 72–90.

Mayer, J. (1975) 'Management of famine relief', *Science*, 188(4188): 571–7.

National Centre for Health Statistics (1977) 'NCHS growth curves for children, birth–18 years, United States', *Vital Health Statistics*, 165: 11–74.

Olsen, G., Carstensen, N. and Hoyen, K. (2002) 'Humanitarian crises: what determines the level of emergency assistance? Media coverage, donor interests, and the aid business', Paper presented at 'Forgotten Humanitarian Crises: Conference on the Role of the Media, Decision-makers and Humanitarian Agencies', 23 October, Copenhagen.

Prendiville, N. (2003) 'Nutrition and food security information systems in crisis-prone countries', Paper presented at the International Workshop on 'Food Security in Complex Emergencies', 23–25 September, Tivoli, Italy: Food and Agriculture Organisation.

Rangasami, A. (1985) ' "Failure of exchange entitlements" theory of famine: a response', *Economic and Political Weekly*, 20(41 and 42): 1747–52; 1797–1801.

Rangasami, A. (1993) 'The masking of famine: the role of the bureaucracy', in J. Floud and A. Rangasami (eds), *Famine and Society*, New Delhi: Indian Law Institute.

Rivers, J., Holt, J., Seaman, J. and Bowden, M. (1976) 'Lessons for epidemiology from the Ethiopian famines', *Annales Société Belge de Médecine Tropicale*, 56: 345–57.

Salama, P., Assefa, F., Talley, L., Spiegel, P., van der Veen, A. and Gotway, C. (2001) 'Malnutrition, measles, mortality and the humanitarian response during a famine in Ethiopia', *Journal of the American Medical Association*, 286(5): 563–71.

Seaman, J. and Holt, J. (1980) 'Markets and famines in the Third World', *Disasters*, 4(3): 283–97.

Sen, A. (1981) *Poverty and Famines: An Essay on Entitlement and Deprivation*, Oxford: Clarendon Press.

Singh, K. S. (1993) 'The famine code: the context and continuity', in J. Floud and A. Rangasami (eds), *Famine and Society*, New Delhi: Indian Law Institute.

Sphere Project (2004) *Humanitarian Charter and Minimum Standards in Disaster Response*, Geneva: The Sphere Project.

Spiegel, P., Sheil, M., Gotway-Crawford, C. and Salama, P. (2002) 'Health programmes and policies associated with deceased mortality in displaced people in post-emergency phase camps: a retrospective study', *Lancet*, 360: 1927–34.

Swift, J. (1989) 'Why are rural people vulnerable to famine?', *IDS Bulletin*, 20(2): 8–15.

The Times Editor (1998) 'Hope in hell: there is no famine in Sudan yet, nor need there be one', *The Times*, April 30: 25.

United Nations Sub-Committee on Nutrition (UNSCN) (1999) 'Report on the nutrition situation of refugee and displaced populations', *Refugee Nutrition Information System* (RNIS) 26 (available at www.unsystem.org/scn/archives/rnis26).

Walker, P. (1989) *Famine Early Warning Systems: Victims and Destitution*, London: Earthscan Publications.

Watson, F. (2002) 'Why are there no longer "war famines" in contemporary Europe? The case of the besieged areas of Bosnia 1992–5', *IDS Bulletin* 33(4): 39–47.

Watts, M. (1983) *Silent Violence: Food, Famine and Peasantry in Northern Nigeria*, Berkeley, CA: University of California Press.

World Food Programme (2000) *Food and Nutrition Handbook*, Rome: WFP.

Young, H. (2001) 'Nutrition and intervention strategies', in S. Devereux and S. Maxwell (eds), *Food Security in Sub-Saharan Africa*, London: ITDG Publishing.

3 The criminalization of mass starvations

From natural disaster to crime against humanity[1]

Jenny Edkins

Introduction

On 31 March 2005 the United Nations Security Council passed Resolution 1593, referring 'the situation prevailing in the Darfur region' of the Sudan to the International Criminal Court (ICC) in The Hague (United Nations 2005). This resolution was notable in being the first instance of a case being referred to the fledgling court by the Security Council.[2] It was also, significantly, the first time that anyone responsible for a situation described as a famine had faced the prospect of being brought to justice and held accountable in this way. What at one time could be passed off as a natural disaster was now indictable as a crime against humanity.

According to the International Committee of the Red Cross, Darfur was facing a food crisis 'worse even than the African famines of the 1980s and 1990s' (Foulkes 2004). A report commissioned by the UN following a Security Council Resolution in September 2004 had strongly recommended that the Council refer the situation to the ICC. They found that:

> A body of reliable information indicates that war crimes may have been committed on a large scale, at times even as part of a plan or a policy. There is also a wealth of credible material which suggests that criminal acts were committed as part of widespread or systematic attacks directed against the civilian population, with knowledge of the attacks. In the opinion of the Commission therefore, these may amount to crimes against humanity'.
> (International Commission of Inquiry on Darfur 2005: 5)

The acts they were talking about included 'extensive destruction and displacement [that] resulted in a loss of livelihood and means of survival for countless women, men and children' (International Commission of Inquiry on Darfur 2005: 3).

In the Sudan, both victims of the famine and its perpetrators had only one place on their minds: The Hague. Those who had been persecuted wanted to go to The Hague to testify; the militia leaders were eager to assure the world that they didn't belong there (Power 2005). However, The Hague seemed an unlikely scenario at this point. The Sudan was not a party to the ICC, and the rules were that any prosecution for criminal acts in such a country could only come from a referral by the UN Security Council – but the US, a vociferous opponent of the court (Sands 2005), had veto powers on the Security Council. However, despite the odds against it, UN Resolution 1593 was passed, and a list of fifty-one named suspects was handed to the ICC Prosecutor. It remains to be seen what the outcome of the Security Council's action will be as far as the Sudan is concerned, and how the ICC will respond to its first major challenge, but this was undoubtedly a significant moment in terms of strengthening calls for famine crimes and mass starvations to be actionable in international law (Edkins 2002a; Marcus 2003; Howe and Devereux 2004).

The response in 2005 was very different to what had happened twenty years earlier in Ethiopia, where a government similarly engaged in an internal military conflict that led to widespread disruption of civilian life and the displacement or forcible resettlement of thousands of people was able successfully to lay the blame for famine and starvation on a natural disaster. Even much later, when it was widely known that many if not most of the deaths in 1984–1985 were attributable more to war than to drought, Ethiopia remained synonymous in the public eye with food shortage and the absence of rains. When we call something a famine it seems no one is to blame; it is only when we call it a genocide that we look for perpetrators. This chapter explores why this is the case, and how we might think differently. I will argue that it is important to ask *who* might be responsible for a famine, rather than *what* caused it: nothing 'caused' the war crimes or crimes against humanity in Darfur. People committed these acts. Similarly, I argue in this chapter, nothing 'causes' famines: people commit the crime of mass starvation.

We begin by exploring the dangers of a common thread that runs through much theorizing about famine in the development literature, and that is linked to the search for cause: technologization. Famine is seen as a failure, a breakdown of an otherwise benign system that just needs fixing. Many of the existing ways of defining and theorizing famine are trapped in this framework, one that regards famine as a failure to which scientific or technical solutions can be found. Approaches of this sort, which include ways of thinking that see famines as evidence of an economic failure as much as those that see it as a natural disaster, lead to responses that are not only incapable of responding adequately to the politics of mass starvations but are themselves implicated in such politics. These responses are technologized (Edkins 2000): they seek a better technical 'fix' for the problem of famine by first investigating what 'causes' it.

The chapter suggests an alternative way of thinking, where the important question is not 'What causes famine and what is the appropriate response if famine is to be avoided?' but 'How were acts of mass starvation committed and by whom, and how can those responsible be brought to justice?'. In this view, mass starvation is seen as a crime against humanity. The language changes, and the issue becomes not what response there should be to famine, but where responsibility lies for producing it in the first place and how those responsible can be held to account.

One obvious way in which perpetrators of crimes against humanity can be held to account is through the ICC, as is beginning to happen. The Rome Statute of the ICC was signed in 1998 and came into force in July 2002 (Schabas 2001; Broomhall 2003). In the second section of this chapter I outline the ways in which the Rome statute already provides for mass starvation as a criminal act, as we have seen in the Darfur case. David Marcus has elaborated four degrees of famine crime committed by government officials, two of which he demonstrates are already covered in international law in a variety of ways, including through the ICC as I have elucidated (Marcus 2003). He proposes that they are in need of codification. The other two forms of what he calls 'faminogenic activity' he does not regard as suitable for inclusion in international law. However, it could be argued that these correspond fairly closely to the duties laid on states by the Intergovernmental Right to Food signed in 2004, and could usefully be pursued in that context.

In the end it is necessary to consider whether it is worth retaining the term 'famine' at all. It has always been a difficult and contested term, often sidelining the experiences of people most closely involved (de Waal 2005: 9–32) and focusing attention on only one part of a process of oppression (Rangasami 1985). There are clearly a number of organizations, both governmental and non-governmental, whose work is focused on food and nutrition and whose *raison d'être* would be threatened if the term were dropped. However, these approaches are contaminated by the associations that the term 'famines' inevitably conjures up: food shortages, agricultural failure, drought and overpopulation. Starvation is no more 'natural' than suffocation; the former is no more a shortage of food than the latter is a shortage of air. Why persist with a word which is disliked by those closest to what it is supposed to signify, and convenient to those who wish to abdicate or conceal their responsibility for what is happening?

Technologized responses and their limitations

There have been numerous attempts to establish what is meant by famine and to determine what its causes might be. The search for an adequate definition is seen by many writers to be an essential precursor to both theoretical analyses and practical action. Donors cannot be motivated to act unless they are convinced that what is taking place is actually a famine. Analysts cannot begin to study the causes of famine until they know what it is they are looking at. And yet to define famine is perhaps already to adopt a particular position in relation to its cause.

In the Malthusian or neo-Malthusian view, for example, famine is a question of the excess of population over the means of subsistence (Malthus 1993). It is an instance where population growth has outstripped food production. Massive starvation almost inevitably follows until the balance is restored. For others, famine is seen as a natural disaster that occurs when a failure of food production, through drought for example, leads to conditions of scarcity. The land can no longer support the population that relies upon it.

The view of famine as caused by a shortage of food was challenged by Amartya Sen (1981). He argued that a decline in what he called 'food availability' was not in fact necessary for a famine to occur. It did not matter what the total food supply per head in any area was; what was crucial was whether particular individuals or households had access to sufficient food. In the famous opening words of *Poverty and Famines*, Sen argues: 'Starvation is the characteristic of some people not *having* enough food to eat. It is not the characteristic of there not *being* not enough food to eat' (Sen 1981: 1). Starvation, according to Sen, is not about food as a commodity, but about the relationship of people to that commodity. This was an important insight, as far as it went, and it brought academic theorizing of famine back into the realm of social science – though, as Amrita Rangasami (1985) was later to argue, it was an insight that was already incorporated in practice, in the Famine Codes of India for example.

Sen's work, with its shift away from an emphasis on quantities of food to questions of entitlements, was an important move in three respects. First, it stressed the need to examine each famine in its own particularity. Sen claimed to present not a general theory of famine but also a framework in which individual famines could be analysed. Second, it involved a move from the examination of overall 'populations' in the Malthusian mode to the study of specific 'persons' or households. Finally, and most importantly, it focused attention on relationships. In order to understand starvation, it is necessary to look at the structure of ownership relations and other forms of entitlement relations within any particular society.

These moves within Sen's work were potentially very radical, and could have produced a new approach to famine studies. However, they did not, for two reasons. First, although Sen moved away from the notion of famine as a failure of food production, he retained the idea of breakdown or collapse, this time of a person's entitlements. Thus famines were still seen as failures, but entitlement failures rather than failures of food supply. He did not consider the possibility that famines could be a *product* of the social or economic system rather than its *failure.*[3]

When something is identified as a failure, whether of the natural or the economic system, it appears as a technical or managerial problem. An otherwise benign system has collapsed and needs putting right. The appropriate response is to try to identify what went wrong and then to intervene in some way to correct it. Expert knowledge of the system and how it works enables those versed in such technologies to apply their pro-grammes unproblematically and provide solutions. So, for example, once Sen's notion of entitlements was accepted, plans could be put in place to replace lost entitlements. Instead of studying populations and food per capita, the experts in famine relief examine the individual household, its vulnerability and its coping strategies. These responses are depoliticized, technologized responses. I shall say more about what I want to suggest by these terms shortly, but briefly this means that solutions are implemented by experts, without consultation with or authorization from those involved. The victims are seen as just that: victims who have no political voice.

The second reason why the radical potential of Sen's approach was blunted is to be found in Sen's very limited view of what politics is. He sees politics as separable from economics, and the state as ultimately benign and non-violent. He excludes two things from consideration in his entitle-ments approach: instances of deliberate starvation, and what he calls 'non-entitlement transfers'.[4] Both of these routinely occur during famines. In addition, Sen does not question the way in which the legitimate violence of the state can be used to uphold the ownership rights of certain sections of the community while others starve, although he does acknowledge that 'starvation deaths can reflect legality with a vengeance' (Sen 1981: 166). Sen's approach, 'which purports to provide a framework for understand-ing starvation and famines, excludes any adequate understanding of pre-cisely those conditions that obtain *whenever there is a famine* – the denial of access to food *by force* employed on behalf of those who possess food' (Edkins 2000: 59).

The distinction being made here between technologized, managerial responses and fully politicized responses needs to be clarified. It is not the same as the distinction often made between practitioners on the one hand and academics on the other, nor is it a question of responses that attend to the symptoms not the causes. A technologized response, in my use of the term here, is a response that claims to rely on a theoretical framework and a set of rules, practices or techniques derived from it. The theory is deemed to be applicable in a series of different historical and geographi-cal locations. In this view, the job of the practitioner is to become an expert in the various theories and their application. The expert is accepted as politically neutral.

A fully politicized response recognizes that there is no one theory that will apply everywhere, and that in any case, first, theoretical analyses already embody political assumptions, and second, the application of general rules to particular cases is not straightforward. Practitioners, however well versed in theoretical studies, and however comprehensive the procedure manual they carry, always in the end have to make judge-ments. They have to go beyond the knowledge or expertise they have, beyond the rules or the guidance they are equipped with. They always, in other words, have to act politically. They have to decide what is to be done in the particular situation in which they find themselves. Their decision will always be political. And as such, it embodies responsibility.

Repoliticizing mass starvations

One of the reasons Sen's entitlement approach falls into the same trap as theories of famine as natural disaster and leads to technologized responses is that he retained a definition of famine which, like other definitions current in the mid-1980s, focused on demographic and biological factors and saw famine as a breakdown. His definition of famine was: 'A particularly virulent manifestation of starvation causing widespread death' (Sen 1981: 40).

Rangasami (1985) questions this definition on two grounds. First, she argues that mortality is not a necessary condition of famine but only its biological culmination. Famine should be seen as a protracted politico-social-economic process of oppression comprising three stages: dearth, famishment and mortality. The culmination of the process comes well before the final stage of disease and death. If the process is halted before people die, it is nonetheless still a famine. Second, famine cannot be defined solely with reference to the victims. The process is one in which 'benefits accrue to one section of the community while losses flow to the other' (Rangasami 1985: 1748). To study only the responses or coping strategies of victims while paying no attention to the actions (or inaction) of the rest of the community is to miss what is going on.

Since Rangasami's work, other writers, including Alex de Waal (2005), have developed the notion of famine as a process and examined the coping strategies that those suffering from famine employ at different stages. Only one writer, David Keen (1994), has taken up directly the challenge of examining the strategies of the beneficiaries of famine: its perpetrators and its bystanders.[5] In his study of the famine in the Sudan in the 1980s, Keen poses the questions 'what use is famine, what functions does it assure, in what strategies is it integrated?'[6] (Keen 1994: 12).

Such questions are not easy ones for the academic community, particularly the development community, to ask. They involve moving away from an approach that is restricted to the level of cause. Asking for the 'cause' of something like famine makes mass starvation appear 'as a sort of disease or abscess ... an obstacle to be removed, a dysfunctioning to be rectified' (Foucault 1980: 135). The question should rather be posed in a positive sense. It is necessary to ask who benefits from mass starvations, not just who the victims are. To do this reinstates mass starvations as a political process.

It is necessary to be clear how the term 'political' is being used here. A political process is one that involves taking decisions when the information needed is insufficient but the decision still needs to be taken, and, in addition, taking responsibility for that decision (Edkins 2000: 148–9). It is a process without guarantees: there is no way of knowing whether the decision taken was the right one. It is not a question of the realm of what is generally called 'politics' (political parties, elections or other struggles for state control), as distinct from economics or the social realm. Those distinctions are unhelpful: what I am calling 'political' is no more likely to take place in the realm of 'politics' than in the realm of 'economics' or 'society'.

To treat mass starvations as political processes is to pay attention to them as processes that involve relationships between people (not just between persons and commodities, as in entitlements theory). Social relations take place on a day-to-day basis through small-scale actions and interactions of people on the ground. The best action to take in particular circumstances cannot in the end be decided by expert knowledge or determined by manuals, though both may help. Those cast in the role of expert or sent out equipped with procedures know this perhaps better than anyone. In the end, for them as for anyone else, it is a question of responsibility and judgement in arriving at decisions and acting.

To study mass starvations as political processes is to examine how they come about, what small actions or inaction on the part of which people make them happen, and who exactly the beneficiaries and the victims are. It brings in questions of responsibility. It requires a detailed investigation rather than a grand general theory. It means addressing minutiae or details. Raul Hilberg is a historian who adopts this approach in his work on the Nazi genocide. He says: 'In all my work I have never begun by asking the big questions, because I was always afraid that I would come up with small answers ... I look at the process ... as a series of minute steps' (Lanzmann 1995: 55).

Once we recognize that we are dealing with political processes that have beneficiaries as well as victims, we cannot assume that famine or mass starvation is something that the whole of the international community would fight against if only it knew how. This belief is reinforced by reliance on experts, scientific research and codes of practice. However, to take this for granted is to forget that, as Rangasami reminds us, many people benefit in some way from famine and oppression. And it is to forget that even under the rule of law in democratic states, violence is present (Edkins 1996). David Keen (1994) and Mark Duffield (1993, 1994, 1998) have shown that there are numerous beneficiaries of the famines and mass starvations in the Horn of Africa. They acknowledge the violence inherent both in so-called peaceful democratic states and in international structures of dominance and oppression.

Attributing responsibility

If it is accepted that mass starvation is the result of a series of small acts, at least some of them deliberate and some carried out with the intention of producing what are called famines, or what I would like to call 'mass starvations', then it is necessary to begin to pay attention to the question of responsibility. Alex de Waal has used the phrase 'famine crimes' (de Waal 1997) and suggested that a possible solution would be 'anti-famine contracts' between rulers and people. If such a political contract is in place 'famine is a political scandal. Famine is *deterred*' (de Waal 1997: 5).

Such political contracts may seem to be more likely in democratic political regimes rather than authoritarian ones (de Waal 2000). However, it is important to avoid concluding that 'democracy prevents famine'. Such an inference risks reinstating a grand theory of famine. A return to theory requires definitions, abstractions and generalizations, and leads once more to technical solutions. Grand theories take the politics and responsibility out of the situation, replacing it with expert knowledge that pretends to objectivity. This is the case even when the theory concerned is a theory of politics. Such theories play into the hands of those whose power is built on a culture of expertise and scientific objectivity. It is also important to avoid framing anti-famine contracts as simply measures against governments that fail to respond quickly enough to an emerging crisis: to say this would be to return promptly to the language of failure, breakdown and disaster. Although one may want to allocate responsibility for an inadequate response, and we return to this shortly, this is merely a first stage. It is clearly the case, as Devereux (2000: 27) argues, that 'famines occur because they are not prevented: they are allowed to happen'. It is also unfortunately the case that sometimes famines occur because they are *made* to happen.

Once mass starvations are considered crimes, and the parallels are made with other crimes like genocide or war crimes, two things happen. First, the vocabulary changes. When genocide is discussed, it is not so much a question of causes and solutions but one of responsibility, criminal liability, perpetrators, bystanders, victims and survivors. Keen suggested that the question of famine should be phrased in a positive sense – 'what functions does famine have?' – rather than the negative sense – 'what causes the failures that lead to famine?' Using the language of genocide, appropriate questions become: 'Who committed the famine?', 'How was it committed and why?', 'Who were the victims?', 'Who was involved (e.g. state, societal institutions, various people – ethnic groups, individuals with certain job roles/professions, bystanders, etc.)?'[7] Or, substituting 'mass starvations' for 'famine': 'Who committed the mass starvation?' If mass starvation is a crime, the appropriate language should be used. Crimes don't happen, they are committed. Crime is not 'ended', as we often talk of 'ending famine', but criminals are deterred, detained and prosecuted.

The second consequence of mass starvation being considered a crime is that those who commit it are prosecuted. For this to happen there must be a legal framework of some sort that specifies the crime as a crime, and a juridical mechanism for prosecution. The Rome Statute of the ICC already explicitly includes mass starvation under three headings (ICC 2002). It is (1) a *war crime* if it is used as a weapon of war; (2) a *crime against humanity* if it is the deliberate extermination of a civilian population by the deprivation of food; and (3) a *genocide* if it is carried out with the intention of destroying in whole or in part a national, ethnic, racial or religious group.

During the discussions establishing the ICC there was a considerable expansion of the list of crimes against humanity. These crimes are no longer linked with warfare; they can take place in peacetime. Certain proposals did not have sufficient support to make the list: currently, terrorism, economic embargo and mass starvation do not appear separately (Schabas 2001: 38). However, Article 7 of the Rome Statute defines 'extermination' as a crime against humanity 'when committed as part of a widespread or systematic attack directed against any civilian population' where ' "extermination" includes the intentional infliction of conditions of life, *inter alia* the deprivation of access to food and medicine, calculated to bring about the destruction of part of a population' (ICC 2002: 10). In conditions of armed conflict, 'intentionally using starvation of civilians as a method of warfare by depriving them of objects indispensable to their survival, including wilfully impeding relief supplies as provided for under the Geneva Conventions' is defined as a war crime in Article 8 (ICC 2002: 10). At present this applies only when starvation takes place in international conflict: it is not yet included in the statute in respect of armed conflict not of an international character. However, customary international law 'extends many of the protections of law applicable to international conflicts to internal armed struggles' (Marcus 2003: 269). The International Criminal Tribunal for the former Yugoslavia (ICTY) has accepted this logic in its decisions (Marcus 2003: 270). Genocide is defined in Article 6, and includes 'deliberately inflicting on the group conditions of life calculated to bring about its physical destruction in whole or in part' (ICC 2002: 9). The term 'conditions of life' is further defined as including 'deliberate deprivation of resources indispensable for survival, such as food or medical services, or systematic expulsion from homes' (Schabas 2001: 250).

David Marcus has examined in some detail the question of famine crimes and international law. He coins the term 'faminogenic' to mean 'creating or aiding in the creation of famine' (Marcus 2003: 245n9). Taking Sen's definition of famine as a starting point,[8] he identifies four 'degrees' of faminogenic behaviour, characterized by different degrees of intentionality. The first two, fourth-degree and third-degree faminogenic behaviour, are the least deliberate, and in Marcus' view do not entail criminal responsibility under international law. They include, first, cases where 'incompetent or hopelessly corrupt governments, faced with food crises created by drought or price shocks, are unable to respond effectively to their citizens' needs' (Marcus 2003: 246). Starvation follows, although this was not necessarily the result the government wanted. Second are cases where the government is not incompetent but indifferent: 'authoritarian governments, impervious to the fate of their populations ... turn blind eyes to mass hunger' (Marcus 2003: 246–7). Mismanagement such as this, though deplorable, is, Marcus argues, not sufficient to warrant criminalization. There is a case, he argues, for criminalization of second- and first-degree faminogenic behaviour. Second-degree faminogenesis involves recklessness: 'Governments implement policies that themselves engender famine, then recklessly ... pursue these policies despite learning that they are causing mass starvation' (Marcus 2003: 247). Finally, first-degree famine crime is where governments or others deliberately use hunger as a tool of extermination against troublesome populations.

In all these cases, those responsible may be government officials or any others who 'create, inflict or prolong famine' (Marcus 2003: 247n19). Paul Howe and Stephen Devereux (2004) emphasize the importance of extending accountability beyond officials of national governments. In many cases, rebel groups or non-government militia are the culprits. More controversially, donors and humanitarian agencies also need to be held to account where they fail to respond in a timely way to prevent famines or where they withhold aid for political reasons. In situations where the international community has assumed effective responsibility for emergency relief, donor agency and international officials should be as accountable as officials of national governments (Howe and Devereux 2004: 367).

Marcus demonstrates in detail how the two higher degrees of famine crime are already contained in international criminal law. Formal codification would bring these scattered elements together. More important however, Marcus argues, is the signal that codification would send (Marcus 2003: 279):

> codification will convey expressive value that will force the international community to address outbreaks of famine appropriately. In part because the popular imagination associates famine with cracked earth and dry riverbeds, the international community has been able to avoid accusing the responsible government officials of crimes against humanity.

Without codification, it will remain easy to 'evade responsibility by portraying ... mass starvation as a regrettable by-product of unfortunate weather' (Marcus 2003: 247).

Third- and fourth-degree famine crimes, where there is no reckless pursuit of policies known to be faminogenic and no deliberate intent to starve, are not covered in international criminal law and should not be, Marcus argues. Incompetence or indifference on the part of those responsible for their citizens' well-being is not generally sufficient for criminal responsibility in his view. However, it seems to me dangerous to rule out third- and fourth-degree famine crimes so easily. Although the climate of opinion is clearly not right at the moment for any action on this front, it might be useful to think of this level of negligence in relation to violations of the right to food. At present, the right to food, although universally recognized and expressed both in the Universal Declaration of Human Rights and the International Covenant on Economic, Social and Cultural Rights, is seen not as an immediate obligation under international law but as something to be achieved progressively (Marcus 2003: 249). However, developments such as the agreement reached in September 2004 on Voluntary Guidelines to support the progressive realization of the right to food by states are hopeful (FAO 2004).

There is an obvious question that must be raised over the strategy being proposed here, which is one of criminalization. It could be argued that criminalization is nothing but another form of depoliticization or technologization.[9] We put in place, quite literally, a rule-book, and alongside it a set of criteria for what counts as evidence. By naming famine as a 'crime' and defining what is to count as 'mass starvation' in a statute or in case law, are we not merely removing it once more from the realm of the political? Michel Foucault in particular saw the production of a criminal class as a form of depoliticization. As a disciplinary practice, it functions to delineate a certain group of people and to label their acts as criminal, not political (Foucault 1991: 277). States have used legislation in this way to outlaw certain forms of protest and to reserve to themselves the monopoly of legitimate violence within a society.

What is proposed here is somewhat different, of course. First, in the case of the ICC, like the International Tribunals in the former Yugoslavia and in Rwanda, the state is not in the same place as usual. The state is not necessarily on the side of the prosecutor, but in the dock with the accused. The tables have in a sense been turned, and those not generally subject to the rule of law, those who have sovereignty, those who can declare a state of emergency and suspend the law, are the ones being made accountable. Second, in the courts it is recognized that what is taking place is a specific judgement or a decision. The evidence of what happened, precisely and in detail, must be investigated. The application of the law to a particular case is accepted as problematic.

However, the important point is that the distinction between a technical act and a political act is not a simple opposition. The aim of the critique offered here is not merely to argue for politicization in the place of technologization, but to point to the way in which what we call techniques, or experts, or theories, are already intensely political. There is a tension between technologization and politicization. It is not really possible to replace one with the other. Any repoliticization can be assimilated and depoliticized once more. This is what has happened to successive attempts to repoliticize famine theory, from Sen's entitlement approach onwards. A radical repoliticization has been followed by the incorporation of the new approach as nothing more than a new technology. And any technologization remains at root a political move.

Conclusion

Any definition of famine that sees it as a failure of some sort is missing the point. Whether famine is seen as a failure of food supply, a breakdown in the food distribution system or a multi-faceted livelihoods crisis, the outcome is the same. These definitions or concepts blind us to the fact that famines, and the deaths, migrations or impoverishments that they produce, are enormously beneficial to the perpetrators: they are a success not a failure; a normal output of the current economic and political system, not an aberration.

This chapter has suggested that it might be useful to replace the notion of famine. It has begun to substitute the phrase 'mass starvations' in an attempt to get away from the idea of scarcity as a cause and famines as a breakdown or failure. To talk of mass starvations is to evoke the parallel of mass killings and genocides. In many ways famines, though distinct from genocides, share more with these acts than they do with natural disasters. In many if not most cases they are the result of deliberate actions by people who can see what the consequences of those actions will be. If they are not produced deliberately, then they are often allowed to progress beyond the stage of 'famishment' to that of 'morbidity', through deliberate or negligent inaction on the part of those who could intervene to save lives and livelihoods.

There is already an embryonic provision in international law that allows for the prosecution of those responsible for mass starvations. Those provisions have finally been invoked in the case of the persecutions that led to hunger and mass starvation in Darfur between 2002 and 2005. Rather than assuming that it is surprising that 'famines' are still with us in the twenty-first century, when our technical know-how is much advanced, it might be as well to acknowledge that technical competence is not the issue. We should instead consider campaigning to improve and codify the provisions in international law to remove immunity from those who, nationally or internationally, commit famine crimes or the crime of mass starvation. This would take place alongside action to establish robust anti-starvation political contracts locally and internationally, through right to food protocols.

The referral by the UN Security Council of the situation in Darfur to the ICC in March 2005 made no mention of either famine or starvation. The Report of the International Commission on Darfur heard credible accounts of 'wanton and deliberate' acts of destruction of 'all essential structures and implements for the survival of the population [including] oil presses, flour mills, water sources ... crops and vegetation'

(International Commission of Inquiry on Darfur 2005: 82). They conclude that this can only be interpreted as 'having the objective of driving out the population through violence and preventing their return by destroying all means of survival and livelihood' (International Commission of Inquiry on Darfur 2005: 83). They conclude that in legal terms not only does this destruction go against the provisions of Article 11 of the International Covenant on Economic, Social and Cultural Rights that provides the right of everyone to adequate food, clothing and housing, it also constitutes a war crime under customary international law, and in addition it 'may well amount to the crime of persecution, as a crime against humanity' (International Commission of Inquiry on Darfur 2005: 84).

The example of Darfur is interesting in relation to the discussion in this chapter. Initially it seems to support the contention that unless mass starvations are more explicitly criminalized, or in other words famine crimes are codified, as Marcus (2003) argues, the law may prove inadequate to the task of prosecuting offenders. In the case of Darfur, the destruction of their means of survival clearly put large sections of the population at risk of starvation, to put it no more strongly. It is remarkable that the Commission's report did not highlight this aspect. The word 'famine' does not occur in the document at all, and the word 'starvation' occurs only once, when the report lists among the relevant provisions of customary international law, in this case Article 14 of the Second Additional Protocol to the Geneva Convention, 'the prohibition on the destruction of objects indispensable to the survival of the civilian population' and notes that 'violence to the life and person of civilians is prohibited, whatever method is adopted to achieve it. It follows that the destruction of crops, foodstuffs, and water sources, to such an extent that starvation is likely to follow, is also prohibited' (UK Ministry of Defence 2004: 15.19.1, quoted in International Commission of Inquiry on Darfur 2005: 49n90). Fortunately on this occasion, existing provisions such as Article 14 provide other avenues for indictment; this might not be the case in future instances of mass starvations.

On the other hand, the Darfur case raises questions as to whether 'famine' is really the right word to use. Here was an instance widely regarded by those in the aid business as a question of famine or starvation. However, when it came to finding grounds for a referral to the ICC, the absence of codified famine crimes did not prove a hindrance. The more general provisions against violence against civilians were adequate. It will be interesting to see how the case develops if a prosecution is indeed brought. The precise grounds for the prosecutions and the development of international law that comes out of the proceedings will be instructive.

The question is whether steps such as the codification of famine crimes would help debunk the myth of famines as 'the result of natural disasters, not human misconduct', as Marcus (2003: 280) argues, or reinforce it. Certainly, given the way in which the attribution of 'genocide' has been ducked notoriously on several occasions since the Genocide Convention, it is hard to be convinced that 'if famine crimes were codified, the international community would be forced ... to determine whether a famine had erupted as a result of criminal behaviour' (Marcus 2003: 280).

At the very least there is a need for a new language that talks of mass starvations, faminogenic behaviours or famine crimes which, like mass killings, are regarded as crimes against humanity.[10] There might well be a case, as argued here, for dropping the use of the word 'famine', with its connotations of natural disaster, altogether. The term is at present so strongly connected with images of failures of climate, food supply or entitlements that it may not be possible to wrest it free. On the other hand the value of a successful reconnection of the term 'famine' with the figures responsible for crimes against humanity, for genocide or for war crimes would be very great.

The starvation of significant numbers of people is brought about through the sometimes deliberate, sometimes unintentional acts or omissions of other people or groups of people. It is people who are responsible for mass starvation – with degrees of responsibility that vary depending on the circumstances – and they should be held accountable in an appropriate way. Abandoning the word 'famine' and adopting instead the terms 'mass starvations', 'faminogenic behaviours' or 'famine crimes', or even working with the broader terms 'war crime' or 'crime against humanity', may help to ensure that this happens.

Notes

1 The argument in this chapter draws on and extends my original call for the criminalization of mass starvations as crimes against humanity in relation to the then embryonic ICC (Edkins 2002a).

2 At the time of writing, early April 2005, there has been robust reaction to this move; the Sudan is voicing strong objections to the UN decision and refusing to countenance its citizens being brought before the ICC. See, for example, IRIN (2005) and McDoom (2005).

3 Complex political emergency approaches retain this idea that famines are unexpected 'emergencies' rather than a product of 'normal' social and political life.

4 Both where a person starves deliberately and where a person is deliberately starved. Non-entitlement transfers are those that fall outside the legal system of the society concerned.

5 Mark Duffield examines this question on a broader canvas as part of a system of global governance (Duffield 2001).

6 In framing these questions, Keen is drawing on Michel Foucault's remarks on the Soviet Gulag (Foucault 1980: 135).

7 These questions are taken from Totten *et al.* (1997: xxv) substituting 'famine' for 'genocide'.

8 'A particularly virulent form of [starvation] causing widespread death' (Sen 1981: 40). For another approach to defining famine, one potentially more useful in terms of attributing responsibility, see Howe and Devereux (2004).

9 I am indebted to Haris Gazdar for drawing my attention to this point in

discussion. In another context, that of international terrorism after September 11, I have argued against criminalization for precisely these reasons (Edkins 2002b). This question is an important one and deserves more space than is available here. For a discussion that unpacks some of the complexities and philosophical implications of the notion of 'crimes against humanity' see Richard Vernon (2002); for a discussion of the relation between justice, law and the political in the context of decisioning, see Jacques Derrida (1992).

10 For a general discussion of crimes against humanity as part of a fight for global justice see Robertson (2000). Interestingly, neither famines nor starvations are mentioned.

References

Broomhall, B. (2003) *International Justice and the International Criminal Court: Between Sovereignty and the Rule of Law*, Oxford: Oxford University Press.

Derrida, J. (1992) 'Force of law: The 'mystical foundation of authority', in D. G. Carlson, D. Cornell and M. Rosenfeld (eds), *Deconstruction and the Possibility of Justice*, New York, NY: Routledge.

Devereux, S. (2000) 'Famine in the twentieth century', *IDS Working Paper* 105, Brighton: Institute of Development Studies.

de Waal, A. (1997) *Famine Crimes: Politics and the Disaster Relief Industry in Africa*, Oxford: African Rights and the International African Institute in association with James Currey.

de Waal, A. (2000) 'Democratic political process and the fight against famine', *IDS Working Paper* 107, Brighton: Institute of Development Studies.

de Waal, A. (2005) *Famine that Kills: Darfur, Sudan* (revised edition), Oxford: Oxford University Press.

Duffield, M. (1993) 'NGOs, disaster relief and asset transfer in the Horn: political survival in a permanent emergency', *Development and Change*, 24: 131–57.

Duffield, M. (1994) 'Complex emergencies and the crisis of developmentalism', *IDS Bulletin*, 25(4): 37–45.

Duffield, M. (1998) 'Containing systemic crisis: the regionalisation of welfare and security policy', in J. N. Pieterse (ed.), *World Orders in the Making: Humanitarian Intervention and Beyond*, Basingstoke: Macmillan.

Duffield, M. (2001) *Global Governance and the New Wars: The Merging of Development and Security*, London: Zed Books.

Edkins, J. (1996) 'Legality with a vengeance: famines and humanitarian intervention in 'complex emergencies'', *Millennium: Journal of International Studies*, 25: 547–75.

Edkins, J. (2000) *Whose Hunger? Concepts of Famine, Practices of Aid*, Minneapolis: University of Minnesota Press.

Edkins, J. (2002a) 'Mass starvations and the limitations of famine theorising', *IDS Bulletin*, 33(4): 12–18.

Edkins, J. (2002b) 'Forget trauma? Responses to September 11', *International Relations*, 16: 243–56.

FAO (2004) 'Intergovernmental Working Group for the elaboration of a set of voluntary guidelines to support the progressive realization of the right to adequate food in the context of national food security', Final Report of the Chair, Rome, 23 September 2004.

Foucault, M. (1980) *Power/Knowledge: Selected Interviews and Other Writings 1972–1977*, Brighton: Harvester Press.

Foucault, M. (1991) *Discipline and Punish: The Birth of the Prison*, Harmondsworth: Penguin Books.

Foulkes, I. (2004) 'Darfur villagers 'facing famine'', BBC News (available at www.news.bbc.co.uk, accessed 18 October 2004).

Howe, P. and Devereux, S. (2004) 'Famine intensity and magnitude scales: a proposal for an instrumental definition of famine', *Disasters*, 28(4): 353–72.

International Commission of Inquiry on Darfur (2005) *Report to the Secretary-General pursuant to Security Council Resolution 1564 of 18 September 2004*, Geneva: United Nations, Geneva, 25 January (available at www.un.org/News/dh/sudan/com_inq_darfur.pdf).

International Criminal Court (2002) *Rome Statute of the International Criminal Court*, The Hague: Public Information and Documentation Centre of the ICC (available at www.icc-cpi.int).

IRIN (2005) 'Sudan: Darfur war-crimes suspects won't go to ICC, government says', *IRIN News*, 4 April, Reuters AlertNet (available at www.alertnet.org/).

Keen, D. (1994) *The Benefits of Famine: A Political Economy of Famine and Relief in Southwestern Sudan, 1983–1989*, Princeton, NJ: Princeton University Press.

Lanzmann, C. (1995) *Shoah: The Complete Text of the Acclaimed Holocaust Film*, New York, NY: Da Capo Press.

Malthus, T. (1993) *An Essay on the Principle of Population*, Oxford: Oxford University Press.

Marcus, D. (2003) 'Famine crimes in international law', *American Journal of International Law*, 97: 245–81.

McDoom, O. (2005) 'Sudanese march against UN war crimes resolution', *Reuters*, 5 April, Reuters AlertNet (available at alertnet.org/).

Power, S. (2005) 'Court of first resort', *New York Times*, 10 February.

Rangasami, A. (1985) '"Failure of exchange entitlements" theory of famine: a response', *Economic and Political Weekly*, 20(41 and 42): 1747–52; 1797–1801.

Robertson, G. (2000) *Crimes Against Humanity: The Struggle for Global Justice*, London: Penguin.

Sands, P. (2005) *Lawless World: America and the Making and Breaking of Global Rules*, London: Penguin; Allen Lane.

Schabas, W. A. (2001) *An Introduction to the International Criminal Court*, Cambridge: Cambridge University Press.

Sen, A. (1981) *Poverty and Famines: An Essay on Entitlements and Deprivation*, Oxford: Clarendon Press.

Totten, S., Parsons, W. S. and Charny, I. W. (1997) *Century of Genocide: Eyewitness Accounts and Critical Views*, New York, NY: Garland.

UK Ministry of Defence (2004) *The Manual of the Law of Armed Conflict*, Oxford: Oxford University Press.

United Nations (2005) 'Security Council refers situation in Darfur, Sudan, to Prosecutor of International Criminal Court', *United Nations Press Release* SC/8351, Security Council 5158th Meeting (Night), 31 March.

Vernon, R. (2002) 'What is a crime against humanity?' *Journal of Political Philosophy*, 10: 231–49.

4 Sen's entitlement approach

Critiques and counter-critiques

Stephen Devereux

Introduction

Within a few years of the publication of Amartya Sen's *Poverty and Famines: An Essay on Entitlement and Deprivation* in 1981, the 'entitlement approach' had effectively displaced Malthusianism as the dominant theoretical framework for explaining and analysing famines. The contribution of the entitlement approach to famine studies cannot be underestimated: it revolutionized famine thinking. On the other hand, it has also attracted much controversy, and its claims as a robust theory of famine causation remain contested.

This chapter begins with a brief exposition of the entitlement approach. I then briefly examine its credentials as a theory of famine causation, before focusing on the main issues I want to address: the four 'limitations' of the entitlement approach that Sen himself acknowledged. These four limitations I characterize as 'choosing to starve', 'starvation or epidemics?', 'fuzzy entitlements' and 'extra-entitlement transfers'. I want to interrogate the entitlement approach through Sen's self-critiques, asking the question in each case: to what extent does each limitation undermine or even invalidate the entitlement approach overall?

The entitlement approach has been subjected to critical scrutiny many times before, ranging from a favourable 'assessment' by Osmani (1995) to less favourable 'reassessment' by de Waal (1990), 'critique' by Nolan (1993), even 'refutation' by Bowbrick (1986) and dismissal as a theoretical 'failure' by Rangasami (1985) and Fine (1997). My intention here is partly to synthesize and comment on several strands of this literature, and partly to evaluate the extent to which Sen anticipated his critics and dealt adequately with the problems they raise. Following Osmani (1995: 254), I do not dwell on the empirical criticisms arising from Sen's applications of the entitlement approach to specific famines; instead I examine its credentials as a conceptual framework and an analytical tool.

The entitlement approach to famine analysis

Entitlements have been defined by Sen (1984: 497) as 'the set of altern-ative commodity bundles that a person can command in a society using the totality of rights and opportunities that he or she faces'. It should be noted immediately that this is a descriptive rather than a normative concept; entitlements are derived from legally-based property rights rather than morality or human rights. Sen (1981: 166) concludes *Poverty and Famines* with this famous observation: 'The law stands between food availability and food entitlement. Starvation deaths can reflect legality with a vengeance.' There is clearly something odd – at best uncomfortable, at worst 'defective' (Sen 1981: 49) – with an analytical approach that appro-priates a normative term like 'entitlement' and strips it of all ethical con-notations. In Sen's framework, people left destitute by famine are not entitled to food; instead they are 'entitled to starve' (Edkins 1996: 550). Despite its normative connotation, entitlements 'does not reflect in any sense a concept of the right to food' (Edkins 1996: 559).[1]

A person's 'entitlement set' is the full range of goods and services that he or she can acquire by converting his or her 'endowments' (assets and resources, including labour power) through 'exchange entitlement map-pings'.[2] In the context of poverty and famine, the entitlement approach aims comprehensively to describe all legal sources of food, which Sen (1981: 2) reduces to four categories: 'production-based entitlement' (growing food), 'trade-based entitlement' (buying food), 'own-labour entitlement' (working for food) and 'inheritance and transfer entitle-ment' (being given food by others).[3] Individuals face starvation if their full 'entitlement set' does not provide them with adequate food for subsis-tence. Famine scales this up: occupationally or geographically related groups of people face famine if they simultaneously experience catas-trophic declines in their entitlements.[4]

Perhaps the most valuable contribution of the entitlement approach to famine theorizing is that it shifts the analytical focus away from a fixation on food supplies – the Malthusian logic of 'too many people, too little food' – and onto the inability of particular groups of people to acquire food. Food insecurity affects people who cannot access adequate food (e.g. because of poverty) irrespective of food availability – a famine can occur even if food supplies are adequate and markets are functioning well. This is a crucial insight. As Sen emphasized, there is no technical reason for markets to meet subsistence needs – and no moral or legal reason why they should. An equally important insight – and one that has generated much confusion and controversy in the literature – is that famine can be caused by 'exchange entitlement decline' (adverse shifts in the exchange value of endowments for food – e.g. falling wages or livestock prices, rising food prices) as well as by 'direct entitlement decline' (loss of food crops to drought, for instance). The entitlement approach does not exclude the latter possibility.

It is common for defenders of the entitlement approach to dismiss critics as 'misreading', 'misinterpreting' or even 'misrepresenting' Sen's intentions.[5] But this begs the question: how could so many academics have misunderstood what Sen was trying to say in *Poverty and Famines* – which is, after all, a brief monograph written with great elegance and clarity? I suggest that the confusion is largely of Sen's own making. Although Sen is careful to emphasize that the entitlement approach is descriptive rather than theoretical, and empirical rather than normative – 'a general framework for analyzing famines rather than one particular hypothesis about their causation' (Sen 1981: 162) – he sets up the entitlement approach in theoretical opposition to something he labels 'FAD', or 'food availability decline', and he invests much intellectual energy in *Poverty and Famines* in attempting to demonstrate that the four twentieth-century famines he chooses as case studies were not precipitated by significant declines in food availability but instead by declines in exchange entitlements.[6] The danger is that setting up 'FAD' as a hypothesis to be refuted by the entitlement approach places the latter in an equivalent status, as a theoretical proposition requiring theoretical justification and empirical verification. Thus Sen first presents the entitlement approach as a generic framework for analysing famine processes, but then deploys his *approach* to refute a *theory* of famine causation with which he profoundly disagrees.

I would suggest that the confusion has arisen because *Poverty and Famines* makes not one but two pathbreaking contributions to the famine literature. Sen has provided both a general analytical framework for examining *all* famines (the 'entitlement approach') and at the same time put forward a 'new' theory of causation:[7] that *certain* famines are characterized by declines in access to food for identifiable population groups, irrespective of food availability at national level ('exchange entitlement failure').[8] The first achievement is subject to critical scrutiny on analytical or conceptual grounds, while the second is open to attack only on empirical grounds.[9] I will deal only briefly with the empirical attacks on the entitlement 'theory', since they are both less interesting and epistemologically flawed.

Early critiques of entitlement 'theory' concentrated on the complex relationship between 'FAD' and 'entitlement decline' in famine events, and specifically on Sen's assertion that several twentieth-century famines were not triggered by catastrophic declines in food production or food availability. A vigorous empirical debate followed around the analysis or interpretation of food production and food availability data for specific famines. This literature has two strands:

1   *Refutation of 'entitlement theory' by reinterpretation (or re-reinterpretation) of data.* In *Poverty and Famines*, Sen recalculated data from four famines to demonstrate (a) adequate food availability and/or negligible decline from pre-famine food availability; (b) exchange entitlement

collapse for specific population groups as a proximate cause of famine. Some critics have challenged Sen's use of food production, trade and price statistics, to claim that Sen underestimated the extent to which food availability decline was in fact an important element in these famines.[10]

2 *Refutation of 'entitlement theory' by counter-example.* A related strand of the critical literature attempts to demonstrate that the entitlement approach does not adequately explain some famines that were not examined by Sen in *Poverty and Famines.*[11] The argument is that Sen's preoccupation with exchange entitlement collapse (adverse shifts in food price/wage or food price/livestock price ratios) understates the significance of FAD – specifically food production failure – as a causal trigger of many famines, especially in Africa, and that if famines can be found that were not triggered by catastrophic 'exchange entitlement failures', this somehow refutes entitlements' claims as a general 'theory' in opposition to 'FAD'.

Whatever the merits of the competing analyses of various famines, this strand of the debate is fatally flawed. It is predicated on the false premise that food availability decline is a 'non-nested alternative' to entitlement decline (Ravallion 1996), whereas in fact FAD is incorporated within the entitlement framework as 'direct entitlement decline' or failure of 'production-based entitlement'. A more significant challenge is provided by cases of famine that are characterized by radical violations of legally defined entitlement relations – such as recent famines in the Horn of Africa, where assets are transferred or destroyed not by voluntaristic exchange in markets nor by natural disaster such as drought but by political conflict and war. I will return to this issue in detail later, but suffice it to say for now that this 'refutation by counter-example' approach is unconvincing.

My preferred reconciliation of this unnecessarily acrimonious debate would be to propose a taxonomic approach, identifying some famines as clearly triggered by 'FAD' (old-style droughts or floods), others by 'exchange entitlement decline' (where food supplies are adequate but certain groups face catastrophic collapses in their access to food) and others by political crisis (unfavourable or hostile government policies, conflict and war, failures of international response). In every case, however, identifying the trigger does not explain the famine, which requires a more complex analysis of conjunctural triggers as well as structural or underlying causal factors. Entitlement collapse offers a fresh perspective on the famine process, but its critics (both 'friendly' and 'hostile') are correct to complain that 'entitlements' is too apolitical and ahistorical to tell us much about the structural causes of famines. However, the point remains that the entitlement approach is not a theory of famine causation in competition with other theories such as 'FAD' or

Malthusianism. It is a framework for the analysis of famine processes at the micro-level, and its claim to be a comprehensive framework is the focus of this chapter. I turn now to more specific critiques of entitlements as an analytical construct.

Sen's four 'limitations' of the entitlement approach

In *Poverty and Famines*, Sen recognized four 'limitations' of the entitlement approach, each of which he mentions with little elaboration:

1   'First, there can be ambiguities in the specification of entitlements' (Sen 1981: 48–9)
2   'Second, while entitlement relations concentrate on rights within the given legal structure in that society, some transfers involve violations of these rights, such as looting or brigandage' (Sen 1981: 49)
3   Third, people's actual food consumption may fall below their entitlements for a variety of other reasons, such as ignorance, fixed food habits, or apathy' (Sen 1981: 50)
4   'Finally, the entitlement approach focuses on starvation, which has to be distinguished from famine mortality, since many of the famine deaths – in some cases *most* of them – are caused by epidemics' (Sen 1981: 50).

I next examine each of these individually (though in a different sequence).

'Choosing to starve'

> ... people's actual food consumption may fall below their entitlements for a variety of other reasons, such as ignorance, fixed food habits, or apathy ... Also, people sometimes choose to starve rather than sell their productive assets, and this can be accommodated in the entitlement approach using a relatively long-run formulation (taking note of future entitlements).
>
> (Sen 1981: 50)

Entitlement analysis is predicated on the implicit assumption that a food shortage triggers an automatic behavioural response, namely the conversion of endowments into food for survival. Thus a person's 'starvation set' is defined as 'those endowment bundles such that the exchange entitlement sets corresponding to them contain no bundles satisfying his [*sic*] minimum food requirements' (Sen 1981: 47). Sen's concession that people 'sometimes *choose* to starve' [emphasis added] in the short term to enhance their future entitlements drew on findings from Indian droughts (Jodha 1975), and anticipated research into 'coping strategies' during

African famines of the 1980s that would highlight consumption rationing as a strategic response to livelihood shocks.[12] However, Sen later stressed that he regards such choice behaviour as applying to 'persistent hunger' rather than to 'famine' (Sen 1986: 9–10):

> If the focus of attention is shifted from famines as such to less acute but possibly persistent hunger, then the role of choice from the entitlement set becomes particularly important, especially in determining future entitlement. For example, a peasant may choose to go somewhat hungry now to make a productive investment for the future, enhancing the entitlement of the following years and reducing the danger of starvation then. For entitlement in a multi-period setting the initial formulation of the problem would require serious modification and extension.

While the early literature on 'coping strategies' reflected an assumption that strategic behaviour is dominated by the search for food, later research found that consumption rationing is an austerity measure that is adopted almost routinely. Evidence from many famines confirms that 'coping strategies' during food crises are preoccupied with avoiding asset depletion rather than with maintaining consumption levels.[13] People facing food shortage make strategic decisions not only about how to bridge their consumption deficit, but also how to balance this priority against its longer-term economic – and social – costs. The sequence of coping strategy adoption is determined not only by each strategy's *effectiveness* in terms of bridging a food gap, but also by the *cost* and *reversibility* of each action (Watts 1983). Strategies that incur little long-run cost are adopted first (including rationing food consumption), while those that incur higher costs and are difficult to reverse are adopted later (e.g. selling land rights or draught oxen to buy food, thereby undermining the household's future potential to produce food).

Seen in this light, decisions to ration food consumption, even severely, can be understood as attempts to manage the current endowment set, including food, to maximize the individual's or household's long-term entitlements. Endowments are not always exchanged for food because consuming productive assets undermines future viability. Thus de Waal (1989: 194) argues that people who suffered hunger and malnutrition in Darfur 'were not "choosing to starve", with its implications of choosing to risk death. Instead, under enormous stress, they were choosing to suffer hunger in order to try to preserve their way of life'.[14]

Osmani (1995: 280) argues that this behaviour can easily be accommodated within an entitlement analysis in which, *pace* Sen and de Waal, choices made from the entitlement set reflect a multi-period planning horizon. People who die during famines are '*having* to starve': strategic management of their endowments leaves them no 'intertemporal entitlement set' that would allow them to avoid starvation both now and in the future. However, even this 'multi-period entitlements analysis' cannot explain the coexistence of famine mortality and unrealized entitlements – household members dying while the household retains assets that it could exchange for food.

Ravallion (1987) has attempted to explain the apparent paradox in terms of risk and uncertainty. People who 'choose to starve' are not choosing to die – which would make preservation of their assets and livelihoods meaningless[15] – but are accepting an increased *risk* of dying, which rises steeply as nutrition status declines but is, at the margin, uncertain (Young and Jaspars 1995). Forced to choose between selling assets to buy food (and the certainty of destitution to follow) and going hungry to preserve future livelihoods (with the unknown probability that excessive rationing will lead to death) the 'rational peasant' logically chooses the latter.

In my view, these arguments are flawed because they erroneously conflate the individuals making decisions about resource allocation (asset disposal, food procurement and intrahousehold food distribution) within the household, with the people who will face the consequences of these difficult choices and trade-offs (in terms of increased nutritional, morbidity and mortality risk). This error arises because of Sen's methodological individualism, which his critics and supporters, on this issue at least, all appear to share. The brutal reality is that famine mortality is a function of 'social vulnerability' as much as individual 'biological vulnerability'. People facing subsistence crises are forced into making the cruellest of choices, and these choices might even involve 'sacrificing' weaker household members. Children consume scarce resources; cattle and goats *are* scarce resources. Famine mortality statistics reveal that it is the weakest and most dependent family members – children and the elderly – who suffer disproportionately and are the first to die (Caldwell and Caldwell 1992; Seaman 1993). Conversely, economically active adults who earn the household income and control the household's assets are most likely to survive famines. These cohorts are the productive and reproductive core of the family unit; their survival is essential for the reproduction and future viability of the household. These individuals – particularly adult males – also dominate the decision-making process within the majority of households. The separation between decision-making power and mortality risk within households is no coincidence.

This could be modelled either as a rational decision to protect the household's core 'productive' members, by neglecting the 'unproductive' consumers of its diminishing resources, or as a reflection of adult (especially male) power over disempowered age-sex cohorts. The problem for the entitlement approach is that it is silent about such apparent violations of the fundamental right to life: as long as a household has any endowments (such as livestock) that can be exchanged for food, the entitlement approach predicts that this exchange will happen. Sen later introduced the notion of 'extended entitlements' (Sen 1986; Drèze and Sen 1989), to cover 'socially legitimated' entitlements to food that were not conferred by the market mechanism. These included intra-family allocation of food, or what has been labelled 'dependency entitlement' (Bongaarts and Cain 1982). But how can even an 'extended entitlement' approach explain a 'household's' decision to violate these intra-family allocation rules and allow some of it members to die in order to preserve entitlements for the survivors?[16]

Here, as elsewhere, Sen's focus on the household as the principal unit of analysis confounds the entitlement approach, as does its failure to engage with social relations and power inequalities, in this case at the intra-household level. Curiously, Sen has never drawn on his related work (e.g. on 'cooperative conflict' (Sen 1990), his seminal contribution to the intra-household bargaining models literature, or on female mortality risk in South Asia) to examine how differential power within the household translates into differential mortality risk during famines.[17]

Starvation or epidemics?

... the entitlement approach focuses on starvation, which has to be distinguished from famine mortality, since many of the famine deaths – in some cases most of them – are caused by epidemics, which have patterns of their own. The epidemics are, of course, partly induced by starvation but also by other famine characteristics, e.g. population movement, breakdown of sanitary facilities.

(Sen 1981: 50)

Conventional wisdom asserts that people who perish during famines die of starvation due to inadequate food consumption. In *Poverty and Famines*, Sen (1981: 47) writes about people being 'plunged into starvation' when their entitlement to food collapses. In fact, frank starvation is rarely recorded as the cause of death in famines. More often, death is attributed to hunger-related diseases such as diarrhoea or gastro-enteritis, and is explained by heightened susceptibility as lack of food undermines biological resistance to these illnesses. This is not of course incompatible with a 'food entitlement decline' theory of famine. For entitlement failure to retain explanatory power, however, requires demonstrating an association between mortality during famines (due to whatever proximate cause) and entitlement collapse, as proxied, say, by destitution. Sen (1981) finds an association between occupation status and mortality risk during the Bengal famine of 1943 and the Bangladesh famine of 1974, with low-paid occupations such as landless labourers suffering the highest rates of destitution and death. However, the evidence is less clear for African famines, and sometimes appears to contradict Sen.

A potentially serious challenge to Sen's privileging of 'entitlements collapse' as the primary cause of famine mortality is presented by Alex de Waal's research on the western Sudan famine of the mid-1980s. De Waal (1989: 182–3) found that: 'Indicators of poverty had no evident relation to mortality' in Darfur in 1985, and that 'mortality in the very poorest house-holds ... was not significantly higher than in the others'. This finding led de Waal to conclude that mortality risk was more closely associated with patterns of migration and exposure to new disease vectors than with rela-tive wealth and access to food. It is known that most mortality in recent African famines is explained by neither starvation nor hunger-related dis-eases, but by epidemics of communicable diseases such as cholera, measles or typhus – especially among displaced populations on the move or in crowded refugee camps – that are not directly related to inadequate food consumption. The key determinants of mortality during the Darfur famine, according to de Waal (1990: 481), were not poverty or lack of enti-tlements, but 'quality of water supply, sanitation and overcrowding'. De Waal's 'health crisis' model sees famine mortality following a very differ-ent causal pathway to the 'food crisis' model (see Figure 4.1). In famines where mortality is triggered by epidemics, 'it is not the undernutrition caused by the famine but the social disruption caused by it that is critical in causing excess deaths' (de Waal 1990: 481). The conclusion is that famine mortality is often a consequence of the social process of famine, rather than the economic process (entitlement collapse and destitution) at the individual level.

Where does the 'health crisis' model leave the entitlement approach, predicated as it is on a posited causal pathway from disrupted access to food through to death by starvation or hunger-related disease? There are two ways in which the entitlement approach can be salvaged on this issue. One is to attribute vulnerability even to communicable diseases to height-ened susceptibility due to undernutrition (weakened biological resis-tance). Nutritionists such as Young and Jaspars (1995: 105) favour this view, arguing that de Waal underestimates 'the synergism between malnu-trition and morbidity' which they regard as best explaining famine mortal-ity. The second defence is to assert that people who become exposed to

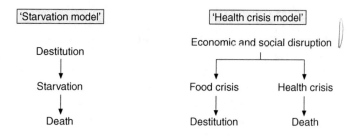

Figure 4.1 Famine mortality models (source: de Waal (1989: 187–9)).

communicable diseases (for instance, displaced populations in refugee camps) left their villages and migrated in search of relief precisely because they had lost their entitlements to food. Ravallion (1996: 9), for instance, suggests that the relationship between food shortage and morbidity or mortality outcomes reflects 'behavioural synergies' (which might include increased exposure due to famine-induced distress migration) as well as 'biological synergies' (increased susceptibility to infection). In terms of both explanations, exposure to disease is accepted as the proximate cause of death, but the underlying cause of death remains as 'entitlement failure'.

A reconciliation of this debate might be to accept the merits of both explanations.[18] Famine mortality reflects both increased *susceptibility* and increased *exposure* to diseases, some of which are hunger-related while others are not – but both reflect a common origin in disrupted access to food (epidemics that are not triggered by food scarcity are not, definitionally speaking, famines). The relative contribution to mortality of starvation, hunger-related morbidity and epidemic diseases will vary from one famine to another, but all three contributory factors are intrinsic to the famine process, and all three can arguably be accommodated within a broadly framed entitlement analysis. One feature that the 'health crisis' model does highlight, though, is the recognition of famine as a social crisis rather than an economic crisis scaled up from the household to the group level. Once again, the entitlement approach proves unable to explain collective outcomes (in this case, disease epidemics) because of its analytical focus on the individual or household unit.

'Fuzzy entitlements'[19]

> ... there can be ambiguities in the specification of entitlements ... in pre-capitalist formations there can be a good deal of vagueness on property rights and related matters. In many cases the appropriate characterization of entitlements may pose problems, and in some cases it may well be best characterized in the form of 'fuzzy' sets and related structures.
>
> (Sen 1981: 48–9)

In his original formulation of the entitlement approach, Sen was concerned only with legal ownership by individuals of alienable commodities. He ignored possibilities for weaker claims over resources (such as access and usufruct rights) as well as contexts where property rights are exercised institutionally (such as common property regimes) rather than individually. These two sources of 'fuzziness' confound the central tool of entitlement analysis: namely the 'mapping' between individuals' endowments and their entitlements.

Fuzziness with respect to units of analysis

In his elaboration of the entitlement approach, Sen (1981) chooses the individual, the household, or an 'economic class' of people (sharecroppers, pastoralists) as his unit of analysis, and he shifts seamlessly between these levels of aggregation as if they are interchangeable.[20] Osmani (1995: 254) justifies this blurring of individuals and groups as follows:

> The basic unit of analysis is an individual person. For practical purposes, however, the analysis can also be conducted at collective levels such as household, group, or class by using the standard device of assuming a 'representative individual'.

In any context where ownership relations between individuals or institutions and resources or commodities are multi-layered, complex and even contested by different individuals or groups of people, the 'standard device' that Osmani endorses becomes difficult to justify. This is particularly the case when 'fuzziness' in terms of units of analysis arises because different individuals and institutions exercise distinct claims over the same resource.[21] In such cases, agreed rules must be established for allocating rights over the resource to the various claimants. When several groups of people each hold socially legitimated rights over the same resource endowment, entitlements flowing from that resource cannot be modelled as if they accrue to a single person, and the notion of a 'representative individual' simply cannot be applied.

Throughout rural Africa, natural resources are owned (*de jure*) or controlled (*de facto*) by private individuals, households, extended families or lineage groups, communities, ethnic groups or 'tribes', and the state. These 'resource decision units' (Bromley 1989) overlap, since all individuals are simultaneously members of most institutional groupings as well. Conflicts and 'ambiguities' can occur at or between any of these levels, because institutional ownership or control of a resource such as land does not necessarily imply equal or equitable access to that resource by each individual member of that institution.[22]

Instead, access to such resources (or to entitlements derived from these resources) is strictly governed by rules and norms that are established on the basis of 'belonging' (citizenship, ethnicity), 'seniority' (age, gender) and other axes of inclusion or exclusion. These filters act as rationing mechanisms, selectively allocating resources to individuals who display the preferred characteristics and marginalizing the claims of others who do not share these characteristics – which are often inherited (ascribed) attributes, such as ethnicity or age, that cannot be changed (or acquired). To the extent that a community or society is structured along rules or norms of inclusion and exclusion, an individual's personal characteristics become a major determinant of his or her ability to access resources (i.e.

to accumulate endowments and to realize entitlements). As Gasper (1993: 694) points out: 'Beyond legal rights, effective access within institutions typically depends not only on formal rules but on particular relationships of authority and influence.'

Leach *et al.* (1997) agree that Sen's definition of entitlements as *legal* rights only is too restrictive, and they develop a concept of 'environmental entitlements', which attempts to 'extend the entitlements framework to the whole range of socially sanctioned as well as formal-legal institutional mechanisms for gaining resource access and control' (Leach *et al.* 1997: 16). This formulation recognizes that certain entitlements – for example usufruct rights to land or trees in communal tenure regimes – are neither conferred nor enforceable by formal legal systems, but instead are validated by community-level institutions on the basis of social membership rather than private ownership.

On the face of it, this would attempt to rescue the entitlement framework from the straitjacket of private property rights that Sen wrapped around it. After all, as Osmani (1995: 254) notes, Sen himself broadened his original narrowly legalistic definition of ownership to incorporate all 'socially accepted' norms of ownership. But is this sufficient? Fine (1997: 625) thinks not: 'the ambiguity in property rights is not resolved by pressing legitimacy into service as a criterion'. As Leach *et al.* (1997: 18) point out, 'resource claims are often contested, and within existing power relations some actors' claims are likely to prevail over those of others'. Socially determined entitlements are more dynamic and fluid, and – crucially for entitlement analysis – less amenable to specification at the individual level than are market-determined entitlements.[23] 'An extended entitlements approach therefore sees entitlements as the outcome of negotiations among social actors, involving power relationships and debates over meaning, rather than as simply the result of fixed, moral rules encoded in law' (Leach *et al.* 1997: 23).

Elsewhere, in his important work on modelling intra-household relations, Sen (1990) recognizes that entitlements are differentially distributed between household members, and that the distribution of entitlements can be a locus of negotiation and contestation between individuals who have very different objectives and decision-making power. Sen's exposition of 'cooperative conflict' within households implies a rejection of 'unitary' household models in favour of 'collective' models (see Kabeer 1994; Haddad *et al.* 1997). This chapter argues for a similar rejection of unitariness with respect to all resource decision units above the level of the individual – such as the extended family, the lineage group or clan, the 'community', and occupation groups or economic classes – and for the application instead of a collective or bargaining analysis. Within each of these institutions, the distribution of endowments – and of decision-making power over both endowments and entitlements – is typically extremely skewed, and is likely to be a source of tension and conflict rather than consensus.

Fuzziness with respect to property rights

> The absence of genuine rights of private property in productive assets is a well-known feature of traditional village societies. It means that no single owner can claim exclusive property in those assets nor use them at discretion in whatever way he likes. In particular, he [*sic*] is not entitled to dispose of them (to transfer them, to donate them, and so on) by an act of will: assets are not freely alienable and, therefore, they may not be 'commoditized'.
>
> (Platteau 1991: 121)

The notion of entitlements is conceptually and empirically inseparable from an economic system founded on private property and the legal rights associated with exclusive ownership by individuals of assets as commodities:

> Exchange entitlements' are defined by the conventions of commodity exchange in capitalist regimes, being subject to the laws of contract and occurring as an impersonal 'exchange of alienable things between transactors who are in a state of reciprocal independence'. By contrast, traditional precapitalist societies are the domain of non-commodity (gift) exchange defined as 'an exchange of inalienable things between transactors who are in a state of reciprocal dependence'.
>
> (Platteau 1991: 119, citing Gregory 1982: 12)

This implies that the entitlement approach is analytically weakest in precisely those socio-economic contexts for which it was designed, namely, famine-prone communities whose vulnerability is partly defined by their weak or unfavourable incorporation into markets, where common property and open access regimes for resources dominate private property and market-based exchange. To the extent that commodity exchanges in precapitalist communities (or in poor communities that retain significant precapitalist features) occur outside the contractual rules of the marketplace, the entitlement approach is effectively inapplicable.

Of the four main resource regimes – private property, state property, common property and open access (Bromley 1989: 871) – entitlements are 'fuzziest' with respect to common property regimes. Under private- and state-property regimes, entitlements are clearly defined and ownership is vested in individuals or state institutions. In open-access regimes, entitlements are freely available to whoever chooses to take advantage of the resource. Under common-property regimes, however, it is necessary to separate out ownership, control of and access to a *resource* (endowment) from ownership, control of and access to the *utilities* derived from that resource (entitlement). This introduces a critical 'ambiguity' (though not necessarily, as Sen puts it, 'vagueness') around the specification of owner-ship relations. Take the case of 'communal land' which is *owned* by the state, *controlled* by community leaders (village headmen) and accessed or *utilized* by individual farmers. In return for allocating usufruct rights over land to local farmers, village headmen might extract rent for its use in the form of tribute or 'gifts'. The state might also extract rent, in the form of a head tax on livestock or grazing fees. There is, in this example, a struc-tural separation between the resource *endowment* and *entitlement* to utilities derived from that resource (see Figure 4.2).

Figure 4.2 expands the conventional entitlement analytical framework, in terms of which an endowment set of resources is transformed into an entitlement set of goods and services, via an entitlement mapping rela-tionship (Osmani 1995: 256). Households which do not enjoy security of tenure over the land that they farm face threats of exclusion or reduction in their entitlements on two fronts: loss of access to land if the community or state exercises its greater authority over this land to dispossess the household; or if taxes or tribute demanded for access rights becomes pro-hibitive.

The pyramid under 'Claims' is inverted to indicate that the strongest claim on the land rests with the state, which owns it. Individual house-holds have the weakest claim – they can be required to pay taxes for its use to both community leaders and the state, and they can be forcibly removed from the land they occupy should the government decide, for example, to convert this land into a state farm or a dam.

'Extra-entitlement transfers'

... while entitlement relations concentrate on rights within the given legal structure in that society, some transfers involve violations of these rights, such as looting or brigandage. When such extra-entitlement

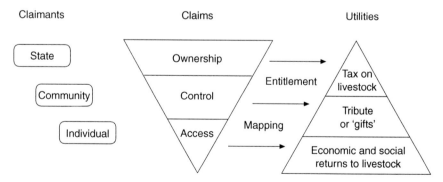

Figure 4.2 Entitlements to resources and entitlements to utilities derived from resources: the case of 'communal' land (source: Devereux (1996: 13)).

transfers are important, the entitlement approach to famines will be defective. On the other hand, most recent famines seem to have taken place in societies with 'law and order', without anything 'illegal' about the processes leading to starvation.

(Sen 1981: 49)

Edkins (1996), following a deconstructive approach, has argued persuasively that what Sen chooses to marginalize or exclude from the entitlement approach is more significant than Sen acknowledges. Two crucial exclusions are 'extra-entitlement transfers' and deliberate starvation. By confining his analysis to legally enforceable property rights, Sen (1981: 162) explicitly favours a restrictive view of famine as an 'economic disaster' and he privileges 'poverty and market forces as the root of famine' (Keen 1994: 4). This characterization had earlier been criticized for neglecting the determination of entitlements (Watts 1991). It also avoids engaging with the highly politicized context within which famines invariably occur.

Contra Sen's assertion, most recent famines, particularly in the Horn of Africa, have been triggered either by political instability or civil war, or by the lethal combination of war plus drought.[24] It might be argued that the emergence of 'complex emergencies' (Duffield 1993) or 'war famines', displacing drought as the dominant trigger, has occurred since the publication of *Poverty and Famines* in 1981. However, despite popular perceptions of famines as natural or economic disasters, the politicization of famines is not a recent phenomenon, nor is it confined to African 'war famines'. An overview of twentieth-century famines found that twenty-one out of thirty-two major famines had adverse politics at the local, national or international level as a principal cause (Devereux 2000: 6).[25] Many other famines that had 'natural' or economic triggers, such as drought, flood or food hoarding, became politicized by failures of government or international response – sometimes involving deliberate withholding of food aid for political reasons.[26]

The entitlement approach overlooks the centrality of political processes, many of which involve gross violations of human rights, including the right to food, in precipitating or exacerbating famines.[27] Sen's characterization of famine as 'entitlement failure' excludes intentionality as a possible causal trigger, and ignores the reality that famine produces beneficiaries as well as victims (Rangasami 1985; Keen 1994), who may play an active role in creating or prolonging famine conditions.[28]

For example, the entitlement approach is unable to explain recent famines in the 'asset transfer economy' (Duffield 1993) of south Sudan, where vulnerability is associated more with wealth than poverty. During the 1980s and 1990s the livelihood systems of Dinka agro-pastoralists were systematically undermined by repeated cattle raiding from aggressive neighbouring groups – either tacitly condoned or actively sponsored by the government in Khartoum – until they were unable to resist livelihood shocks like drought (Keen 1994; Deng, Chapter 11, this volume). During the 1990s over half a million people were displaced and their livestock herds were halved, and in the 1998 famine 70,000 people died (Deng 1999). These 'extra-legal transfers' occurred outside the market mechanism, which is for Sen the primary institution for commodity exchanges and asset transfers.

It is often asserted that the entitlement approach by definition cannot address 'war famines', since 'entitlement theory has no place for violence' (de Waal 1990: 473). In a general sense this is true, but the impact of war and violence needs to be unpacked before any analytical role for the entitlement approach is rejected, since one of its most powerful contributions is in examining the distributional impact of a livelihood shock, whatever its source. Clearly, conflict impinges on all sources of entitlement to food, but not all of these involve 'extra-entitlement transfers':

1   *Production-based entitlements.* During a war, the ratio of food producers to food consumers falls: farmers are conscripted, displaced, disabled or killed; soldiers requisition food and livestock. 'Scorched earth' tactics include destruction of granaries, burning of fields of standing crops and poisoning of wells. Before the famines of the 1970s and 1980s in Ethiopia, Angola, Mozambique and Cambodia, thousands of hectares of farming land had been taken out of production because of landmines.

2   *Employment-based entitlements.* During a war, cash crop production and marketing networks collapse, employment opportunities (demand for agricultural labour, petty trading activities) contract, farmers and pastoralists are attacked for food and livestock. Internally displaced persons and refugees lose their normal livelihoods. Lacking assets, incomes and access to food, they become dependent on external assistance.

3   *Trade-based entitlements.* Conflict disrupts normal trading activities in various ways, including: (1) by disrupting trade routes – roads are mined and bridges are destroyed, trucks and fuel are diverted to military uses; (2) by direct attacks on markets – e.g. the Ethiopian government bombed village markets in Tigray and Eritrea during the 1980s until markets had to be held at night (de Waal 1997: 118); (3) by appropriating food from traders or looting food stores; (4) by laying siege to towns or districts, thereby blockading movements of people and food. All these disruptions reduce food supplies and raise food prices in conflict zones, thus creating famine conditions.

4   *Transfer entitlements.* War disrupts both 'private' and 'public' transfers. Conflict shatters social support networks. The 1998 famine in southern Sudan was named the 'famine of breaking relationships' by local people (Deng 1999). Transport problems and road-blocks might

make it impossible for relatives to send remittances. Food aid is frequently prevented from entering conflict zones, either by government decree or because of security risks. Relief convoys and planes are attacked and food aid is seized: 80 per cent of food aid sent to Somalia in 1986 was taken by the army or militias. During the 1980s famine in Ethiopia the Dergue regime appropriated food aid to support its forced resettlement programme, which exacerbated the famine.

These effects of war can be disaggregated into three distinct clusters. The first covers the disruptive effects of conflict on local economies and livelihoods. In theory, these disruptions – such as farmers volunteering for military service, or the contraction of local markets – could be incorporated within the entitlement approach, much as the effects of drought can be modelled insofar as they affect endowments and entitlement mappings.[29]

The second cluster is Sen's illegal 'extra-entitlement transfers', such as the requisitioning of grain from farmers, raiding of livestock from pastoralists, or seizing of food aid from relief convoys. There is no escaping Sen's own judgement that these typical features of 'war famines' render the entitlement approach 'defective'.[30] The third cluster of effects is equally problematic for the entitlement approach, and describes various 'unruly practices' (Gore 1993) associated with war that do not directly transfer entitlements but create 'conditions which are deliberately and socially engineered to undermine entitlement' (Fine 1997: 627). Perhaps the paradigmatic case is a siege that denies access to food, in order deliberately to bring about starvation of the inhabitants.[31]

Conclusion

This chapter differs from many other critical contributions to the entitlement literature, in that I have not attempted to refute Sen's empirical analysis of specific famines, nor do I dispute his seminal insight that famines can occur because of shifts in the distribution rather than the availability of food. Instead, I have interrogated Sen's concept of 'entitlement' as an analytical construct, and I have confined the discussion to four possible problems that Sen himself identified. On these four 'limitations' the following conclusions can be drawn.

1 *Choosing to starve.* Rationing one's own food consumption to protect assets and livelihoods beyond an immediate crisis is entirely consistent with a 'multi-period entitlements analysis'. 'Choosing to starve *others*' within the household requires an understanding of intra-household power relations that cannot be captured within the entitlement framework, which is severely undermined by the reality that those household members who make decisions concerning entitlements and

those household members who die during famines are two distinct groups. Choosing to starve others could presumably be incorporated within the entitlement framework by adopting an extreme utilitarian view in which 'dependent' household members were modelled as 'endowments' that are expendable during livelihood crises, but this would remove any claim to being a normative or ethical concept that the word 'entitlement' implies.

2   *Starvation or epidemics?* Although Sen's view of famine mortality as 'death by starvation' is naïve, de Waal's 'health crisis model' does not refute a narrative of famine causation based on direct or exchange entitlement decline. Although increased *exposure* to disease might not be hunger-related, if this exposure is due to the social disruption triggered by a food crisis, then entitlement decline remains as the underlying cause of death. Conversely, if the social disruption was not caused by a food crisis (e.g. distress migration during a war) then this is not a famine at all.

3   *Fuzzy entitlements.* The existence of property regimes such as communal land tenure gives rise to two sets of 'fuzziness' around entitlement relations: first, over the unit of analysis, and second, over the nature of property rights. Rights or claims over resources that are held *collectively* (by groups of people, or institutions) are incompatible with the entitlement approach, which is conceptually grounded in private-property regimes, where resources are commoditized and owned by individuals. Rights can also be exercised at varying levels, from ownership (the strongest form, including rights of disposal) to access and usufruct rights (the weakest form, where ownership and use are often separated). The entitlement approach is effectively inapplicable in contexts where the relationship between individuals and resources is mediated by (non-market) institutions.

4   *Extra-entitlement transfers.* The entitlement approach can be used to analyse the 'normal' disruptive effects of war on local economies and livelihoods. It cannot, however, explain violations of entitlements such as requisitioning of grain, raiding of cattle and appropriation or withholding of food aid. Nor can it explain 'unruly practices' such as deliberate starvation, or the use of famine as a weapon. 'Complex emergencies' expose most sharply the limitations of what is essentially an economistic analytical framework: its failure to engage with famine as both a social process and a political crisis.

All four 'limitations' discussed by Sen and scrutinized in this chapter share two common underlying themes: first, a failure to recognize individuals as socially embedded members of households, communities and states, and second, a failure to recognize that famines are political crises as much as they are economic shocks or natural disasters. The result is an elegant analytical framework that privileges the economic aspects of famine and excludes the social and the political: the importance of institutions in determining entitlements (at intra-household or community level), famine as a social process (mortality due to communicable diseases), and violations of entitlement rules by others (complex emergencies). Without a complementary social and political analysis of famine, the entitlement approach can illuminate only part of this complex, multi-faceted phenomenon.

Notes

1 The right to adequate food is enshrined in the Universal Declaration of Human Rights of 1948 and in the International Covenant on Economic, Social and Cultural Rights of 1966. Little progress has been made in enforcing this 'entitlement to food' to date, notwithstanding commitments made by governments and international organizations at the 1974 World Food Conference and the 1996 World Food Summit. The adoption in 2004 of 'voluntary guidelines to support the progressive realization of the right to adequate food' (FAO 2004) is an encouraging recent development.

2 One example: a pastoralist can sell her cow for a 50-kg bag of millet. The cow is an endowment, the bag of millet is one entitlement (among many) that the cow provides; the exchange entitlement mapping includes the livestock/grain price ratio (1 cow = 50-kg of millet). Since famines in rural areas are characterized by collapsing livestock prices and escalating food prices, the livestock/grain price ratio is often used as an indicator of pastoralists' 'exchange entitlements' in famine early warning systems (Swift and Hamilton 2001: 71–4).

3 These are defined respectively as follows: the right to own what one produces with one's own (or hired) resources; the right to own what one acquires through exchange of commodities with willing parties; the right to self-employment or to sell one's labour power; the right to own what is willingly given by others.

4 As Fine (1997) argues, this 'scaling up' from individual to mass starvation does not adequately capture the social dynamic of famine, and this represents the first of several tensions that are explored in this chapter between Sen's 'methodological individualism' (Fine 1997: 618) and famine as a social process.

5 See Sen (1986) on Bowbrick (1986); Osmani (1995: 274) on Kula (1988) ('An extreme form of misunderstanding is revealed by Kula'); Ravallion (1996) on Devereux (1988).

6 It is significant that one of Sen's earliest published papers on the entitlement approach is titled 'Famines as failures of exchange entitlements' (Sen 1976).

7 Early, hostile critics complained that the entitlement approach offered no original insights into famine causality and processes, but merely introduced new jargon to what had long been known (see Mitra 1982; Rangasami 1985).

8 In asserting that the entitlement approach does incorporate a theory of famine causation I am disputing the current conventional wisdom, which holds that 'the entitlement approach is best seen as an *investigative* method rather than as providing a *causal* theory' (Fine 1997: 621; see also Gasper 1993; Osmani 1995: 262). However, I am not endorsing the naïve view that the entitlement approach is a theory which asserts 'that famine is *not* caused by a 'fall in food availability'' (Rangasami 1985: 1797).

9 Critics who challenge Sen on empirical grounds often confuse the two, believ-

ing that by demonstrating that specific famines were triggered by food availability decline they have 'refuted' the entitlement 'theory' of famine (see especially Bowbrick 1986). In fact, the best they can hope to do is refute the
'exchange entitlement decline' hypothesis for individual famines, since the
entitlement approach incorporates the possibility of food availability decline as
'direct entitlement' failure.

10 See Bowbrick (1986) on the 1943 Bengal famine; Cutler (1984) and Devereux
(1988) on the 1970s Ethiopian famine.

11 See Kula (1988) and Nolan (1993) on the Chinese 'Great Leap Forward'
famine; Baulch (1987) on the 1980s famine in northern Ethiopia; and de Waal
(1990) on the 1985 famine in western Sudan.

12 Corbett (1988) synthesized the 1980s 'coping strategies' literature. The term
was subsequently criticized for embodying unrealistic optimism, most pithily by
Seaman (1993: 14): 'In contemporary development jargon, Africans do not
starve, they 'cope'.' A more neutral term might be 'risk management behaviour' (Siegel and Alwang 1999).

13 See, *inter alia*, Wolde Mariam (1986) and Dessalegn Rahmato (1987) for evidence from Ethiopia; Watts (1983) on northern Nigeria; de Waal (1989) on
western Sudan; also (in non-emergency contexts) Campbell and Trechter
(1982) on northern Cameroon; Devereux (1993) on northern Ghana; Davies
(1996) on Mali.

14 See also Gasper (1993: 685): 'Even during real but 'moderate' starvation,
people may not use all of their food entitlements, but instead balance their
own increased risk (due to malnutrition) of morbidity and mortality, against
their wish and need to maintain assets such as livestock.'

15 As Fine (1997: 619–20) puts it, given the fact that the entitlement approach is
grounded in neoclassical individualism, 'it would appear to be impossible to
explain how famines occur since no one maximizing utility would choose
death (and negative infinite expected utility) even with a low risk'.

16 How, for that matter, can the entitlement approach explain systematic deprivation of girl children in parts of the world such as south Asia, and the resulting
'100 million missing women' that Sen himself has written about (Drèze and
Sen 1989: 51–3)?

17 Reviewing Sen's extensive work on poverty, food insecurity and famine, it is
striking not only how diverse this body of work is (see Devereux and Singer
1999), but also how rarely Sen attempts to unify various strands of his thinking
where the potential and rationale for synthesis seem powerful.

18 See Watkins and Menken (1985: 650): 'Some of the increase in infectious
disease may be due to increased susceptibility that is thought to accompany
malnutrition and some may be due to the peculiar conditions that accompany
scarcity, for example, a breakdown of systems of water supply and waste disposal, an increase in the number of vagrants, or the crowding and dismal conditions of refugee camps.'

19 This section draws on arguments elaborated in Devereux (1996) and Devereux
and Seely (1996).

20 To take just one example: 'It is, in fact, possible for a group to suffer both
direct entitlement failure and trade entitlement failure, since the group may
produce a commodity that is both directly consumed and exchanged for some
other food. For example, the Ethiopian pastoral nomad both eats the animal
products directly and also sells animals to buy foodgrains (thereby making a
net gain in calories), on which he is habitually dependent' (Sen 1981: 51).

21 This is by no means atypical. As Woldemeskel (1990: 493) observes: 'There are
no good *a priori* reasons to prefer possession-based entitlement accounts to
institutionally-based entitlement accounts. On the contrary, we have reason to

believe that the latter will have more explanatory power, and be more comprehensive, than the former.'

22 Since Namibia achieved independence in 1990, for example, restitution of ancestral land has been a source of conflict between the state and various ethnic groups or communities who were dispossessed by the South African colonial administration. Within rural Namibian communities a crisis has developed over the 'illegal' fencing of communal rangelands, a phenomenon which can be explained as an attempt by pastoralists to 'privatize' access to grazing lands that remain communally controlled but state owned. Within Namibian households, a married woman's access to land is secured through her husband under customary law, and if she is widowed she is at risk of being dispossessed of her residential and farming land by her late husband's relatives. (Devereux 1996 elaborates on these three case studies.)

23 Of course, when resources become privatized and commodified, socially dictated rules of 'endowment' allocation and 'entitlement' determination become superseded by market-based rules (or 'exchange entitlement mappings'), and the market is famously blind with respect to the personal characteristics of transactors.

24 Von Braun *et al.*(1998: 3) list twenty-one famines worldwide since 1970. All but two – Bangladesh in 1974 and North Korea in the late 1990s – occurred in sub-Saharan Africa, and fifteen of the twenty-one had war or counter-insurgency as a trigger, either in combination with drought (as in Ethiopia, Somalia and Sudan) or alone (as in Angola, Liberia or Zaire).

25 These include several famines in China, the Soviet Union (notably 'Stalin's famine' in the 1930s, during which 7–8 million Ukrainians died), Biafra, Cambodia and elsewhere, which can be directly attributed to war and/or the malevolent exercise of state power.

26 Well-documented examples include Bangladesh (1974), Ethiopia (1984) and Sudan (1990). In each case, the United States delayed relief deliveries because it had difficulties with the regime in power at the time. The literature has not examined the question of precisely when a transfer-based entitlement such as food aid enters an individual's 'entitlement set'. I suggest that this occurs not at the time of delivery, but at the moment when the state or donor makes a commitment to deliver, say, food aid and establishes eligibility criteria. If the donor then fatally delays its delivery of food aid such that eligible people die, then in terms of the entitlement approach these deaths were caused by violations of 'transfer entitlements'.

27 Elsewhere, Sen has drawn attention to political factors in other writings on famine. Specifically, he has highlighted the importance of democratic institutions – a vigilant press to disseminate information about food crises, free elections to ensure state accountability to its citizens – in preventing famines, notably in post-independence India (Drèze and Sen 1989: 212; see also Banik, Chapter 13, this volume). Here again, there would appear to be great potential for drawing synergistic connections between entitlements as an economistic construct and entitlement to food and freedom from famine as a political or moral imperative.

28 This technocratic bias extends to Sen's policy prescriptions for redressing hunger and famine, which privilege top-down 'public action' (Drèze and Sen 1989) such as food or cash distribution and public works projects, over 'political action' such as measures to empower the poor and reduce their structural vulnerability. Sen's package of interventions – essentially welfarist transfers to targeted individuals or households – follows logically from the methodological individualism of the entitlement approach, which fails to recognize that a famine 'is plainly social in character, something other than a number of individuals facing starvation' (Fine 1997: 624).

29 One of Sen's case studies in *Poverty and Famines*, the Bengal famine of 1943, was triggered by wartime food price inflation due to disrupted food supplies, which Sen (1981: Chapter 6) analyses convincingly in terms of exchange entitlement failure for market-dependent groups such as wage labourers.

30 'There is, of course, a very *general* hypothesis underlying the approach, which is subject to empirical testing. It will be violated if starvation in famines is shown to arise not from entitlement failures but either from choice characteristics ... or from non-entitlement transfers (e.g. looting)' (Sen 1981: 162–4). Sen (1981: 164) recognizes that 'non-entitlement transfers have played a part in some famines of the past', and he cites the 1925 famine in Szechwan, China, which followed the requisitioning of local grain reserves and livestock by troops.

31 Examples include Leningrad and parts of the Netherlands during the Second World War (see Watson, Chapter 12, this volume), and the town of Juba in southern Sudan, which was besieged for several years during the 1980s and early 1990s.

References

Baulch, B. (1987) 'Entitlements and the Wollo famine of 1982–1985', *Disasters*, 11(3): 195–204.

Bongaarts, J. and Cain, M. (1982) 'Demographic responses to famine', in K. Cahill (ed.), *Famine*, New York, NY: Orbis Books.

Bowbrick, P. (1986) 'The causes of famine: a refutation of Professor Sen's theory', *Food Policy*, 11(2): 105–24.

Bromley, D. (1989) 'Property relations and economic development: the other land reform', *World Development*, 17(6): 867–77.

Caldwell, J. and Caldwell, P. (1992) 'Famine in Africa: a global perspective', in E. van de Walle, G. Pison and M. Sala-Diakanda (eds), *Mortality and Society in Sub-Saharan Africa*, Oxford: Clarendon Press.

Campbell, D. and Trechter, D. (1982) 'Strategies for coping with food consumption shortage in the Mandara Mountains region of north Cameroon', *Social Science and Medicine*, 16(24): 2117–27.

Corbett, J. (1988) 'Famine and household coping strategies', *World Development*, 16(9): 1099–112.

Cutler, P. (1984) 'Famine forecasting: prices and peasant behaviour in northern Ethiopia', *Disasters*, 8(1): 48–56.

Davies, S. (1996) *Adaptable Livelihoods*, London: Macmillan.

Deng, L. (1999) 'The 1998 famine in the Sudan: causes, preparedness and response', *IDS Discussion Paper* 369, Brighton: Institute of Development Studies.

Dessalegn Rahmato (1987) 'Famine and survival strategies: a case study from northern Ethiopia', *Food and Famine Monograph Series 1*, Addis Ababa: Institute of Development Research.

Devereux, S. (1988) 'Entitlements, availability and famine: a revisionist view of Wollo, 1972–74', *Food Policy*, 13(3): 270–82.

Devereux, S. (1993) 'Goats before ploughs: dilemmas of household response sequencing during food shortages', *IDS Bulletin*, 24(4): 52–9.

Devereux, S. (1996) 'Fuzzy entitlements and common property resources: struggles over rights to communal land in Namibia', *IDS Working Paper* 44, Brighton: Institute of Development Studies.

Devereux, S. (2000) 'Famine in the twentieth century', *IDS Working Paper* 105, Brighton: Institute of Development Studies.

Devereux, S. and Seely, M. (1996) 'Fuzzy entitlements and natural resources: the case of Namibia', Paper prepared for 'Livelihoods from Resource Flows: Environmental Awareness and Contextual Analysis of Environmental Conflict' conference, Linköping, Sweden: IUAES/IGU.

Devereux, S. and Singer, H. (1999) 'A tribute to Professor Amartya Sen on the occasion of his receiving the 1998 Nobel Prize for Economics', *Food Policy* 24(1): 1–6.

de Waal, A. (1989) *Famine That Kills: Darfur, Sudan, 1984–1985*, Oxford: Clarendon Press.

de Waal, A. (1990) 'A re-assessment of entitlement theory in the light of the recent famines in Africa', *Development and Change*, 21(3): 469–90.

de Waal, A. (1997) *Famine Crimes: Politics and the Disaster Relief Industry in Africa*, Oxford: James Currey.

Drèze, J. and Sen, A. (1989) *Hunger and Public Action*, Oxford: Clarendon Press.

Duffield, M. (1993) 'NGOs, disaster relief and asset transfer in the Horn: political survival in a permanent emergency', *Development and Change*, 24: 131–57.

Edkins, J. (1996) 'Legality with a vengeance: famines and humanitarian relief in 'complex emergencies'', *Journal of International Studies*, 25(3): 547–75.

FAO (2004) 'Intergovernmental Working Group for the elaboration of a set of voluntary guidelines to support the progressive realization of the right to adequate food in the context of national food security', Final Report of the Chair, Rome, 23 September 2004.

Fine, B. (1997) 'Entitlement failure?', *Development and Change*, 28: 617–47.

Gasper, D. (1993) 'Entitlements analysis: relating concepts and contexts', *Development and Change*, 24(4): 679–718.

Gore, C. (1993) 'Entitlement relations and 'unruly' social practices: a comment on the work of Amartya Sen', *Journal of Development Studies*, 29(3): 429–60.

Gregory, C. (1982) *Gifts and Commodities*, London: Academic Press.

Haddad, L., Hoddinott, J. and Alderman, H. (eds) (1997) *Intrahousehold Resource Allocation in Developing Countries*, Baltimore, MD: Johns Hopkins University Press.

Jodha, N. (1975) 'Famine and famine policies: some empirical evidence', *Economic and Political Weekly*, 10, 11 October.

Kabeer, N. (1994) *Reversed Realities: Gender Hierarchies in Development Thought*, London: Verso.

Keen, D. (1994) *The Benefits of Famine: A Political Economy of Famine and Relief in Southwestern Sudan, 1983–1989*, Princeton, NJ: Princeton University Press.

Kula, E. (1988) 'The inadequacy of the entitlement approach to explain and remedy famines', *Journal of Development Studies*, 25: 112–17.

Leach, M., Mearns, R. and Scoones, I. (1997) 'Environmental entitlements: a framework for understanding the institutional dynamics of environmental change', *IDS Discussion Paper 359, Brighton: Institute of Development Studies*.

Mitra, A. (1982) 'The meaning of meaning', *Economic and Political Weekly*, 17(13): 488.

Nolan, P. (1993) 'The causation and prevention of famines: a critique of A.K. Sen', *Journal of Peasant Studies*, 21: 1–28.

Osmani, S. (1995) 'The entitlement approach to famine: an assessment', in K. Basu, P. Pattanaik and K. Suzumura (eds), *Choice, Welfare and Development*, Oxford: Oxford University Press.

Platteau, J.-P. (1991) 'Traditional systems of social security and hunger insurance:

past achievements and modern challenges', in E. Ahmad, J. Drèze, J. Hills and A. Sen (eds), *Social Security in Developing Countries*, Oxford: Clarendon Press.

Rangasami, A. (1985) '"Failure of exchange entitlements" theory of famine: a response', *Economic and Political Weekly*, 20(41 and 42): 1747–52; 1797–1801.

Ravallion, M. (1987) *Markets and Famines*, Oxford: Oxford University Press.

Ravallion, M. (1996) 'Famines and economics', *Policy Research Working Paper* 1693, Washington, DC: World Bank.

Seaman, J. (1993) 'Famine mortality in Africa', *IDS Bulletin*, 24(4): 27–32.

Sen, A. (1976) 'Famines as failures of exchange entitlements', *Economic and Political Weekly*, 11(31–33): 1273–80.

Sen, A. (1981) *Poverty and Famines: An Essay on Entitlement and Deprivation*, Oxford: Clarendon Press.

Sen, A. (1984) *Resources, Values and Development*, Oxford: Basil Blackwell.

Sen, A. (1986) 'Food, economics and entitlements', *Lloyds Bank Review*, 160: 1–20.

Sen, A. (1990) 'Gender and cooperative conflicts', in I. Tinker (ed.), *Persistent Inequalities: Women and World Development*, New York, NY: Oxford University Press.

Siegel, P. and Alwang, J. (1999) 'An asset-based approach to social risk management: a conceptual framework', *Social Protection Discussion Paper* 9926, Washington, DC: World Bank.

Swift, J. and Hamilton, K. (2001) 'Household food and livelihood security', in S. Devereux and S. Maxwell (eds), *Food Security in Sub-Saharan Africa*, London: ITDG Publishing.

von Braun, J., Teklu, T. and Webb, P. (1998) *Famine in Africa: Causes, Responses and Prevention*, Baltimore, MD: Johns Hopkins University Press.

Watkins, S. and Menken, J. (1985) 'Famines in Historical Perspective', *Population and Development Review*, 11(4): 647–75.

Watts, M. (1983) *Silent Violence: Food, Famine and Peasantry in Northern Nigeria*, Berkeley, CA: University of California Press.

Watts, M. (1991) 'Entitlements or empowerment? Famine and starvation in Africa', *Review of African Political Economy*, X(X): 9–26.

Wolde Mariam, Mesfin (1986) *Rural Vulnerability to Famine in Ethiopia: 1958–1977*, London: ITDG Publishing.

Woldemeskel, G. (1990) 'Famine and the two faces of entitlement: a comment on Sen', *World Development*, 18(3): 491–5.

Young, H. and Jaspars, S. (1995) 'Nutrition, disease and death in times of famine', *Disasters*, 19(2): 94–109.

5 AIDS, hunger and destitution

Theory and evidence for the 'new variant famines' hypothesis in Africa

Alex de Waal

Introduction[1]

The HIV/AIDS epidemic is the biggest health disaster in modern history, and has the potential to bring secondary disasters of comparable magnitude in its wake. In sub-Saharan Africa, the concern of this chapter, AIDS has intensified and widened poverty, left millions of children orphaned and is destroying the capacity of institutions to function. The 'new variant famine' hypothesis (henceforth, NVF) is concerned with one aspect of this impact, namely how the epidemic creates new and unfamiliar vulnerabilities to famine. This chapter examines the NVF hypothesis, elucidating what it claims (and, equally importantly, what it does not claim), assessing what current evidence can tell us and situating it within existing models and frameworks for famine and famine prevention.

The NVF hypothesis is still in its academic infancy,[2] although advocates have raced ahead and made strong and largely unsubstantiated claims on its behalf. For this reason, it is important to note from the outset what the NVF hypothesis is *not*. It is not a claim that HIV/AIDS was the sole, or even the prime, cause of the 2002 food crisis in southern Africa. It does not claim that HIV/AIDS is causing a decline in aggregate food production (though that may occur in some places).

The chapter first outlines the claims that are made by the NVF hypothesis. Second, it evaluates recent empirical evidence for NVF's sub-hypotheses. A growing number of studies provide empirical evidence that supports or refutes components of NVF. However, there have as yet been no studies specifically designed to test it. In the light of what can be said with confidence, and what cannot, the chapter then locates NVF within four of the dominant frameworks for analysing food security and famine in Africa, namely: entitlement theory; livelihoods and vulnerability analyses; the political economy of famine; and the malnutrition-health crisis model of famine mortality. Although they have different emphases, for the most part these are interlocking and mutually compatible approaches. A final section of the chapter projects into the future and inquires into the possibility of a crisis in social reproduction associated with the HIV/AIDS epidemic. This goes well beyond the evidence, to suggest what may occur if generalized HIV/AIDS epidemics are allowed to proceed unchecked.

There are sensitivities over the use of the word 'famine'. Political leaders and staff of international agencies fear that the term carries with it the implications of failure. They are correct: governments and international agencies should be profoundly ashamed of the famines that they have allowed to happen, or (in the case of some governments) that they have created. The word 'famine' is also considered extreme and alarmist. It is remarkable that the crises that have struck Africa in recent years, causing such widespread impoverishment, hunger and death, should not be considered worthy of an 'alarmist' label. However, it is also worth recalling that African definitions and diagnoses of famine are typically made for adverse events that cause hunger and destitution, but not 'mass starvation unto death' (de Waal 2005). In this chapter I follow the practice of using 'famine' in this broader sense.

The NVF entails the following sub-hypotheses. First, there are new categories of poor and vulnerable people, namely those affected directly or indirectly by HIV/AIDS and its impacts. These include families directly hit because an adult has fallen sick or died of AIDS, and the second-generation impacts that play out over a longer time period, in the form of children orphaned by AIDS who grow up with reduced life chances, and older people whose own adult children have died of AIDS and who are thus left with reduced family support systems and perhaps orphaned grandchildren to support as well. This 'AIDS poverty' and 'AIDS vulnerability' has two components: it leads to new patterns of vulnerability to destitution and hunger, and it changes the 'normality' from which well-being deviates during crisis. Second, the advent of HIV/AIDS leads to new patterns of coping (or failing to cope) when there is an additional shock such as a drought: the trajectory of destitution when a famine occurs is sharper, and recovery is slower. Third, a generalized epidemic of HIV/AIDS in a poor and vulnerable population changes the ecology of nutrition and infection, and thereby the pattern and level of child mortality. Available evidence supports a *prima facie* confirmation of the first two sub-hypotheses, but there are not yet sufficient data to test the third.

The NVF hypothesis also makes predictions about what may happen if HIV prevalence continues at a high level, causing widespread illness and death in poor and food-insecure countries. It hypothesizes that there will be a new kind of crisis marked by unprecedented patterns of mortality – specifically, widespread death among mature adults, especially women. It also argues that there may be a vicious cycle in which poverty, migration and lower educational achievement in turn create greater susceptibility to HIV infection. This can then cause a crisis of social reproduction. There are no data in support of this conjecture.

It is important to stress that the NVF supplements rather than displaces other explanations for famine. The NVF claims that HIV/AIDS changes the pattern of vulnerability to famine, but this does not mean that economic, climatic and (most importantly) political factors are unimportant. To the contrary, the NVF hypothesis derives from the view that the HIV/AIDS epidemic exacerbates existing social and economic problems. It is the interaction between the impact of HIV/AIDS and other shocks and stresses that creates destitution and hunger. The NVF hypothesis does not exonerate national governments and the international community from political responsibilities for failure to prevent food crises.

Empirical evidence for the NVF hypothesis

This section discusses empirical evidence in support or refutation of the NVF. None of the studies cited were designed specifically to test the NVF, so the interpretation of results must be cautious.

Evidence for new patterns of vulnerability associated with HIV/AIDS

Evidence for this takes the form of studies of the livelihoods of households impacted by HIV/AIDS, not during periods of additional stress (e.g. in food-secure areas or during non-drought periods), and nutritional surveillance data from southern Africa during the drought of 2002–2003. This evidence almost all relates to the first generation of AIDS-poor, namely households in which a working-age adult is sick or has died, and not to the socio-economic profile of second-generation impacts on children orphaned by AIDS as they themselves enter maturity.

An array of small-scale studies indicates that HIV/AIDS causes serious losses at household level, including lower incomes, decreased food cultivation and depletion of assets. The first of these studies dates from Uganda in the late 1980s (Barnett and Blaikie 1992). Subject to differences relating to the structure of agrarian livelihoods, especially labour demand and labour roles, this finding has been replicated across southern Africa (Webb and Mutangadura 1999; Baylies 2002). This literature is well reviewed elsewhere (Toupouzis 1999; Haddad and Gillespie 2001; Haddad and Frankenberger 2003; Harvey 2004).

AIDS-affected households do, however, show a remarkable ability to cope. Good evidence for this comes from (among other places) a series of studies in the Kagera region of Tanzania in the early 1990s, financed largely by the World Bank (Killewo *et al.* 1994; Tibaijuka 1997; Dayton and Ainsworth 2002; Beegle 2003). Kagera was hit early and hard by HIV/AIDS, but the region has shown remarkable resilience, and most indicators show significant improvements over the last decade. Possible reasons for the effectiveness of coping include a farming system that includes heavy reliance on tree crops (which require little labour), effective social support systems (such as burial associations, which help spread the costs of funerals) (de Weerdt 2001), and the absence of any concurrent shocks such as drought or commodity price collapses. Currently, a ten-year follow-up study on the 1991–1994 panel survey is being undertaken, which should provide fascinating evidence for the long-term impacts of HIV/AIDS.

Studies from different parts of Africa indicate that many households impacted by an adult death respond by drafting in new adults, thus maintaining the household workforce (Yamano and Jayne 2002). The strategy (and hence the impact) differs according to the gender of the deceased. In Mozambique, the death of a father led to a marked adverse shift in the dependency ratio and great difficulties in adjusting, while households suffering the death of an adult female were more able to cope, both by shedding children and by acquiring another adult woman (Mather *et al.* 2003). Evidence from tea-pluckers in Kenya (Fox *et al.* 2004) and cotton growers in Zambia (Larson *et al.* 2004) shows that declines in production can be offset by households drafting in the labour of relatives or children to sustain production. However, this coping response is necessarily short term. These studies concern households that are not subject to additional stresses such as drought, suggesting that, as they suffer such external stress, they will be less able to respond effectively and are thus more vulnerable to destitution.

Structural factors in the farming system determine its resilience or vulnerability to the impacts of AIDS morbidity and mortality. The robustness of Lake Victoria farming systems is related to well-distributed rainfall and the reliance on tree crops without seasonal labour bottlenecks. It may also be related to a favourable economic environment in the late 1980s and early 1990s, when the AIDS epidemic was at its worst. We are currently awaiting re-studies of the sample sites investigated in the early 1990s, to see if the cumulative impacts of the AIDS epidemic over a decade are more severe. In dry areas of Zambia, where such a seasonal labour constraint is critical to farming activities, adult deaths have a more severe immediate impact on production (Barnett *et al.* 1995). In rural South Africa, half of a sample of 700 households affected by AIDS reported that their children were going hungry as a result (Steinberg *et al.* 2002). Again, we do not have information regarding the long-term impacts of the epidemic in these areas, but a planned re-study of early 1990s survey sites in Zambia should provide important evidence.

The burden on rural households may be increased by a number of other factors. The sick may move from urban to rural homes – especially if they originate from there. A study of rural Tanzanian households suffering an adult death found that about one-third of those who died had joined the household recently – they had relocated because they were terminally ill (Beegle 2003: 18). Urban households may also send children orphaned by AIDS to the village for care, often because of the presence of grandparents. When urban families lose income they may choose to return to rural areas where they have, at least, an entitlement to food. As a result the rural economy is bearing a disproportionate burden of the costs of the HIV/AIDS epidemic, while also being less able to call upon support from the urban economy in times of distress (Rosen and Simon 2002).

Other households may suffer from the negative externalities of their AIDS-afflicted neighbours. Factors include the afflicted households no longer hiring labour (Food Economy Group 2002), and the burden of upkeep of orphaned children left in need of support when the household ultimately dissolves. On the other hand, some neighbouring households may be able to benefit, for example by acquiring the land or assets of the distressed household. The exploitation of orphans for domestic labour, agricultural work and income generation, and sexual services is documented (Daniel 2003), though the scale of these phenomena has not been quantified. There is evidence that, in some places and at some times, wealthier households are more likely to suffer AIDS deaths (Ainsworth and Semali 1998), complicating the picture of assessing the socio-economic impact.

Another source of evidence is nutritional surveillance data. An overview of nutritional surveys in southern Africa conducted by UNICEF in collaboration with John Mason (UNICEF Southern African Humanitarian Unit 2003; Mason *et al.* 2004) found some evidence that indicates an adverse impact of HIV/AIDS. This included clear signs that double orphans have much higher prevalence of malnutrition compared with children with one or both parents living. However, the locational correlation between HIV prevalence and undernutrition was complicated by the fact that urban areas tend to have higher HIV prevalence than rural areas, but have better access to food markets and relief supplies.

The data available did not allow analysis according to HIV/AIDS proxy indicators at the household level. However, these studies pointed to an important conclusion – that although malnutrition rates were higher in rural areas, which tended to have lower HIV prevalence, the *decline* in nutritional status was most marked in locations closer to towns, which traditionally enjoyed higher food security but were now hit by higher prevalence of HIV/AIDS. If this is correct and generalizable, this points to the emergence of a new category of the vulnerable – namely children in high-prevalence urban and peri-urban communities.

Concerning the socio-economic profile and life chances of children orphaned by AIDS, there is considerable debate and many gloomy prognoses. However, data on the long-term economic prospects of these children as they attain adulthood and establish their own households are so far lacking.

Evidence for new trajectories of destitution during crisis

The household studies cited above suggest that AIDS-impacted households may be able to 'cope' in the absence of additional stresses. All coping has a cost, which implies either a secular long-term decline in well-being or a greater vulnerability to downward pressures without the prospect of corresponding increases. What happens when there is a drought?

The second and major prediction of the NVF hypothesis is that AIDS-affected households and communities should follow a new trajectory of impoverishment during crisis. They should more rapidly move from the more sustainable coping strategies to the less sustainable ones. Specifically, there should be less reliance on kinship networks and less collection of wild foods, and greater disposal of assets and earlier resort to commercial sex work. This prediction has yet to be tested.

Some of the best data concerning the household-level impact of the southern African food crisis come from the surveys by the SADC Food, Agriculture and Natural Resources Vulnerability Assessment Committees (SADC FANR VAC). During 2002 these surveys did not look for potential impacts of HIV/AIDS, although they were collecting data on potential proxy indicators such as household demography or the presence of a chronically sick adult. A reanalysis of data in early 2003 found that many of these proxies were strongly correlated with household food insecurity (SADC FANR VAC 2003). There is plentiful evidence of households going hungry during food crises. According to the VAC survey in early 2003, 57 per cent of households with a chronically ill adult (taken as a proxy for AIDS-affected) had gone entire days without eating (SADC FANR VAC 2003). However, a study of two districts in Tanzania found no association between socio-economic variables and households' AIDS-impacted status (Tanzania Food and Nutrition Centre 2004) – a finding that may be explicable by the fact that in one location (Monduli), households identified as AIDS-impacted had a markedly better socio-economic profile to begin with.

The analysis of nutritional surveillance data by John Mason and colleagues found an interaction between HIV/AIDS and drought in increasing child malnutrition levels. While drought and the presence of an HIV/AIDS epidemic were each independently associated with a decline in the nutritional status of children in the general population, the decline was multiplied with a concurrence of the two. What we need to know is whether this deterioration continued, slowed or halted, or reversed, during the non-drought year of 2003. Preliminary findings indicate a modest rebound in the middle of 2003, followed by a subsequent deterioration.[3]

We do not have detailed household-level qualitative studies of coping (or failing to cope) during the drought of 2002–2003, which might back up these findings. However, there are anecdotes implying an increase in young women and girls entering commercial sex work (SCF 2002) and widespread sale of assets (SADC FANR VAC 2003). In parts of Malawi, an old practice known as *kupimbira* reportedly resurfaced in 2002, whereby very poor families 'sold' or 'loaned' pubescent girls as 'wives' to older and wealthier men in return for 'gifts' of food (SAHIMS 2003; Semu-Banda 2003).

Evidence for new mortality risks

There is evidence for changes in the ecology of malnutrition associated with the southern African drought and the HIV/AIDS epidemic. However, we do not know how this translates into risks of mortality. There are no data on mortality for the southern African drought of 2002–2003 that can be used to test this aspect of the hypothesis. Overall, levels of child mortality have risen in parts of Africa in ways that are suggestive of a link to the HIV/AIDS epidemic.

Evidence for aggregate food production impacts

Although the 'food availability decline' theory of famine was refuted by Sen (1981) more than twenty years ago, it has a remarkable after-life and still commands respect among many. The NVF makes no claims about aggregate food production. However – reflecting the ambitious claims made for NVF by some advocates – some critics have argued that it *should*, and therefore it can be tested against aggregate production statistics (Scott and Harland 2003).

Looking at aggregate crop production, the correlations between HIV prevalence and production are weak or non-existent. For example, the Zambia VAC survey attributed the geographical distribution of food short-ages to climatic conditions, environmental degradation, food marketing and pricing factors, rather than HIV levels (Zambia National VAC 2003). Another analysis, by Scott and Harland (2003), came to a similar conclusion, arguing that rural HIV levels were relatively low (11 per cent) and had no clear correlation with food insecurity, that there were no indications of a rural labour shortage (especially in the cotton sector) and that the food crisis had in any case been somewhat exaggerated. Comparable findings were reported by Bruce Larson's team investigating the impact of adult illness and death on Zambian farm production (Larson *et al.* 2004: 4):

> Despite the relatively large losses at the level of the individual household, the impacts ... do not yet 'add up' to large effects on aggregate measures of agricultural production. Among the households we surveyed, just under 5 per cent experienced a death of a working aged adult each year. If all of these deaths occurred in median households, the annual impact on agricultural production across all the households in the sample would be less than 1 per cent for all the outcome measures we considered. Importantly, although 1 per cent is a modest

share of total output, it is considerably larger relative to typical agricultural growth estimates (typically in the 1–3 per cent range annually).

Households that are already labour-constrained suffer greater proportionate losses in production following the death of a working-age adult. However, given that they are poorer than average and thus producing less, 'even the large losses they suffer have little impact on aggregate output' (Larson *et al.* 2004).

Summary of empirical evidence

The empirical evidence is suggestive but not conclusive. None of the studies cited were specifically designed to test the NVF hypothesis; rather, they are parts of a jigsaw with many missing pieces. There are indications of a time-lag effect, namely coping for a while followed by collapse, and a concurrent shock effect, whereby households and communities are able to withstand the impact of an AIDS death provided there are favourable external circumstances. The three major gaps at present are: first, the absence of a livelihoods study of households concurrently impacted by HIV/AIDS and another shock such as drought or commodity price crash; second, the lack of mortality data; and third, the paucity of studies of second-generation impacts, specifically the long-term socio-economic prospects of children orphaned by AIDS. In addition, the two main existing data sources, namely livelihoods studies focusing on the impact of adult deaths, and nutritional surveillance, need to be considerably expanded in scope before firm general conclusions can be drawn.

NVF and entitlement theory

The starting point for any theoretical analysis of the economics of famine is Amartya Sen's entitlement theory (Sen 1981). This needs only modest revision to account for the potential impacts of HIV/AIDS on a household or population. Specifically, entitlement theory needs to adjust to the changed dependency ratio in some AIDS-impacted households, communities and populations, consequent on adult mortality due to AIDS; to the higher level of expenditure and food consumption required in such households, communities and populations, on account of HIV/AIDS; and to the impacts of the epidemic on the likelihood and severity of entitlement failure. Such an analysis has been undertaken by Gabriel Rugalema (1999), and a simple revision of the entitlement model is presented here. The analysis looks first at how AIDS changes the nature of the 'starvation set', and second, at how it increases vulnerability to entitlement collapse along different dimensions.

How HIV/AIDS expands the household starvation set

HIV/AIDS can directly cause entitlement failure at the level of the household. This can be modelled simply. It has been presented elsewhere (de Waal 2004) and will not be elaborated here. The essential point is to analyse the individual's or household's ability to meet minimum consumption needs, based on its command over entitlement of various kinds: own production, labour-based trade-based, and transfer-based. When the sum of all these forms of entitlement fails to meet the minimum requirements for food consumption, the household falls into the 'starvation set'.

What Sen, and other theorists of famine, did not analyse was vulnerability based on household-level scarcity of labour. Even though this was self-evidently a vulnerability factor at the household level (and has historically been the cause of much poverty), his implicit assumption was that the population-level dependency ratio[4] would not change adversely during famine, and thus that this variable could be held constant and thereby discounted as a causal factor. Under conditions of a generalized HIV/AIDS epidemic, this assumption should be questioned (Toupouzis 1999: 10–12; Brown *et al.* 1994). Entitlement theory can easily be adapted to allow for an adverse shift in dependency ratios among substantial numbers of households as a contributing cause for the collapse in a household or community's entitlement to sufficient food. In the affected households, each productive individual simply has to be more productive to a specified degree in order to feed his or her dependants, and those with fewer endowments will find this impossible to do. The difficulty that arises is the practical one of identifying vulnerability scattered throughout society in this way, rather than the theoretical one of understanding why it has occurred.

Demographic modelling indicates that a generalized AIDS epidemic may not lead to substantial adverse shifts in the dependency ratio in a general population. However, this constancy conceals two important adverse shifts. One is an inequality effect: mature households that are AIDS afflicted suffer adverse shifts (due to either loss of adult breadwinners or an increased burden of dependants, or both), while the proportion of unattached young adults increases. There is a greater inequality between households' dependency ratios. The affected households are more vulnerable to being plunged into the starvation set. An adverse shift in household dependency ratio can be modelled in entitlement theory (de Waal 2004: 57–8). This analysis does not supplant the remedies identified by classic entitlement theory but adds an additional one: lessening the burden of dependants.

HIV/AIDS has the potential to affect every component of household entitlement. On each axis there is a double effect. Affected households lose assets and deplete social claims, while also losing the skills and labour necessary to utilize them effectively. Households lose cash income while also needing to spend more resources and time on care, treatment and upkeep of dependants. Households need to produce more food to feed a greater number of dependants (orphans and sick adults) while suffering labour shortages. *In extremis*, such households simply cannot reproduce themselves. Even without an additional shock such as a drought, they are not 'coping' but are trapped in a slow downward slide of impoverishment (Rugalema 2000).

The second caveat we must register is that the composition of the adult population itself is shifting, as the population pyramids for high-prevalence countries show. Specifically, there are more young adults and fewer mature adults, and more men than women. This represents a 'dependency disjuncture': the adults who do most of the work of supporting dependent children and the elderly are relatively scarce, while those who are least socially engaged are relatively plentiful. The extent to which a household can engage young adults in socially productive activities is likely to be an important determinant of its resilience when faced with threat. This can be modelled as 'social capital' (Carter and Maluccio 2002).

Lastly, in the midst of a generalized HIV/AIDS epidemic some adults will be sick and unable to work, while also imposing additional burdens on the household. The concept of 'effective dependency ratio' (EDR), which includes sick adults among the dependants, has been coined in response to this. Households with an adverse EDR are at greater risk. The period of sickness of a person living with AIDS may be more stressful and impoverishing than the bereavement itself (Kwaramba 1998).

These two methodological innovations – the dependency disjuncture and EDR – are gendered in a way that conventional dependency ratio calculations are not. Any measure of social engagement and participation in care activities will necessarily place greater emphasis on women's work.

How HIV/AIDS makes entitlement failure more likely and more severe

Not only does an AIDS-impacted household suffer an expanded 'starvation set', but in the midst of an HIV/AIDS epidemic it is possible that households may be more likely to suffer entitlement failure, and certain that the impact of any such entitlement failures will be even more adverse. It is this concurrence between HIV/AIDS and other shocks and stresses that is most likely to bring disaster.

Entitlement theory supposes that individuals or households may suffer entitlement failure because of unemployment or a collapse in incomes, an increase in the price of staple foods or a failure of markets. Are any or all of these more probable because of the HIV/AIDS epidemic? A thorough discussion of the economic effects of HIV/AIDS is beyond the scope of this chapter, and current macroeconomic models for the impacts of the epidemic are at best 'confused' (Nattrass 2004: 160). However, there are two common themes in the literature. One is that HIV/AIDS is bad eco-nomic news. The second is that the poorest will be hardest hit. It is quite plausible that failure of exchange entitlements will become more common in an AIDS-impacted society (or, in other words, exposure to shock is increased).

One criticism of entitlement theory is that it fails to take account of intra-household allocation of food and other resources, and in particular the disadvantages suffered by women. It is clear that HIV/AIDS exacer-bates gender inequalities in many different ways, not least in that women are more vulnerable to HIV and bear the greater part of the burden of caring for the sick and bringing up orphans.

The core of the NVF hypothesis is that HIV/AIDS aggravates the con-sequences of entitlement failure. Households affected by AIDS are both directly impoverished and also have their vulnerability to falling into the starvation set increased in many different ways at the same time. This implies that when any additional shock co-occurs with the stress of AIDS, the adverse impact will not simply be an additive product of the two factors but is likely to be multiplicative. This can be modelled within enti-tlement theory by introducing new factors, including dynamic or feedback elements, into the analysis. Alternatively, we can utilize the livelihoods approach to understanding famine as a framework for assessing the impact of AIDS.

NVF within livelihoods and vulnerability analyses

The concepts of livelihoods and vulnerability have provided intellectual scaffolding for much of the most insightful work on destitution, hunger and famine in the last decade. This has been formalized and adapted for policymakers in models such as the sustainable livelihoods framework (SLF), while new and expanded models for social protection are being canvassed (Devereux 2002a). This section locates NVF theory within a cluster of livelihoods and vulnerability analyses.

First, some methodological caveats. Both empirical evidence and analy-sis based on entitlement theory point to the emergence of a new class of vulnerable individuals and households, rendered destitute or likely to become so through the impacts of HIV/AIDS at the household level. There is reason to suppose that some members of this class of 'AIDS poor' will be concealed in aggregate statistics. Some AIDS-impacted households simply disappear when an adult dies. There are almost insuperable prob-lems for surveys to track dissolved households, with the result that they underestimate the effects of AIDS. One study in Zimbabwe found that 65 per cent of households where a deceased female used to live had dissolved by the time of a subsequent visit (Mutangadura 2000), though such high levels of AIDS-related household dissolution have not been recorded else-where – for example, Kagera (Lundberg *et al.* 2000). (The different findings appear to relate to the different prior socio-economic status of the households and the differing nature of kinship and social support systems.) A second reason for this is that aggregate economic statistics do not measure unremunerated contributions of women and girls to the domestic economy (de Waal 2003a). Thus the loss of this input is statistically unrecorded but is crucial to household reproduction.

A complementary methodological problem arises from the very complexity of livelihoods analyses. The empirical evidence cited above indicates how environmental and climatic factors interrelate with household composition, socio-economic status, livelihood options and coping strategies, and sources of support to help deal with shocks and stresses, all influenced in different ways by the impact of HIV/AIDS at the household level. All these different factors could be incorporated as factors within the sustainable livelihoods framework (to take one example). Every single part of the SLF model is impacted by the HIV/AIDS epidemic. This is both a strength of the SLF and a weakness. Through its capacity to incorporate everything, it risks losing the capacity to predict or explain anything. The challenge facing the NVF hypothesis is not to identify that something has changed with the advent of AIDS, but to isolate the truly significant changes.

The SLF provides a means of capturing the complexities of how rural communities function and respond to stress (Scoones 1998: 5). With some slight annotations, Jeremy Swift and Kate Hamilton (2001) provide an overview:

> [S]ituated in particular *settings* (historical, environmental, policy and other), particular assets or forms of *capital* [and liabilities] are accessed by households, and used to construct *livelihood strategies*, which result in positive or negative *outcomes*. The role of *institutions and organizations* [including gender relations, property rights etc.], which determine in large part the access of households to resources and strategies, is critical.
>
> Sustainability is a key quality of successful livelihoods. Sustainability means both the ability of the livelihood system to deal with and recover from shocks and stresses (short-term, reversible responses) or adaptation (a longer-term change in livelihood strategy), and also the ability of the livelihood system and the natural resources on which it depends to maintain or enhance productivity over time.

The impacts of the HIV/AIDS epidemic can be seen throughout the *entire* system: in the vulnerability context, on all five different categories of assets (all may be adversely affected – the 'asset pentagon' is shrinking) (Haddad and Gillespie 2001) and on policies, institutions and processes (notably, institutions function less well, and processes of development and institutional progress are halted or reversed) (de Waal 2003b). Systemic shocks of this nature challenge our analytical capacity. Our task is to identify what individual component of the shock, or which nexus within the system, is most significant in its potential to create destitution and hunger.

The NVF hypothesis presupposes that the HIV/AIDS epidemic creates new categories of people who are vulnerable to hunger and destitution, and that, for a population suffering a generalized AIDS epidemic, the outcome of an extraneous shock is different and more adverse. Note again that the pivotal area of concern is the interaction between HIV/AIDS and other sources of shock or stress. The key concepts to appropriate from livelihoods analysis are sensitivity and resilience (Davies 1995). Sensitivity refers to the extent to which a household (or community or population) suffers adverse outcomes consequent on an external shock (such as a drought). This in turn is related to the extent to which the household has been able to diversify its sources of income and food, build up reserves and invest in assets and social networks. Resilience refers to the household's ability to recover after such a shock, depending in turn upon its social networks and ability to cope. When combined with exposure to shock, we have the compound concept of vulnerability.

This approach can be represented in simplified form by Figure 5.1, in which the vertical axis represents well-being in a general sense and the horizontal axis represents time.

The NVF hypothesis predicts that two specific subsets of households would have a different trajectory. One category is those that have been relatively recently hit by the illness or death of a prime-age adult. The second is those that were affected at an earlier stage of the household cycle – for example, children orphaned by AIDS who have not inherited sufficient assets from their parents and may have failed to obtain an education. The two categories are somewhat different. Almost all socio-economic research to date has been on the recently affected. The study of

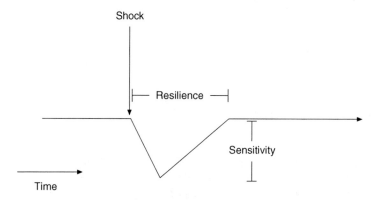

Figure 5.1 Sensitivity and resilience in a 'traditional' community (source: adapted from Davies (1996:26)).

long-term social and economic outcomes for children orphaned by AIDS is necessarily a more extended research project.

Both these 'AIDS poor' categories may suffer declining welfare even before the advent of a shock. Households with a recent AIDS illness or death may be losing income and assets, or struggling to cope. Maturing AIDS orphans may not anticipate achieving the standard of living of their parents or grandparents. This has important implications, because it undermines the concept of 'normality' to which the decision-makers in the household aspire to return after the crisis. Among the two categories of 'AIDS poor', we expect that sensitivity to an external shock will be increased. The stresses on households associated with AIDS morbidity and mortality mean that they need to adjust their food production and income-generation activities. In some circumstances, this will leave them significantly poorer. In other cases, households are able to cope because of favourable economic and ecological factors and social support. Despite the appearance of coping well, the NVF hypothesis predicts that both categories of AIDS-affected households will have a reduced margin for absorbing shocks: the concurrence of HIV/AIDS and an additional shock or stress will substantially increase sensitivity.

The literature on social protection provides us with further tools for analysing this phenomenon (Devereux 2002b). Poverty can be disaggregated into chronic poverty associated with low labour productivity, vulnerability to a transient collapse in income and consumption (itself a compound of sensitivity, resilience and exposure), and dependency arising from an inability to generate an independent livelihood, usually because of infirmity. Vulnerability analysis further distinguishes between idiosyncratic shocks (such as, in pre-AIDS times, workplace accidents or disabling illnesses, which tend to affect one household but not its neighbours) and covariant shocks (such as droughts, which affect an entire community). Idiosyncratic shocks are much easier to protect against, using both formal insurance mechanisms and traditional means such as rotating credit associations.

The impact of a generalized HIV/AIDS epidemic cannot be confined readily to any of these categorizations. The epidemic contributes to each of the three clusters of poverty: it reduces returns to labour, both absolutely and by increasing dependency ratios; it creates transitory high, irreducible expenditure; and it leaves people unable to work. It contributes to all components of vulnerability including exposure, insofar as it is a shock in itself. At low incidence AIDS is an idiosyncratic shock, but as it becomes more common it is less easy to absorb within established social insurance mechanisms geared for such shocks. However, it is unlike a covariant shock, in that even during the high-death phase of a generalized epidemic, adult deaths still affect only a minority of households at any one time, and it is a protracted and systemic stress, not a one-off event. In important respects, HIV/AIDS can be seen as a chronic, background stress factor.

This leads us to introduce a third type of shock, namely concurrent shock. The basic insight here is that a household or community can withstand one shock, but not two at the same time (or perhaps it can withstand two but not three, or maybe it can withstand two but only if there are good support mechanisms, etc.). AIDS lowers the threshold of vulnerability to an additional shock. This in turn has important implications for social protection measures.

Who is vulnerable to this impact? The NVF hypothesis predicts that both categories of the AIDS poor will register as vulnerable, in different ways. How is this adverse impact manifest? Livelihoods and vulnerability frameworks give us only the most general guidance: they are tools for exploring possible areas of impact, not predicting precise outcomes. The NVF hypothesis specifically predicts that resilience will be reduced: AIDS-afflicted households will find it more difficult to manage, and famine coping strategies will be less available and less viable. These households may find that they are unable to call upon the support of their neighbours and kin, because these support networks are already saturated due to the demands of caring for orphans and supporting the sick. If the household has a shortage of labour, its members may be unable to undertake labour-intensive coping strategies such as gathering wild foods and finding casual employment. Children are more likely to be withdrawn from school in order to supplement the household labour force (Fox *et al.* 2004). In addition, households without mature adults may lack the experience and skills necessary for effectively following these strategies. Knowledge of which wild foods are edible and how to prepare them is a specialized skill, handed down from mother to daughter in times of crisis. Knowledge of kin networks is another specialist skill, acquired over many years by adults, which younger people may not possess. Hence, NVF predicts that members of AIDS-impacted households are likely to resort more rapidly to responses that include selling essential assets, crime and commercial sex work – i.e. to shift from 'coping strategies' to 'survival strategies' (Toupouzis 1999: 18–19).

A final consideration is that the *motivation* for engaging in a difficult coping regimen, involving hunger, hardship and hard work, may be reduced. This could arise because the adults and older children in the household no longer have a realistic expectation of returning to 'normality' following the end of the period of food shortage. The subjective expectation that things are on a secular downward path may kill off the seasoned determination to see things through, and lead to fatalism and apathy. Although hard to measure, this subjective consideration may be the most important element in the adverse transformation of livelihoods that occurs during an HIV/AIDS epidemic. When life expectancy plunges to the levels currently anticipated in southern Africa, it is certain to have a serious impact upon how people make major life decisions.

The adjusted sensitivity and resilience trajectory for an AIDS-impacted

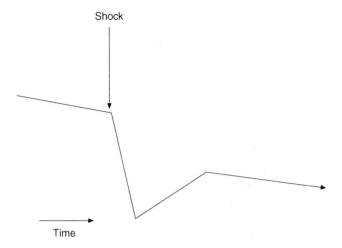

Figure 5.2 Sensitivity and resilience in an AIDS-impacted community.

community is represented in Figure 5.2. This shows a secular downward trajectory.

This changed trajectory is the most important implication of the NVF hypothesis. Efficacious household coping strategies can maintain welfare despite HIV/AIDS and other shocks, but not without cost, and not indefinitely. External assistance, including social protection mechanisms, will be required.

The political economy of AIDS and famine

All famines and epidemics are political events. Our third approach to the analysis of HIV/AIDS and famine examines the thesis that democracy prevents famine, and its application to NVF. This section will elaborate on this theory, at each turn discussing, first, how it is to be understood with reference to 'traditional' famines, and second, what is new in NVF.

The thesis that liberal rights are guarantees against famine is derived from Amartya Sen's remarks on the subject (Sen 1990):

> The diverse political freedoms that are available in a democratic state, including regular elections, free newspapers and freedom of speech, must be seen as the real force behind the elimination of famines. Here again, it seems that one set of freedoms – to criticize, publish and vote – are usually linked with other types of freedoms, such as the freedom to escape starvation and famine mortality.

A full elaboration and critique of Sen's point would take us well beyond the remit of this chapter.[5] However, several points are in order. The first is

to clarify what Sen actually meant. He did not mean that liberal democracy was sufficient to overcome hunger and all other social ills. In fact, he
clearly demonstrated that, whereas India had been free from major
famine since it achieved independence in 1947 – in contrast to communist
China, which suffered the century's most disastrous famine during the
'Great Leap Forward' period – democratic India had fared less well in
reducing chronic malnutrition and in raising life expectancy. Second, it is
only fair to point out that while Sen strongly believes in this thesis, he has
not explored it systematically; it does not form part of his major body of
work, and it is not for this that he was awarded the Nobel Prize for economics. Third, there are a number of scholars of Indian famines who
argue that the post-independence history of Indian famine prevention is
more complicated than Sen claims (Banik 2003). Some have argued, for
example, that a famine occurred in Bihar in 1966, despite the best efforts
of the free press (Myhrvold-Hanssen 2003). More recently, starvation
deaths have occurred in Rajasthan (Jha 2002) and Uttar Pradesh (Shankar
2002), illustrating the shortcomings of drought response and the public
distribution system (PDS), which has emerged as the principal state
response to the threat of famine. The PDS has been a particular target of
critique, on the grounds that it does not respond to the needs of the
poorest states such as Bihar and Jharkhand. Politics, poor bureaucratic
procedures and corruption are singled out (Mooiji 2001).

An exploration of Sen's hypothesis must focus upon the processes
whereby liberal civil and political rights translate into the protection of
social and economic rights. These include the provision of information
through a free press, the pressures on officials seeking electoral office,
and the processes of accountability that are brought into play through
public examination of the record in responding to food crises. None of
these work perfectly. Press coverage can be useful in sparking government
action (Ram 1990), but is often uneven. Banik concludes, 'The English-
language press enjoys greatest credibility but has poor in-depth coverage
of starvation-related issues; in contrast the local vernacular press is very
active but their open political ownership and management deprives their
reports of credibility' (Banik 2003: 3). Electoral pressures work only when
the issue of famine has been politicized and therefore becomes an issue of
concern for the majority of voters. Most famines strike only a minority of
people, and usually that minority is poor, remote and with little political
influence. Direct public pressure, through the threat of strikes, demon-
strations and riots by the hungry themselves, is relatively rare, but its
threat can be effective. Jean Drèze quotes a labourer during the Maha-
rashtra relief operations of 1973: 'they would let us die if they thought we
would not make a noise about it' (Drèze 1990: 92–3).

What are the conditions that must prevail for the liberal theory to
work? Among others, they include technical capacity and knowledge of
what interventions can be effective. The basic technology of famine pre-

vention is well-established, and has been known since the Indian Famine Codes were drafted in the late nineteenth century. The bureaucratic procedures necessary for speedy and effective implementation are similarly well-known, though there is a perhaps inevitable tendency for bureaucracies to become ensnared in their own politics, thereby impeding action. Governments can be readily chastised for failing to implement these proven technologies, and international relief agencies criticized for ignoring these lessons (de Waal 1997).

The advent of a generalized HIV/AIDS epidemic changes the situation in three ways. First, the nature of the crisis is different and, thus far, poorly understood. The HIV/AIDS epidemic has simply not been on the radar screen of most food-policy planners, as evidenced by its complete absence from an otherwise excellent state-of-the-art collection on food security published as recently as 2001, which makes no mention of the topic (Devereux and Maxwell 2001). The well-established package of famine early warning and prevention technologies is not readily applicable to AIDS-related food crises. Labour-based relief schemes, for example, are less applicable for poor people who suffer a labour shortage. The press, civil society and the general public have also been perplexed. Thus, for example, Carolyn Baylies reported that rural people in Zambia tend to see HIV/AIDS as a personal misfortune deserving only of individual charity, in contrast to drought, which is a collective problem requiring an official response (Baylies 2002). Analysis of the Afrobarometer public opinion surveys across southern Africa points to a similar conclusion (Whiteside *et al.* 2002). The extent to which HIV/AIDS, and government responses to it, have not been a political issue also reflects the levels of stigma associated with AIDS. Most people, especially those in political life, prefer not to talk about the disease and the attendant social problems. There has been impressive political mobilization around certain AIDS-related issues, notably treatment access, but this has not transferred to activism around AIDS-related hunger and poverty. As a result, there is a vacuum of political authority and legitimacy to act against AIDS-related famine.

Second, the capacity of the government itself is undermined by AIDS-related morbidity and mortality. There is plentiful evidence for the institutional crises brought about by the haemorrhage of human resources on account of HIV/AIDS. This extends to the institutions that need to be able to respond to food security challenges, such as agricultural extension systems.

Third, the HIV/AIDS epidemic itself poses immense challenges for public action by resource-strapped governments, most clearly seen in the challenge of providing anti-retroviral treatment (ART). Most African governments simply do not have the funds and capacity for all citizens living with HIV to access ART. Even those that do have the resources, such as South Africa, have argued that they do not, or that the treatment is not 'sustainable'.[6] To the extent that governments have begun to fund ART, it has usually been quietly provided for senior army officers, civil servants and politicians. There is no inclusive social contract regarding AIDS treatment. It is in effect a moral economy of triage. This may change as the finance and organization for expanding treatment is provided, but the reality thus far is that universal treatment access is not a right recognized by most governments. Curiously, it is not a right that is (yet) claimed by most citizens, who continue to see HIV/AIDS as a private affair. However, as deaths from AIDS mount and the demand for treatment access grows, democratic values will be imperilled in those countries that are unable to respond.

If governments are not recognizing equal citizenship in the sphere of access to ART, does this mean they will be similarly callous in responding to hunger? Not necessarily. While responding to HIV/AIDS itself is not (yet) high on the list of politically legitimated public actions, responding to hunger remains so. A 'moral economy' is one that is legitimated by history, and the history of hunger remains deeply embedded in political cultures. Therefore, governments are likely to see responding to famine as a necessary political action, giving it priority over responding to AIDS – even if the latter is killing more people. Where the two problems are superimposed, it is politically easier to pretend that the immediate challenge is a traditional one of feeding the hungry.

These changes come on top of a trend in international development assistance that pays lip service to 'partnership' and 'participation', but which in reality subordinates democratic involvement in policymaking to the dictates of economic orthodoxies. Most poor governments have lost autonomy or control over economic policymaking. Highly-indebted countries – a category that includes most poor and famine-vulnerable countries – are obliged to obtain a favourable assessment from the IMF before their debt burden is reduced. This assessment is based not on the effectiveness of measures to reduce poverty or prevent famine, but on the achievement of macroeconomic stability, which is defined in terms of low inflation, a low fiscal deficit and policies that encourage the private sector. Another condition is the adoption of a poverty reduction strategy paper (PRSP). However, if a country tries to design its PRSP in such a way that it conflicts with the macroeconomic prescriptions of the Bretton Woods institutions, it cannot expect the latter's endorsement or support (Oxfam 2003). Several countries have struggled hard to obtain flexibility from the IMF and World Bank, and one or two have won concessions. Rwanda, for example, succeeded in raising its spending ceilings in the post-genocide period, on the argument that post-conflict reconstruction was a form of investment rather than current account spending. However, in most cases stringent economic orthodoxy has prevailed, even when it entails abandoning any serious prospect of achieving poverty reduction.

One of the principles underlying the PRSP process is popular participation. The PRSP is supposed to be a document endorsed by all national stakeholders, including civil society. However, in reality the process has always been steered in such a way that the outcome is predetermined. The PRSP will be compatible with a growth-based approach to poverty reduction, which in turn is premised upon the same economic prescriptions that the IMF uses for debt relief assessments. While 'best practice' in development partnership moves towards direct budget support for recipient governments and a reduction in formal conditionalities, the PRSP process has become an alternative means whereby the donors, led by the World Bank, determine the details of a recipient government's economic policies. The term 'donorship' has been coined to describe this (Oxfam 2004), and both bad and good examples exist. An interesting aspect of the PRSP process and the associated shifts in approaches to development partnership is the fact that, while poverty reduction lies at the centre of the strategies (at least in theory), humanitarian aid has been wholly delinked from the strategy. In Ethiopia, this led to the absurd situation in 2002 in which the government was required to reduce its public spending in order to meet the Highly-Indebted Poor Countries' initiative (HIPC) completion point criteria (which it duly did), in the midst of a drought that left more than 14 million people in need of assistance. Ethiopia and its donors mounted its largest ever relief operation, based almost entirely on food aid provided from abroad. There seemed to be no thought given at all to the obvious contradiction between the two approaches.

In this context of near-complete powerlessness by African governments, it is unsurprising that there is little popular enthusiasm for engagement with famine prevention strategies. These considerations point to the need for a political contract for the prevention of famine, revised in the light of the HIV/AIDS epidemic and the current international political economy of development 'partnership'. Such a political contract will need both domestic and international dimensions.

We should therefore consider NVF a political (as well as an economic and social) disaster with new dimensions. Because the path of the epidemic is readily foreseeable (no early warning system for AIDS deaths is needed once HIV prevalence is known), the advent of a secondary disaster should have come as no surprise to political authorities. The first time it struck, the precise nature of a novel crisis such as NVF could not have been known in advance, so that no government could be expected to have fully efficacious responses in place, but its imminence was not difficult to predict. Subsequently, since the debate on HIV/AIDS and famine has become part of the mainstream discussions of both the HIV/AIDS epidemic and food security, there is no excuse for ignoring warning signs and failing to act accordingly. Even if the NVF remains unproven, the consequences of failing to act appropriately are sufficiently alarming to indicate that it must be taken seriously.

In conclusion, the 'democracy prevents famine' hypothesis demands significant reconsideration in the context of an HIV/AIDS epidemic and its implications for famine. There is no exculpation from political responsibilities. However, the complexities of the linkages between the HIV/AIDS epidemic, famine and political processes, are such that a substantial revision of the account is needed.

Malnutrition and the health crisis framework for famine mortality

This section applies two closely-related frameworks to the NVF hypothesis: the first is UNICEF's 'underlying causes of malnutrition' approach, and the second is concerned with how malnutrition and disease contribute to increased mortality. At the outset, we should note that this model is concerned with child malnutrition. Adult malnutrition and starvation have been of less concern to nutritionists and policymakers, for the reasons that adults are less vulnerable to death during nutritional crisis, and adult anthropometry is less advanced than the measurement of child malnutrition.

HIV/AIDS and the causes of child malnutrition

How is a generalized HIV/AIDS epidemic likely to impact upon child malnutrition? The hypothesis of this chapter is that in poor and vulnerable communities, the impact is likely to be significant. Clearly, children who are living with HIV have special nutritional needs and are more vulnerable to malnutrition and early death. But it is probable that an AIDS epidemic also contributes to higher background levels of malnutrition, thus increasing child mortality rates. The evidence on this issue is as yet insufficient and inconclusive.

Paediatric AIDS is implicated in 8 per cent of child deaths in sub-Saharan Africa. Mortality among children born with HIV is estimated at 26–45 per cent by age twelve months and 35–59 per cent by two years (Dabis and Ekpini 2002; Walker *et al.* 2002). However, the Bellagio Study Group on child survival concludes that the traditional threats to child health – neonatal causes, malaria, measles, diarrhoeal diseases and respiratory infections – which still cause over 90 per cent of child deaths, should remain the priority for health interventions. Without disputing the importance of these other diseases, the 8 per cent figure surely underestimates the impact of HIV/AIDS on overall child mortality. If we broaden our focus to the underlying causes of malnutrition, the impact of HIV/AIDS is likely to be much more systemic. Figure 5.3 provides one framework for understanding the causes of child malnutrition, which in turn allows us to identify the causal role of HIV/AIDS.

Each of the boxes is impacted by HIV/AIDS, both directly (through interactions with paediatric HIV) and indirectly (the wider impacts of an HIV/AIDS epidemic on a general population of children). Household

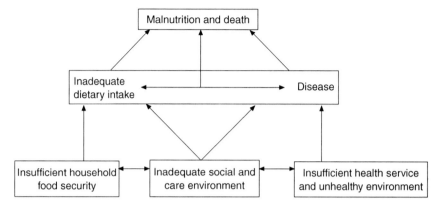

Figure 5.3 Underlying causes of malnutrition (source: Adapted from: UNICEF (1990)).

Note
That the lower part of the figure, the 'basic causes' located in the socio-economic system, has been omitted.)

food security, discussed above, is a major determinant of the nutritional status of children. Infection with HIV exacerbates inadequate dietary intake, through three mechanisms. It decreases the amount of food consumed (through loss of appetite), it impairs nutrient absorption and it changes the metabolism of the infected individual – in particular, energy and protein requirements increase (Piwoz and Preble 2002; WHO 2003: 5).[7] This is discussed in greater detail below. In their review of the subject, Piwoz and Preble point out that: 'For many years before the AIDS epidemic, the impairment to immune function caused by malnutrition was called the 'Nutritionally Acquired Immune Deficiency Syndrome' or NAIDS' (WHO 2003: 8).

It is a reasonable surmise that the HIV/AIDS epidemic is decreasing the quality of care-giving for children, both for those living in a household where an adult (especially a mother) is living with HIV/AIDS and for children orphaned by AIDS. There are reasons to suspect wider effects too. In some countries, the epidemic is eroding the human resources necessary to sustain a water and sanitation system. Water engineers are highly mobile and are therefore a high-risk group for HIV infection (Cohen 2002). Lower standards of sanitation and poorer water provision are of particular concern because of the higher demand for water in households that include individuals sick with AIDS-related infections (especially diarrhoea) (Holden 2003: 47; Kamminga and Wegelin-Schuringa 2003). As with so many other issues, in this area it is important to move beyond surmise based on anecdote to rigorous research.

HIV/AIDS is undermining health services. There are three major impacts: an increased workload on health capacity; morbidity and mortality of health workers due to HIV/AIDS; and demoralization of health professionals because they are unable to provide more than palliative care for AIDS patients, while also facing the stresses of caring for their own family members who are sick and for children orphaned by AIDS (Tawfik and Kinoti 2003; Joint Learning Initiative 2004). Claudia Hudspeth has adapted UNICEF's 'underlying causes of malnutrition' model to capture these effects (see Figure 5.4).

How does a generalized HIV/AIDS epidemic impact upon the health environment of a rural population in normal times and during a food crisis? A population with a substantial proportion of immuno-suppressed individuals is a more fertile ground for the spread of infectious diseases. Certain diseases are already thriving in this favourable environment, afflicting both HIV-positive and -negative individuals. HIV-infected persons are at dramatically increased risk for primary or reactivation tuberculosis and for second episodes of tuberculosis from exogenous re-infection (Havlir and Barnes 1999), and there is a concurrent epidemic of TB affecting the general population. There is also a vicious interaction between HIV and malaria (Harms and Feldmeier 2002). Similar interactions of HIV and childhood infectious diseases have not yet been documented, but are plausible, particularly with regards to parasitic infestations.[8] A famine-induced health crisis in such an immuno-suppressed population could create even more favourable conditions for the spread of many infectious diseases.

However, we should note several important caveats. The first is that the main immuno-suppressed population category is adults, while famine-related health crisis is primarily a threat to young children. A second is the complexity of the relationship between a child's age and HIV-related vulnerability to malnutrition.[9] The HIV/AIDS epidemic is changing the age pattern of child malnutrition in several ways. A child who is vertically infected with HIV (from its mother) is unlikely to reach his or her fifth birthday (Walker *et al.* 2002), with most dying before three years, and is doubly at risk both of dying from HIV-related causes and because of the indirect impacts of HIV/AIDS on the household. Due to paediatric HIV, underweight prevalence peaks earlier than for non-AIDS impacted populations. However, for a child who is not HIV-infected but is *affected* by the HIV-positive status of a parent, the principal (but not only) effects of HIV/AIDS are associated with orphanhood. The risk of orphanhood rises in relationship to the age of the child, because the risk of parental death increases as the child ages. Therefore, the traditional focus on children under five years may miss a category of children seriously affected by HIV/AIDS.

It is safe to conclude that a generalized HIV/AIDS epidemic is a negative factor adversely affecting each of the underlying causes of malnutrition in children, thereby contributing to the pressures for increased childhood mortality.

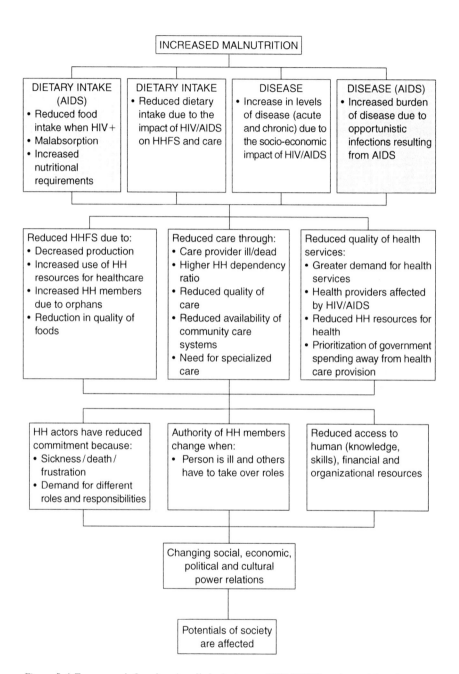

Figure 5.4 Framework for showing links between HIV/AIDS and nutrition (source: Modified by Claudia Hudspeth, UNICEF, from the work of Yambia and Wagt (2003)).

Risk of mortality during crisis

How does malnutrition relate to risk of mortality during a crisis? This is a surprisingly difficult question to answer (Young and Jaspars 1995). Most deaths during famines are caused by infectious diseases. Commonly, most deaths are among children, and their immediate causes include diarrhoeal diseases, measles, malaria and acute respiratory infections. Factors related to the crisis but not a direct outcome of malnutrition, such as distress migration, cause an increase in exposure to disease. Studies of the association between malnutrition rates and mortality levels in normal and refugee populations have produced differing results. While high malnutrition levels in a displaced or refugee population predispose to higher mortality rates among children (Toole and Waldman 1990; Toole and Malkki 1992), the relationship is affected by a number of factors, notably exposure to disease (Nieburg *et al.* 1992). In some situations high malnutrition has not been associated with high death rates, usually because the environment is relatively healthy (good water supplies, perhaps even a drop in certain kinds of infection such as malaria). In others, relatively lower malnutrition rates appear to have contributed to escalating death rates, apparently as a consequence of an unhealthy environment. One finding is consistent: co-infection with different diseases (e.g. measles and respiratory infection) leads to a much higher risk of mortality than a simple addition of individual disease risk. A review of child mortality data indicates that co-infection increases mortality risk 8.7 times (Black *et al.* 2003). The overall picture is therefore marked by two factors. First, the 'healthiness' of the environment determines the mortality risk for a given level of malnutrition. Second, holding that environment constant, there is a logarithmic relationship between malnutrition and mortality risk. Although strictly speaking this is not a threshold effect, it is akin to a variable threshold at which the risk of mortality accelerates.

We would expect a generalized HIV/AIDS epidemic to cause deterioration in the background healthiness of the environment and thereby to increase the risk of mortality for a given level of malnutrition. This would occur because of the increased exposure to infections, and/or the increased virulence of those infectious agents, and/or the lower quality of care, reduced food security and other indirect impacts of the epidemic. Among children living with HIV and AIDS, we might also expect an increased risk of mortality for any given level of malnutrition, independently of these background factors.

These links between nutrition and crisis epidemiology can be further elucidated using a model from the work of Young and Jaspars (1995) (see Figure 5.5).

This model demonstrates the variable mortality risk associated with child malnutrition, showing the interaction between the background health factors (such as exposure to measles or waterborne infections

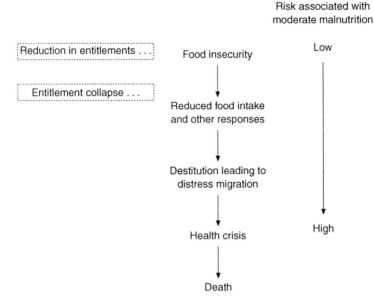

Figure 5.5 Nutritional status and health crisis framework for famine mortality (source: Young and Jaspars (1995: 23)).

consequent on distress migration) and the logarithmic increase in mortality risk.

How does a concurrent HIV/AIDS epidemic impact upon these factors? AIDS itself kills children. HIV infection is both a risk factor for acquiring other infections, and increases the risk of death from any such concurrent infection (Black *et al.* 2003). However, we should notice that paediatric HIV prevalence varies independently of background child mortality, which is closely associated with food insecurity (Zaba *et al.* 2003). In some very high HIV-prevalence countries (e.g. Botswana) child mortality from non-HIV causes is low, leading to HIV being implicated in 40–60 per cent of child deaths. In countries with low HIV prevalence but high child mortality from other causes (e.g. Niger) it is implicated in well under 5 per cent, whereas in countries with both high HIV prevalence and high background mortality (e.g. Tanzania and Malawi) HIV is directly implicated in 10–20 per cent of child deaths (Walker *et al.* 2002; Zaba *et al.* 2003: 9–10). What we do not know is how a food crisis affects the proportional increase in deaths among children who are HIV-positive and -negative.

There is evidence that HIV infection increases the risk of malnutrition (Piwoz and Preble 2002). A person with asymptomatic HIV is estimated to have an increased energy requirement of about 10 per cent, rising to 30 per cent in the case of symptomatic HIV infection, with parallel additional protein requirements (ACC/SCN 1998: 3–4; Semba and Tang 1999; WHO and FAO 2002). Severe wasting and symptomatic starvation[10] are signs of advanced AIDS. However, definitive clinical and epidemiological evidence for an accelerated progression from HIV infection to AIDS or opportunistic infections on account of malnutrition is still lacking, for both adults and children (WHO 2003). Still, the implications are clear and common-sense: HIV infection and malnutrition are likely to combine in a vicious interaction.

Given our concern with the health status of the general population, we should attend to the negative health externalities of HIV-negative persons living in an immuno-suppressed population suffering a health crisis.[11] An increased level of infections in the population will increase their exposure to infectious pathogens. As noted above, mortality risk rises geometrically as risk of co-occurrence of separate infections increases.

The hypothesis that a generalized HIV epidemic is associated with an increase in child mortality from all causes can be tested. Using data from the Kenya Demographic and Health Surveys, Kenneth Hill and colleagues show that the onset of the HIV/AIDS epidemic in Kenya was associated with a halting and reversal of child survival gains, an association that holds up strongly under multivariate analysis (Hill *et al.* 2004: 15). They find that:

> the prevalence of HIV at the district level at the time of the birth of the child is found to be associated with increased mortality risk for children in the 1990s in Kenya. The association does not prove causation, but the strength and consistency of the association across a variety of analyses would require a remarkable degree of coincidence if the effect were not causal.

They conjecture that the indirect impacts of HIV may provide the causal link. A cohort study of malnutrition and mortality among children orphaned by AIDS in Malawi shows mixed results, including increased mortality among maternal orphans but no measurable increases in wasting or stunting among surviving children (Crampin *et al.* 2003). These findings indicate the importance of context and the need for caution in drawing general conclusions. More such studies are needed.

It is likely that the figure of 8 per cent of child deaths in sub-Saharan Africa attributable to HIV/AIDS is a significant underestimate. However, as the Bellagio Study Group (2003) concludes, the technologies for preventing child deaths, including those for which HIV/AIDS has been an indirect contributory factor, remain unchanged.

The HIV/AIDS epidemic reinforces the need for a new attention to traditional child survival interventions, such as measles vaccination, insecticide-treated bed-nets, oral rehydration therapy and safe breastfeeding.

These bring clear benefits to all children (including those living with HIV) and have the positive externality that they hinder the deterioration of the background disease environment and thus help prevent or mitigate the emergence of other epidemics of infectious diseases in partially immuno-compromised populations. Any emphasis on treatment for HIV/AIDS, including paediatric HIV, should not come at the expense of existing child survival interventions.

However, we need also to be alert to the fact that the deteriorating general health environment brought about by the direct and indirect effects of the HIV/AIDS epidemic may mean that child mortality proves less sensitive to existing interventions, such as those advocated by the Bellagio Study Group. It is probable that these technologies will have the best positive impact on child survival only if they are combined with measures to tackle the secondary or indirect impacts of the HIV/AIDS epidemic.

In short, in most African countries there is a potential indirect adverse impact of the HIV/AIDS epidemic on child survival – through poverty and food crisis – which demands further investigation. The principle of minimizing child deaths in famine through established health technology remains valid. It also follows that in assessing the efficacy of PTMTC and ART, we should pay attention to the extent to which these interventions operate to protect against orphanhood, food insecurity and other social ills (Nattrass 2004).[12]

Unfortunately, our knowledge about malnutrition, infection and mortality in older children and adults is much more limited. However, it is important to note that although fewer older children and adults die during famines, their *relative* risk of mortality compared to normal times is increased more than for young children (Dyson 1993). Can we expect a geometric increase in adult mortality due to the co-occurrence of HIV infection, malnutrition and other infections? This is plausible, but as yet untested.

In summary, the malnutrition and health crisis model of famine mortality, revised to take account of a generalized HIV/AIDS epidemic, predicts relatively little impact in the short term, but several channels for potentially significant escalation of health crises and excess mortality in the longer term. It also predicts that existing low-cost child survival technologies could still prevent most of the excess deaths among children. It means we should also assess the efficacy of interventions in terms of their capacity to mitigate the wider impacts of the epidemic, especially orphanhood and food insecurity.

A crisis of social reproduction

The implication of the models for NVF and the evidence cited are that AIDS-related destitution and hunger are not transient phenomena. There will not be a rapid bounce back to 'normality'. Rather, the combination of

HIV/AIDS and recurrent external shocks threatens to leave a substantial proportion of the population in chronic extreme poverty. This scenario has the potential of leading to the second reference for NVF: a crisis of social reproduction. Thus far, there is no evidence for an increase in mortality levels directly associated with AIDS-related livelihood crises. However, this possibility should not be ruled out in the future. Already in some places that are suffering concurrent high levels of HIV/AIDS and other socio-economic crises there are signs of such collapse, brought about by both heightened mortality and out-migration. For example, in Makete district, Tanzania, where such conditions exist in extreme form, the population is declining (Government of Tanzania 2004).

Famine, in any variant, leads to impoverishment, migration, social dislocation and an increase in commercial sex workers. All of these in turn are risk factors for an increase in HIV incidence. Communities that are high on 'social cohesion' are likely to have lower levels of HIV than those that are disrupted (Barnett and Whiteside 1999), and are also better placed to achieve successful health transitions. A vicious cycle of feedback between famine and the structural causes of vulnerability to HIV is a real possibility.

Mortality patterns in 'traditional' famines are remarkably consistent and clearly adaptive for the long-term survival of the population affected (Watkins and Menken 1985). The first and most universal demographic response to the stress of reduced food intake is lower fertility. This conserves energy and means that adult females are less encumbered by infants during a period of food shortage. During famine, mortality is concentrated among the very young and the very old. Adult females are the most resilient population category. In all recorded famines in a general population, women have survived better than men – even in those populations in which there is a male lifespan advantage in normal times (Macintyre 2002). This means that the productive and reproductive core of the population is kept intact, and dependency ratios temporarily improve. It is a cruel logic but a sound one for populations on the margin. It leaves the population well placed for a post-famine demographic rebound, and evidence suggests that, in most cases, the demographic impact of famine is erased within a generation or less (Watkins and Menken 1985).

A generalized HIV/AIDS epidemic in the phase of mass death reverses the demographic logic of collective famine survival. AIDS selectively kills adults in their key reproductive years, and kills women more than men. It worsens dependency ratios and the social and economic basis for demographic resilience. It may create demographic sinks in which death rates exceed birth rates over extended periods of time. This prospect led to the first coinage of the concept of a 'new variant' of famine. In contrast with the age-old threat of famine, unpleasant but not lethal to the body politic, I wrote that we faced 'a new and uniquely virulent variant of the familiar famine pathogen' (de Waal 2003c: 180). This pathology was still seeking a name: '[j]ust as HIV is a pathogen that has not yet reached any form of equilibrium with its human host, the as-yet-nameless social catastrophe that it brings in its wake is one for which we have no measure and no remedy' (de Waal 2003c: 178).

The most striking manifestation of this inverted demographic response is widespread orphanhood. In traditional famines orphanhood was rare, as children were far more likely to die than their parents (Iliffe 1987). Many children orphaned by AIDS are cared for by grandparents, a category that is already suffering health problems and economic hardship consequent on the premature deaths of their adult children (Ainsworth and Dayton 2001). This particular combination of stresses has no obvious precedent. However, old-style famines were marked by mass migration of adults, abandonment and fostering of children and other dislocations. It is possible that many African societies have absorbed even greater stresses in the past, and the social fabric is more resilient than we expect. There is a striking lack of data on these issues. We simply do not know about the socio-economic profiles of children orphaned by AIDS as they enter adulthood.

In extremis, this new pattern of mortality could jeopardize the basic biological and social reproduction of a population. This would operate through pressure on women's numbers, energies and time. Women's numbers are being depleted through their greater susceptibility to HIV. We are on the threshold of major excess mortality among adult women – a phenomenon truly unprecedented in recent times. We simply do not know what this will entail. The greater parts of the burden of caring for the sick and for children orphaned by AIDS fall upon women, in addition to their existing and extremely onerous burdens in the domestic and productive spheres. We do not know the implications of this.

The scenario of a crisis in biological reproduction – a population crash – is not in prospect. As with most historical famines, out-migration is likely to be a more significant demographic outcome, including selective exodus of the most skilled and dynamic. It is this that is causing communities such as Makete to become demographic sinks. Across Africa, the crest of the wave of AIDS deaths in the coming decade is certain to bring profound traumas in its wake.

Conclusion

The framework of 'new variant famine' is a useful means of analysing the actual and potential impacts of HIV/AIDS on entitlements, livelihoods, malnutrition and child mortality. There is no evidence to support some of the more dramatic claims made on its behalf. The NVF approach is compatible with existing frameworks for understanding and responding to food crises and can also be assimilated to analyses of the political economy of famine. In each case, the NVF hypothesis draws explanatory power from its coherence and compatibility with established approaches. The NVF hypothesis allows us to organize and understand the recent deterioration in food and livelihood security in southern Africa, and to make a set of predictions about what may occur in the coming years.

The NVF hypothesis is both supported and refined by a growing number of micro-level studies. There is no doubt that there is an AIDS-related food, livelihood and health crisis afflicting millions of poor households in Africa. This impact is slow and protracted, and is complicated both by other adversities and by the efficacy of short-term coping responses. The increased vulnerability of many households has been masked and postponed by coping strategies, including labour replacement, but we should be aware of the costs of these strategies.

The concurrence of a generalized HIV/AIDS epidemic with other shocks is the key factor that pushes households into destitution and hunger. African rural households are typically able to withstand single shocks, especially when they do not strike the entire community at the same time. Double or multiple concurrent shocks are far more dangerous. Insofar as a generalized HIV/AIDS epidemic represents a chronic shock, it thereby increases the systemic vulnerability of livelihood systems to other shocks.

When we look at aggregates, the impact of HIV/AIDS is less clear. This is partly because of the way in which the effects of HIV/AIDS are masked at the macro-level, and partly because there is an array of formidable methodological difficulties in measuring the impacts of the epidemic. In addition, some writers have mistaken the NVF hypothesis to be an argument about AIDS and food production or a claim that AIDS causes famine. There is no evidence in support of either contention. An important criticism that has been made of the NVF approach is that using the word 'famine' is extreme and alarmist. If 'famine' is taken to mean mass starvation unto death, that is correct. If it refers to the immiseration of millions of families scattered across sub-Saharan Africa, the alarm is warranted. The scale of the social crisis that is unfolding in southern Africa is such that even the most severe words in our lexicon of disaster, such as 'famine', fail to do it justice.

The worst-case scenario is that the recurrent socio-economic shocks combine with the HIV/AIDS epidemic to create a wide, severe and intractable famine, marked by excess adult mortality, widespread social disruption and the establishment of a new and dangerous ecology for infectious disease. While improbable, this scenario must be considered seriously. A less severe outlook is for continuing impoverishment of a wide section of the southern African rural populace and a continued high prevalence of HIV. A chronic pattern of destitution and hunger ('famine' in my lexicon) may coexist with a veneer of normality, even prosperity. National and international mobilization of resources, capacity, programmes and political will can prevent this. Unfortunately, time is not on our side: compound crises of AIDS, hunger and poverty may well be upon us before we fully understand what they are, or have the tools and means to respond.

Notes

1 This chapter has benefited from collaborative work with Alan Whiteside, background literature research on HIV/AIDS and malnutrition by Annie Sparrow, on famine and democracy by Anna Mecagni, and comments from Helen Young, Sue Lautze, Stuart Gillespie, Lauren Carruth, Samantha Willan, Girum Zeleke, John Mason, Urban Jonsson and Claudia Hudspeth.
2 The first peer-reviewed publication on NVF was in 2003 (de Waal and Whiteside 2003).
3 John Mason, pers. comm. June 2004.
4 Defined as the ratio between adults (assumed to be productive) and dependent children and the elderly.
5 See Banik, Chapter 13, this volume, for a detailed analysis.
6 See Nattrass (2004) for a critique of the South African Government's position.
7 Note that there is no evidence for extra protein needs additional to those provided by a diet with sufficient energy.
8 For example, Annie Sparrow, in a comment on this chapter, suggests that gastro-enteritic parasitic infestations, particularly helminthiasis (including schistosomiasis), might be more likely to compound the nutritional depletion due to HIV, and *vice versa*, and one might speculate that the parasitemia may increase viral load of HIV in similar ways to malaria.
9 This paragraph draws heavily on unpublished papers by and correspondence with Claudia Hudspeth.
10 Starvation is both the process of not eating enough (causative or consumptive starvation) and the symptomatic manifestation of not absorbing enough nutrients (symptomatic starvation).
11 We should also note that HIV-positive individuals are likely to have greater mortality risks in an environment with a higher prevalence of infectious diseases.
12 Similarly, it is important that ART programmes at scale include nutritional support, shelter, clean water, etc., to those on medication.

References

ACC/SCN (Administrative Committee on Coordination/Subcommittee on Nutrition of the United Nations) (1998) 'Overview to the feature: nutrition and HIV/AIDS', *SCN News*, 17: 3–4.

Ainsworth, M. and Dayton, J. (2001) 'The impact of the AIDS epidemic on the health of the elderly in Northwestern Tanzania', *Policy Research Working Paper* 2649, Washington, DC: World Bank.

Ainsworth, M. and Semali, I. (1998) 'Who is most likely to die of AIDS? Socio-economic correlates of adult deaths in Kagera region, Tanzania', in M. Ainsworth, L. Fransworth and M. Over (eds), *Confronting AIDS: Evidence from the Developing World*, Brussels: European Commission and Washington, DC: World Bank.

Banik, D. (2003) 'Democracy, drought and starvation in India: testing Sen in theory and practice', unpublished Doctoral Thesis, Oslo: University of Oslo, Department of Political Science.

Barnett, T. and Blaikie, P. (1992) *AIDS in Africa: Its Present and Future Impact*, London: John Wiley.

Barnett, T. and Whiteside, A. (1999) 'HIV/AIDS and development: case studies and a conceptual framework', *European Journal of Development Research*, 11(2): 100–34.

Barnett, T., Tumushabe, J., Bantebya, G. *et al.* (1995) 'The social and economic impact of HIV/AIDS on farming systems and rural livelihoods in rural Africa: some experience and lessons from Uganda, Tanzania and Zambia', *Journal of International Development*, 7(1): 163–76.

Baylies, C. (2002) 'The impact of AIDS on rural households in Africa: a shock like any other?', *Development and Change*, 33(4): 611–32.

Beegle, K. (2003) 'Labor effects of adult mortality in Tanzanian households', *World Bank Policy Research Working Paper* 3062, Washington, DC: World Bank.

Bellagio Study Group on Child Survival (2003) 'Knowledge into action for child survival', *Lancet*, 362: 323–7.

Black, R. E., Morris, S. S. and Bryce, J. (2003) 'Where and why are 10 million children dying every year?', *Lancet*, 361: 2226–34.

Brown, L. R., Webb, P. and Haddad, L. (1994) 'The role of labour in household food security: implications of AIDS for Africa', *Food Policy*, 19(6): 560–71.

Carter, M. R. and Maluccio, J. A. (2002) 'Social capital and coping with economic shocks: an analysis of stunting of South Africa's children', *Food Consumption and Nutrition Division Discussion Paper* 42, Washington, DC: IFPRI.

Cohen, D. (2002) 'Poverty and HIV/AIDS in Sub-Saharan Africa', *HIV and Development Program Issues Paper* 27, New York, NY: UNDP.

Crampin, A., Floyd, S., Glynn, J., *et al.* (2003) 'The long-term impact of HIV and orphanhood on the mortality and physical well-being of children in rural Malawi', *AIDS*, 17(3): 389–97.

Dabis, F. and Ekpini, E. R. (2002) 'HIV-1/AIDS and maternal and child health in Africa', *Lancet*, 359: 2097–104.

Daniel, M. (2003) 'Children without parents in Botswana: the safety net and beyond', Paper presented at Scientific Meeting on Empirical Evidence for the Demographic and Socio-Economic Impact of AIDS, Durban, 26–28 March.

Davies, S. (1995) *Adaptable Livelihoods: Coping with Food Insecurity in the Malian Sahel*, London: Macmillan Palgrave.

Dayton, G. J. and Ainsworth, M. (2002) 'The elderly and HIV/AIDS: coping strategies and health consequences in rural Tanzania', *Working Paper* 160, New York: Population Council, Policy Research Division.

Devereux, S. (2002a) 'Social protection for the poor: lessons from recent international experience', *IDS Working Paper* 142, Brighton: Institute of Development Studies.

Devereux, S. (2002b) 'Can social safety nets reduce chronic poverty?', *Development Policy Review*, 20(5): 657–75.

Devereux, S. and Maxwell, S. (eds) (2001) *Food Security in Sub-Saharan Africa*, London: ITDG Publishing.

de Waal, A. (1997) *Famine Crimes: Politics and the Disaster Relief Industry in Africa*, London: IAI and James Currey.

de Waal, A. (2003a) 'HIV/AIDS and emergencies: challenges of measurement and modelling', Paper for the RIACSO Consultation, 'Vulnerability in the Light of the HIV/AIDS Pandemic', Johannesburg, 9–11 September.

de Waal, A. (2003b) 'How will HIV/AIDS transform African governance?', *African Affairs*, January, 102(406): 1–23.

de Waal, A. (2003c) 'Aids, aid and famine: new variant famine in Southern Africa', *Index on Censorship*, January 32: 176–81.

de Waal, A. (2004) 'AIDS-related famine in Africa: questioning assumptions and developing frameworks', in N. K. Poku and A. Whiteside (eds), *The Political Economy of AIDS in Africa*, Aldershot: Ashgate.

de Waal, A. (2005) *Famine that Kills: Darfur, Sudan*, revised edition, New York, NY: Oxford University Press.

de Waal, A. and Whiteside, A. (2003) ' "New variant famine": AIDS and food crisis in Southern Africa', *Lancet*, 362: 1234–7.

de Weerdt, J. (2001) 'Community organisations in rural Tanzania: a case study of the community of Nyakatoke, Bukoba rural district', February, Bukoba: Economic Development Initiatives.

Drèze, J. (1990) 'Famine prevention in India', in J. Drèze and A. Sen (eds), *The Political Economy of Hunger, Vol. II: Famine Prevention*, Oxford: Clarendon Press.

Dyson, T. (1993) 'Demographic response to famines in South Asia', *IDS Bulletin*, 24(4): 17–26.

Food Economy Group (2002) 'Household food economy and HIV/AIDS: exploring the linkages', Food Economy Group.

Fox, M., Rosen, S., MacLeod, W., *et al.* (2004) 'The impact of HIV/AIDS on labour productivity in Kenya', *Tropical Medicine and International Health*, 9(3): 318–24.

Government of Tanzania (2004) 'Report of the joint multisectoral team visit to Makete District on human resource capacity due to HIV/AIDS', mimeo, February, Dar es Salaam: President's Office.

Haddad, L. and Frankenberger, T. (2003) 'Integrating relief and development to accelerate reductions in food insecurity in shock-prone areas', *USAID Office of Food for Peace Occasional Paper* 2, Washington, DC: USAID.

Haddad, L. and Gillespie, S. (2001) 'Effective food and nutrition policy responses to HIV/AIDS: what we know and what we need to know', *Food Consumption and Nutrition Division Discussion Paper* 112, Washington, DC: IFPRI.

Harms, G. and Feldmeier, H. (2002) 'Review: HIV infection and tropical parasitic diseases – deleterious interactions in both directions?', *Tropical Medicine and International Health*, 7(6): 479–88.

Harvey, P. (2004) 'HIV/AIDS and humanitarian action', *Humanitarian Policy Group Report* 16, April, London: Overseas Development Institute.

Havlir, D. V. and Barnes, P. F. (1999) 'Tuberculosis in patients with human immunodeficiency virus infection', *New England Journal of Medicine*, 340(5): 367–73.

Hill, K., Cheluget, B., Curtis, S., Bicego, G. and Mahy, M. (2004) 'HIV and increases in childhood mortality in Kenya in the late 1980s to the mid-1990s', USAID and Measure Evaluation, June (available at www.dec.org/pdf_docs/PNADA259.pdf).

Holden, S. (2003) 'AIDS on the agenda: adapting development and humanitarian programmes to meet the challenge of HIV/AIDS', Oxford: Oxfam.

Iliffe, J. (1987) *The African Poor: A History*, Cambridge: Cambridge University Press.

Jha, M. K. (2002) 'Rajasthan: hunger and starvation deaths: call for public action', *Economic and Political Weekly*, 29 December.

Joint Learning Initiative (2004) *Human Resources for Health*, Cambridge: Global Equity Initiative.

Kamminga, E. and Wegelin-Schuringa, M. (2003) 'HIV/AIDS and water, sanitation and hygiene', *IRC Thematic Overview Paper*, February (available at www.irc.nl/top, accessed 30 May 2004).

Killewo, J., Dahlgren, L. and Sandstrom, A. (1994) 'Socio-geographical patterns in HIV-1 transmission in Kagera region, Tanzania', *Social Science and Medicine*, 38(1): 129–34.

Kwaramba, P. (1998) 'The socio-economic impact of HIV/AIDS on communal agricultural production systems in Zimbabwe', *Working Paper* 19, Economic Advisory Project, Harare: Friedrich Ebert Stiftung.

Larson, B., Hamazakaza, P., Kapunda, C., Hamusimbi, C. and Rosen, S. (2004) 'Morbidity, mortality and crop production: an empirical study of smallholder cotton growing households in the central province of Zambia', *Agricultural Policy Brief*, Boston: Boston University, Center for International Health and Development and FASAZ.

Lundberg, M., Over, M. and Mujinja, P. (2000) 'Sources of financial assistance for households suffering an adult death in Kagera, Tanzania', East Lansing: Michigan State University and Washington, DC: World Bank.

Macintyre, K. (2002) 'Famine and the female mortality advantage', in T. Dyson and C. Ó Gráda (eds), *Famine Demography: Perspectives from Past and Present*, Oxford: Oxford University Press.

Mason, J. B., Bailes, A. T. and Mason, K. E. (2004) 'AIDS, drought and malnutrition in Southern Africa: preliminary analysis of nutritional data on the humanitarian crisis', *Population Health Nutrition*, 8(6): 551–63.

Mather, D., Donovan, C., Weber, M., Marrule, H. and Alage, A. (2003) 'Prime age mortality and household livelihood in Rural Mozambique: preliminary results and implications for HIV/AIDS mitigation efforts', 20 November, Maputo: Government of Mozambique, Ministry of Agriculture and Rural Development, and East Lansing: Michigan State University.

Mooiji, J. (2001) 'Food and power in Bihar and Jharkhand: PDS and its functioning', *Economic and Political Weekly*, August 25–31.

Mutangadura, G. (2000) 'Household welfare impacts of mortality of adult females in Zimbabwe: implications for policy and program development', unpublished paper, AIDS and Economics Symposium.

Myhrvold-Hanssen, T. J. (2003) 'Democracy, news media and famine prevention: Amartya Sen and the Bihar famine of 1966–67', Lund: Swedish South Asian Studies Network.

Nattrass, N. (2004) *The Moral Economy of AIDS in South Africa*, Cambridge: Cambridge University Press.

Nieburg, P., Person-Karell, B. and Toole, M. (1992) 'Malnutrition-mortality relationships among refugees', *Journal of Refugee Studies*, 5(3/4): 247–56.

Oxfam (2003) 'The IMF and the Millennium Goals: failing to deliver for low income countries', *Oxfam Briefing Paper* 54, September, Oxford: Oxfam.

Oxfam (2004) 'From 'donorship' to ownership? Moving towards PRSP round two', *Oxfam Briefing Paper* 51, January, Oxford: Oxfam.

Piwoz, E. G. and Preble, E. A. (2002) 'HIV/AIDS and nutrition: a review of the literature and recommendations for nutritional care and support in Sub-Saharan Africa', Washington, DC: USAID.

Ram, N. (1990) 'An independent press and anti-hunger strategies: the Indian experience', in J. Drèze and A. Sen (eds), *The Political Economy of Hunger, Vol. I: Entitlement and Well-Being*, Oxford: Clarendon Press.

Rosen, S. and Simon, J. (2002) 'Shifting the burden of HIV/AIDS', February, Boston: Boston University, Center for International Health.

Rugalema, G. (1999) 'Adult mortality as entitlement failure: AIDS and the crisis of livelihoods in a Tanzanian village', unpublished PhD thesis, The Hague: Institute of Social Studies.

Rugalema, G. (2000) 'Coping or struggling? A journey into the impact of HIV/AIDS in Southern Africa', *Review of African Political Economy*, 26(86): 537–45.

SADC FANR VAC (2003) 'Towards identifying impacts of HIV/AIDS on food insecurity in Southern Africa and implications for response: findings from Malawi, Zambia and Zimbabwe', Harare, Zimbabwe.

SAHIMS (2003) 'Girls exchanged for food', SAHIMS editorial (available at www.sahims.net/countries/Malawi/editorial/review_mal_06_08_03.htm, accessed 9 March 2004).

SCF (2002) 'The livelihoods of commercial sex workers in Binga', March, Harare: Save the Children Fund.

Scoones, I. (1998) 'Sustainable rural livelihoods: a framework for analysis', *IDS Working Paper* 72, Brighton: Institute of Development Studies.

Scott, G. and Harland, C. (2003) 'Food insecurity, HIV/AIDS and children', unpublished manuscript.

Semba, R. D. and Tang, A. M. (1999) 'Micronutrients and the pathogenesis of human immunodeficiency virus infection', *British Journal of Nutrition*, 81(3): 181–9.

Semu-Banda, P. (2003) 'Daughters for loan under fire', *The Nation Online*, 24 July.

Sen, A. (1981) *Poverty and Famines: An Essay on Entitlement and Deprivation*, Oxford: Clarendon Press.

Sen, A. (1990) 'Individual freedom as a social commitment', *New York Review of Books*, 14 June.

Shankar, K. (2002) 'Starvation deaths in UP and PDS', *Economic and Political Weekly*, October 19.

Steinberg, M., Johnson, S., Schierhout, G., *et al.* (2002) 'Hitting home: how households cope with the impact of the HIV/AIDS epidemic: a survey of household affected by HIV/AIDS in South Africa', Durban: Health Systems Trust, and Washington, DC: The Kaiser Family Foundation.

Swift, J. and Hamilton, K. (2001) 'Household food and livelihood security', in S. Devereux and S. Maxwell (eds), *Food Security in Sub-Saharan Africa*, London: IT Publishing, and Pietermaritzburg: University of Natal Press.

Tanzania Food and Nutrition Centre (2004) 'Report on the assessment of effects of HIV/AIDS on household food security and nutrition in drought-affected areas', March, Dar es Salaam.

Tawfik, L. and Kinoti, S. N. (2003) 'The impact of HIV/AIDS on the health workforce in Sub-Saharan Africa', September, Washington, DC: USAID, Support for Analysis and Research in Africa Project (SARA).

Tibaijuka, A. (1997) 'AIDS and economic welfare in peasant agriculture: case studies from Kagabiro village, Kagera region, Tanzania', *World Development*, 25(6): 963–75.

Toole, M. J. and Malkki, R. M. (1992) 'Famine affected, refugee and displaced populations: recommendations for public health issues', *Morbidity and Mortality Weekly Report*, 41RR: 13.

Toole, M. J. and Waldman, R. (1990) 'Prevention of excess mortality in refugee and displaced populations in developing countries', *Journal of the American Medical Association*, 263(24): 3296–320.

Toupouzis, D. (1999) 'The implications of HIV/AIDS for household food security in Africa', Addis Ababa: UN Economic Commission for Africa, Food Security and Sustainable Development Division.

UNICEF (1990) 'Strategy for improved nutrition of children and women in developing countries', *UNICEF Policy Review Paper*, New York, NY: UNICEF.

UNICEF Southern African Humanitarian Unit (2003) 'Drought, AIDS and child malnutrition in Southern Africa: preliminary analysis of nutritional data on the humanitarian crisis', March, Nairobi: UNICEF.

Walker, N., Schwartlander, B. and Bryce, J. (2002) 'Meeting international goals in child survival and HIV/AIDS', *Lancet*, 360: 284–9.

Watkins, S. C. and Menken, J. (1985) 'Famines in historical perspective', *Population and Development Review*, 11(4): 647–76.

Webb, D. and Mutangadura, G. (1999) 'The socio-economic impact of adult morbidity and mortality in households in Kafue District Zambia', Harare: Southern Africa AIDS and HIV Information Dissemination Service (SAfAIDS).

Whiteside, A., Mattes, R., Willan, S. and Manning, R. (2002) 'Examining HIV/AIDS in Southern African through the eyes of ordinary Southern Africans', *Afrobarometer Paper* 21, Cape Town: Institute for Democracy in South Africa.

WHO (2003) 'Nutrient requirements for people living with HIV/AIDS', report of a Technical Consultation, Geneva: WHO.

WHO and FAO (2002) *Living Well with HIV/AIDS: A Manual on Nutritional Care and Support for People Living with HIV/AIDS*, Rome: FAO.

Yamano, T. and Jayne, T. (2002) 'Measuring the impacts of prime-age adult death on rural households in Kenya', East Lansing: Department of Agricultural Economics, Michigan State University.

Yambia, O. and de Wagt, A. (2003) 'Nutrition and HIV/AIDS', *UNICEF Priority Actions Paper*, New York, NY: UNICEF.

Young, H. and Jaspars, S. (1995) *Nutrition Matters: People, Food and Famine*, London: ITDG Publishing.

Zaba, B., Marston, M. and Floyd, S. (2003) 'The effects of HIV on child mortality trends in Sub-Saharan Africa', UN Population Division, Training Workshop on HIV/AIDS and Adult Mortality in Developing Countries, UN/POP/MORT/2003/10, 11 August.

Zambia National VAC (2003) 'Zambia emergency food security assessment', Lusaka: Zambia National Vulnerability Assessment Committee in collaboration with the SADC FANR Vulnerability Assessment Committee.

6 Pre-modern, modern and post-modern famine in Iraq, 1990–2003[1]

Haris Gazdar

Introduction

This chapter is about conditions that prevailed in Iraq between 1990 and 2003, particularly until around 1999 – a period marked by economic sanctions and large increases in mortality. Humanitarian crises took a qualitatively new and dramatic turn with war and the invasion of the country in 2003. The sanctions period remains an important historical epoch for an understanding of Iraq's post-invasion prospects, but also as a case study of a policy-induced famine at the end of the twentieth century. Events relating to the war and the post-invasion period will not be directly addressed here, though some comments will be offered (in a postscript) on new information that has come to light as a consequence of the invasion.

Famine conditions in Iraq since 1990

The UN Security Council imposed economic sanctions against Iraq in August 1990, in response to Iraq's military invasion of Kuwait. The sanctions banned all trade with Iraq, virtually isolating its economy from the rest of the world. There was a limited lifeline through Jordan, but this was a mere trickle compared with Iraq's historical dependence on foreign trade for its basic sustenance. Prior to the imposition of sanctions, between 60 and 85 per cent of Iraq's food consumption was imported and the export sector accounted for up to 90 per cent of the GDP.

Tested against current standards of economic liberalization, the Iraq of 1990 was not a market-friendly economy: there were internal restrictions, state controls and a war-oriented command system. But at the same time Iraq was not autarkic. The country was highly dependent on international trade due to the historical importance of the oil sector to its economy.

It was suspected from the outset that Iraq would face severe food shortages as a result of the sanctions. A country that had relied heavily on food imports had been virtually cut off from the rest of the world. With the imposition of sanctions it was estimated that aggregate food availability had declined by around 60 per cent of its pre-1990 level. Early attempts at measuring changes in nutritional conditions and mortality rates led to estimates of the doubling of malnutrition and mortality among children, and suggested excess mortality in the hundreds of thousands (International Study Team 1991; Zaidi and Smith Fawzi 1995; Center for Economic and Social Rights 1996). While these early assessments helped to highlight the possible extent of the crisis, their results were subjected to much controversy, leaving many questions unanswered.

It was only in 1999, almost a decade after the sanctions were imposed, that an international agency finally conducted a large-scale national statistical survey of the country (UNICEF 1999; Ali and Shah 2000). A study by UNICEF – based on parallel surveys in the autonomous north and government-controlled south/centre – found that for children aged under five there had been nearly half a million excess deaths between 1991 and 1998 (Ali *et al.* 2003). Mortality rates for children had doubled in the south/centre of the country during the sanctions period. In the period prior to the sanctions, mortality rates had been declining at a rapid rate. Child mortality estimates might provide a useful lower benchmark for the overall increase in mortality (reliable data on excess adult mortality are not yet available). The fact that around 85 per cent of the excess mortality among children (aged five or under) occurred among the youngest group (infants aged under one year) provides an indication that the adult population might have been better protected.[2]

Mortality estimates corroborated the evidence from nutritional surveys conducted in Iraq throughout this period. These surveys too focused mainly on children and their results were – like the early work on mortality – subject to much debate and controversy. There is broad agreement, however, that child malnutrition increased rapidly between 1990 and 1996, and then stabilized or declined somewhat in the subsequent years. The incidence of acute (weight-for-height) malnutrition increased from 3 per cent in 1991 to 11 per cent in 1996. The proportion of children suffering from chronic malnutrition went up between these two years from 19 to 32 per cent.[3]

The Iraq case is sufficiently nuanced to provoke questions about whether the sanctions period might, justifiably, be labelled a famine or not. Iraq in the 1990s clearly answers to Ravallion's definition: 'a geographic area experiences famine when unusually high mortality risk is associated with an unusually severe threat to the food consumption of at least some people in the area' (1997: 1205). The fact that the excess mortality – though widely anticipated – was eventually confirmed through *post hoc* survey evidence rather than through graphic images of emaciated bodies hardly constitutes grounds for disqualification.[4] Another objection to the use of the term 'famine' to describe the sanctions period might be that Iraq was successful in preventing mass starvation and that disease was the probable cause of excess mortality. Famine studies have, for good reason, long departed from narrow etymological definitions of the subject.[5]

From the point of view of understanding contemporary and future episodes of policy-driven large-scale excess mortality, it is perhaps more relevant to ask what *type* of famine Iraq experienced. It is argued here that, faced with a sharp reduction in aggregate food availability, Iraq's Government was able to protect food entitlements to a great degree. Sustained stresses on food consumption and the decline in public health conditions, however, led to a collapse in 'capabilities' and a fall in the life chances of the population.

Sen's entitlement approach moved the understanding of famines into the realm of 'exchange' economies. In subsistence economies with limited potential for exchange (and no labour market), food availability decline (FAD) would be indistinguishable from an entitlement failure. The entitlement approach allows for a more complex and modern relationship between food production and food consumption. The entitlement approach in its original formulation, however, stipulated a simple relationship between food entitlement failure and the risk of famine (de Waal 1990; Drèze 1999). What is ultimately of interest, however, is the ability of an individual or a population to lead healthy lives or to avoid the risk of malnourishment. The concept of 'capabilities', also due to Sen, has been suggested as a way of extending the entitlement approach to account for factors such as prolonged exposure to hunger and disease, typically encountered as major causes of mortality in famines (Ravallion 1997).

It is possible to imagine circumstances under which an economy or a segment of an economy might get reduced to pre-modern conditions – or a notional non-exchange subsistence economy. For Robinson Crusoe, for example, there would be complete correspondence between a collapse of food availability and entitlement failure. The term 'pre-modern famine' can be used to identify those crises where the absence (or extraordinarily high costs) of exchange imply a high degree of correspondence between availability and entitlement.[6] Much of the imagery of famine, and indeed the 'theory' behind the 'FAD' approach to famines, was essentially a depiction of the pre-modern famine. In modern exchange economies, famine might occur due to a collapse in entitlements independently of any change in food availability. Finally, 'post-modern famine' refers to excess mortality in spite of protected food entitlements but due to non-food crises: notably, the stresses of macro-shocks on relatively sophisticated public health and social welfare systems.

Economies with modern infrastructure and the ability to protect food entitlements are likely to be ones that have also experienced gains in mortality reduction through public health and social welfare. If these economies go into freefall for some reason – as Iraq did in the 1990s – they may revert to high mortality rates despite protecting food entitlements. Famine is substantially about *excess* mortality – increases in deaths above the norm. If the norm happened to have been low mortality rates due to social and economic development, any collapse in capabilities can result in dramatic increases in mortality rates, and in excess mortality.

Iraq under sanctions, it will be argued, represents one of the most disastrous examples of the famine of the future – where essentially policy-induced macroeconomic shocks in a globally integrated economy can lead to dramatic increases in mortality over sustained periods of time.

Functioning modern economy and government

Pre-sanctions Iraq was a country of untargeted food subsidies. The government subsidized the prices of most imported commodities, including food, through the partial maintenance of a highly overvalued exchange rate. While imports of most other commodities faced quantitative restrictions which were administered through the regulated issue of import licences, the government itself was the main importer of staple food items such as wheat-flour. The subsidy was administered by the Ministry of Trade through its monopolistic control of food imports.

In August 1990 the untargeted general subsidy on wheat-flour was replaced with a ration system. Wheat-flour and other food items were still subsidized, but the government relinquished its monopoly over the import of food and allowed the private sector to import food at the market exchange rate. Subsidized food was now available in limited quantities through the government ration system. From August 1990 onwards, therefore, there was a dual market for staple foods – one with highly subsidized prices and rationed quantities, the other an unregulated open market. Much of the Iraqi population relied on a combination of these two sources of food during the sanctions period and beyond.

The food ration system was organized quickly to replace the generalized price subsidy. The fact that this system was controlled by the Ministry of Trade emphasized its origins in the generalized import price subsidy of the pre-sanctions period. The system functioned efficiently, and its operation improved over time. It was supported by an efficiently managed food procurement system. The ration system was supplemented with a well-functioning market for imported food. There were restrictions and regulations, particularly those relating to the ability of local farmers to sell staple foods in the open market, but by and large the market system worked without too much government interference.

Iraq in the 1990s presented the case of a government and market economy that functioned effectively internally, despite facing severe external military, political and economic pressures. Perhaps even more surprisingly, the government and market systems as they related to food functioned without undue interference or predation from a ruling elite that had otherwise proven itself to be both intrusive and predatory. It is in the context of modern and effective governmental and market systems that Iraq witnessed dramatic increases in mortality. The Iraqi crisis, therefore, is quite unlike other famines of the late twentieth and early twenty-first centuries that have been associated with breakdowns in administrative and market systems. Even though its origins were to be found in war, the Iraqi crisis was structurally similar (though more severe and prolonged) to recent crises in countries such as Argentina, Indonesia and Russia that experienced macroeconomic free-fall leading to dramatic increases in poverty, and possibly in morbidity and mortality.

Three phases of the sanctions

The sanctions regime can be divided, broadly, into three phases: (1) August 1990 to March 1991 – total ban on imports and exports; (2) April 1991 to December 1996 – total ban on exports, but exemption of food, medicines and designated humanitarian supplies from the import ban; (3) January 1997 until 2003 – 'oil-for-food' (OFF) agreements allowing Iraq to export oil in return for restricted (but increasing) imports of designated humanitarian supplies.

From August 1990 until April 1991, there was a strictly enforced total ban on all external trade. Iraq was not allowed to import or export anything, with the exception of a small trickle of trade with Jordan – an exemption agreed by the UN Security Council to gain Jordan's compliance with the overall aims of the sanctions.

The first war between Iraq and the American-led coalition began in January 1991 and ended in March. There were large-scale rebellions in the north and the south of the country in the aftermath of the US-led attack, which took the shape of a civil war. Foreign military intervention in the north led to the creation of a Kurdish enclave, while in the south the civil rebellion and conscript mutiny were brutally suppressed by the Iraqi regime. Towards the end of March some semblance of order had been restored to the entire country – with the north achieving partial autonomy from Baghdad, and the south having been militarily 'pacified'. Pockets of resistance continued in the southern marshes for some time after, but these did not present a major threat to the military and civil order of the main population centres.

In March and April 1991, there were several missions into Iraq for the assessment of humanitarian conditions. These included two influential UN-led missions which reported to the Secretary-General. There were also new UN Security Council resolutions that led to a modification of the sanctions regime. The main change was that Iraq was now allowed to import food, medicines and other designated humanitarian supplies.[7]

The new resolutions also included a provision for export exemptions in order to allow Iraq to regain the ability to pay for essential imports. Negotiations on these OFF arrangements remained stalled for several years, until 1996, when Iraq and the UN finally agreed on an OFF deal which once again modified the sanctions regime. The original OFF was highly restrictive, both in terms of the value of oil that Iraq was allowed to export as well as the procedures for approving imports financed by the foreign exchange thus earned. Subsequent negotiations led to some loosening on both counts, with the result that Iraqi exports reached the limits of the country's productive capacity.

The ration system and the market under sanctions

The ration system and the open market functioned with varying degrees of effectiveness after August 1990 in meeting the food needs of Iraqi people. The ration system had been well organized and its coverage in government-controlled areas was widespread.[8] However, the extent to which the ration system actually met the population's food needs varied from time to time, depending on the economic resources available to the government. In 1991, for example, the ration provided the equivalent of around 1,400 kcal per person per day. By 1996, six years into the sanctions, the caloric value had dropped to around 1,200 kcal. These two amounts represented, respectively, around two-thirds and three-fifths of recommended minimum requirements. After the OFF provisions were agreed in 1996, and following their subsequent liberalization, the amount of food available through the ration increased to cover basic minimal nutritional requirements.[9]

The open market existed alongside the ration system. Benchmark prices for staple foods in the market were found to be close to the cost of importing these foods from neighbouring countries, using the unofficial exchange rate, which varied according to anticipated changes in Iraq's external political environment. There had been an inflationary tendency in Iraq since 1991, when the government began raising nominal wages of public sector employees by resorting to monetary expansion. The value of the currency declined to historically low levels in 1995, resulting in historically high open-market dinar prices. Improvements in the value of the dinar led to lower relative prices for food.

The market was robust and efficient. Transport and communication between different parts of government-controlled Iraq functioned well, and market prices in various population centres fluctuated within narrow margins. Prices in the open market, however, were typically several times higher than ration prices. Purchasing power of Iraqi households measured in terms of market prices was estimated to have dropped by over 90 per cent in just the first year of sanctions (Drèze and Gazdar 1992).

Pre-modern famine: food availability crises

There were crucial periods and places in Iraq where the modern administrative and market systems broke down, leading to food availability crises. One such period was around January to March 1991, during which there was excess mortality directly resulting from combat, but also due to the widespread disruption of existing systems caused by the war and civil conflict. There were refugee crises in both the northern and southern parts of the country. Public as well as private systems of food delivery broke down. During this period, conditions of pre-modern, food availability-driven famine existed over large parts of Iraq. There were reports of hunger and starvation, of people reducing their number of meals or subsisting on simple staples alone, or even relying on famine foods such as edible matter in reed stalks.

Those regions where the war and civil conflict were particularly severe also experienced greater hardship in food availability. The Kurdish areas of northern Iraq already had a long history of military repression and economic disruption. Similar conditions prevailed over large parts of the south. Order was restored, however, through brutal military action in which many civilians were killed and injured. The re-establishment of government control was quickly followed by the resumption of the food ration system and the restoration of the market.

Iraq as an economy underwent a severe 'FAD' when food imports were banned following the imposition of sanctions in August 1990. For individuals, families and communities this might have translated into a food availability crisis through two channels: first, the disruption of the modern exchange economy through war, destruction of infrastructure and civil strife; and second, state-led attempts to control food supply causing localized shortages. In the event, the former channel did come into play and did have an impact on nutrition and mortality. State response, however, as shown below, turned out to be judicious and protective.

Modern famine: food entitlement failures

War and civil conflict caused acute food availability crises across the country in general, and in areas of fighting such as the north and the south in particular. Nonetheless, for most of the time, and over much of the country, government and market systems of food delivery functioned relatively well. In the early part of the sanctions period the government relied heavily on the stockpiles of food that had been accumulated in anticipation of the crisis. As the sanctions wore on, the ability of the government to sustain the ration system came under increasing stress.

From 1991 onwards there were attempts to revive the agricultural sector that had suffered a decade of neglect during the Iran–Iraq war. There were strong economic incentives for people to return to farming, and to some extent the efforts of the government were rewarded. There was an increase in the number of people employed in the agricultural sector, increases in farmed area, and some increase in domestic food output.

Economic conditions continued to deteriorate, however, and this was reflected in small declines in the amount of the food ration. Real wages had fallen dramatically – by a margin of around 90 per cent between 1990 and 1991 – and they fell again, by around 40–50 per cent of their 1991 values, up to 1996. By 1996 the purchasing power of an Iraqi office worker had declined to just around 2–3 per cent of its 1990 value. Government transfers in the shape of the subsidized monthly ration, which was available at nominal prices, amounted to around three-quarters of the purchasing power of the office worker's family. The collapse in the real value of private incomes meant that the food entitlements of ordinary Iraqis were dependent on the ration system, and the ration system provided only partial protection against hunger.

It can be argued that the protection provided by the state ration was instrumental in preventing the onset of mass starvation in Iraq. However, six years after the sanctions had been imposed and five years after the end of the war even this system was under severe stress. The war and civil conflict in early 1991 was a period of serious hardship for most people. The restoration of administrative and market systems after this period had led to the alleviation of local food availability crises. By 1996, however, the government of Iraq as well as the private household economy were close to breaking point once again.

The government had held out against the OFF deal for many years, in the vain hope that sanctions might be lifted altogether. In 1996, faced with an imminent macro-economic meltdown, the Government of Iraq finally agreed to the terms of OFF. This led to some immediate relief both in the ration system – which was expanded – and in the market economy, where the value of the Iraqi currency appreciated.

Post-modern famine: capabilities failures

The OFF agreement was a provisional measure aimed at allowing the flow of emergency supplies to Iraq. In the initial years its scale and operation were highly restrictive. Iraq was allowed to export only a fraction of its productive capacity and its import requests were subject to lengthy bureaucratic – and allegedly politically motivated – delays. Although the operation of the OFF was liberalized over the years, its one essential feature – that the government of Iraq did not have direct access to Iraq's export earnings – remained in place.

This implied that while Iraq was able to import certain commodities such as food, selected medicines and other essential supplies, the OFF deal prevented any significant revival of domestic economic activity or the non-imported component of public services. For example, the OFF allowed for the importation of certain medicines, but it did not allow the Iraqi Government to use Iraq's export revenues to retain the services of trained Iraqi doctors or paramedics at remunerative salaries. Even under the most benign conditions, the OFF only allowed Iraq to be run as a relatively efficient refugee camp in which people received just about enough food to eat. The people living in this refugee camp were not allowed to import goods such as spare parts and raw material supplies that might have been essential for running their enterprises. The managers of the refugee camp, moreover, got virtually no budget for hiring local people or paying them a living wage.[10]

The post-OFF scenario led to anticipated improvements in food availability and entitlements. It also threw into relief, however, some of the binding causes of excess mortality in Iraq that had existed since August 1990. Iraq before 1990 was a repressive but welfarist state where people enjoyed high standards of nutrition, water supply and public health.[11] The welfarist interventions of the Iraqi state were responsible for notable improvements in life expectancy and declines in mortality. After August 1990 Iraq reverted to conditions of poor nutrition, water supply and public health. Successive changes in the sanctions regime led to improvements in food entitlements, but these improvements were not sufficient to lead to the restoration of a relatively sophisticated urban economy and systems of public services.

After 1996 the Iraqi people were relatively well-fed, following a long period of malnutrition interspersed with acute food availability crises. In the autonomous northern region, in particular, the improvement in conditions was significant. There was a decline in mortality rates to historically unprecedented levels.[12] Even in the south and centre, where the mortality rate did not decline (but stabilized), there were indications of other improvements after 1996, such as declines in child malnutrition (FAO/WFP 2003).[13] However, Iraqis were still much poorer and much less healthy than they might have been under different sets of international and national policies. Their poverty and ill-health was a direct contributor to excess mortality.

The blame game

The successive sanctions regimes provided the context for Iraq's economic engagement with the rest of the world. The period between August 1990 and 2003 saw drawn-out detailed negotiations between the Iraqi Government and the UN Security Council over every minute change in the sanctions regime. The formal objective of the sanctions was to secure Iraq's compliance with various resolutions of the UN Security Council dealing with Iraq's demilitarization. Both protagonists – the leading members of the Security Council and the Government of Iraq – however, treated the debate about sanctions as a struggle over their respective strategic goals, which had little to do directly with the formal objectives of the Security Council Resolutions. The Government of Iraq's detractors in the Security Council viewed the sanctions as a way of keeping Iraq 'in the box', while the Iraqi Government's positions were geared to breaking its diplomatic, political and economic isolation.

The common factor in this struggle over the sanctions was the attempt by the US and its allies to limit as much as possible the Government of Iraq's access to the country's actual and potential export earnings. This was an extremely severe restriction, given that the state sector had historically been the main mechanism through which primary commodity producers had channelled export earnings into the domestic economy.

The debate on sanctions evolved into a 'blame game' in which the two sides had well-established positions absolving themselves of responsibility. Opposite policy conclusions would be drawn, often from the same evidence on the humanitarian crisis facing the civilian population.[14] The typical posture of the US and its allies in the Security Council went something like:

> The Iraqi Government is repressive and cynical – it could put an end to the sanctions by cooperating with the UN Security Council, and by using available resources for welfare. The Government uses civilian suffering for political advantage.

The Government of Iraq's position, on the other hand, can be summarized thus:

> The powerful states that dominate the Security Council have unstated and illegal political objectives in isolating Iraq. The Security Council resolutions are simply a convenient cover, and Iraqi civilians are the real victims.

Both positions were simplistic and did little justice to the political economy of sanctions. The Iraqi Government was repressive but also welfare-oriented, and the unstated political objectives of world powers were not entirely autonomous of the nature of the Iraqi Government. The blame game was disingenuous, because it concealed the fact that the prevention of excess mortality was not the primary concern of either party to the conflict.[15]

Beyond the blame game

The blame game conveyed the impression that what had happened in Iraq was something quite peculiar to the nature of conflict in the Gulf, and that it had little bearing on humanitarian policy, food security and famine prevention elsewhere. While it is true that there were aspects of the Iraqi situation that were probably unique, it is worth noting that some of the key features of the crisis in Iraq are more widely applicable.

First, whatever the precise politics of the sanctions, and whichever side one might want to take in the 'blame game', the sanctions were, substantively, a severe and sustained macroeconomic shock. In particular, sanctions represented the policy-induced economic isolation of a national economy from an otherwise integrating world economy. Unilateral and multilateral sanctions of various types affect a large number of countries, and continue to be regarded as humane tools of ensuring political compliance. Their effects on individual countries are likely to be more severe the greater the overall integration of the global economy. Even a poor economy such as post-Taliban Afghanistan – which is nevertheless integrated into the world economy due to its dependence on remittances of migrant workers and the export of opium – can be vulnerable to policy-induced isolation such as restrictions on the operation of the informal foreign exchange system.[16] If the tendency towards economic integration is inevitable, then so is the increased vulnerability of diverse economies to unilateral or multilateral acts of 'regulation'.

Second, the breakdown in relatively sophisticated economic and public services systems can give rise to dramatic increases in poverty, malnutrition, morbidity and mortality. Countries that have experienced improvements in economic and health conditions can revert back to higher rates of malnutrition, morbidity and mortality in the face of sustained macroeconomic shock and decline. In these situations the quantum of excess mortality can be very high, precisely because the initial conditions were relatively benign.

Third, unlike conspicuous food availability failures or even entitlement failures, which tend to be associated with natural disasters and wars, a post-modern famine could occur quietly as a result of economic shock, and be revealed *post hoc* through the analysis of demographic data (for an example, see Garenne, Chapter 8, this volume).

Iraq provides a gruesome glimpse of possible future famines – i.e. famine in a context where other problems of modernization find benign solutions. Iraq was a well-functioning state (in terms of administrative functions), closely integrated with the world economy (through the export of oil), with a domestic economy that was well-integrated internally. On the scale of modernization, Iraq was much ahead of most developing countries; indeed, many developing countries would have regarded the modernization of countries such as Iraq as a benchmark to be aspired to.

The excess mortality associated with the collapse of Iraq's economy and its welfare infrastructure is unique only in its scale and in the persistence of the sanctions regime. The post-modern famine is not a chronologically determined event. The conditions of the global economy imply that post-modern famine conditions will coexist with pre-modern food availability crises as well as modern famines due to entitlement failures. Indeed, in Iraq, all three types of famine were experienced, sequentially and simultaneously.

Postscript

The war and invasion of Iraq by US-led forces in 2003 unleashed a new and qualitatively distinct humanitarian crisis in the country. Estimates of excess mortality in this period range from several thousand to around 200,000, with a figure of 100,000 excess deaths being cited as a conservative benchmark from a cluster sample survey conducted in September 2004 (Roberts *et al.* 2004). The survey, understandably, focused on deaths due to violence. However, given the large-scale disruption to physical and institutional infrastructure, non-violent mortality increases are also to be expected.[17] While sanctions came to an end, and there were indications of a revival of private economic activity, the adverse effects of the invasion were likely to dominate prospects for rapid improvement in health and social welfare.

There were indications that conditions identified in this chapter as pre-modern, modern and post-modern famine might all have returned to Iraq to varying degrees after the invasion. It was reported, for example, that military actions were often preceded by many days, even weeks, of enforced isolation of entire cities and localities, including bans on food and medical supplies, and the shutting down of water and electricity systems.[18] The United Nations Human Rights Commission food specialist testified that acute malnutrition among children had doubled since the invasion, and cited war-related destruction of infrastructure as well as military blockades as probable causes.[19]

The invasion also brought to the fore new information that might help with understanding the sanctions period better. The foreign military powers in Iraq were embarrassed by their inability to find weapons of mass destruction – proving that the previous Iraqi regime was, in effect, in compliance with Security Council resolutions when it had demanded the lifting of the sanctions. Attention, in the meanwhile, turned to other aspects of the sanctions regime, most conspicuously the OFF programme. The OFF was closed down in May 2004 following allegations that it had been used as a cover by the former regime illegally to appropriate funds through fraudulent deals, and several investigations were launched into the operation of this programme (Gordon 2004).[20]

Something that did not receive a great deal of public coverage, however, was the fact that the food ration system pioneered by the Iraqi Ministry of Trade in August 1990 had been retained by the incoming military powers and their successor Iraqi regime. The allegations of corruption and fraudulent practices around the OFF did not seem to have filtered down to the micro-level into the workings of the food ration system. After initial speculation in the immediate post-invasion period that the ration would be disbanded, the occupying powers chose to continue with a system that had helped to protect the Iraqi population from mass starvation for over a decade. It is, of course, another matter that the international stakeholders, both the UN agencies as well as the occupying powers, chose to portray the ration system as their own rather than the previous regime's achievement.[21]

Confirmation of the effective universal coverage of the ration system came from other unusual sources. Politicians demanding the holding of early elections argued for the use of ration cards in lieu of electoral rolls as authentic records of citizenship and residence.[22] While the occupying powers did not agree with this suggestion in early 2004, towards the end of the year it was reported that the Iraqi interim government had decided to use the ration system to enrol voters (BBC 2004b).

What these observations reveal is that the ration system in Iraq did represent a genuine, effective and successful attempt by a politically repressive regime to protect the food entitlements of a population faced with the threat of mass starvation. The implicit acceptance of the welfarist credentials of the previous regime – through the actions of its local and foreign enemies – simply confirms that the politics of welfare can be complex, and that repressive regimes can be sensitive to the goal of famine prevention. It also implies that, despite the prevalence of repression and corruption, some Iraqi state institutions did operate with a surprising degree of organizational competence and integrity. The summary disbanding of many of these institutions in the first few months of the occupation might go down, in retrospect, as an act of institutional vandalism with tragic humanitarian consequences.

Notes

1 This chapter draws heavily upon Drèze and Gazdar (1992), Gazdar and Hussain (2002) and Mahdi and Gazdar (2002).

2 This appeared not to have been the case during the invasion and war of 2003, when adults as well as children experienced increased rates of mortality (Roberts *et al.* 2004).

3 Various sources compiled by FAO/WFP (2003).

4 The Russian and Soviet famines of the twentieth century were also demographic events that continue to yield varying estimates of mortality (Adamets 2002), as does China's 'Great Leap Forward' famine of 1959–1961 (Yao 1999). A more recent example is the Madagascar famine of the 1980s (Garenne, Chapter 8, this volume).

5 De Waal (1990) is not alone in insisting that starvation need not be an essential feature of a famine. Even the Great Irish Famine is thought to have killed many more people through disease than outright starvation (Mokyr and Ó Gráda 2002). Drèze (1999) shows, for example, that the timely 'declaration' of famine under the Famine Code in British India, was an essential *prerequisite* of famine prevention.

6 Devereux (Chapter 4, this volume) makes the same point when he points out that FAD is in fact incorporated within Sen's entitlement framework.

7 The two UN missions were led, respectively, by Martti Ahtisaari and Sadruddin Aga Khan. For details and references see Drèze and Gazdar (1992).

8 The secretive and repressive character of the Iraqi regime prompted suspicion about the reach and effectiveness of the public distribution system. In particu-

lar, there were fears that some segments of the population would have been systematically excluded due to their political opposition to the regime. While independent assessments of the ration system did not bear out these apprehensions, they continued to worry commentators, particularly in the US and Britain. The post-invasion scenario discussed further below brought some clarification of the issue.

9 The caloric value of the ration had risen to 2000 kcal/person per day by 2003 (FAO/WFP 2003).

10 There was much suspicion, of course, that the OFF was used by the 'managers' of this refugee camp to cream away resources through fraudulent deals. These suspicions and their implications are discussed further below with reference to new post-invasion information.

11 Welfarism, according to one prominent Iraqi dissident of the time, was as essential to the Ba'athist model of dictatorship as was repression (al-Khalil 1989).

12 Detractors of the Iraqi regime pointed to the relatively better position of the northern autonomous region as evidence that the government was holding back support to the people in areas under its control. The actual position was more complex. Under OFF, the per capita allocation in the northern region was double that for the south/centre. Also, unlike the south/centre, in the north OFF funds could be used for budgetary support. Moreover, the northern economy was not under sanctions, had relatively open access to neighbouring countries and had developed as a major conduit for informal trade.

13 Within the centre/south, the south was not only poorer to begin with but it also suffered more during the various episodes of violence and crisis. While there were indications that government systems functioned better in the centre than in the south, and that the centre might have been better protected against humanitarian crises due to its political influence, empirical evidence on relative decline does not highlight substantial inter-regional differences.

14 This duality was not restricted to debating chambers of international organizations; it spilled over into academic discussion too. See, for example, correspondence in the medical journal the *Lancet* (1996) following publication of the results of a health and mortality survey in 1995.

15 It turns out in retrospect that the position of the Iraqi Government might have been somewhat less cynical than that of its detractors, given that it was, effectively, in compliance with most of its Security Council obligations. There are any number of voices now that recall the 'success' of the sanctions in disarming Iraq. The cost of that 'success' to ordinary Iraqis is rarely acknowledged.

16 International action against opium and heroin production and export from Afghanistan might play out as a massive macroeconomic shock to the fledgling economy. The case of Iraq clearly demonstrates that in the contemporary globalizing economy the expected effects of trade sanctions of any sort need to be understood within a general equilibrium framework.

17 See contributions to the *Lancet* for discussion of the health crisis associated with the invasion: for example, Kapp (2003), Ashraf (2003), Aziz (2003), and Burkle and Noji (2004). See also UNICEF (2003) for an assessment by an international agency.

18 See, for example, CASI (2004).

19 See Ferri-Smith (2005) for a summary of the UNHRC report as well as rebuttals by US government sources.

20 The charge against OFF was that the Iraqi Government had fraudulently gained access to export revenues generated from the sale of oil. Some of the investigations have concluded that the main source of leakage in the sanctions regime was not the OFF but the oil Iraq was allowed to export outside of the OFF arrangements (BBC 2005).

21 It is particularly interesting to note that the USAID website claims among its major accomplishments that it 'worked directly with WFP and Coalition Forces to re-establish the Public Distribution System (PDS) in less than 30 days, avoiding a humanitarian food crisis and providing food security throughout the country' (USAID 2004).
22 Ayatollah Sistani, a respected religious leader of the Shi'i community who was incarcerated by the previous regime, was at the forefront of those making this demand (Kubba 2004; BBC 2004a).

References

Adamets, S. (2002) 'Famine in nineteenth and twentieth-century Russia: mortality by age, cause, and gender', in T. Dyson and C. Ó Gráda (eds), *Famine Demography: Perspectives from the Past and the Present*, Oxford: Oxford University Press.

Ali, M. M. and Shah, I. H. (2000) 'Sanctions and childhood mortality in Iraq', *Lancet*, 355(9218): 1851–7.

Ali, M. M., Blacker, J. and Jones, G. (2003) 'Annual mortality rates and excess deaths of children under five in Iraq, 1991–98', *Population Studies*, 57(2): 217–26.

al-Khalil, S. (1989) *Republic of Fear: the Politics of Modern Iraq*, London: Hutchinson.

Ashraf, H. (2003) 'World Food Programme gears up to help entire Iraq population', *Lancet*, 361(9364): 1189.

Aziz, C. (2003) 'Struggling to re-build Iraq's health system', *Lancet*, 362(9392): 1288–9.

BBC News (2004a) 'No Iraq poll before 2005 – Bremer', 21 February 2004 (available at www.bbc.co.uk/go/pr/fr/-/1/hi/world/middle_east/3509241.stm, accessed 17 November 2004).

BBC News (2004b) 'Q&A: Iraqi elections', 10 November 2004 (available at www.bbc.co.uk/go/pr/fr/-/1/hi/world/middle_east/3971635.stm, accessed 17 November 2004).

BBC News (2005) 'US and UK blamed for oil scandal', 15 April 2005 (available at www.news.bbc.co.uk/go/pr/fr/-/2/hi/americas/4447165.stm, accessed on 23 April 2005).

Burkle, F. M. and Noji, E. K. (2004) 'Health and politics in the 2003 war with Iraq: lessons learned', *Lancet*, 364(9442): 1371–5.

CASI (2004) 'Denial of water to Iraqi cities' (available at www.casi.org.uk/briefing/041110denialofwater.pdf, accessed 23 April 2005).

Center for Economic and Social Rights (1996) 'Un-sanctioned suffering', mimeo, New York, NY: CESR.

de Waal, A. (1990) 'A re-assessment of entitlement theory in the light of recent famines in Africa', *Development and Change*, 21(3): 469–90.

Drèze, J. (1999) (ed.) *The Economics of Famine*, Cheltenham: Elgar.

Drèze, J. and Gazdar, H. (1992) 'Hunger and poverty in Iraq, 1991', *World Development*, 20(7): 921–45.

FAO/WFP (2003) 'Special report: FAO/WFP crop, food supply and nutrition assessment mission to Iraq, 23 September 2003' (available at www.wfp.org/newsroom/in-depth/Middle_East/Iraq0309_Iraq.pdf, accessed 18 November 2004).

Ferri-Smith, D. (2005) 'Iraq health and infrastructure digest #7', Voices in the Wilderness (available at www.vitw.org/archives/877#more-877, accessed 23 April 2005).

Gazdar, H. and Hussain, A. (2002) 'Crisis and response: a study of the impact of economic sanctions in Iraq', in K. A. Mahdi (ed.), *Iraq's Economic Predicament*, Reading: Ithaca Press.

Gordon, J. (2004) 'Scandals of oil for food', *Middle East Report (MERIP) Online*, 19 July (accessed 17 November 2004).

International Study Team (1991) 'Health and welfare in Iraq after the Gulf War', mimeo, London: Medical Education Trust.

Kapp, C. (2003) 'United Nations reveals aid plans for war in Iraq', *Lancet*, 361(9358): 622.

Kubba, L. (2004) 'Who's afraid of elections in Iraq?', *Guardian*, London, 2 January.

Lancet (1996) Correspondence on 'sanctions against Iraq', *Lancet*, 347(8995): 198–200.

Mahdi, K. A. and Gazdar, H. (2002) 'Introduction', in K. A. Mahdi (ed.) *Iraq's Economic Predicament*, Reading: Ithaca Press.

Mokyr, J. and Ó Gráda, C. (2002) 'Famine disease and famine mortality: lessons from the Irish experience, 1845–50', in T. Dyson and C. Ó Gráda (eds), *Famine Demography: Perspectives from the Past and the Present*, Oxford: Oxford University Press.

Ravallion, M. (1997) 'Famines and economics', *Journal of Economic Literature*, 35(3): 1205–42.

Roberts, L., Lafta, R., Garfield, R., Khudhairi, J. and Burnham, G. (2004) 'Mortality before and after the 2003 invasion of Iraq: cluster sample survey', *Lancet*, 29 October (available at www.image.thelancet.com/extras/04art10342web.pdf, accessed 16 November 2004).

UNICEF (1999) 'Iraq Child and Maternal Mortality Survey 1999' (available at www.unicef.org/reseval/iraqr.html, accessed 18 November 2004).

UNICEF (2003) 'Press Release: Iraq Survey Finds Child Health Sliding', UNICEF Press Centre (available at www.unicef.org/emerg/media_9419.html, accessed on 18 November 2004).

USAID (2004) 'Accomplishments: food security' (available at www.usaid.gov/iraq/accomplishments/foodsec.html, updated 13 October 2004, accessed on 18 November 2004).

Yao, S. (1999) 'A note on the causal factors of China's famine in 1959–61', *Journal of Political Economy*, 107(6): 1365–9.

Zaidi, S. and Smith Fawzi, M. C. (1995) 'Health of Baghdad's children', *Lancet*, 346(8988): 1485.

7 Malawi's first famine, 2001–2002

Stephen Devereux and Zoltan Tiba

Introduction[1]

In 1949, the British colony of Nyasaland suffered a minor famine.[2] More than half a century later, four decades after Nyasaland achieved independence in 1964 and eight years after Malawi's first multi-party elections in 1994, the democratic state of Malawi suffered its first ever famine. How this could happen early in the twenty-first century is the subject of this chapter. Despite generating an extraordinary amount of media and academic attention, this famine remains a puzzle. Some elements of the story have received disproportionate attention – an example being the sale of the Strategic Grain Reserve – while others remain obscure. There is no consensus on how many people died, for instance, or even on whether the label 'famine' is appropriate at all.

The next section of this chapter reviews what happened in Malawi in 2001–2002. We ask the question *'what happened'?*, discuss whether it was food crisis or famine, and answer this partly by presenting new mortality estimates that classify this event as a 'major famine'. We next ask the question *'what made it happen?'* and assess the explanatory power of two theoretical frameworks – 'food availability decline' (FAD) (a 'famine as natural disaster' explanation) and 'exchange entitlement failure' (an economic crisis of markets and poverty). We also propose a new theoretical explanation – the 'controlling institution' hypothesis (a political economy analysis) – which suggests that certain powerful groups may have had an interest in creating and perpetuating food crisis conditions in Malawi in 2002. Since these approaches only explain proximate factors around the crisis itself, we then ask the question *'what made it possible?'*. While there are many underlying vulnerability factors, we focus on three – demographic/health (the 'new variant famine' hypothesis, which highlights the role of HIV/AIDS), economic (failures of economic liberalization) and political (failures of the democratic transition). The chapter concludes by arguing that the Malawi famine was not simply a failure on the part of those who should have prevented it; it was in many significant – and explanatory – respects a 'success' for those who benefited.

What happened?

Food crisis or famine?

While popular conceptualizations of famine are dominated by its defining outcome – 'mass death by starvation' – there remains a lack of consensus in the academic and policy literatures regarding the specific parameters by which a famine can be identified and differentiated from lesser intensities of food crisis (cf. Howe and Devereux, Chapter 2, this volume). In the case of Malawi, some analysts labelled the events of 2001–2002 a 'famine' (Devereux 2002; Owusu and Ng'ambi 2002), but this remains a minority view. The Government of Malawi (GoM) and the donor community in Malawi have never publicly accepted that this was a famine. The government (belatedly) declared a 'State of Disaster' on 27 February 2002, while donors preferred terms like 'food crisis' (IMF 2002a) or 'humanitarian crisis' (International Development Committee 2003). When food aid was eventually mobilized – after the famine was effectively over – it was with the stated objective of '*averting* famine in Malawi' (World Bank 2002).

While disagreement persists about the appropriate label, it is generally acknowledged that even the lowest official estimates of 300–500 hunger-related deaths in 2002 are higher than the number of people who died during the Nyasaland famine of 1949, which was indisputably a 'minor famine' that resulted in an estimated 200 deaths (Vaughan 1987). This chapter provides statistical evidence from several sources for much higher hunger-related mortality in early 2002 than was previously believed. Evidence is also presented on many other famine indicators, including extremely high food prices, oedema in adults, the adoption of irreversible and sometimes fatal 'coping strategies', and social breakdown within affected communities. Given these consistent and complementary indicators of severe distress, it would be remarkable if this 'famine process' had not resulted in extensive mortality. Together with the personal testimonies of survivors, the circumstantial evidence about famine processes and the statistics on mortality add up to a familiar narrative. In terms of both severity and scale, Malawi 2001–2002 was incontrovertibly a famine.

Mortality

The question of how many people died during the Malawi famine is highly controversial, and will probably never be known with any certainty.[3] In this section we present crude estimates derived from our respective surveys, extrapolated to the national level (Devereux *et al.* 2003; Tiba 2005). In the Malawi Food Crisis Impact Survey, a total of fifty-nine hunger-related deaths were recorded in 1,203 households interviewed: thirty-five in the central region, twenty-one in the southern region and three in the northern region.[4] Reported deaths were higher in female-headed households (9.5 per cent) than in male-headed households (3.9 per cent). If these proportions were replicated throughout the country, national excess mortality due to famine would amount to 84,955.[5] To triangulate the household survey findings, key informants (e.g. traditional leaders, teachers) from 111 villages visited were asked to provide actual numbers of people who died during and because of the food crisis of 2001–2002. These informants enumerated a total of 255 deaths (2.3 per village). Assuming that these communities were typical of all of rural Malawi, this equates to a national famine death toll of 46,200. We therefore conclude – by extrapolation from two stratified random samples of households and key informants – that famine-related mortality in Malawi in 2001–2002 was in the range of 46,000 to 85,000. This figure considerably exceeds previous estimates – such as 300 to 500 deaths (Taifour 2002: 2), or 1,000 to 3,000 deaths (Catholic Commission for Justice and Peace, cited in Devereux 2002: 18) – which were based on smaller, localized fieldwork. Another NGO in Malawi informally 'guesstimated' total famine deaths at 10,000 to 15,000, but with no empirical basis.[6]

Our mortality estimates make this a relatively small famine in global and historical terms, equating to 0.5 to 0.9 per cent of the rural population (in the Bangladesh 1974 and Ethiopia 1984–1985 famines, approximately 2 per cent of the national populations died). In terms of 'magnitude scales', which distinguish five categories of famine based on excess mortality levels (Howe and Devereux, Chapter 2, this volume), Malawi 2001–2002 would rank as a 'minor famine' (less than 1,000 deaths) in terms of the lowest estimates but as a 'major famine' (10,000 to 99,000 deaths) if our survey estimates are correct.

In a survey in rural Zomba district, southern Malawi, Tiba (2005) enumerated 122 hunger-related deaths among a population of 19,752 people in forty-three villages. Scaling up this proportion (2.8 deaths per village) to the national rural population, total deaths would amount to 57,050, which falls within the range of the national Food Crisis Impact Survey. A clear indicator that this mortality was hunger-related is that 90 per cent of all reported deaths occurred in the hungry season months of January to March 2002, with over 50 per cent occurring in February, at the peak of the food crisis (Tiba 2005: 268). A comparison with annual mortality in these same villages during the previous five years reveals that nearly as many people died during the three peak famine months as the average annual death rate in previous years – so absolute mortality in the area increased by a factor of four. The age distribution of mortality reveals that, among adults, it was mainly those over fifty years old who died during the famine. This is consistent with demographic evidence from famines elsewhere, which reveal that 'young children ... and the elderly experience the greatest absolute increases in death rates' (Dyson and Ó Gráda 2002: 10). This also supports our contention (see below) that most mortality during the famine period cannot be attributed to HIV/AIDS, because the age group that was worst affected – the elderly – is a low-risk cohort for HIV infection.

In April 2002, WHO Malawi and the Ministry of Health conducted a rapid assessment of the health impacts of the humanitarian crisis. The team visited forty communities in ten of Malawi's twenty-seven districts and surveyed over 1,000 households. Elevated levels of malnutrition and mortality were found, 'with a crude mortality in some areas exceeding one per 10,000 people per day which means we are already facing a severe humanitarian crisis' (WHO 2002a: 1). The crude mortality rate (CMR) was calculated as 1.96/10,000 per day, and the under-five mortality rate (U5MR) was 3.9/10,000 per day (WHO 2002b). More than one in four communities reported cases of oedema during the previous six months. Maternal mortality rates in local health facilities had increased by 71 per cent, 'due to malnutrition and poor health status' (WHO 2002a: 1). Reported mortality in 1,076 households totalled 233 for the period October 2000 to March 2001, and 277 for October 2001 to March 2002, an increase of 18.9 per cent. Among children under-five, total deaths had increased by 79.2 per cent, from ninety-six to 172 (WHO 2002c). Assuming these additional deaths can be attributed to the famine conditions prevailing in 2002 (at 0.0087 famine deaths per household – remarkably close to the figure of 0.0092 from the Food Crisis Impact Survey), and extrapolating to the national level, total famine deaths in rural Malawi amounted to 80,360. Like the estimate derived from Tiba's survey, this falls within the range of the Food Crisis Impact Survey, but since WHO's ten districts were selected purposively rather than randomly – on the basis of being 'among the most affected' by the crisis – this should be regarded as an upper estimate. Some deaths also reflected synergies between hunger and disease. For example, WHO reported 609 deaths in a cholera epidemic in early 2002, with a case fatality rate three times above normal. 'This is a clear indication that people, weakened by the lack of food, more easily succumb to disease' (WHO 2002c: 1).[7]

Throughout rural Malawi, respondents to the Food Crisis Impact survey reported that the food crisis was associated with an increased incidence of hunger, disease and premature death. Two explanations were given. First, shortages of maize forced people to eat substitute foods, some of which were not fit for human consumption. (For instance, a wild tuber called *zikhawo* is poisonous unless soaked and boiled for several hours, and several people died because they did not prepare *zikhawo* thoroughly enough.) Second, many people lost weight due to hunger ('People started looking taller'), and this rise in malnutrition made them vulnerable to hunger-related diseases. In severely affected communities the famine was known as 'the swelling', because many individuals suffered from oedema of parts of their bodies – notably the legs, arms and face. They understood this as being caused by eating nothing but wild foods and fluids for lengthy periods. Adult men and women were equally affected by oedema, as were children and the elderly. Almost one-third (31 per cent) of 1,200 households interviewed had a household member who fell ill as a result of lack of food. Symptoms included stomach pains, wasting, fainting, anaemia and oedema.

Apart from malnutrition and diarrhoea, outbreaks of dysentery and cholera were reported. Several communities also mentioned that there were fewer births and a higher incidence of miscarriages during the food crisis, which they attributed to women being too undernourished to conceive or to nourish their foetus, respectively. These findings are consistent with empirical evidence on the demographic impacts of famine, which include fertility declines as well as mortality increases (Dyson and Ó Gráda 2002).

Below are extracts from the life histories of a Mulanje woman who was widowed by the famine, and a woman from Ntcheu whose mother suffered oedema and died in March 2002.

> Although food is a problem in my house most years, last year things got much worse. Many days we could go without eating any food. The entire family was eating vegetables. My husband then started suffering because we could not find food to eat. Due to failure to eat *nsima* [maize porridge, the staple diet] my husband's body started swelling. During the period his body was swollen he used to eat ripe mangoes whenever they were available. When the season for these fruits ended, there was nothing else to eat and he passed away.
>
> (A widow from Mulanje District)

> I lost my mother on 17 March 2002 due to hunger. Due to regular lack of food that my family used to experience it was difficult for my old mother to find anything to eat. She could also sleep without taking anything. This then resulted into swelling of her feet, face and even arms. She then did not take long after her body had swollen. She eventually died. My husband too started swelling and fortunately enough he survived. However, the unfortunate part was that he could not go out to assist in looking for food, since he was sick.
>
> (A woman from Ntcheu District)

Villagers distinguished clearly between HIV/AIDS-related deaths and hunger-related deaths. One focus group in Phalombe explained that 'a person who dies of starvation does so quite quickly, while a person with AIDS suffers for a long time and takes many months to die'. A focus group in Zomba added that someone who dies from AIDS first gets abnormally thin – a common nickname for AIDS in much of southern Africa is 'slim' – whereas 'if one dies of hunger they first suffer from *kutupa mapazi* [swelling]'. Oedema of the limbs clearly marks these symptoms as being hunger-related. This community also pointed out that a person suffering from starvation will recover quickly if given adequate food, whereas someone who has AIDS can eat a lot 'but the body doesn't show any response'. This is important because sceptics have argued that there were no famine deaths in Malawi in 2001–2002, only deaths from AIDS which people chose to misreport as hunger-related – either out of shame or denial about AIDS, or in an effort to secure food aid. On the other hand, there are negative synergies between HIV/AIDS and hunger – each raises vulnerability to the other – and many deaths that occurred during the crisis period were certainly due to a combination of both.

Social impacts

The famine had a range of negative social impacts in affected communities. Social ceremonies – harvest festivals, initiation rites, weddings and funerals – were cancelled or postponed. More generally, the crisis contributed to a rise in individualism and anti-social behaviour in rural Malawi, accelerating an erosion of communal values and reciprocal arrangements that may have been ongoing for several years (Devereux 1999). People stopped sharing with their neighbours, and resented others who had food: 'In those days you could not even go to visit your friends'. In Phalombe, it was said that anybody who had smoke coming from their house was hated because it was inconceivable that some people were cooking food while others were starving.

The famine was responsible for a nationwide increase in crime and physical insecurity. Over 70 per cent of community focus groups reported a rise in cases of theft during the crisis period. 'Due to the famine, some people resorted to stealing from other people's fields'. Assets were also stolen – everything from livestock to bicycles – and sold or exchanged for food. In rural Lilongwe district, respondents described stealing at that time as 'normal' behaviour: 'Everybody stole during the famine period. Anyone who says that they did not steal, would say so only because they were not caught'. People interviewed in Karonga readily admitted their personal involvement in theft: 'We were stealing bananas and livestock. We cooked the bananas and sold the livestock'. Thieves attacked women returning home from milling their maize, and men returning with food from Mozambique.

One consequence of the collapse of trust in neighbours and strangers was that people guarded their assets more carefully. Instead of storing grain in granaries, all harvested and purchased food was brought inside the house, both to protect it against theft and to conceal stocks from neighbours and relatives. Some people even brought their animals indoors, while others reduced their livestock holdings by selling them, to buy food and to minimize the risk of losing their animals to thieves. In southern Malawi, people reported sleeping outdoors or sitting up all night in their gardens, guarding their vegetables and fruit trees. Looting of these crops had never happened before, because fruits are considered inferior to maize, and fruit trees are often regarded as communal property. In one village in the Chikala Mountains, the hungriest households were said to have survived the food crisis thanks to several communal avocado trees located in the middle of the village. Conversely, violence was reported from other villages in the same district, where fruit trees were owned by individuals and access was restricted.

More disturbing than the rise in criminality was a corresponding rise in 'vigilante justice' within communities against people accused of stealing. Violent punishments were often meted out, even when those caught could legitimately claim that they were committing these acts out of desperation. In Dowa district, thieves were beaten, stripped naked and paraded through the village. More severe punishments were reported from Zomba and Machinga, where people caught taking crops from fields or selling stolen goods were attacked with *pangas* (machetes) or knives: 'The consequences of stealing were very disastrous, as people caught stealing were hacked and some of their body parts, especially their arms, were removed'.

Stress around the inability to acquire food caused domestic disputes and marital breakdowns. Several marriages broke up when men left to search for *ganyu* (casual work) and food, in Mozambique and elsewhere ('A lot of husbands ran away from their families, leaving the wife and children to fend for themselves. Some never came back'). In other cases, when husbands returned home they found that their wives had moved in with other men who could provide food for their children ('during the crisis women were not refusing any proposals for partnership from men, actually they were actively looking for men who could help them with a little food'). Intra-household conflicts were also associated with complaints – mostly by men – that the crisis had led to 'moral degeneration' in rural communities, with women who managed to find food being accused of exchanging sex for cash or food.

On the other hand, the famine period was also associated with a rise in early marriages. In Karonga, young men looked for wives on the local rice schemes, where food was available. Other early marriages happened at the initiative of parents, who encouraged their daughters to marry during this time, either to reduce the size of the household and the number of mouths to feed, or as a way of securing cash or food from their new son-in-law's family. On rare occasions, the phrase 'selling daughters for food' was used (Devereux *et al.* 2003).

Children were affected in many ways by the food crisis. One health centre in Zomba district found that malnutrition rates for children under five were ten times higher in February 2002 than a year before (Tiba 2005). Enrolment figures from a local primary school in January 2002 were 42 per cent down on the average for preceding years, with the sharpest fall experienced in the two lowest classes. Equally revealing are statistics on the number of graduate students who failed the national exam in November 2002. While during the previous five years 48–70 per cent of students finishing primary school had passed their final exam, in the 2002 academic year 93 per cent failed. The headmaster of the school attributed this to hunger-related absenteeism (Tiba 2005: 221): 'Pupils were not coming to school between January and March 2002 because of hunger. If a student does not attend school for three months, what could be the result of the exam?'

What made it happen?

Explanations for famine divide broadly into theories that explain the event (what caused the decline in food production, or the disruption in food access? Why was food aid not mobilized in time?) and theories that focus on contextual factors (what made the affected population vulnerable to these triggers?). This section focuses on four trigger factors: 'FAD' (the production shock and import failure of 2001); 'entitlement failure' (rapid food price rises and limited income-earning opportunities); 'humanitarian response failure' (lack of food aid); and the 'controlling institution' hypothesis (which explains interventions – or non-interventions – by people with the intention of creating food crisis conditions).

Food availability decline

Maize is the staple food in Malawi. It is produced by the majority of smallholder households, and accounts for over 90 per cent of total calorie consumption from cereals in an average year. The immediate trigger for the food crisis was a collapse in maize production in 2001, to a level 32 per cent below the harvest of 2000. At first glance, this appears to provide sufficient evidence for a FAD on a scale that could trigger a famine in the absence of alternative sources of food. However, during the 1990s the production of maize fluctuated considerably, and the food crisis year was preceded by two bumper harvests, with aggregate maize production well above the ten-year average. If the maize harvest in 2001 is compared with the five-year average the decline is 12 per cent, but compared to the ten-year average it is actually 6 per cent *higher* (Figure 7.1). Also, the 'maize gap' in 2002 was smaller than in 1992, 1994 and 1997, three years when production also fell sharply from the previous harvest, but no food crisis ensued.[8] It follows that the fall in maize production cannot on its own explain the food crisis of 2002.

Household survey data reveal the impact of the production decline on maize self-sufficiency. Respondents were asked to state the month in which they had depleted their maize stocks following the 2001 harvest (the year of the food crisis) as well as the season before the crisis (2000–2001) – a good harvest – and the season after (2002–2003) –

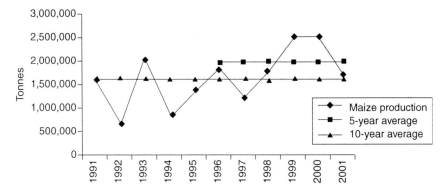

Figure 7.1 Maize production in Malawi, 1990–2001 (metric tonnes) (source: Tiba (2005: 91)).

another poor harvest, though less severe. The comparison between 2000–2001 and 2001–2002 is striking. Almost twice as many households harvested no maize in 2001 compared to 2000 (14 per cent *versus* 8 per cent), or less than three months' supply (23 per cent *versus* 11 per cent). By the start of the hungry season in January 2002, more than nine in ten households faced empty granaries compared to six in ten in 2001, and only thirty-two households out of 1,217 (2.6 per cent) were self-sufficient in maize, against a much higher 23 per cent in 2000–2001 (Figure 7.2). Taking maize production self-sufficiency – which most farmers strive to achieve – as an indicator of household food security, less than one rural Malawian in four is food secure, even in a good year like 2000–2001. The effect of the production failure in 2001–2002 was to lengthen the 'hungry season': many households that normally faced empty granaries for three to four months of the year had to find food from other sources for six to nine months, or even longer.

Maize self-sufficiency in Malawi is geographically distributed, following regional differences in population densities. The proportion of self-sufficient households in a good agricultural year (2000–2001) was highest in the northern region (52.5 per cent) and lowest in the southern region (17.6 per cent). In the famine year (2001–2002), these proportions collapsed to one household in ten in the northern region (10.5 per cent) and one household in a hundred in the southern region (0.9 per cent).

Maize production is not total food production. Starchy roots and tubers (cassava, Irish potatoes, sweet potatoes) make an important contribution to agricultural production and food consumption in Malawi. In the run-up to the 2001 harvest, the famine early warning system predicted the maize gap but confidently predicted a national food *surplus* overall: 'maize production dropped by 32 per cent ... in 2001. Nonetheless, Malawi will experience 437,775 tonnes food surplus this year due to high root crop

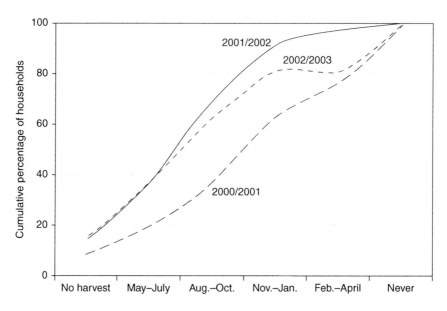

Figure 7.2 Depletion of maize stocks in rural Malawi, 2000–2001 to 2002–2003 (source: Devereux *et al.* (2003: 29 [*n*=1,217])).

production' (FEWS NET 2001: 1). It subsequently became clear that this was a massive over-estimate, and that root crops were not in fact able to bridge the maize gap. Cassava production had been exaggerated during the 1990s by anything between 2.5 and ten times. In the early 1990s starchy roots provided 4.4 per cent of total calorie production in Malawi, and the Integrated Household Survey (IHS 1998) found that roots and tubers provided only 5.4 per cent of average daily calorie intake in the late 1990s. According to the Ministry of Agriculture, however, roots and tubers contributed 18 per cent of national food production in 2001 (FAOSTAT 2001). Already in 1998, informed observers had pointed to an unex-plained difference 'in perception between farmers, doctors and nutrition-ists on the one hand who are concerned at declining per capita food availability and the MoA figures on the other which record a massive surplus of energy supplying foods, well beyond the consumption capacity of the population' (Carr 1998: 4).

The reasons for this systematic over-estimation have much to do with the politics of data and information management. The UDF Government that succeeded President Banda in 1994 pursued a policy of crop diversifi-cation away from white maize, which had distorted agricultural policy and dietary preferences for decades. USAID supported the Ministry of Agricul-ture in this objective, notably with a million-dollar cassava project (pro-moting production, multiplication and marketing) from the mid-1990s.

Demonstrating the success of this project required reporting rapid and sustained increases in cassava hectarage and yields, which the Ministry of Agriculture duly did, and FEWS NET duly repeated.[9]

Although these methodological problems with cassava production estimates were well known for many years before the 2001–2002 food crisis (cf. Carr 1998), the Ministry of Agriculture's refusal to adjust its estimates and the persistence of FEWS NET (another USAID-funded project) in reporting these figures without qualification or confidence intervals were largely responsible for the complacency regarding the national food availability situation in mid-2001. When food shortages and rising maize prices in rural markets suggested an evolving food crisis, FEWS NET (2002b: 3) attributed this to Malawians' 'rigid consumption preferences' for maize. In fact (as shown below), the evolution of cassava prices closely tracked the evolution of maze prices during the crisis period, indicating similar supply shortages for both food staples.

Official confirmation that food balance-sheet statistics in Malawi were subject to enormous over-estimation errors came immediately after the famine, when cassava production figures for the previous five years were retrospectively adjusted downwards to less than half their previous values – by applying a conversion factor of 0.437 – in an explicit (but unexplained) acknowledgement of the mistakes of previous years. Applying these adjustments to the famine year, FEWS NET's projected food surplus for Malawi of 271,000 tonnes becomes a *deficit* of –435,000 tonnes (Tiba 2005: 139).[10]

Total food availability during the famine is not only about food production in Malawi, it also includes international commodity movements during the period between the 2001 and 2002 harvests. Even in terms of this broader definition, there are reasons to question whether FAD was a significant causal factor of the crisis. During the 1997–1998 season, for instance, the amount of maize officially available in Malawi (production+commercial imports–exports) was 360,000 tonnes *less* (27 per cent) than during the crisis year (Tiba 2005: 88). Taking into account population growth over the period, and assuming that in 1997 the SGR was fully stocked (at 180,000 tonnes) and released onto the market, per capita maize availability was almost identical in the two years. One reason for the different outcomes was a massive market intervention by ADMARC (the Agricultural Development and Marketing Corporation), which sold 563,000 tonnes of maize (equivalent to 46 per cent of the maize harvest) during the 1997–1998 agricultural year. This maize was sourced from SGR carry-over stocks, official imports, and ADMARC purchases and resale of informal maize imports. Although informal cross-border trade is problematic to quantify, it is known to be significant (Whiteside 2003), with net maize imports from Mozambique and Tanzania estimated in the range of 60,000 to 200,000 tonnes per year (VAC 2003: 19; FAO/WFP 2004: 3). ADMARC's intervention was effective in maintaining adequate food supplies in Malawi through the 1997–1998 hungry season, and – importantly

– in keeping food prices affordable. During the 2001–2002 crisis, however, ADMARC's intervention in the market was limited and ineffective, which is indicative of fundamental changes in food-security institutions and policy over the period (as discussed below).

Exchange entitlement failure

As Sen's entitlement approach has demonstrated, food security crises are about losing access to food, and production is just one of several sources of access to food. When harvests fail and farmers switch from being largely self-sufficient food producers to being market-dependent consumers, they exert upward pressure on food prices that, if not offset by inflows of supplies from elsewhere, can quickly become unaffordable for the poor. In this sense poverty and famines are closely related, because it is the poorest who get priced out of the market first.[11] This is one key insight of the entitlement approach. In addition, as people rush to sell their assets (including labour) to buy food, they flood the market until asset prices and real wages collapse, compounding the terms of trade decline between assets and food. Sen (1981) labels this process 'exchange entitlement failure'.

Malawi's rural economy is remarkably undiversified, with few income-earning options other than casual labour (*ganyu*) on neighbouring farms or estates. During the 2001–2002 hungry season more people searched for *ganyu* than normal, but at the same time *ganyu* became more scarce and competitive ('If nine people went out looking for *ganyu*, seven would not succeed in finding it'). Even people who had often hired daily labour in previous years were in food deficit and were looking for employment themselves. When people did find *ganyu*, they complained of being paid much less for the same work than in other years. In Ntcheu, one pail of cassava was offered for ridging one acre of land; the year before, this task had earned three to four pails. Asked why they were willing to work for such low pay, focus group discussants replied that they had no choice: 'We just took the payment to have something to eat'.

A participatory methodology based on proportional piling was devised in the Food Crisis Impact Survey, to indicate trends in demand for and supply of *ganyu* in rural communities over the decade leading up to the crisis. The results from one focus group in Zomba are typical (Figure 7.3). This group asserted that more work was available than was needed during most of the 1990s – even in the drought years of 1992 and 1994 – but that the search for *ganyu* to bridge annual hunger gaps started increasing around 1996, until by 1999 people looking for *ganyu* exceeded its availability for the first time. This indicates that rural labour markets had been constricting for several years, with persistent excess supply of labour since the late 1990s, and locates the origins of the livelihood crisis in rural Malawi in the mid-1990s.

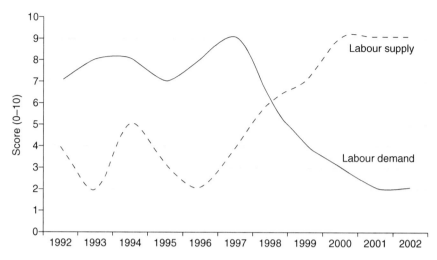

Figure 7.3 Supply and demand for 'ganyu' labour, 1992–2002, rural Zomba (source: Devereux *et al.* (2003: 64)).

Following the poor harvest of 2001, shortages of maize in farmers' granaries and village markets resulted in sharp price rises, exacerbating problems of accessing food. According to the Ministry of Agriculture's 'Market Information System', retail maize prices increased by 500 per cent or more in many markets across the country, starting at around 6 Malawi Kwacha per kg (MK6/kg) in April–May 2001 and peaking at over MK30/kg in January–February 2002 (Figure 7.4). Important to note is that cassava prices tracked maize prices closely during the crisis period, contradicting FEWS NET's argument that cassava was available but Malawians were choosing not to consume it because of their 'inflexible' preference for white maize. In Zomba district, people reported queuing overnight at village markets and outside grinding mills, hoping to purchase maize, cassava, or even maize bran (*madeya*) and 'sawdust' from the grinding mill floor, before supplies sold out in the morning. Fights often broke out as people accused others of queue-jumping, and the police were sometimes called to restore order. Even *madeya*, which was prepared and consumed as an alternative to *nsima* made from maize flour, proved to be beyond the reach of some households: in some markets in Mulanje district, *madeya* sold at MK35/kg in early 2002 – double the official price of maize.

Before agricultural liberalization, until the mid-1990s, ADMARC had a range of maize price-stabilization mechanisms at its disposal, including pan-territorial and pan-seasonal pricing, counter-seasonal market interventions (purchasing maize after the harvest for resale in 'social markets' during the hungry season) and price banding (floor prices for producers, ceiling prices for consumers) (Devereux 1997). By 2001, these mechanisms had been

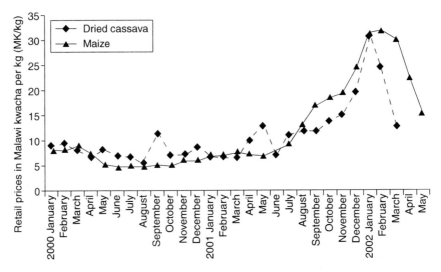

Figure 7.4 Average prices of maize and dried cassava across 27 districts in Malawi, 2000–2 (source: Tiba (2005: 92)).

abolished or undermined to the point of ineffectiveness. Market prices for maize throughout Malawi were substantially higher than the official ADMARC price of MK17/kg, confirming that the government's attempts to contain price rises by imposing a ceiling price on maize traded through its parastatal had little effect on the market. This was mainly because supplies of maize through ADMARC were severely constrained, but also because traders purchased ADMARC maize and resold it at much higher prices. According to John Seaman, an expert witness who gave oral evidence to the UK inquiry into 'The humanitarian crisis in Southern Africa', this unprecedented rise in maize prices was the main trigger factor: 'if you had stabilized the price of maize in 2001 in Malawi no crisis would have occurred' (International Development Committee 2003: EV67).

During the peak of the hunger in late 2001 and early 2002, various household assets were sold for cash or bartered for maize or cassava. These included livestock, farm tools, furniture, kitchen utensils, means of transport (e.g. bicycles), consumer goods (radios, cassette players) and clothing (trousers, shirts, women's clothes). Some households even removed and sold their doors and window-frames, while others exchanged puppies for a basket of cassava.

Survey respondents who sold or exchanged assets for food were asked about the selling price – in cash or cash equivalent – and for how much they could have sold these assets in the year before the famine. The responses were used to estimate the loss in asset value that households incurred by liquidating their assets during the crisis period. The average value loss across all assets sold was 53 per cent. Prices simply collapsed as supply exceeded demand. In Zomba district, a bicycle was bartered for a single bag of dried cassava (*makaka*). One man in rural Lilongwe sold a bicycle for MK150, knowing it would cost him MK800 to replace it. Households that owned no valuable assets like radios or bicycles were forced to sell basic household items like pots and plates, or tables and chairs – even blankets. A woman in Dowa District sold a blanket she had bought in Lilongwe at MK450, for MK80. Another woman from Dowa exchanged a *chitenge* (a wrap-around cloth) for a small plate of maize flour.

Livestock ownership is lower in Malawi than in most African countries. Nonetheless, by October 2001 people with livestock had started selling them to buy food, but the terms of trade fell rapidly: while maize prices were rising due to excess demand, livestock prices started collapsing due to excess supply. People in Chikwawa district reported that by December a cow was selling for as little as MK2,000, when under normal conditions the minimum price would have been MK6,000. In Mchinji district, goats which would have sold for MK600–1,000 in November fetched MK150–500 in February 2002. Across all 577 households in the Food Crisis Impact Survey that sold livestock during the food crisis, the average value loss on livestock sales was 57 per cent. Because the fall in livestock prices coincided with maize being scarce and expensive, those who bartered livestock for maize faced rapidly deteriorating terms of trade, which magnified the value losses. While the cash value of livestock halved, on average, the barter value collapsed to a quarter or less of pre-famine exchange rates. Hens that normally cost MK150 were exchanged for two plates of unrefined maize worth MK20–30. Elsewhere, goats were traded for a pail of maize, and in some village markets the exchange value of one head of cattle fell to two to three bags of maize.

Humanitarian response failure

A further puzzle in the Malawi famine is why the GoM and the donor community failed to mobilize and distribute free or subsidized food aid, to compensate for production and market failures. One explanation might be related to information failures. Certainly the donors defended their failure to react to signals of an impending food crisis by claiming to have been misled about cassava production forecasts, and deceived about mismanagement of the SGR. If the cassava estimates had been accurate, and if the SGR had not been ransacked, the national food gap would have been much less – indeed, as noted above, FEWS NET predicted a food surplus despite the poor maize harvest. However, this is inadequate justification for inaction. As we have seen, the false optimism regarding cassava production had been exposed several years before the food crisis, and the donors in Lilongwe strongly suspected that the SGR had already been sold by late 2001. The donors were also highly selective about which information they chose to accept or reject. In general, official data were accepted, no matter how flawed, while unofficial data were dismissed, despite often being more persuasive and accurate.

As early as August 2001, NGOs working in rural communities reported abnormal maize price rises and warned of rapidly declining food security, but the credibility of this information was questioned and the signals were ignored. In October, Save the Children (UK) published a report that revealed alarming indicators of food stress in Mchinji district: maize prices had risen by 340 per cent since January and 40 per cent of households were already out of food (Sawdon 2001). In November, Save the Children made a public presentation in Lilongwe, calling for immediate intervention. Still, the government and donors remained sceptical, arguing that according to official statistics there was no food availability problem. Around this time, the Malawi Economic Justice Network (MEJN) – an umbrella grouping of forty-five civil society organizations concerned with 'economic governance' – was mobilizing activist groups, lobbying the media and pressurizing the government to declare a famine. Religious groups affiliated to MEJN – such as the Catholic Commission for Justice and Peace – collected statistics on starvation deaths and presented these to the government and the local and international press. In December 2001 and February 2002, Save the Children commissioned two nutrition surveys, which found an alarming deterioration in global malnutrition rates for Salima district, from 9.3 per cent to 19.0 per cent (Taifour 2002). This provided the first 'hard evidence' that donors found credible, and it finally provoked a response. President Muluzi, having at first denied the crisis, declared a State of Disaster – though not a 'famine' – on 27 February 2002. In March, while farmers were starting to harvest green maize, the government set up a Task Force on the Food Shortage Situation, and the World Food Programme launched an Emergency Operation ('EMOP') to provide food aid to 300,000 Malawians (International Development Committee 2003: 97).

When donors are as active and interventionist in domestic policies as they are in Malawi, they have to accept some responsibility for catastrophic policy failures. Instead of sharing the blame, however, the donor community in Malawi distanced itself from the policy decisions that precipitated the food crisis, preferring to blame the GoM entirely. A case in point is the controversy surrounding the sale of the SGR. The SGR had been stocked to full capacity (180,000 tonnes) since 1999. The IMF, World Bank and European Commission were increasingly concerned that this level was fiscally unsustainable – especially since they had insisted that the SGR be run on a cost-recovery basis. By early 2001 the SGR maize was almost two years old and needed replenishment, while the National Food Reserve Agency (NFRA), which had taken a commercial loan to purchase this maize in 1999, remained heavily in debt. The IMF therefore advised the GoM to export SGR maize (rather than dump it on local markets, which would depress prices and undermine producer and trader incentives) and replenish it to a much lower 'cost-effective' level (30,000–60,000 tonnes) to release funds to repay the NFRA loan. In an interview with one of the authors in May 2002, the IMF conceded that with hindsight this advice proved to be wrong, but insisted that: 'this was the correct decision based on information available at the time. An average harvest was forecast, the maize stock was old, and someone was willing to buy it. The advice would have been correct if the information was correct' (Devereux 2002: 10).

Whatever the merits of the IMF advice (including its earlier insistence that the operations of the national grain reserve be commercialized), it is clear that the sale of the SGR maize was corruptly handled in that senior civil servants and politicians (including Cabinet Ministers) purchased this maize cheaply and later resold it at scarcity prices, making sizeable personal profits. There is no doubt that this issue delayed the donors' humanitarian response. 'Concerns about the sale of the SGR 'clouded' discussions between the Government of Malawi and DFID about how to respond to the emerging food crisis' (International Development Committee 2003: 21). When it emerged that the grain reserve was empty and rumours circulated in Lilongwe that political elites had profiteered from its sale, several donors demanded an explanation before they would agree to mobilize food aid. DFID argued that if the maize had been sold to Malawians who were hoarding it to make speculative profits, then the food crisis was artificial and this maize should be released onto local markets. On the other hand, USAID claimed that the export of SGR grain left them with their hands tied: 'If a government exports food, the US has prohibitions on bringing in emergency food in the same year' (Devereux 2002: 15). The consequence of this sequence of events was that the humanitarian response to the food crisis was fatally delayed.

The 'controlling institution' hypothesis

The maize trade in Malawi has been centrally controlled and heavily regulated since before independence in 1964. Under the dictatorship of Dr Hastings Banda, power and information were concentrated in the hands of the President and his narrow circle of political affiliates. The dominance of the parastatal ADMARC in maize marketing was overwhelming. During the 1980s and 1990s, state intervention in agriculture was gradually reduced, and a major step towards full liberalization of the maize market was the abandonment of the maize price band in 2000 (Chirwa and Zakeyo 2002: 23). Political and economic power have been transferred, through liberalization and privatization policies, from the previous regime to a different set of agents. However, no in-depth analysis has yet been carried out into the functioning of private maize-trading companies.

It remains unknown how market-dominant maize traders or companies interlink with political circles which influence not just private maize marketing in the country but also the operation of state-led food security institutions. The different set of interests that now control and regulate the maize market in Malawi can be termed a 'controlling institution', which stands between maize availability in the *country* and maize availability on the *market*, and has the political and economic power to influence the national maize market.

The 'controlling institution' hypothesis puts forward the argument that certain forces were present during the food crisis which may have: (1) prevented or deliberately delayed imports of maize before and during the crisis; (2) used contentious data and manipulated information to justify inaction in order to avoid intervention in the market; and (3) intentionally denied the existence of a crisis – finally declaring a State of Disaster on 27 February 2002 when the famine was almost over – despite ample evidence that a food crisis was happening. If these forces were present, it is reasonable to assume that they were driven by a combination of political and economic interests, strongly related to purchases, sales and prices of maize. This hypothesis challenges commonly accepted claims that 'a key lesson from Malawi seems to be of *ignorance* – those who advised and took decisions were *unaware* of the true state of affairs and, consequently, took wrong decisions' (Stevens *et al.* 2003: 12; emphasis added).

Most of the evidence for the controlling institution hypothesis is circumstantial. Perhaps the strongest evidence relates to the fact that those who purchased maize from the SGR during 2000–2001 managed to acquire this commodity at an average price of MK3–4 kg (GoM 2002: 9) – and some individuals acquired this maize without paying for it at all – but within a year maize was retailing in some local markets at ten times this price. Assuming that those who purchased or stole the Grain Reserve did so for speculative purposes, it follows that they had a vested interest in driving up maize prices and creating an artificial shortage on the market – in other words, making this a *planned* famine.[12]

This scenario makes it easier to explain the various institutional 'failures' that occurred during the famine. As the SGR was emptied by August 2001, the controlling institution, now in possession of this maize, made every effort to delay humanitarian intervention and block food imports into Malawi. The Ministry of Agriculture produced cassava production figures that were known to be grossly exaggerated, other decision-makers chose to accept the erroneous indicators of a national food surplus, as published in the food balance sheet and early warning reports, and all available (and more reliable) information about increasing maize and cassava prices and rising food insecurity in rural areas was deliberately ignored. The government subsequently ordered maize imports of less than half the official maize gap (and substantially lower than maize imports during 1998).

Another controversial decision by the government is inexplicable except in terms of the controlling institution hypothesis. According to Whiteside (2003: 53), early in 2002 the Malawian authorities stationed a phyto-sanitary inspector at the Mozambican border, which disrupted and delayed maize imports from Mozambique into southern Malawi at the height of the famine, causing large quantities of maize to be rejected and provoking a riot during which one trader was killed. Under competitive market conditions, private traders should respond promptly to incentives and price signals. The historically high maize and cassava prices recorded in Malawian markets during the early months of 2002 suggest either catastrophic market failure, or institutional interventions that restricted the free movement of food from surplus to deficit markets. Posting an inspector on a major trade route, with instructions to enforce unrealistic and inappropriate phyto-sanitary standards on food imports, is one such interference, and provides strong evidence that a 'controlling institution' within government was deliberately blocking informal maize imports into the country at a time of dire need.

A related case in point was imports into northern Malawi from Tanzania. Despite wide maize price differentials in late 2001 and early 2002, cross-border trade from Tanzania was a trickle (2,000 to 3,000 tonnes per month) that made little impact either on Malawi's maize gap or on prices in Malawian markets. Imports actually increased by five to seven times in late 2002 – *after* the crisis was over, when cross-border price differences were much narrower. According to Whiteside (2003: 34), 'this is probably due to the institutional orders from NFRA and WFP eventually coming through'. The question of why orders by major institutional actors like the NFRA and the WFP were not placed during the crisis period itself remains an unexplained paradox. There are also unconfirmed reports that a Malawi Cabinet member sent instructions to customs officials in early 2002, to stop trucks carrying food from crossing the border from Tanzania into Malawi.

If true, this evidence of political interference in the maize market suggests that the political economy of maize marketing in Malawi played a decisive role in generating and sustaining the food crisis of 2001–2002. The competitive sector (maize wholesalers and retailers) in Malawi is supplemented by a set of dominant agents which make strategic decisions about large-scale commercial maize imports. If some of these institutions and individuals collaborate and act in a harmonized manner, their decisions will significantly influence maize availability in the country and on the market. Furthermore, if strategic decisions are made by the same people as those who decide about government imports, food-security interventions, ADMARC prices, market interventions or administrative regulations, then the profit-making private food trade business overlaps with the loss-making food-security business, and the vulnerability of those whose food security is undermined (rather than enhanced) by artificial scarcity and high food prices is greatly elevated.

Different commentators on the food crisis nominated different people or institutions who may have been behind the key decisions. Rubey (2002: 2) notes: 'There are legitimate questions as to how maize was sold from the strategic grain reserve (SGR) and who benefited from these sales. There are also questions about the final destination of the sales proceeds that, if true, may indicate embezzlement of government revenues'. Devereux (2002: 11) concludes that rising prices 'enabled many wealthy and influential people who had bought maize from the SGR earlier in the year to sell it back to ADMARC at the higher price, earning large profits. These well-connected people knew about the coming price hike, so they bought grain from the SGR and withdrew these stocks from the market driving prices up and creating an artificial shortage'. Carr (2003: 2) notes about the sale of the SGR: 'the whole stock was transferred into the hands of powerful families who controlled supply to the market so as to drive up the price of maize'. Owusu and Ng'ambi (2002: 11) prefer to blame grain traders: 'Private grain traders have followed the market signals all too well – they have hoarded supplies and made money out of food shortages'. The GoM also accused traders of profiteering from hunger, and banned traders from purchasing maize from ADMARC in December 2001. But this measure, like other token actions such as limiting the amount of ADMARC maize that individuals could purchase, was ineffectual – such actions were easily circumvented, and the amount of maize sold through ADMARC was insignificant. Recent reports have suggested that the senior management of ADMARC was itself heavily involved in corruption and mismanagement of government resources (GoM 2004).

Further research is needed into the precise relationships between 'wealthy and influential' people and 'powerful families' in Malawi on the one hand, and the institutions of political and economic power on the other. Certainly, the existence of an interlinking set of interests between politicians, civil servants and private traders would explain many of the puzzles and paradoxes described above: why there was no official declaration of a food crisis until too late; why all available and timely information about the impending crisis was ignored; why food balance-sheet estimates that erroneously projected a food surplus were used to justify inaction; why official maize imports were not ordered and unofficial maize imports were deliberately blocked; and why the government and the donor community – who at best are embarrassed by being duped about the cassava figures and the SGR corruption – continue to deny that a famine occurred in Malawi in 2001–2002.

What made it possible?

FAD, entitlement failure, humanitarian response failure and 'controlling institutions' can explain *how* famines happen, but not *why* famines happen. A comprehensive understanding of the Malawi famine requires examining a wide range of underlying structural vulnerabilities. Three sources of vulnerability in Malawi are reviewed here – demographic (HIV/AIDS), economic (failures of liberalization) and political (failures of the democratic transition).

HIV/AIDS and 'new variant famine'

HIV-prevalence in Malawi is estimated at over 20 per cent of the national population, one of the highest in Africa (National AIDS Commission 2001). By 1999, AIDS had reduced life expectancy at birth from fifty-one to thirty-seven years – one of the lowest in the world (Haacker 2002: 4). In 2001 alone, there were an estimated 80,000 AIDS-related deaths (UNAIDS 2002) – higher than five of the seven mortality estimates for the 2001–2002 famine reported above. In cumulative terms it is estimated that 550,000 Malawians have died of AIDS, dwarfing the highest estimate for famine-related mortality of 85,000. Within Malawi, HIV-prevalence is highest in the southern region, where the 2001–2002 famine was also concentrated. The negative synergies between HIV/AIDS and food security are not only biological, but also operate at the level of livelihood sustainability. Livelihood impacts of HIV/AIDS include loss of labour, reduced agricultural productivity and depletion of household assets. Since women bear the heaviest burden of caring for the sick and play a pivotal role in agriculture, AIDS has significantly undermined food production and household food security in Malawi (CARE 2002).[13]

Alex de Waal has conceptualized the adverse impacts of HIV/AIDS on food security and national economies, first in a scenario labelled 'AIDS-Related National Crises' (ARNC) (de Waal 2002), and second in a hypothesis known as 'New Variant Famine' (de Waal, Chapter 5, this volume). An ARNC is likely to evolve 'slowly and insidiously', through steadily eroding state capacity, and to be 'relatively unnoticed' until an economic crisis exposes its effects. 'In a food insecure country, an ARNC may be first manifest in a famine partly brought about by government mismanagement and market crisis' (de Waal 2002: 122–3). Although de Waal highlights the contributory role of AIDS in undermining economies and governance in Africa, he emphasizes that 'the NVF hypothesis is *not* a claim that HIV/AIDS was the sole, or even the prime, cause of the 2002 food crisis in southern Africa'. Instead, the NVF hypothesis asserts that HIV/AIDS creates 'new categories of poor and vulnerable people', and that this 'AIDS poverty' and 'AIDS vulnerability' undermines the ability to cope with 'an additional shock such as a drought: the trajectory of destitution when a famine occurs is sharper, and recovery is slower' (de Waal, Chapter 5, this volume). For this reason, and despite the methodological difficulties of quantifying the impacts of HIV/AIDS on household and national food security, elements of both ARNC and NVF must be invoked as partly explaining the heightened vulnerability of affected Malawians to the food crisis of 2001–2002. Certainly, one crucial difference between the 'non-famine' in Malawi in the early 1990s (Eldridge 2002) and the famine of 2001–2002 – which followed a production shock of comparable magnitude – is the rapid rise in HIV-prevalence during the 1990s.

Failures of economic liberalization

Many observers have linked the 2001–2002 food crisis in southern Africa to problematic processes of agricultural liberalization, as implemented in Malawi and other countries in the region during the 1980s and 1990s (Devereux 2002; Owusu and Ng'ambi 2002; Dorward and Kydd 2004). The key assertion is that liberalization raised vulnerability and food insecurity, mainly by undermining smallholder access to input and output markets, culminating in the inability of many smallholders to survive a relatively minor production shock and subsequent commodity market failures in 2001–2002. An important nuance of this argument over conventional 'market failure' analyses of famine – which correctly identify these market failures as a *proximate* cause of disrupted access to food (see the discussion of 'exchange entitlement failure' above) – is that the *underlying* cause of input, output and commodity market failures is understood as 'liberalization failure', i.e. a flawed policy process.

Agricultural liberalization was promoted as a central component of 'Washington consensus' policy prescriptions, which emerged in the early 1980s as a reaction against the perceived failure, in Africa and elsewhere, of state interventionism in agriculture and other economic sectors. After independence, many African governments established monopolistic marketing parastatals that dominated the provision of inputs and marketing of outputs for smallholder farmers, as well as setting prices and regulating food supplies through strategic management of grain reserves. These policies were intended to achieve national and household food security,[14] and to compensate for weak infrastructure and lack of incentives for private sector investment in agricultural production and marketing. However, parastatals like ADMARC in Malawi were susceptible to mismanagement, corruption, political interference and operational inefficiencies that undermined their performance and often exacerbated rather than solved the problems that smallholders faced. 'Washington consensus' thinking, which was vigorously promoted by the World Bank and IMF through their policy advice and loan conditionalities, was based on neo-classical economic arguments that market forces could achieve positive outcomes, without the costs and distortions associated with government subsidies and parastatal institutions.

By the late 1990s it was apparent that liberalization policies had not produced the expected boost to agricultural production and trade across sub-Saharan Africa. In Malawi and many other countries, agriculture was stagnating and rural poverty was static or rising. Explanations for the failure of agricultural liberalization in Africa have taken three broad positions: (1) partial liberalization; (2) weak institutions; and (3) coordination failures (Kydd and Dorward 2003). The first two positions are supportive of the liberalization agenda, but argue that liberalization was not properly and fully implemented, due to lack of political commitment or capacity by governments that had structural adjustment policies imposed on them (Jayne *et al.* 2002). As discussed below, 'neo-patrimonial' theorists have argued that many African governments are more preoccupied with 'preserving political power and protecting rent-seeking opportunities' (van de Walle 2001: 13) than with achieving economic growth and poverty reduction, and this logic makes them understandably hostile to liberalization, which requires ceding control over public institutions and resources that are important sources of power and rents. In Malawi, pressures to commercialize ADMARC were vigorously resisted, and the Fertilizer Subsidy Removal Programme (FSRP) took eight years to complete (1988–1995) – not least because fertilizer subsidies were used by the Banda regime as a source of political patronage. Similarly, one reason for the victory of the UDF party over Banda's MCP in the 1994 elections was that the UDF pledged to write off farmers' debts to the Smallholder Agricultural Credit Association (SACA).

The third position is sceptical about the potential for agricultural liberalization to deliver poverty reduction and food security in economies characterized by market failures, high transaction costs and coordination risks, and believes that 'Washington consensus' policy prescriptions are misguided. Kydd and Dorward (2003) point out that successful agricultural transformations in Asia were preceded by heavy government intervention to reduce transaction costs (e.g. by investing in physical infrastructure like roads) and to compensate for market and coordination failures (by subsidizing agricultural inputs, stabilizing food prices and setting up parastatal marketing agencies). In Africa, the enforced withdrawal of the state from agriculture under structural adjustment conditionality often occurred before investments in infrastructure had reduced transaction costs sufficiently to attract traders. The result was that when the state – with all its inefficiencies and shortcomings – finally withdrew, it left a vacuum. Complementary institutions and infrastructure were either absent or too weak to support the emergence of private actors and competitive markets in the agriculture sector. In Malawi, as elsewhere, smallholder farmers simply lost their access to vital input and output markets and became exposed to the same market failures that had motivated state interventionism in the first place (Peters 1996).

Many agriculture sector reforms impacted negatively – and unambiguously – on household food security. For example, to reduce its 'losses', ADMARC was forced to close 15 per cent of its low-volume markets in the late 1980s. Most of these were located 'in remote areas, inaccessible to private traders' (Chilowa 1998: 562). Addressing the question, 'who are the losers and winners from agricultural marketing liberalization in Malawi?', Chilowa (1998: 563) concludes that the losers were 'smallholder farmers in the category of net food buyers, low-income or wage earners in urban and semi-urban areas and smallholder farmers in remote areas'. These groups (especially smallholders who are net food buyers and/or live in 'remote areas') were also worst affected by the 2001–2002 famine.

In 1997, reflecting on the failures of economic liberalization in Malawian agriculture, one of these authors wrote about 'the deepening livelihood crisis facing Malawi's smallholders' and predicted 'the inevitable day when Malawi ... becomes permanently dependent on massive inflows of aid to bridge chronic food production deficits' (Devereux 1997: v). The analysis centred on the erosion of institutions and policies that were implemented by the Banda regime with a specific mandate to protect household food security, but were 'reformed' or abolished under structural adjustment programmes that gave no consideration to how these essential functions would be maintained, or were based on naïve assumptions about the latent entrepreneurial spirit that would be released once the 'dead hand' of the state was lifted from the market (cf. USAID's 'market-oriented approach to food security in Malawi' (Brown *et al.* 1996)).

Van de Walle (2001) argues that African governments are adept at managing donor expectations to minimize the reforms they actually implement, while ensuring continual access to international financial assistance. But it is important not to lose sight of the culpability of donors in supporting bad governance and promoting bad policies in Africa. Thus Malawi's political transformation in the mid-1990s coincided with the near-completion of the 'Washington consensus' project, which could be interpreted as an attack on the viability of smallholder livelihoods. Although their interests were defended to some extent by the Banda regime, the UDF Government effectively ignored the needs of smallholders, whose political marginalization was mirrored in a rapid deterioration of their food security status. The period between 1991–1992, when a major drought did not result in famine, and 2001–2002, when erratic weather resulted in a famine that should have been averted, was a protracted period of rising livelihood vulnerability that was not addressed because there was insufficient political will from the government to intervene, and because donor-driven agricultural policies were undermining the state's capacity to protect household food security in rural areas.

A final point to make in this regard concerns the political economy of liberalization. Most analysts of agricultural liberalization have focused on its direct economic consequences – the impacts of fertilizer subsidy removal on maize production, or of parastatal commercialization on maize price volatility. However, another important dimension has been largely neglected in the literature to date, namely, the impacts of radical institutional and policy reforms on the configuration of private and political interests involved in the food security 'business'. While it is often asserted that food security is loss-making in financial terms (hence the pressure on poor-country governments to desist from 'subsidizing' it), it is equally well known that food *insecurity* can be highly profitable for those well placed to take advantage of the basic human need for food. (The 'controlling institution' hypothesis builds on this insight, that powerful but largely unaccountable politicians and traders have incentives and opportunities to manipulate institutions and markets, to create conditions of food insecurity which they can then exploit for personal gain.) To our knowledge, no detailed political economy analysis has been carried out on the transformation of interests in Malawi's maize sector that accompanied agricultural liberalization – specifically around the ongoing restructuring of input and output marketing – yet the failure (or cynical manipulation) of both parastatal and commercial maize markets played a pivotal role in turning the 2001 production decline into the 2002 famine.

Failures of the democratic transition

The Malawi famine was a failure of political liberalization as much as it was a failure of economic liberalization. In May 1994, Malawi's first multi-party elections since independence saw Dr Bakili Maluzi's southern-based United Democratic Front (UDF) winning a decisive victory over Dr Banda's Malawi Congress Party (MCP), while the Alliance for Democracy (AFORD), with its power base in the least populated northern region, came third.[15] When the UDF Government took power, according to 'Sen's law' – 'no substantial famine has ever occurred in a democratic country – no matter how poor' (Sen 1999: 51) – democracy should have protected Malawians against famine threats. However, no 'anti-famine political contract' (de Waal 1997) was 'signed' between the elected government and its citizens. Instead vulnerability intensified, culminating in a food crisis in 2002 that, as we have seen, caused thousands of premature deaths. Why?

Part of the explanation lies in the flawed nature of the democratic transition in Malawi. President Banda may have been a repressive dictator, but he was canny enough to behave like a 'benevolent dictator' in certain key respects. He pacified the rural poor by subsidizing food production and marketing, and he pacified urban elites by subsidizing food consumption. Because these objectives – incentivizing farmers to produce more food while simultaneously controlling food prices for consumers – were fiscally incompatible (Chilowa 1998), this strategy eventually became unsustainable; however while it lasted it brought political stability and a gloss of successful economic management to Malawi. Ironically, it was only after a democratically elected government took power that famine became politically feasible. The 1994 elections launched Malawi into an era of interest-group politics, where the interests of the powerful and well-connected are effectively represented while the interests of the poor and powerless are neglected or marginalized.

This process has been theorized in a growing literature on the 'neo-patrimonial state' in Africa (Chabal and Daloz 1999; van de Walle 2001; Ayittey 2005). Although Malawi is hardly an extreme case, several symptoms of neo-patrimonialism can be identified in Malawi, including:

- weak or ineffective mechanisms of accountability between the state and its citizens
- government hostility towards civil society and other non-state actors that strive to hold the government to account
- direct or indirect control of large sections of the press and other media
- persistent allegations of corruption involving high-level government members, and reluctance to act decisively against these allegations
- attempts to consolidate and concentrate power in the hands of the incumbent elite, for instance by amending the constitution to allow the President to rule for multiple terms.

As is typical of many recent democratization processes in Africa, one effect of the transition from one-party dictatorship to multi-party democracy in Malawi was to reduce politics to a competition among interest groups for preferential access to public resources. Although Dr Banda presented himself as a 'father of the nation' figure, whereas Dr Muluzi's UDF represented the interests of an urban-based business elite, there was more continuity than change between the two political regimes. The rhetoric of 'uniting the nation' may have been superseded by the rhetoric of 'democratization' and 'poverty reduction', but both the unelected and elected leaders pursued policies that served their respective interest groups. According to Nugent (2004: 407): 'it did not take too long before some of the worst practices of the ousted regime began to repeat themselves ... Government Ministers were not slow in cashing in on the privileges of office and in cornering scarce resources for themselves.'[16]

Despite campaigning during the 1994 election on a platform of improved public services, universal free primary education, and transparent and efficient government, the UDF and opposition parties like AFORD have been described as equally driven by a 'hunger for raw power ... Malawi's opposition movements are basically opportunistic movements and have not put in place any serious agenda for genuine democratization' (Ihonvbere 1997: 239). According to Chinsinga (2003: 19), 'all the major parties have invariably degenerated into platforms for select selfish individuals. Their institutional frameworks have become highly manipulable in order to gratify personal aggrandizement. The parties have thus turned into instruments of patronage targeting particular constituents ... for their help to maintain themselves in power.'

The UDF's power base and natural constituency is in southern Malawi (where Muluzi won 91 per cent of the 1994 vote in his home district of Machinga), and the UDF government has attempted to skew allocations of government and donor resources (food aid, fertilizer and seed 'starter packs') to the south. Nonetheless, when the opportunity arose to profiteer from selling the SGR, the government showed little hesitation in prioritizing its collective and individual self-interest above the food security needs of its vulnerable constituents. This was politically possible because of a lack of real democratic accountability. Malawian voters, especially in rural areas dominated by a single party, are ineffectively represented by their Members of Parliament. The Food Crisis Impact Survey found that local MPs were generally unresponsive to reports of food insecurity in their constituencies in 2001–2002. Several respondents stated that: 'We do not know our Member of Parliament'. Their MPs live in the urban centres of Lilongwe or Blantyre, and rarely visit except during elections, to encourage people to vote for them. Some MPs even exploited the food crisis as a campaigning opportunity – they held political rallies and distributed maize to those who attended. In another village, local people who tried to protest about the famine to their MP were chased away at gunpoint by policemen hired by the MP (Devereux *et al.* 2003).

Van de Walle (2001: 20) attributes the high degree of autonomy that most African states enjoy to 'the weakness of organized pressure groups that would hold the state more accountable'. Civil society in Malawi remains weak, though the role of groups like the Civil Society Agriculture Network (CISANET), Malawi Economic Justice Network (MEJN) and the Catholic Commission for Justice and Peace in mobilizing international awareness of the food crisis in 2001–2002 has raised their profile and influence. As for the media, the press in Malawi has always been under state control, either directly (through legislation) under Dr Banda or indirectly (through ownership). Most newspaper reporting is either politically biased or passive rather than campaigning in nature. 'The vast majority of the newspapers today are party- or politician-owned (mostly UDF affiliated) ... None has used the press to run concerted campaigns around food-related issues, e.g. the sale of the grain reserve, the closure of Admarc depots ...' (Cammack *et al.* 2003: 9–11).

Failures of accountability 'from below' (citizens and civil society) were mirrored by failures of accountability 'from above' (donors and international financial institutions). In the late 1990s, a series of corruption scandals soured relations between the GoM and the international community. In July 2000, the parliamentary Public Accounts Committee published a highly critical report on corruption and fraud within the government. Donors also complained about economic mismanagement and 'bad governance'. In October 2000, the British High Commissioner publicly rebuked the GoM and threatened to withdraw aid unless corruption was tackled.[17] In November 2001 several major donors, including the

UK (DFID), European Union and the US (USAID), did in fact suspend their development assistance to Malawi, alleging corruption involving donor funds, economic mismanagement and political violence by government supporters against its opponents. The IMF withheld balance of payments support, while Denmark closed its development programmes and withdrew from Malawi entirely. This deterioration of relations came at the worst possible time, as the food crisis was gaining momentum in rural communities, and undoubtedly contributed to the slow humanitarian response.

Although the donors did eventually make substantial pledges of emergency assistance, most food aid arrived only after the crisis was over, and in subsequent years the donors over-compensated for their failure to intervene in 2001–2002 (Tiba 2005). Relations did not improve for some time, not least because the government and donors indulged in mutual recriminations about who was to blame for the food crisis. In May 2002, the IMF delayed disbursement of US$47 million in loans, because the GoM had overspent its budget by US$45 million:

> Lack of good governance has resulted in a misallocation of resources, increased the cost of doing business, created a general distrust in public sector activities, and weakened civil service morale. There is a need to recognize that corruption and weak governance in tandem with bad policies make financial aid ineffective, even counterproductive.
>
> (IMF 2002b)

The IMF also took the opportunity to blame government policies for creating famine conditions in Malawi earlier in the year: 'Government interventions in the past may have contributed to the current crisis by eroding initiatives for producing food'.

The famine itself had little impact on government efforts to consolidate its grip on power. Malawi's new constitution of 1995 prescribed a limit of two five-year terms on the presidency. Soon after the UDF was re-elected in 1999, the government initiated a campaign to amend the constitution to allow President Muluzi to stand for a third term. The 'third term debate' coincided exactly with the 2002 famine. In late 2001 and 2002 the government was preoccupied with campaigning for the constitutional amendment, rather than preventing famine in remote rural villages. Ironically, Muluzi himself complained about this inappropriate prioritization in an address to the nation in September 2002: 'at this time, when our people are starving, it seems irresponsible and hard-hearted to preoccupy ourselves with politics, especially when the next general elections are not due until 2004' (quoted in Chinsinga 2003: 8). Ultimately, political resistance proved just strong enough to prevent the Constitution being amended: needing a two-thirds majority in the 193-seat Parliament, 125

MPs voted for the 'Open Terms Bill' in July 2002, just three votes short of the 128 required (Ross 2004).

Symptomatic of the limited accountability and absence of an anti-famine contract is the fact that the UDF Government was not punished in the 2004 elections for the famine of 2002. Despite the food crisis, the controversy over the third-term issue, the SGR scandal and several other highly-publicized cases of corruption, Bakili Muluzi's designated successor, Bingu wa Mutharika, was elected President (with 36 per cent of the popular vote) ahead of the MCP candidate, John Tembo (27 per cent).

President Banda had resisted pressures for political pluralism for several years, arguing that 'democracy would increase tribalism and regionalism' (Ihonvbere 1997: 231). It is also true that 'Banda had strongly identified his populist legitimacy with domestic maize availability, contrasting colonial famines with post-independence food security' (Harrigan 2003: 850). Nonetheless, the failure of democratization in Malawi to prevent famine in 2002 is not an argument against multi-party democracy (nor, incidentally, does it refute 'Sen's law'). Instead it is an argument for *more* democracy, especially increased accountability. The democratic transition has not yet delivered an 'anti-famine contract' to Malawi, because it is not yet a 'consolidated democracy' (Chinsinga 2003). As long as democratic institutions and political accountability remain weak, the vulnerability of poor and powerless Malawians will persist. In the interim, democracy must be actively promoted and gains must be vigorously protected. The successful campaign against the Open Terms Bill is one positive sign in this regard.

Conclusion

One of many unresolved puzzles about the 2002 famine in Malawi is why a relatively small maize gap had such a devastating human cost. As noted above, Malawi had experienced three significant food production shocks during the 1990s – in 1992, 1994 and 1997 – but with no comparable impact in terms of famine process or outcome indicators. Our analysis suggests that several important factors had changed during the decade, all of which combined to make rural Malawians more vulnerable to livelihood shocks than ever before. These vulnerability factors included the following:

1   A rapid rise in prevalence of HIV/AIDS and its economic, demographic and social consequences, which undermined incomes and labour power in affected households and compromised the ability of communities to provide support
2   Lowered resilience of rural economies, with food prices at historically high levels due to weak markets, and *ganyu* (casual employment) least available when it was needed most[18]

3   Weakened institutional capacity to respond, due to the abolition of policies and manipulation of institutions that had a food security mandate, including ADMARC, the National Food Reserve Agency, and the SGR
4   Diminished political will to protect household food security, due to a shift from an authoritarian but effective regime to a multi-party democracy that was minimally accountable to vulnerable sections of Malawian society.

The conventional view of famine is that it represents a failure, or a succession of failures – of production, of markets, of 'entitlements', of coping, of information, and of response. Since at least the 1980s, the reality that there are winners as well as losers from famine has been well understood, but this insight has yet to be incorporated into theoretical frameworks for famine analysis, except in conflict situations or 'complex emergencies' (see Deng, Chapter 11, this volume). The possibility that famine conditions can be orchestrated, manipulated and perpetuated has also been understood for some time by political analysts. Nonetheless, the dominant perception of famines remains that they represent economic and political 'failure'.

Famines rarely affect an entire country; they affect its poor and powerless citizens. This chapter has reflected on the failures of production, marketing and aid that precipitated the 2001–2002 famine in Malawi, and the failures of economic liberalization and political transition that made the famine possible. However, by asserting that information was cynically manipulated by a 'controlling institution', that the SGR was stolen, and that trade was deliberately disrupted, we also want to suggest that this famine was a *success*, an entirely avoidable tragedy from which many powerful individuals profited opportunistically. As a final piece of support for this hypothesis from popular culture, consider the lyrics of a song titled '*Njala*' ('hunger'), by Joseph Phungu Nkasa (translated from Chichewa):

> In 2002 we had a very bad year.
> ADMARC sometimes had maize
> but they were selling it only for funerals.
> Those people who bought ADMARC maize
> could sell it at very high prices.
> If you didn't get rich last year
> you will never get rich!

Notes

1 Two main sources provided the empirical data reported in this chapter. The first is the 'Malawi Food Crisis Impact Survey', a research study conducted in

2003 by the Institute of Development Studies (IDS), Sussex and the Centre for Social Research, University of Malawi (Devereux *et al.* 2003), which included a questionnaire survey of 1,200 households in forty-eight Enumeration Areas from eleven districts throughout rural Malawi, and qualitative fieldwork (focus groups, case studies and key informant interviews) in twenty-two communities. Our second source is fieldwork conducted by Zoltan Tiba for a PhD at the School of Oriental and African Studies (SOAS), University of London (Tiba 2005). During this fieldwork, 256 households were interviewed in a village in Zomba district, over a period of six months. This research also involved focus group discussions and qualitative interviews in thirteen village communities in the area, and a regional survey about famine mortality in forty-three villages.

2 An excellent account of the Nyasaland famine is provided by Megan Vaughan, in her book *The Story of an African Famine* (Vaughan 1987).

3 Possibly the only 'official' figures related to famine mortality were CMRs, though none attempted to estimate total famine deaths. Taifour (2002) recorded a CMR of 1.23/10,000 per day in Salima District. In February 2002, USAID's famine early warning system noted that: 'There have been widespread reports in the press about people dying because of hunger', and reported CMR peaking at 1.9/10,000 per day (FEWS NET 2002a: 10).

4 In the Food Crisis Impact Survey, respondents were asked several questions about morbidity and mortality during the crisis period, including: (1) 'Did any of your household members suffer from any hunger-related condition like malnutrition, oedema (swelling), marasmus, kwashiorkor, etc? What were the major signs?'; (2) 'Did your household lose anyone through death due to hunger and starvation during the famine?'; and (3) 'Did any household member get injured or killed in a situation related to the famine?'

5 The official population of Malawi in 2001 was 10.791 million, and in the 1998 Population and Housing Census 85.6 per cent of the population was rural (NSO 1998). This implies a total rural population in 2001 of 9,237,096.

6 To put our relatively high mortality estimates into context, consider that Wiggins (2005: 9) estimates under-5 mortality alone in Malawi at 72,000 in a 'normal' year.

7 In August 2002 the Director-General of the World Health Organization predicted hundreds of thousands of excess deaths in Malawi, due to the ongoing 'Southern Africa famine': 'Weakened by hunger, many people will die of diseases. They could have survived these if properly nourished – if they had produced adequate food or been able to purchase the food they need ... We fear there could be at least 300,000 'extra' deaths during the next six months because of this crisis' (WHO 2002c: 1).

8 In 1997 the maize harvest in Malawi was officially 1.226 million tonnes; in 2001 it was 1.713 million tonnes. Applying the FAO's annual cereal consumption requirement of 165 kg per person to the national population of 10.26 million in 1998 and 11.44 million in 2002, the 'maize gap' was 470,000 tonnes in 1997–1998, but only 170,000 tonnes in 2001–2002.

9 Incredibly, according to the Ministry of Agriculture, cassava yields trebled in a single year, from 5,390 tonnes/Ha in 1998–1999 to 15,253 tonnes/Ha in 1999–2000 (Tiba 2005: 93).

10 Before the famine, national cassava production officially increased from 692,000 tonnes in 1998 to 752,000 tonnes in 1999 and 874,000 tonnes in 2001. Applying the conversion factor of 0.437, national cassava production for the same three years would officially have been 302,000 tonnes, 329,000 tonnes and 382,000 tonnes respectively (Tiba 2005: 139).

11 This does not apply to cases where markets play a minor role during famines,

as in socialist economies ('centrally planned' famines) or where markets are disrupted by conflict.

12 Purchasing and hoarding grain in advance of an anticipated food shortage, either for precautionary (survival) or speculative (profiteering) reasons, is a feature of many famines, and was responsible for exacerbating the Bangladesh famine of 1974 (Ravallion 1987).

13 Although HIV/AIDS rightly receives a great deal of attention, it is important not to forget that there are many other 'killer diseases' in Malawi, not least malaria, which is the 'leading cause of morbidity and mortality in Malawi' (DHS 2000: 185) and accounts for about 40 per cent of the deaths in children below the age of two.

14 In fact, the goals of national and household food security sometimes contradicted each other: in attempting to secure reliable supplies of inexpensive food for the 'nation' (including the non-farming population), government parastatals frequently offered farmers such low prices for their produce that the production of surpluses was discouraged and farmers' incomes dwindled.

15 The UDF won seventy-one out of seventy-six seats in the south; the MCP won fifty-one of sixty-eight seats in the centre; and AFORD won all thirty-three seats in the north.

16 Ayittey (2005: 48) has generalized this tendency in his graphic depiction of the 'vampire state' in post-colonial Africa: 'The centralization of both economic and political power turns the state into a pot of gold that all sorts of groups compete to capture. Once captured, power is then used to amass huge personal fortunes, to enrich one's cronies and tribesmen, to crush one's rivals, and to perpetuate one's rule in office. All others are excluded.'

17 'The UK High Commissioner to Malawi has warned the country's ministers that Britain will not support corrupt governments. Mr George Finlayson said Britain would not subsidize economic mismanagement nor would it give backing to leaders who were unwilling to take tough decisions. Mr Finlayson's remarks, made in the capital Lilongwe, come after a series of corruption allegations against members of President Bakili Muluzi's administration. The comments did not go down well with the Malawian government' (BBC 2000).

18 After the 1994 drought shock, Pearce et al. (1996) reported that many better-off rural Malawians offered employment to their affected neighbours, even if they had no need to hire labour, as a gesture of solidarity and support. In 2001–2002, however, local employment was non-existent in many affected villages, and people were forced to travel to Mozambique and elsewhere in search of work. Eldridge (2002) explains the 'non-famine' of 1992 in southern Africa in terms of the strength of rural communities' coping strategies at that time, rather than the effectiveness of the government and donor response to the drought-triggered food shortage.

References

Ayittey, G. (2005) *Africa Unchained: The Blueprint for Africa's Future*, New York, NY: Palgrave Macmillan.

British Broadcasting Corporation (BBC) (2000) 'Malawi graft: UK talks tough', 12 October (available at www.news.bbc.co.uk/world/africa).

Brown, G., Reutlinger, S. and Thomson, A. (1996) *Food Security in Malawi: A Market Oriented Approach*, Lilongwe: USAID-Malawi.

Cammack, D., Chulu, O., Khaila, S. and Ng'ong'ola, D. (2003) 'Malawi Food

Security Issues Paper', *Forum for Food Security in Southern Africa*, London: Overseas Development Institute (available at www.odi.org.uk/food-security-forum).

CARE (2002) *Impact of HIV/AIDS on Agricultural Productivity and Rural Livelihoods in the Central Region of Malawi*, Lilongwe: CARE International.

Carr, S. (1998) 'Root crop production in Malawi: some anomalies in the data', mimeo, Zomba, Malawi.

Carr, S. (2003) 'Food shortages in Malawi 2001–2003', mimeo, Zomba, Malawi.

Chabal, P. and Daloz, J.-P. (1999) *Africa Works: Disorder as Political Instrument*, London: Zed Press.

Chilowa, W. (1998) 'The impact of agricultural liberalisation on food security in Malawi', *Food Policy*, 23(6): 553–69.

Chinsinga, B. (2003) 'Lack of alternative leadership in democratic Malawi: some reflections ahead of the 2004 general elections', *Nordic Journal of African Studies*, 12(1): 1–22.

Chirwa, E. and Zakeyo, C. (2002) 'Impact of economic and trade policy reforms on food security in Malawi', Paper presented at FAO Trade and Food Security Project Workshop, 5–6 December, 2002, Rome: FAO.

Demographic and Health Survey (DHS) (2000) *Demographic and Health Survey*, Zomba: National Statistical Office.

Devereux, S. (1997) 'Household food security in Malawi', *IDS Discussion Paper 362*, Brighton: Institute of Development Studies.

Devereux, S. (1999) '"Making less last longer": informal safety nets in Malawi', *IDS Discussion Paper 373*, Brighton: Institute of Development Studies.

Devereux, S. (2002) *State of Disaster: Causes, Consequences and Policy Lessons from Malawi*, Lilongwe: ActionAid Malawi.

Devereux, S., Chilowa, W., Kadzandira, J., Mvula, P. and Tsoka, M. (2003) *Malawi Food Crisis Impact Survey: A research report on the impacts, coping behaviours and formal responses to the food crisis in Malawi of 2001/02*, Brighton, UK and Lilongwe, Malawi: Institute of Development Studies and Center for Social Research.

de Waal, A. (1997) *Famine Crimes: Politics and the Disaster Relief Industry in Africa*, Oxford: James Currey.

de Waal, A. (2002) '"AIDS-Related National Crises" in Africa: food security, governance, and development partnerships', *IDS Bulletin*, 33(4): 120–26.

Dorward, A. and Kydd, J. (2004) 'The Malawi 2002 food crisis: the rural development challenge', *Journal of Modern African Studies*, 42(3): 343–61.

Dyson, T. and Ó Gráda, C. (eds) (2002) *Famine Demography: Perspectives from the Past and Present*, Oxford: Oxford University Press.

Eldridge, C. (2002) 'Why was there no famine following the 1992 southern African drought? The contributions and consequences of household responses', *IDS Bulletin*, 23(4): 79–87.

FAOSTAT (2001) *FAO Online Statistical Database*, Rome: Food and Agricultural Organisation (available at www.fao.org).

FAO/WFP (2004) *Special Report: Crop and Food Supply Assessment Mission to Malawi*, Rome: FAO/WFP.

FEWS NET (2001) *Malawi – Monthly Food Security Report: mid-May–mid-June, 2001*, Lilongwe: FEWS NET.

FEWS NET (2002a) *Malawi – Monthly Food Security Report: mid-January–mid-February, 2002*, Lilongwe: FEWS NET.

FEWS NET (2002b) *Malawi – Monthly Food Security Report: mid-March–mid-April, 2002*, Lilongwe: FEWS NET.

Government of Malawi (GoM) (2002) *Investigation Report: Allegation that Top UDF Officials and Cabinet Ministers Corruptly Benefited from the Purchase of Maize from the Strategic Grain Reserve*, Lilongwe: Anti-Corruption Bureau.

Government of Malawi (GoM) (2004) *Report of the Presidential Commission of Inquiry on Strategic Grain Reserves*, Lilongwe: Government of Malawi.

Haacker, M. (2002) 'The economic consequences of HIV/AIDS in southern Africa', *IMF Working Paper* 02/38, Washington, DC: International Monetary Fund.

Harrigan, J. (2003) 'U-turns and full circles: two decades of agricultural reform in Malawi, 1981–2000', *World Development*, 31(5): 847–63.

Ihonvbere, J. (1997) 'From despotism to democracy: the rise of multiparty politics in Malawi', *Third World Quarterly*, 18(2): 225–47.

Integrated Household Survey (IHS) (1998) *Integrated Household Survey, Malawi*, Zomba: National Statistical Office.

International Development Committee (IDC) (2003) 'The humanitarian crisis in Southern Africa', *Third Report of Session 2002–2003*, London: House of Commons.

International Monetary Fund (IMF) (2002a) 'Malawi – the Food Crisis, the Strategic Grain Reserve, and the IMF – A Factsheet', Washington, DC: International Monetary Fund.

International Monetary Fund (2002b), 'Malawi – 2002 Article IV Consultation: Concluding Statement of the IMF Mission', Washington, DC: International Monetary Fund.

Jayne, T., Govereh, J., Mwanaumo, A., Nyoro, J. and Chapoto, A. (2002) 'False promise of false premise? The experience of food and input market reform in Eastern and Southern Africa', *World Development*, 30(11): 1967–85.

Kydd, J. and Dorward, A. (2003) 'Implications of market and coordination failures for rural development in Least Developed Countries', Paper presented at the Development Studies Association Annual Conference, 10–12 September 2003, Glasgow: Strathclyde University.

National AIDS Commission (NAC) (2001) *Sentinel Surveillance Report*, Lilongwe: NAC.

National Statistical Office (NSO) (1998) *Population and Housing Census*, Zomba: National Statistical Office.

Nugent, P. (2004) *Africa Since Independence*, Basingstoke: Palgrave Macmillan.

Owusu, K. and Ng'ambi, F. (2002) *Structural Damage: The Causes and Consequences of Malawi's Food Crisis*, London: World Development Movement.

Pearce, J., Ngwira, A. and Chimseu, G. (1996). *Living on the Edge: A Study of the Rural Food Economy in the Mchinji and Salima Districts of Malawi*, Lilongwe: Save the Children (UK).

Peters, P. (1996) 'Failed magic or social context? Market liberalization and the rural poor in Malawi', *Development Discussion Paper* 562, Cambridge MA: Harvard Institute for International Development.

Ravallion, M. (1987) *Markets and Famines*, Oxford: Oxford University Press.

Ross, K. (2004) ' "Worrisome trends": the voice of the churches in Malawi's third term debate', *African Affairs*, 103: 91–107.

Rubey, L. (2002) 'Malawi's food crisis: causes and solutions', Lilongwe: USAID Malawi.

Sawdon, G., 2001, 'A Final Report on the Findings of a Household Economy Assessment and Training in Mchinji District, Malawi', Lilongwe: Save the Children (UK).

Sen, A. (1981) *Poverty and Famines*, Oxford: Clarendon Press.

Sen, A. (1999) *Development as Freedom*, Oxford: Oxford University Press.

Stevens, C., Devereux, S. and Kennan, J. (2003) 'International trade, livelihoods and food security in developing countries', *IDS Working Paper* 215, Brighton: Institute of Development Studies.

Taifour, H. (2002) *Nutrition Survey Report: Salima and Mchinji Districts, Malawi*, Lilongwe: Save the Children (UK).

Tiba, Z. (2005) 'A new type of famine with traditional response: the case of Malawi, 2001–2003', unpublished PhD thesis, London: Department of Economics, School of Oriental and African Studies, University of London.

UNAIDS (2002) *Epidemiological Fact Sheets on HIV/AIDS and Sexually Transmitted Infections: Malawi, 2002 Update*, Geneva: UNAIDS.

van de Walle, N. (2001) *African Economies and the Politics of Permanent Crisis, 1979–1999*, Cambridge: Cambridge University Press.

Vaughan, M. (1987) *The Story of an African Famine*, Cambridge: Cambridge University Press.

Vulnerability Assessment Committee (VAC) (2003) *Malawi: Emergency Food Security Assessment Report*, Lilongwe: Malawi National Vulnerability Assessment Committee.

Whiteside, M. (2003) 'Enhancing the role of informal maize imports in Malawi food security', *Consultancy Report for DFID*, Lilongwe: DFID Malawi.

Wiggins, S. (2005) 'Southern Africa's food and humanitarian crisis of 2001–2004: causes and lessons' *Discussion Paper for Agricultural Economics Society Annual Conference*, London: Overseas Development Institute.

World Bank (2002) 'Averting famine in Malawi', Washington, DC: World Bank.

World Health Organization (2002a), 'Health conditions aggravate Southern Africa famine', August (available at www.who.int/mediacentre/news/releases/who63/en/).

World Health Organization (2002b), 'Report on update of health assessment', September (available at www.who.int/disasters/repo/8416.doc).

World Health Organization (2002c), Preliminary findings on the humanitarian health impact in Malawi', April, Lilongwe: WHO Malawi.

8 An atypical urban famine
Antananarivo, Madagascar 1985–1986

Michel Garenne

Introduction[1]

This chapter documents and discusses the case of an urban famine that occurred in Antananarivo, the capital city of Madagascar, in 1985–1986. This famine is atypical in many respects, since it was an urban famine that occurred in peace-time and remained hidden for a long time. It was discovered *a posteriori* by an in-depth analysis of vital registration and causes of death data in the city. The details of the demographic analysis have been presented elsewhere (Garenne *et al.* 2002). The analysis here focuses on the economic and political factors underlying the crisis. The chapter demonstrates that the crisis of 1985–1986 qualifies as a famine, as defined by Thomas Downing (1990): 'an extreme collapse in local availability or access to food that causes a widespread rise in mortality from outright starvation or hunger-related illnesses'. The first part of this chapter presents a brief background on Madagascar; the second part documents excess mortality due to the famine; the third part explores the political and economic context of the famine; and the fourth part examines several underlying causes.

Background on Madagascar

Madagascar is atypical in many respects. The great island, one of the largest in the world (587,041 sq km), is located off south-east Africa, far from the main trade routes. Its landscape is highly mountainous, which makes communications particularly difficult between regions. Madagascar has several distinctive ecological zones. The central plateau (Antananarivo and Fianarantsoa) has a temperate climate, and is well suited for rice farming and cattle raising. The eastern coast has a tropical climate, favourable to tropical crops (coffee, vanilla, cloves and sugar-cane), and has the largest harbour (Toamasina). The western part (Mahajanga) is more arid, though it harbours fertile valleys. The southern part (Toliary) is very arid, especially the 'Androy' region, also called the 'spiny desert', though this area has the richest mineral deposits (chromite, graphite and

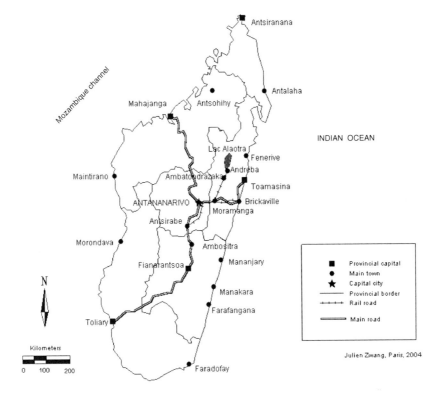

Figure 8.1 Map of Madagascar.

mica). The northern area (Anstiranana) lies behind the highest mountains, and remains topographically isolated from the rest of the country
(Figure 8.1).

Due to its geographical isolation, Madagascar was one of the last areas
to become peopled, probably at the end of the first millennium AD. The
island was settled by several waves of migrants from diverse origins – primarily Indonesians and Africans, with small minorities of Arabs and Jews
who were trading along the East African coast, and more recently by
groups of Europeans, Comorians, Indians and Chinese. The precise
history of this settlement is poorly documented prior to the seventeenth
century, since there are virtually no written documents. It seems that until
the arrival of Europeans the total population was small, and scattered all
over the island. During the eighteenth century a central power emerged
in the highlands, around a new kingdom called the *Imerina*, a dynasty of
Indonesian descent. The country was unified during the nineteenth
century by the Merina kingdom, and colonized by France in 1896.

In the early days of colonization, low population density was felt to be a
handicap to the colonial strategy for economic development, which was

based primarily on cash crops. However, the population increased dramatically during the twentieth century, multiplying seven-fold, and numbered about seventeen million by 2003. Even though population density remains low by European standards (29 inhabitants per square kilometre), it is relatively high given the topography and the arable land potential (5.5 inhabitants per hectare) (calculated from World Development Indicators). The population is unevenly distributed, with the majority living in the central highlands (50.2 per cent), followed by the eastern coast (16.3 per cent), southern province (14.5 per cent), western province (11.2 per cent) and northern province (7.8 per cent). Malagasy people have a strong identity, despite their diversity of ethnic origins. The Malagasy language, of malayo-polynesian origin, is shared by all eighteen official ethnic groups. The level of education is relatively high for Africa (4.53 years of schooling for women born in 1965–1969), especially given the low level of income (the average for sub-Saharan Africa was 4.01 years for the same group of women, according to Demographic and Health Survey (DHS) data).

Madagascar has maintained ambiguous relationships with Europeans over the centuries, sometimes friendly but at other times conflicting. The first Europeans who traded with Malagasy people in the sixteenth and seventeenth centuries were Portuguese, Dutch, British and French. All abandoned the island, after many attempts to control the trade. Europeans returned in the nineteenth century. They were the first military instructors to the new Merina kingdom, and also sent Protestant missionaries. However, the Europeans were expelled by Queen Ranavalona I (1828–1861), and missionaries as well as newly converted Christians were killed in numbers. Her successors, however (King Radama II and Queen Ranavalona II), were more open to European influence, and by 1869 the ruling family and the Prime Minister had converted to Protestantism. During the following decades the rulers tried to develop a modern political system, based on written law. French influence grew at that time, but was fiercely resisted. In 1890 England recognized the French protectorate, and France started to take over the country in 1895. It took about ten years to 'pacify' Madagascar, despite resistance, especially in the southeast. Colonial rule applied until 1960, the year of independence. Opposition to Western influence grew again in the 1970s, as will be seen, and is part of the famine story.

The Madagascan economy remains primarily based on agriculture, both food crops (rice, cassava, peas) and cash crops (coffee, vanilla, cloves), as well as cattle rearing. Rice cultivation seems to have been introduced by the first settlers, and is based on classic irrigation techniques found in Indonesia and India. By the eighteenth century, rice was cultivated in abundance, and Madagascar exported rice and other agricultural products, particularly to nearby Reunion. During the colonial period, many new crops were introduced and developed. However, rice harvests continued to be abundant, and surpluses were exported – for instance to France during the First World War – until as recently as the early 1970s.

Famines did not appear to be a feature of the country in peace-time, except in the dry areas of the south (Gendarme 1960; Campbell 1992). However, famines did occur at times of civil unrest, in particular during the French invasion, and during the period of forced labour imposed by the colonial rulers to promote a cash economy. At these times the local population tended to abandon their rice fields to flee into hiding in the forests. Another famine occurred in the south during the so-called 'cactus war' (1924–1999), when colonial rulers used biological warfare to destroy the pear cactus in order to force farmers to change their production system. This considerably modified the fragile ecological balance between people, plants and animals, and obliged part of the population to move away, probably causing the premature deaths of small numbers of people (Kaufmann 2000). Otherwise, the main adverse climatic events in Madagascar are floods and hurricanes, which can occur all over the country, though they are rather localized in time and space (a situation similar to the West Indies) and are rarely a cause of famine. Only the extreme south (Andriana) is regularly prone to drought. Food shortages and minor famines, called the *kere*, were documented in the south in 1971–1972, in 1991–1992, and most recently in 2002–2003. We will come back to these events in the discussion. However, according to available documentation, no famine due to climatic events was recorded in the central highlands in the twentieth century.

Demographic evidence of the Antananarivo famine

Antananarivo, the capital city of Madagascar, lies in the highlands, in the central part of the country. The city had 577,000 inhabitants in 1985, and is characterized by slow population growth due to low migration inflows compared with most other African capital cities. This is primarily due to lack of economic opportunities and of international aid in the 1970s and 1980s, as will be seen below.

A long tradition of birth and death registration exists in Madagascar. This started before the colonial period under the successful reign of Queen Ranavalona II, was developed under French colonial rule and remained of high quality in the post-independence period. Vital registration seems to be virtually complete in urban areas, especially in Antananarivo. Comparison with DHS data and with demographic models reveals no evidence of under-registration of deaths in the capital city for the 1976–1995 period (Garenne *et al.* 2002). Not only are vital events properly registered, but causes of death are also available for Antananarivo – a rare situation in sub-Saharan Africa. Causes of death are certified by physicians, whether the death occurred in a hospital or elsewhere. These data existed but were not processed, published or analysed until a team led by

Pierre Cantrelle undertook a systematic coding of all mortality data and causes of death for the 1976–1995 period. This is how the 1985–1986 famine was uncovered: by analysing the demographic data and the causes of death before and after the 1985–1986 crisis. A full-scale life table analysis of the 1976–1995 data has been published elsewhere (Waltisperger *et al.* 1998).

The mortality data recorded in Antananarivo for the 1976–1995 period clearly show a typical famine in 1985–1986. Compared to mortality levels before 1985 and after 1987, death rates increased markedly in 1985–1986, and life expectancy in 1986 (at 49.0 years) had dropped by about 10 years compared with 1975 (59.4 years) or 1995 (59.8 years). The mortality increase bears all the characteristics of a famine: a strong relative increase among children, especially five-to-nine year-olds (risk ratio compared to baseline: RR=2.5) and young adults, especially young men aged twenty to thirty-four years (RR=2.2). In absolute terms, it was estimated that about 7,600 people died in 1985–1986 in excess of baseline mortality levels. About half the excess deaths were children under fifteen years old, with a small excess of boys; about a third were adults aged fifteen to fifty-nine, among whom 74 per cent were men; the remainder were elderly people, again with a higher male mortality. This implies that some 1.3 per cent of the city's population died because of the famine – a rate that compares to other moderate famines, though much lower than great famines where larger proportions of the population died of starvation or hunger-related diseases.

The main evidence for this excess mortality being due to famine lies in the profile of causes of death, which is especially clear for young adults. Mortality from malnutrition (starvation) among adults hardly existed before 1984 and after 1988, whereas it showed a pronounced spike in 1986 (Figure 8.2). The same spike can be observed for child deaths over the same period, even though some child mortality from malnutrition occurred before and after the crisis, as elsewhere in Africa. The peak in malnutrition-related mortality is mirrored by a peak of mortality from an exceedingly rare disease: alveolitis of the jaws. This disease occurs primarily in rodent populations, when animals facing food scarcity resort to eating roots and other food too hard for their teeth. It also occurs in human populations as a result of improper dental surgical procedures. This disease produces an infection of the jaws which is often lethal. It seems that in Antananarivo, starving people started eating sugar-cane and destroyed their jaws. Indeed, the few cases of death attributed by physicians to this disease were all concentrated in the crisis years.

In addition to typical starvation, deaths from other causes also increased: in particular, deaths from diarrhoeal diseases (often associated with malnutrition), deaths from acute respiratory infections and deaths from cardiovascular diseases among adults. There was, however, no evidence of significant epidemics of infectious diseases, such as typhoid,

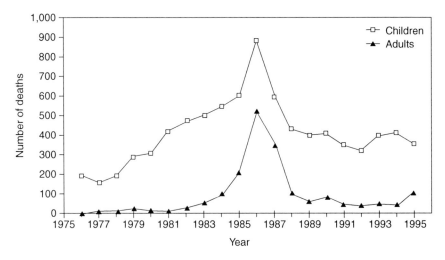

Figure 8.2 Number of deaths due to malnutrition, Antananarivo, 1976–1995.

typhus, measles, cholera or dysentery, as is often seen in famine situations. It seems therefore that the famine deaths were primarily due to starvation and its metabolic consequences. The 1985–1986 period in Antananarivo therefore meets the demographic criteria of a famine, as defined by an increase in mortality from starvation.

Political and economic context of the famine

To understand what happened in 1985–1986 in Antananarivo it is necessary to review the contemporary political history of Madagascar. The great island enjoyed relative stability in the pre-colonial and colonial periods. Decolonization went smoothly: by 1958 a republic was formed under President Tsiranana, two years before formal independence (1960). The first eleven years of independence were quite peaceful, but civil unrest exploded in 1971 around economic and social issues in both urban and rural areas, which was followed by a series of *coups d'état*. In 1972 General Ramanatsoa took power, to be replaced three years later by Admiral Ratsiraka, who started the so-called 'Malagasy revolution' (second republic). The new regime followed a strict Marxist line, cut itself off from Western powers and received support and advice from Russia, China and North Korea. After about ten years of nationalizations and severe economic mismanagement, in particular the 1978–1980 period of 'extreme investment' (*investissement à outrance*), which bears some similarities to the Chinese 'Great Leap Forward', the country went virtually bankrupt. Around 1984 the government started changing its policies, re-established links with the IMF and the World Bank as well as with France and other Western countries, and accepted the structural adjustment policies that were in vogue at that time. Free elections were organized in 1993, and were won by a liberal, Professor Albert Zafy, who changed the constitution (third republic). However, Ratsiraka was re-elected four years later, in 1997, and remained in power until December 2001, when he was replaced by Marc Ravalomanana, a liberal, after a severe crisis around the elections. These dramatic political changes are closely linked to economic performance, and to the 1985–1986 crisis.

During the colonial period Madagascar followed a classic path of rural economic development, with a priority on exported cash crops, in particular coffee and vanilla. In the late colonial period (1950–1959) and the early post-independence period (1960–1971) it followed a liberal import substitution policy, which was moderately successful but did little to promote industrialization. According to Maddison (2001), income per capita expressed in purchasing power parity terms (GNP–PPP) was increasing during this period, from an estimated US$951 in 1950 to US$1,246 in 1971 – a slow but consistent growth of 1.3 per cent per year. Compared with income levels in other African countries in 1971, Madagascar ranked in the middle – eighteenth in a list of thirty-eight for which income estimates were available – even though economic growth was somewhat lower than elsewhere during the 1950–1971 period (the median value for sub-Saharan Africa was 2.0 per cent).

Madagascar's economic situation deteriorated rapidly after 1971, and by 1998 income per capita in parity purchasing power had dropped to US$690, almost half what it was twenty-seven years earlier – a negative economic growth of –2.2 per cent per year. In 1998 Madagascar was in one of the worst economic situations in Africa, ranking twenty-ninth in the same list of thirty-eight countries, having experienced one of the most dramatic economic downturns for the continent, together with countries devastated by civil war such as Sierra Leone and Angola.

The situation in Antananarivo was no better than in the rest of the country. We know more about the capital city because of a series of five detailed household consumption surveys based on representative samples of the population. According to these surveys, real household income per capita in Antananarivo also declined regularly over the 1961–1995 period, from an estimated value of 1.42 million Malagasy Francs (MGF) in 1961 to 1.25 m in 1968–1969, 0.99 m in 1977–1978, 0.93 m in 1993–1994 and 0.79 m in 1994–1995 (Ravelosoa and Roubaud 1996). This decline in real income translated into declining food consumption over the same period, from an estimated 1,713 kcal per person in 1961 to 1,410 kcal in 1993–1994 for the three main food items: cereals, meat and sugar (Table 8.1). The composition of the diet also changed between 1961 and 1995, with decreases of 21 per cent in rice consumption, 42 per cent in bread, 52 per cent in sugar and about 60 per cent in meat consumption. As a result, mean height went down over the period – further evidence of

Table 8.1 Structure of household consumption in various years (from household consumption surveys), Antananarivo, 1961–1995

	1961	1968– 1969	1977– 1978	1993– 1994	1994– 1995
Household consumption (1983 MGF)	1,417,898	1,253,940	997,530	934,256	787,581
% spent on food	37.8	39.1	47.6	50.0	47.3
Caloric value of three main food items	1,713		1,355	1,410	1,217
% rice in caloric value	78.0	81.8	79.3	87.0	

Source: Ravelesoa and Roubaud (1996)

Note
Household expenditures are in constant 1983 Malagasy Francs. Caloric values of three main food items (cereals, meat, sugar) is given in kcal, converted from household consumption.

increasing malnutrition. The decline in mean height for adult women born after 1960, who reached puberty after 1974, is also documented for the whole country in DHS surveys.

Rice production, consumption and marketing

Rice is the main agricultural crop, and the main staple food in Madagascar. The country was largely self-sufficient, and even exported rice, as noted above, until several years after independence in 1960. According to FAO data, per capita rice production was increasing in the 1960s and culminated in 1968 at a peak of 194 kg per capita, exceeding the reference basic needs of 183 kg per adult per year. However, rice production started to decline steeply in the early 1970s, reaching a low point of 140 kg per capita in 1976, before increasing again for a few years to reach 168 kg in 1986 (the famine year) but declining thereafter to reach a new low value of 126 kg in 1996 (Figure 8.3). It should be noted that rice production in 1985–1986 was probably high enough to cover all needs, since children's needs are lower than average, and was rather better than in many preceding and succeeding years that were free of famine. Therefore, food availability decline cannot be considered as a valid causal factor explaining the 1985–1986 famine in Antananarivo.

The price of rice had been quite stable over long periods of time, despite seasonal and yearly fluctuations, with values around 217 MGF per kilogram in constant 1983 prices (Barrett 1994; Azam and Bonjean 1995; Araujo-Bonjean and Azam 1996). During the late colonial period and until 1971 the rice market was free, but the price of rice was stabilized, with minimum (floor) and maximum (ceiling) values, by a specialized government agency (the *Bureau de Commercialisation et de Stabilisation du Riz*, or BCSR). This was a common policy in colonial Africa and in the

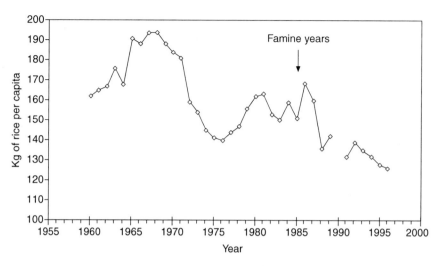

Figure 8.3 Rice production in Madagascar, 1960–1996.

early post-independence period, for the major food crops as well as cash crops. With the installation of a Communist regime, the rice market, both internal and external, was controlled by a state monopoly, and the price of rice was fixed by the government. In addition, the price paid to farmers for their rice was fixed at too low a level – which discouraged local producers, who decreased their production to a point where rice had to be imported and sold at a subsidized price to satisfy the increasing demand of the urban population. With the policy changes initiated in 1984, the internal rice market was opened to private merchants and producer prices increased somewhat. In 1985, price controls on rice were lifted, and internal trade was fully liberalized in 1986. International trade was opened to the private sector only in 1990. The 1985–1986 seasons were therefore years when domestic rice trading and pricing could be fixed by private traders, but imports of rice remained under state control.

Although many crops can be cultivated in tropical areas, rice is grown only once a year in the Madagascan highlands, and is harvested between June and September. In a normal year the price of rice is lowest in May and during the harvest season, then increases steadily until the next harvest – a classic case of rational expectations behaviour by stockholders (Araujo-Bonjean and Azam 1996). The range of price seasonality is moderate in normal years, at roughly ±15 per cent. However, during the crisis years price fluctuations were dramatic, and one consequence of the transition period policies was a massive increase in the price of rice on urban markets (Figure 8.4). The rice price, in constant 1983 Malagasy Francs, was 240 MGF in June 1985 – but increased to 640 MGF by December 1985, three times higher than its baseline average of 217 MGF. This seems to have been due to the speculation of newly authorized merchants, who anticipated a price increase, wanted to increase their stocks, and expected that the government would not import rice (Araujo-Bonjean and Azam 1996). Trade between rural and urban areas had just been liberalized and was controlled by just a few agents. The rice price went down just before the next harvest, and averaged 315 MGF in May–June 1986 – still 45 per cent above the baseline price. It increased again in the months after the harvest and peaked at 415 MGF in October 1986 for the same reasons, before falling to its baseline level at the time of the next harvest, in May 1987. The famine mortality followed quite clearly the evolution of the rice price in Antananarivo (compare Figures 8.2 and 8.4).

The impact of the price increase can be understood by considering income levels and the structure of spending in household budgets. In household consumption surveys, food accounted on average for about half of total expenditure: 47.7 per cent in 1977–1978 and 50.0 per cent in 1993–1994 (Ravelosoa and Roubaud 1996). Among the food products purchased, rice and bread accounted for more than a third of the total (33.1 per cent in 1977–1978 and 43.2 per cent in 1993–1994), and rice accounted for some 90 per cent of cereals purchased (93.6 per cent in 1977–1978 and 85.6 per cent in 1993–1994). Altogether, rice provided about 80 per cent of the total daily caloric intake of Antananarivo households (81.8 per cent in 1977–1978 and 79.3 per cent in 1993–1994). These are average values for all households, rich and poor. When the price of rice trebled in a short period of time, expenditure on rice accounted for more than half of the total budget for the average household, and simply

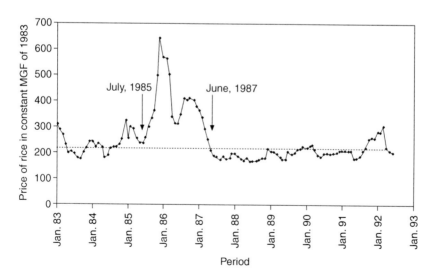

Figure 8.4 Market price of rice in Antananarivo, 1983–1992.

Table 8.2 Relative income of five socio-economic categories, Antananarivo 1961–1995

Category	1961	1968–1969	1977–1968	1993–1994	1994–1995
Professional, upper	2.22	3.21	3.13		2.53
Professional, medium	1.44	2.09	2.02		1.83
Clerical	1.13	1.20	1.05		0.97
Skilled workers	0.80	0.90	0.80		0.73
Unskilled workers	0.58	0.62	0.54		0.62

Source: Ravelesoa and Roubaud (1996)

Note
Relative income is calculated as the ratio of the income for each socio-economic category to the average for the population.

exceeded the total budget of poor households. According to the above calculations, this was the case for those living on less than 55 per cent of the average household income – as was the case for unskilled workers (Table 8.2). Even if there was some substitution between rice and bread over the 1977–1994 period, this was minor since the price of imported wheat was much higher, and did not enable the poor to cope with the massive increase in the rice price.

Discussion: underlying causes of the famine

The mechanisms of the Antananarivo famine appear clearly in the economic analysis. Rapid deregulation of rice prices and rice markets, following a long period of strict state regulation and subsidized prices, but not accompanied by adequate public policies to mitigate the impacts of deregulation, induced a rapid increase in the price of rice – the staple food of a large majority of the population. The exceptional rise in prices lasted for about two years, from July 1985 to June 1987, as did the mortality increase. During this period the poorest strata in the city could not cope with the increasing cost of what constituted 80 per cent of their food intake, and many died of starvation as a result. Mortality fell back to pre-crisis levels as soon as prices reverted to their baseline levels. This famine was due to a combination of market failure and institutional failure, and occurred in a context of widespread poverty. It appears that the combination of adverse economic policies together with extensive poverty was the main immediate cause for the famine. Beyond these immediate reasons, however, several underlying causes played significant roles. We review and discuss some of these below.

Structural adjustment policies

The Antananarivo famine occurred in the mid-1980s – a time when many economic policies were suddenly changed in Africa, ostensibly in response to decades of mismanagement and failed economic experiments. Structural adjustment policies (SAP) were put in place all over the continent, at the express request of the Bretton Wood institutions (IMF and World Bank). Structural adjustment involved stabilization policies (a return to state budget equilibrium and trade balance) and liberalization policies (privatization of parastatal agencies, deregulation of prices, exchange rates and wages). These policies had limited economic impact in the short run, and probably induced a major crisis such as the Antananarivo famine only rarely, although detailed studies in the poorest strata of African cities are lacking.

One might have hoped that the tragedy seen in the 1980s in Madagascar would never occur again. However, the recent Malawi famine of 2001–2002 bears some common features with respect to brutal economic policy changes, even though it was primarily rural and triggered by crop failure. The Malawi famine was analysed in detail by Devereux and colleagues at IDS Sussex.[2] The Malawi crisis also occurred in a context of rapid changes in economic policies and poor interface with the international donor community. In the years prior to the famine, Malawi was required to commercialize the agricultural marketing agency that had been in place for many decades, to remove agricultural subsidies to farmers, to lift price controls on staple foods and to sell its strategic grain reserve in order to reimburse its international debt. Furthermore, the donor community was discouraged by evidence of corruption and economic mismanagement, and some donors had stopped providing aid in 2001. This adverse context made the food deficit much worse than it would otherwise have been: Malawi no longer had any safety net when the crisis arose, and it took several months to find appropriate solutions.

The twentieth century also witnessed other cases of faulty economic policies inducing famines, often with enormous demographic impacts, such as the Ukraine famine (1932–1993) in Russia and the 'Great Leap Forward' famine in China (1959–1961). Fortunately, the more recent adverse events have not been of such magnitude.

Food availability

According to conventional theory, famines usually occur after an external shock – climatic stress (drought, flood) or an epidemiological event (pests or plant diseases) – affects essential food crop production (cereals or tubers) and suddenly reduces staple food availability. However, in the Antananarivo famine overall food availability nationwide did not seem to be a major issue, since rice production per capita was rather better than in preceding and following years. A similar observation was made by economists working on famines in India (1943) and Bangladesh (1974). These famines occurred not because of declining food availability, which remained at average levels during the famine period, but primarily as a dysfunction of the economic system (such as a rapid increase in food prices relative to income, or a rapid decline in employment) which affected the poorest strata of the population (Sen 1981; Ravallion 1987; Drèze and Sen 1989). Rapid price increases as a result of 'price forecasting errors', or speculation by food traders, are not necessarily proportionate to food availability. Similarly, in the Malawi famine of 2001–2002, the deficit in maize production (the main staple food) was comparatively minor (–25 per cent) – lower than in other years during which no famine was noted, such as 1994 or 1997 – and occurred after two good years (1999, 2000) of higher than average production during which stocks could have been accumulated (Devereux 2002). In all these cases, a food deficit was not the leading trigger of the crisis. Even in a case of severe food shortage resulting from a natural disaster, such as the potato famine in Ireland in 1845–1847, food continued to be exported from famine areas towards markets where it could be sold at a higher price, so in this case again the food deficit was made worse by adverse policies or lack of appropriate mitigating policies (Ó Gráda 1993).

Poverty, income distribution and entitlement failure

Another important aspect of the Antananarivo famine, which is common to most famines, is extensive poverty. Madagascar has long been a poor country by international standards. Furthermore, as discussed above, poverty was increasing over the period preceding the crisis, and started to decrease only ten years later, after 1996. However, poverty *per se* was not the sole causal factor of the urban famine, since the years 1987–1995 were even worse in terms of average income per capita. Income distribution was another important element in the Antananarivo crisis. Although we lack data on the distribution of income among those who died, poverty certainly played an important role in the distribution of starvation. Wealthier people in the city did not suffer in the same way, simply because they had the means to cope. In purely arithmetical terms, the poor trapped in the city could not afford the higher cost of rice during the crisis years. Sen (1981) developed a theory that famines are often a consequence of 'entitlement failure', or 'exchange entitlement failure' – that is, a lack of rights to food and an inability to access food from any source, rather than a simple 'market failure'. If people had higher incomes or valuable assets to sell, or if they had access to credit, they would have been able to purchase the food they needed to survive the crisis.

Ravallion (1987: 18), also studying famines in the Indian subcontinent, has noted that even relatively small price increases may entail large mortality increases among the market-dependent poor.

When potential famine victims rely heavily on current foodgrain markets for their consumption needs, high prices will reduce their survival chances. If those survival chances are also sufficiently concave functions of their incomes, foodgrain price instability will induce famine mortality.

Here again, poverty and income distribution appeared as major factors explaining famine. In the case of Madagascar, the proportion of the asset-poor, defined by the number of goods owned by a household, is extremely high. According to DHS surveys conducted in 1992 and 1997, 43 per cent of households own no 'modern' goods. This is one of the highest proportions recorded in all the African DHS surveys, together with Ethiopia and Rwanda, and twice as much as the African average. This very poor stratum had nothing to exchange for food. In Antananarivo, therefore, 'exchange entitlement failure' was another important feature of the famine.

Geographical isolation and transportation

We have noted already that Madagascar is geographically separated from the African continent, and that its various provinces are relatively isolated and linked by a poor road system. Geographical isolation is one factor that self-evidently affects the speed of response to a food crisis. This was the case to a certain extent in the Malawi famine of 2001–2002, because of the landlocked nature of the country, far from any sea route, and more importantly because floods had cut off many roads, bridges and even a railroad. However, this did not seem to be a key factor for Antananarivo. Even though the capital city lies in the highlands, it is linked by train to the major port (Toamasina) and also to the leading rice-growing region (Lake Alaotra). If geographic isolation played a role, it was rather through market segmentation, which was reinforced by public policies during the Marxist regime (see below).

Segmented markets

Historians have documented the role of segmented markets in famines of the past. For instance, Ó Gráda and Chevet (1999) showed that, more than 'market failures', it is 'market segmentation' that explains the Anjou famine in seventeenth century France. Similarly, highly localized markets and high costs of transportation may also explain features of recent Ethiopian famines (Devereux 1988; Ravallion 1997; von Braun *et al.* 1998). In Madagascar, the isolation of the various regions together with the high cost of road transportation and the underdevelopment of sea routes have all contributed to market segmentation. Furthermore, the low fixed-price policy followed during the Marxist period discouraged farmers from increasing production, so by and large they tended to produce for their own needs and to commercialize very little. Had the rice market been flourishing prior to 1985, prices would probably not have increased by such a large amount. In this respect, market segmentation in Madagascar appears as another element of the crisis, and of the overall 'market failure'.

Information and communication

More and more, famines have an international political dimension, and are becoming morally unacceptable for the international community. Sylvie Brunel (2002) has developed a typology of famines in relation to international politics and the international aid business. In her study of recent African famines, Brunel distinguished three categories of famines:

1   Famines 'hidden' by local political powers, primarily to avoid criticism of their own policies – this category applies to cases such as the Ethiopian famine of 1984, the Kivu (Congo) famine of 1996, and many famines in Communist countries
2   Famines 'exposed' (and sometimes exaggerated) by political leaders, in order to maximize the amount of food relief and international aid, which may also be used for other purposes – an example being the Biafra famine of 1968–1970
3   Famine conditions deliberately 'created' by political groups, in order to provoke international aid – such as the Liberia and Sierra Leone famines of the late 1990s – aid on which some guerrilla movements are totally dependent, as pointed out by Pérouse de Montclos (2002).

To follow Brunel's typology, the Antananarivo famine seems to have been 'hidden' from the start – probably to conceal the major failure of previous policies, a common feature of Marxist regimes, and possibly to not put the government's changing policies at risk. One could argue that the government might not have been aware of the food crisis; however, physicians who wrote death certificates with causes obviously related to starvation must have spoken to their peers, and the information must have reached the ministries one way or another. Certainly, as an urban famine with high impacts in the capital city, it is difficult to believe that people in power were totally unaware of it. Further potential sources of information were the economists who were working at that time on the economic reforms. However, their policy recommendations were based more on standard remedies developed in Washington, DC than on detailed local knowledge: the first DHS and Living Standards Measurement Survey (LSMS) in Madagascar was implemented only in 1992. Had the press been free to report the situation, and had economists been properly informed, relief mechanisms could have been put in place. The role of good information and a free press in preventing famines has been stressed by other famine analysts (Drèze and Sen 1989; see also Banik, Chapter 13, this volume).

Madagascar has undergone several natural disasters over recent decades, such as drought, cyclones, flood and locust invasion. Evidence of excess mortality in rural areas is scanty, however, and it remains possible that unreported minor famines have occurred in localized rural areas. However, the country is far more open now than before, and famine relief agencies are very active throughout Africa. Early warning systems such as GIEWS, supported by the FAO, and FEWS NET, supported by USAID, monitor food-security indicators quite closely and are able to mobilize support rapidly for those in need. The publication of data on the Internet is another powerful modern element of information and famine prevention. These services were not available in 1985, and the network of relief agencies was not as extensive as it is now. This new information technology, as well as more integrated markets, makes another famine in Madagascar less likely in the future. A good example is provided by the food crisis caused by drought that occurred in the southern province in 2002–2003. The crisis was rapidly picked up by charitable organizations and by the press, and numerous articles were published in the press and on the web. This induced a massive reaction from the international community (European Union, USAID, GTZ, Care, Japan Aid, etc.). Food aid was made available, and a food-for-work programme was started. In fact, this became a case of an 'over-exposed' famine, much exaggerated, to the point that experts later argued that there were no famine conditions at all. In any case, there was no evidence of increased mortality during the crisis years.

An urban famine in peace-time

The famine process in Antananarivo was not started by a natural disaster, as is the case in many rural famines. Nor was it started by violent events or a military blockade, as in other urban famines of the twentieth century, such as the Dutch famine, the Warsaw ghetto and the siege of Leningrad, all during the Second World War (see Watson, Chapter 12, this volume), or the German occupation of the Greek islands during the same war (Hionidou 2002). It was the changing economic situation of 1984–1986 that created a 'market trap' in Antananarivo. In a sense, this had an effect similar to that of a blockade, producing a sharp rise in food prices and denying access to the poorest. Rice was available in the country or could have been imported, but people could not afford to purchase enough to meet their needs. In this sense – being triggered not by a food availability decline but by an entitlement decline that was related to dubious economic policies, and displaying atypical features (being urban rather than rural, and 'hidden' rather than overt) – the Antananarivo famine is a variant on the 'new famine' concept as developed in this book.

Psychological factors

We know too little about the psychological aspects of famines. In principle, poor people in Antananarivo could have demonstrated in the streets to fight for their rights, or could have led visible political action to awaken the government and force politicians to take the appropriate measures. This did not happen. Devereux (1993, 2000) has noted apparently irrational aspects of human reactions to famine situations. People might make counter-intuitive economic choices by 'choosing to starve' rather than sell their assets for a variety of personal, social or economic reasons. Or they may be simply too weak to fight, after rationing their food consumption for too long. The people most in need in developing countries are often the 'voiceless', those who are never heard by decision-makers.

The situation of rural areas in 1986

We know little of the situation in rural areas during the 1985–1986 crisis. The mortality increase seen among children in the vital registration of Antananarivo over the 1975–1986 period, with a peak in 1985–1986 at the time of the famine, was also visible in the nationally representative sample of the DHS surveys in urban areas, and to a lesser extent in rural areas. No comparable data are currently available for young adults – a highly sensitive age group for famine mortality. It would require a special effort to code vital events throughout the country in order to answer this important question. It might be expected that peasants who grew their own rice or tubers were less likely to be affected by structural adjustment policies, and also had their own coping mechanisms which were not available to the urban poor. However, it should be noted that many of the poorest and most vulnerable farmers in Madagascar, as elsewhere in Africa, are net food buyers, since they produce too little to meet their family's subsistence needs and are dependent on the market for part of the year. These households would have been as adversely affected by sharp price rises as any market-dependent households in towns and cities.

Public policies to avert famine

Many public policies could have been introduced to mitigate the crisis, such as imports of rice to stabilize local food markets, requesting international aid, providing access to credit for the poor, or possibly providing jobs for jobless people. Ravallion (1987, 1997) has noted that in Bangladesh during the 1974 famine, foodgrain price stabilization would have reduced famine mortality. International aid could have been easily mobilized if the government had taken the appropriate steps.

Another element of international aid is the relationship with donors. In the case of the Malawi famine of 2001–2002, donors had stopped much of their non-emergency assistance to the country in 2001 because of alleged mismanagement of aid resources. Had the relationship been better, emergency assistance could have been provided earlier. Similarly in our case, Madagascar had a poor relationship with Western countries in the years leading up to the 1985 crisis because of its political alignment with Communist countries during the previous decade, and the nationalization of many foreign private companies which took place in the early years of the Malagasy revolution. In 1985, links were just being re-established with major donors, but the country had not yet gained full recognition. If these relationships had been stronger, information would have circulated better, donors would have been more responsive and aid might have been provided in time.

Conclusion

Ultimately, modern famines are above all abnormal 'institutional failures', since there are so many options to prevent them. Let us hope that they will tend to disappear in the twenty-first century. However, the turmoil of state development and the many government failures in Africa over the past twenty-five years do not lead to optimism. It seems that, above all, the international community must play an increasingly active role through the many channels available, if future famines are to be avoided.

Notes

1 I would like to thank Milasoa Cherel-Robson for helpful comments on an earlier draft.
2 See Devereux 2002; Stevens *et al.* 2002; also Devereux and Tiba (Chapter 7, this volume).

References

Araujo-Bonjean, C. and Azam, J.-P. (1996) 'La libéralisation du riz à Madagascar ou l'ajustement sans croissance', *Région et Développement*, 4: 34–53.

Azam, J.-P. and Bonjean, C. (1995) 'La formation du prix du riz: théorie et application au cas d'Antananarivo, Madagascar', *Revue Économique*, 46: 1145–66.

Barrett, C. (1994) 'Understanding uneven agricultural liberalisation in Madagascar', *Journal of Modern African Studies*, 32(3): 449–76.

Brunel, S. (2002) *Famines et Politique*, Paris: Presses de Sciences Po.

Campbell, G. (1992) 'Crisis of faith and colonial conquest: the impact of famines and diseases in late nineteen century Madagascar', *Cahiers d'Etudes Africaines*, 32: 409–53.

Devereux, S. (1988) 'Entitlements, availability and famine', *Food Policy*, 13(3): 270–82.

Devereux, S. (1993) *Theories of Famine*, New York, NY: Harvester Wheatsheaf.

Devereux, S. (2000) 'Famine in the twentieth century', *IDS Working Paper* 105, Brighton: Institute of Development Studies.

Devereux, S. (2002) 'The Malawi famine of 2002', *IDS Bulletin*, 33(4): 70–78.

Downing, T. E. (1990) 'Assessing socioeconomic vulnerability to famine: frameworks, concepts and applications', *Famine Early Warning System Project, Working Paper 2*, Arlington, TX: Tulane University.

Drèze, J. and Sen, A. (1989) *Hunger and Public Action*, Oxford: Oxford University Press.

Garenne, M., Waltisperger, D., Cantrelle, P. and Ralijaona, O. (2002) 'The demographic impact of a mild famine in an African city: the case of Antananarivo, 1985–7', in C. Ó Gráda and T. Dyson (eds), *Famine Demography: Perspectives from the Past and Present*, Oxford: Oxford University Press.

Gendarme, R. (1960) *L'Économie de Madagascar*, Paris: Editions Cujas.

Hionidou, V. (2002) ' "Send us either food or coffins": the 1941–2 famine on the Aegean island of Syros', in C. Ó Gráda and T. Dyson (eds), *Famine Demography: Perspectives from the Past and Present*, Oxford: Oxford University Press.

Kaufmann, J. C. (2000) 'Forget the numbers: the case of a Madagascar famine', *History in Africa*, 27: 143–57.

Maddison, A. (2001) *The World Economy: A Millennial Perspective*, Paris: OECD.

Ó Gráda, C. (1993) *Ireland Before and After the Great Famine: Explorations in Economic History*, Manchester: Manchester University Press.

Ó Gráda, C. and Chevet, J.-M. (1999) 'Market segmentation and famine in Ancien Régime France', Paper presented at the European Science Foundation Workshop on Historical Market Integration, Venice International University, 16–19 December.

Pérouse de Montclos, M.-A. (2002) *L'Aide Humanitaire, Aide à la Guerre?*, Paris: Complexe (collection: les enjeux du XXI siècle).

Ravallion, M. (1987) *Markets and Famines*, Oxford: Oxford University Press.

Ravallion, M. (1997) 'Famines and economics', *Journal of Economic Literature*, 35: 1205–42.

Ravelosoa, M. and Roubaud, F. (1996) 'Evolution de la consommation des ménages à Antananarivo', *Économie de Madagascar 1*, Antananarivo.

Sen, A. (1981) *Poverty and Famines: An Essay on Entitlement and Deprivation*, Oxford: Clarendon Press.

Stevens, C., Devereux, S. and Kennan, J. (2002) 'The Malawi famine of 2002: More questions than answers', Institute of Development Studies, University of Sussex (available at www.odi.org.uk/speeches/famine_july2002/devereux.pdf).

von Braun, J., Teklu, T. and Webb, P. (1998) *Famine in Africa: Causes, Responses and Prevention*, Baltimore, MA: Johns Hopkins University Press.

Waltisperger, D., Cantrelle, P. and Ralijaona, O. (1998) 'La mortalité à Antananarivo de 1984 à 1995', *Documents et Manuels du CEPED 7*, Paris: CEPED.

9 North Korea as a 'new' famine[1]

Marcus Noland

Introduction

The Democratic People's Republic of Korea (DPRK) or North Korea has been experiencing a chronic food crisis for well over a decade. A famine during the 1990s resulted in the deaths of perhaps 600,000 to one million people out of a pre-famine population of roughly twenty-two million.[2] At a time in which famine has been increasingly confined to sub-Saharan Africa, it is astonishing that this could occur in an industrialized country in Asia with a level of development comparable to that of Romania, Indonesia or the Philippines (Noland 2000).

There is no standard definition of famine or its associated epiphenomena, and the term lends itself to diverse typologies.[3] The North Korean case is unusual in that while it clearly harks back to the 'state-created' or 'hidden' famines experienced by totalitarian socialist states of the mid-twentieth century, the increasing centrality of internal institutional changes and involvement of external actors in the post-Cold War context of globalization simultaneously situates it in the contemporary milieu of 'post-modern' famine, as discussed by Gazdar (2002). What may have been the last famine of the twentieth century may also be a harbinger of those of the twenty-first.

The North Korean crisis has its origins in a political-economic system characterized by two generations of economic mismanagement and an utterly ruthless political elite, which values the maintenance of political control over public welfare and proved unwilling or incapable of adjusting political or economic practices to changing circumstances when the economic and diplomatic environment changed in the early 1990s. In terms of the notion of a 'political' or 'anti-famine' contract (de Waal 2000), the state's monopoly on social organization and its maintenance of an extensive apparatus for repression and social control denies the populace any mechanism for enforcing such a contract, even if the elite implicitly recognizes its existence. This lack of effective voice at least partly explains the prolonged nature of the crisis.

By standard statistical measures, such as the share of the population under arms or the share of national income devoted to the military, North

Korea is the world's most militarized society, and domestic propaganda incessantly proclaims the virtues of 'military first' politics. The population is classified according to perceived political loyalty, and the share deemed reliable is relatively small, in the order of one-quarter of the population with a core elite of perhaps 200,000 (or roughly 1 per cent of the population).[4] A network of political prison camps holds 200,000 or more political prisoners.[5] Prisoners have been executed for ill-defined political crimes such as 'ideological divergence', and any unauthorized attempt to leave the country is a capital crime. There are numerous eyewitness accounts of public executions, including cases of schoolchildren being forced to witness these killings (Amnesty International 2004; KINU 2004; US Department of State 2004).

Any sign of political deviance, from listening to foreign radio broadcasts, to singing South Korean songs, to sitting on a newspaper containing the photograph of the deified founding leader Kim Il-sung, is subject to punishment. Collective punishment is practised, with up to three generations of a family interned for an individual's offence. Death rates in these camps are high, torture is practised, and there have been unconfirmed reports of prisoners being used for chemical and biological warfare testing. A second network of smaller extra-judicial detention centres exists, many located near the Chinese border, which developed during the 1990s partly as an *ad hoc* response to famine coping behaviour such as foraging, unauthorized internal movement or crossing the border into China. Here as well, death rates are high, torture is practised and there are extensive anecdotal reports of forced abortions and infanticide (Hawk 2003; KINU 2004; US Department of State 2004). There are no firm estimates of the number of people detained in these facilities.

Given the regime's extreme preference for guns over butter, the North Korean economy does not produce enough output to sustain the population biologically, and population maintenance is aid-dependent. Since the mid-1990s a combination of humanitarian food aid and development assistance has ameliorated the situation, but conditions remain precarious and the country could slip back into famine if there were a major interruption in aid. There is already considerable evidence of donor fatigue, at least in the US, Japan and the European Union (EU), and their calls for more transparent and systematic monitoring of aid distribution prompted the North Koreans to reject participation in the 2005 consolidated appeal by UN agencies.

Conventional donor–recipient tensions have been further complicated by the October 2002 revelation of an alleged North Korean nuclear weapons programme based on highly enriched uranium (in addition to a plutonium-based programme acknowledged a decade earlier), undertaken in contravention of several international agreements, and North Korea's subsequent withdrawal from the Nuclear Non-proliferation Treaty. In the case of Japan, North Korean actions with respect to its abductions of Japanese citizens have exacerbated the situation. Nevertheless a major aid cut-off is unlikely as long as South Korea and China fear a collapse of the North Korean regime. From a Chinese perspective, its fraternally allied socialist neighbour, with a population of roughly twenty-two million people, is a relatively small province. Moreover, the Chinese and South Korean governments have displayed far less interest in issues such as transparency and non-discrimination in provision of relief than have other major donors.

Internally, the situation is complicated by economic policy changes initiated in July 2002. These changes have exacerbated pre-existing social inequality and created a new group of food-insecure households among the urban non-elite. According to a WFP survey, most urban households are food insecure, spending more than 80 per cent of their incomes on food. In December 2003, Masood Hyder, the UN's humanitarian relief coordinator in North Korea, told the world press that the food problem was concentrated among up to one million urban workers, a view echoed by Rick Corsino, head of WFP's local operation, who claimed that 'some people are having to spend all their income on food'.[6] According to the FAO, for the period 1999–2001, 34 per cent of North Korea's population was malnourished, though it is unclear on what basis the organization reached such a precise figure – especially in light of the problematic nature of the survey evidence, as discussed below (FAO 2003: Table 1). Nevertheless, given the precarious situation of North Koreans who already lack adequate food, it would not be surprising to observe future increases in mortality rates, especially if China and South Korea were to reduce their assistance.

Background on North Korea

Prior to the partition of the Korean peninsula, most industries were located in the north while the south was the bread-basket. In the period immediately following the end of the Second World War and the expulsion of Japanese colonialists, the peninsula was partitioned into zones of Soviet and American military occupation in the north and south, respectively. In the Soviet-occupied zone, land belonging to Korean landlords and Japanese colonialists was seized and redistributed to the peasantry during 1945–1946. This land reform was accompanied by a dramatic fall in agricultural output, and urban food shortages developed. The new socialist administration prohibited private trade in food and launched compulsory grain seizures in rural areas during the winter of 1945–1946.

In 1950, North Korea invaded South Korea. An armistice was signed in 1953, ending hostilities and more or less restoring the original border. Under Soviet tutelage, the North set about establishing a thoroughly orthodox centrally planned economy, remarkable only in the degree to which markets were suppressed. Following the Korean War, agriculture was collectivized, quantitative production planning was introduced, state marketing and distribution of grain was established, and private production and trade were prohibited. Households obtained food and other items through a ration system (the public distribution system or PDS) that provided for some differentiation on the basis of age and occupation. Two types of farms were established legally: cooperatives and state farms, with the latter considered ideologically more advanced. The country experienced food shortages in 1954–1955, as these changes were undertaken.

In 1955, Kim Il-sung proclaimed *juche*, or self-reliance, as the national ideology. Beginning in 1959, motivated by military security concerns, food security was pursued through self-sufficiency, not only at the national level but also at provincial and even county levels (H. Lee 2000; S. Lee 2003). Collectivization was accompanied by an increase in irrigation and the use of industrial inputs such as tractors. During the 1960s, the country pursued the 'four modernizations' of 'mechanization, electrification, irrigation, and chemicalization', eventually establishing perhaps the world's most input-intensive agricultural system, with the usage of chemical fertilizers and pesticides exceeding even Japan's. The authorities altered planting patterns, specifically by replacing traditional food crops such as tubers, millet and potatoes with maize. Yields increased, but they were susceptible to a fall in inputs.

In response to food shortages in 1970–1973, the degree of centralization of agricultural planning was intensified and local authorities were increasingly marginalized. Food production was subject to the same input–output standardization as any other economic activity, and instructions were specified down to the level of fertilizer usage by individual cooperative farm households. In 1973 a Cultural Revolution-type movement was created, and young Communists were dispatched to initiate ideological, cultural and technical education of farm households. New rural educational institutions were established, and existing rural officials and staff were reassigned and required to enrol in these *juche* curriculum programmes. This social engineering eroded the knowledge of, respect for and influence of traditional farming techniques; rural life was thoroughly regimented by the state, and any sort of individual initiative was stifled (S. Lee 2003).

Origins of the present crisis

The present crisis has its origins in a multi-faceted set of developments in the late 1980s, though the precise causal relationships among these drivers are unclear. Despite its *juche*-inspired declarations of self-reliance, North Korea has been dependent on outside assistance throughout its entire history, with first the Soviet Union, later China and most recently South Korea playing the role of chief benefactor or patron.

In 1987, frustrated by North Korean unwillingness to repay accumulated debts, the Soviets withdrew support. According to US Central Intelligence Agency figures, the net flow of resources turned negative, though some analysts argue that these figures understate implicit Soviet military assistance and fuel subsidies. That same year the North Koreans initiated a number of possibly conflicting policies in the agricultural sector, including the expansion of state farms, tolerance of private garden plots, expansion of grain-sown areas, transformation of crop composition in favour of high-yield items, maximization of industrial inputs subject to availability, and intensification of double-cropping and dense planting. Continuous cropping led to soil depletion, and the over-use of chemical fertilizers contributed to acidification of the soil and eventually a reduction in yields. As yields declined, hillsides were denuded to bring more and more marginal land into production. This contributed to soil erosion, river silting and, ultimately, catastrophic flooding. Isolation from the outside world reduced the genetic diversity of the North Korean seed stock, making plants more vulnerable to disease.

These effects were compounded by the tremendous trade shocks that hit the economy, starting in 1990 as the Soviet Union disintegrated and the Eastern bloc collapsed. Trade with the Soviet Union accounted for more than half of North Korean two-way trade, including most of its fuel imports. The fall in imports from Russia in 1991 was equivalent to 40 per cent of all imports, and by 1993 imports from Russia were only 10 per cent of their 1987–1990 average (Eberstadt *et al.* 1995). North Korea proved incapable of reorienting its commercial relations in the face of this massive trade shock. Imported fuel was used to power irrigation systems and agricultural machinery, as well as for the production of chemical fertilizers. The North Korean industrial economy imploded and, deprived of industrial inputs, agricultural output plummeted.

Food availability

In certain respects the North Korean case represents an archetypal example of what Sylvie Brunel has termed 'hidden famines', because of tight restrictions on information surrounding the event (Garenne 2002). Like everything else North Korean, there is some controversy as to the precise timing and magnitude of the decline in grain output. Data compiled from four sources are shown in Figure 9.1. All show a decline in production in the 1990s compared to a decade earlier, though the FAO series, weirdly, spikes in the early 1990s.[7] There is a broad consensus that in recent years, North Korean grain production has been approximately four million tonnes.

Data on food imports and aid are shown in Figure 9.2.[8] In the period immediately following the collapse of the Soviet Union, China stepped into the breach, offsetting some of the fall in trade with the Soviet Union and emerging as North Korea's primary supplier of imported food, most

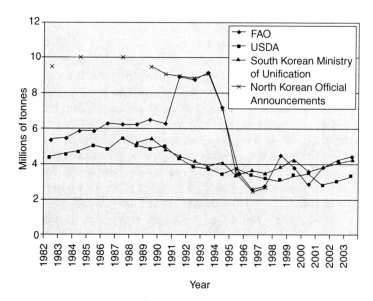

Figure 9.1 Estimates of North Korean grain production, 1982–2003 (sources: FAO
Statistics Database (FAOSTAT: apps.fao.org/default.jsp); USDA FAS
website (www.fas.usda.gov/pecad2/highlights/2002/06/nKorea/index.
htm); Korean Ministry of Unification (data available at www.unikorea.
go.kr/data/eng0302/000047/attach/eng0302_47A.pdf); Woo (2004)).

of it reportedly on concessional terms. However, in 1994 and 1995, a disillusioned China reduced its exports to North Korea. If there was a single
proximate trigger to the North Korean famine, this was it.

By 1994, North Korean radio broadcasts had admitted the existence of
hunger. In May 1995, South Korean President Kim Young-sam made a
public offer of unconditional food assistance to the North. Later that
month, the North Korean Government conceded that the country was
experiencing a food shortage and asked the Japanese Government for
help. (Internally, assistance from Japan could be justified as reparations –
aid from rival South Korea would be harder to rationalize.) In June, the
North Korean Government in Pyongyang reached agreements with the
Japanese and South Korean Governments on the procurement of emergency food aid, and in July, the Pyongyang Government announced to its
public that it was receiving external assistance, though it failed to mention
the South Korean role. In August 1995, North Korea made a formal
request for emergency assistance to the UN and immediately began receiving aid from a variety of UN organizations.

Catastrophic floods in July and August 1995 added to North Korea's
suffering. While the flooding was considerable, the consensus among
outside observers was that the government's claims were exaggerated.[9]

Nevertheless, the floods played an important public relations role, in as much as they facilitated the North Korean Government's portrayal of the famine as a product of natural disaster (the government unit charged with obtaining international assistance was renamed the Flood Damage Rehabilitation Committee or FDRC), a guise that a number of foreign relief agencies found advantageous.[10]

The floods of 1995 were followed by more, though less severe, floods in July 1996, and renewed appeals for help. As the international aid campaign took off, rising aid inflows effectively crowded out food imports on commercial terms, in effect acting as balance-of-payments support (Figure 9.2).[11] The primary suppliers of food assistance were the US, followed by South Korea, Japan and the EU. The provision of aid was highly politicized, reflecting the interests of the main donors. North Korea emerged as the largest Asian recipient of US aid in the 1990s, receiving more than US$1 billion in food and energy assistance between 1995 and 2002. The provision of this assistance has often been used to induce North Korean participation in diplomatic negotiations.[12]

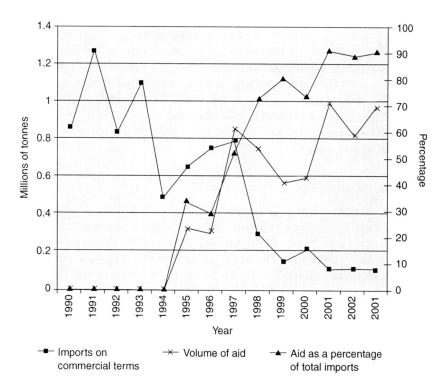

Figure 9.2 North Korean food imports and aid, 1990-2003 (source: Ministry of Unification, FAO Special Reports, various issues (www.fao.org/ WAICENT/ faoinfo/economic/giews/English/alert/index.htm)).

The possible diversion of aid to military uses has been an ever-present issue since relief efforts first began in the mid-1990s. In one sense, this whole argument is a red herring: food aid is fungible (though imperfectly so) and, as the WFP's John Powell testified with admirable frankness before the US Congress: 'the army takes what it wants from the national harvest upfront, in full. And it takes it in the form that Koreans prefer: Korean rice' (Powell 2002: 52). Another WFP official, with first-hand experience, and on the condition of anonymity, described the bargain under which the DPRK military offloads aid from China and thus preserves the WFP's claim that its food does not go directly to the military. If the provision of international assistance has contributed to the ongoing North Korean military build-up, it has been mainly through the channel of implicit balance of payments support, rather than through diversion *per se*.[13]

Although flooding contributed to the food crisis in North Korea, agriculture, like the rest of the economy, had been in secular decline since the beginning of the 1990s. On the basis of their econometric analysis of North Korean agricultural production, Heather Smith and Yiping Huang (2003) conclude that 'the dominant triggering factor in the crisis was the sharp loss of supplies of agricultural inputs following the disruption of the trade with the socialist bloc from the late 1980s . . . The contribution of climatic factors to the agricultural crisis, as stressed by North Korea's policy-makers, was at most a secondary cause'. This conclusion is reinforced by the computable general equilibrium model-based simulation of Noland *et al.* (2001), who find that restoration of flood-affected land and capital would have only a minor impact on the availability of food. Taking at face value WFP's estimates of human consumption needs, even without flooding, North Korea would have entered the mid-1990s with a substantial food deficit.

Distribution of misery

In 1987, as Soviet aid was terminated, daily grain rations distributed through the PDS – which officially had been 600 to 700 grams for most urban dwellers and 700 to 800 grams for high officials, military personnel and heavy labourers – were cut by 10 per cent (Table 9.1). In 1991, as economic difficulties worsened, the government launched a 'let's eat two meals a day' campaign, and the following year rations were cut by another 10 per cent.[14] By 1993, there were rumours that PDS rations were delayed or temporarily suspended in certain northern areas, and persistent (though unconfirmed) reports of food riots. In 1994 the North Korean Government responded by implementing what some observers would describe as 'triage' – ending PDS shipments to four provinces (North and South Hamgyong, Yanggang and Kangwon) and prohibiting internal shipments to these regions. PDS daily rations were cut to 400 to 450 grams, and refugees, mainly from the most heavily affected northern provinces,

Table 9.1 Rice and maize per capita daily rations, 1987

Occupation and age group	Per capita daily ration (grams)	Ratio of rice to maize	
		Pyongyang area	Other areas
High-ranking government officials	700	10:0	10:0
Regular labourers	600	6:4	3:7
Heavy-labour workers	800	6:4	3:7
Office workers	600	7:3	3:7
Special security	800	6:4	3:7
Military	700	6:4	3:7
College students	600	6:4	3:7
Secondary school students	500	6:4	3:7
Primary school students	400	6:4	3:7
Preschool students	300	6:4	3:7
Children under 3 years	100–200	6:4	3:7
Aged and disabled	300	6:4	3:7

Source: Kim *et al.* (1998).

reported that rations had fallen to 150 grams. By 1997 the daily ration had fallen to 128 grams, before rising in subsequent years.

At the same time, the government launched a campaign of coercive seizures of farmers' grain and reduced the annual retained farm allotment from 167 to 107 kilograms per person. Given the government's history of confiscating grain, rural households responded by hoarding, intensifying cultivation of illegal private plots and relatively neglecting production on officially recognized farms and cooperatives. The effect was to constrict the supply of food available to the PDS.[15]

As the economic crisis deepened, fuel shortages and deterioration of the transportation infrastructure contributed to a fragmentation of markets. This process reinforced the rupturing of the social compact, and increasingly desperate local officials adopted entrepreneurial coping strategies. While the state tolerated certain coping mechanisms (such as barter trade managed by local officials), at the same time it intensified human rights abuses, including the establishment of special camps and prisons for those found illegally foraging for food. These forces, together with pre-existing social differentiation, meant that by the mid-1990s, according to eyewitness accounts, conditions varied enormously across geographic regions and social groups, with perceived political loyalty to the state affecting access to humanitarian relief (Noland 2000; Natsios 2001; Hawk 2003).

According to one close observer with a long personal history of dealing with DPRK authorities, 'the interaction between the FDRC and international humanitarian aid organizations was adversarial from its inception'

(Snyder 2003a: 6), while another observed that 'DPRK officials were successfully able to come across not as the beggar, but instead as the recipient of entreaties from the outside world. In contrast, the would-be donors, the NGOs, became the supplicants, asking the DPRK for the 'privilege' of helping the North Korean people.' And the unwillingness of some (especially those motivated by religious ideals) to walk away encouraged some DPRK officials to 'hold their own populace hostage to their demands and conditions' (Flake 2003: 38). Indeed, humanitarian organizations such as *Médecins Sans Frontières*, Oxfam and CARE pulled out of North Korea, citing fundamental violations of international norms of non-discrimination in the provision of relief. This was not a universal reaction, however, and some NGOs remain active in North Korea.

As might be expected in these circumstances, the possible diversion of aid, especially to the North Korean military, has been a hot issue among donors (Noland 2000, 2003). Monitoring of aid distribution for the quantitatively significant official donors still falls below acceptable norms, a decade into the crisis. Furthermore, at its peak, international aid was reputedly feeding roughly one-third of the population. The scale of this assistance forces a reconsideration of exactly what diversion means; with such a large volume of humanitarian assistance entering the country it is almost certainly the case that some aid is reaching needy people while some is diverted to the better connected or less needy. Military stockpiling further complicates this dynamic. Assessment of these issues in North Korea is impeded by fundamental shortcomings in transparency, access and accountability.

What do we know and how do we know it?

As a consequence of the extraordinary isolation of North Korea and the secretiveness of its political regime, there is considerable uncertainty about the timing of the famine and its social and geographical incidence. Even today, outside official observers do not have access to counties accounting for roughly 15 per cent of the population, pre-notification is required for site visits and official relief agencies are not permitted to use Korean-speaking personnel (though WFP personnel are now permitted to take Korean language lessons while in-country) and are unable to monitor aid shipments continuously from port of entry to final distribution (Figure 9.3).[16] Since 1997, USAID, WFP and other official agencies have threatened to make continued assistance conditional on improved monitoring, but have infrequently terminated assistance due to North Korean non-cooperation. (When aid has been cut off, as in the case of the cessations of Japanese assistance in 2002 and 2004, it has been for diplomatic, not programmatic, reasons.) The point is simply that more than a decade into this emergency, we still have remarkably little systematic information about conditions inside North Korea, and some of what we do have appears to be of dubious quality.

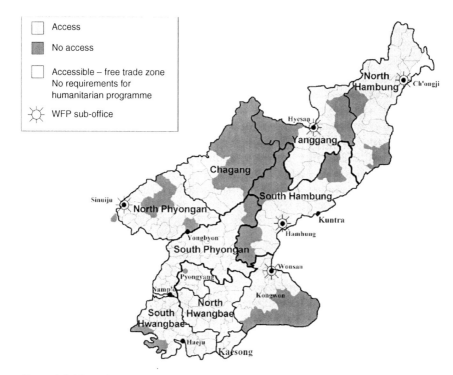

Figure 9.3 Map of the World Food Program's North Korea operations as of January 2004 (source: World Food Programme, Map Resources. Adapted by Manyin and Jun (2003)).

Take, for example, an EU/UNICEF/WFP nutritional survey that found that 16 per cent of surveyed children were wasted (low weight-for-height), 62 per cent were stunted (low height-for-age) and 61 per cent were under-weight (low weight-for-age) (WFP 1998). This implies that the incidence of wasting among children in North Korea was more than double that in Angola, a country in the midst of a thirty-year civil war, and more than 50 per cent worse than in Sierra Leone, a country that had collapsed into virtual anarchy. A 2002 survey conducted by North Korea's Central Bureau of Statistics (CBS), in collaboration with UNICEF and WFP, implied extraordinary improvements in nutritional status – underweight falling from 61 to 21 per cent, stunting from 62 to 42 per cent, and wasting from 16 to 9 per cent. Indeed, the proportion of low birth weights in the North Korean survey (6.7 per cent) is actually lower than that for the US (7.6 per cent).

There are at least two possible explanations for these stunning sets of numbers. The North Koreans, UNICEF and WFP attribute these gains to food aid (CBS 2002; WFP 2003a). Another (admittedly speculative) explanation is mis-measurement. The first survey obtained extremely high stunting and underweight percentages, both in an absolute sense and relative to the much lower wasting percentage. Both of these measures involve age. It might be assumed that the UNICEF/WFP enumerators who conducted the first survey, being unable to speak Korean, may well have misinterpreted the responses to questions about the children's ages, and systematically over-estimated the ages of the children in their sample – hence the shocking figures on the age-related measures. The second survey was conducted by the North Koreans, who presumably got the ages right, hence the disproportionate improvement in the age-related measures. In any event, the surveys may not be representative. The North Korean authorities excluded Chaggang and Kangwon provinces from the surveys – two provinces that still remain largely beyond WFP access.

Excess mortality

Given the secrecy of the North Korean regime, it is unsurprising that contemporaneous estimates of the excess death toll vary enormously, ranging from 220,000 to 3.5 million (Noland 2000). In 2003, USAID Administrator Andrew Natsios testified that '2.5 million people, or 10 per cent of the population' had died in the famine (Natsios 2003). This is almost certainly an exaggeration. If the pre-crisis population of North Korea was approximately twenty-two million, and one assumes that there were no excess deaths among the privileged populations of the armed forces (about one million) or the capital city Pyongyang (around three million), this would leave a total non-privileged or 'exposed' population of around eighteen million people. The work of Robinson *et al.* (1999) implies an excess mortality rate of roughly 12 per cent for North Hamgyong province. Applying the 12 per cent figure to the 'exposed' population of eighteen million yields a figure of just over two million, which would have to be considered an upper estimate. Put another way, if one accepts the Robinson *et al.* estimate of 245,000 excess deaths for North Hamkyong province out of a pre-crisis population of approximately two million, the Natsios statement implies that there must have been roughly 2.25 million deaths among the remaining sixteen million 'exposed' population, indicating an excess mortality rate of 14 per cent – or 15 per cent higher for the country as a whole than Robinson *et al.* calculated for what was, by consensus, the worst affected province.

Taking 1994 as the base, two demographers, Daniel Goodkind and Lorraine West (2001), using official DPRK statistics on crude death rates together with an age-specific death rate model, estimated excess deaths of 236,900 between 1995 and 2000. Using the same model with the much higher mortality rates implied by the Robinson *et al.* interviews generated an estimate of 2,648,939 excess deaths over the same period – a figure more than ten times the estimate derived from the official statistics. Goodkind and West then used data from the 1997 and 1998 WFP nutritional surveys and, calibrating from China's experience in the 'Great Leap Forward' famine, obtained estimates of excess deaths of 605,458 and 1,042,021, respectively – their preferred estimates.

On the basis of a close analysis of official statistics, Suk Lee (2003) argues that there was a significant increase in mortality rates in 1994, which implies that the famine was well underway before the flooding of June 1995. Again, using a sex- and age-specific model of death rates, Lee estimates that, between 1 January 1994 and 31 August 1999, North Korea experienced 668,000 excess deaths. Lee ignores population loss due to refugee flows into China, and, as a consequence, his analysis may misattribute these as famine-related deaths. At the same time, if he is right that the famine really started in 1994, then Goodkind and West have underestimated its impact by taking the already elevated crude death rates in 1994 as their base. Both Goodkind and West, and Lee, assume that fertility rates remained unchanged and hence do not consider births foregone.

In summary, the timing and impact of the famine are still not well understood. The most recent and sophisticated attempts to measure excess deaths put them in the range of roughly 600,000 to one million, or approximately 3 to 5 per cent of the pre-crisis population.

Marketization

As the PDS failed and the famine intensified, food was increasingly allocated through informal markets. As such, the situation more closely resembled past famines in market economies described by Amartya Sen (1981), Martin Ravallion (1987) and others. Access to food appears to be determined by a combination of geographic location (food surplus or deficit region), occupation (urban or rural), access to foreign exchange (either through official employment or non-official economic activities, or remittances – principally from relatives in Japan and, increasingly, China). This is to say that access to food varies positively with physical proximity to its cultivation and access to foreign exchange.

In these circumstances, control of aid potentially confers astronomical rents – a situation abetted by the inability of official relief agencies continuously to monitor the distribution of supplies. Suspicions that aid flows have been diverted for private use have been reinforced by consistent testimonies from refugees that they had not received aid before fleeing the country, and by eye-witness reports of grain in bags with international relief-agency markings being sold in the farmers' markets.[17] Given the North Korean state's long history of illicit commercial activity (drug trafficking, smuggling, counterfeiting, etc.) and the system-fraying that has occurred over the past decade, it is entirely plausible that private individuals and groups have managed substantially to capture these rents.

Indeed, some have argued that international aid agencies should circumvent the government distribution channels entirely, inasmuch as providing aid through the government simply strengthens the power of the totalitarian North Korean state relative to nascent non-state actors. As Scott Snyder (2003b: 119) observes:

> the amount of food distributed through the PDS is no longer an accurate indicator of imminent distress within the North Korean system, yet it has remained the WFP's primary indicator of distress and the primary vehicle through which the WFP distributes food inside the country. In this respect, the WFP is an ally of the government in its efforts to re-establish control over the means of production.

Or, in the words of Fiona Terry, an MSF researcher, 'by channelling [aid] through the regime responsible for the suffering, it has become part of the system of oppression' (Terry 2001).

As the crisis continued, several foreign governmental and private organizations, concerned about political sustainability and donor fatigue, attempted to reorient their programmes from the provision of food aid to agricultural development assistance, with mixed success. Disenchantment with North Korean behaviour coupled with emerging food crises elsewhere caused the WFP in 2002 and 2003 to miss its assistance target and cut back the number of North Koreans that it was in principle assisting, from 6.4 million (almost a third of the population) to 3.5 million.[18] In late 2004 the North Korean Government informed the UN that it was not interested in participating in the 2005 consolidated appeal of the UN agencies. Some observers interpreted this action as a North Korean bargaining ploy, signalling its annoyance with what it considered to be the increasingly intrusive demands of the international donor community. Nevertheless, the North Korean action created an odd situation in which foreign would-be donors were claiming that the North Korean population was in serious distress, while the North Korean Government discounted or downplayed the problem.

Policy changes

In July 2002, the Government of North Korea announced changes in economic policy that could be regarded as having four components: microeconomic policy changes, macroeconomic policy changes, special economic zones and aid-seeking.

With respect to the microeconomic reforms, involving, among other things, an attempt to increase the importance of material incentives, opinions about what the North Koreans are trying to accomplish range widely.[19] In the industrial sector there is some thought that the government was attempting to adopt a dual-price strategy similar to that which the Chinese have implemented in the industrial sphere. In essence, the Chinese instructed their state-owned enterprises to continue to fulfil the plan, but once planned production obligations were fulfilled, the enterprises were free to hire factors and produce products for sale on the open market. In other words, the plan was essentially frozen in time, and marginal growth occurred according to market dictates. Yet the North Korean planning apparatus may have reached such an advanced stage of decline that the conditions under which such an approach might have been viable have passed (Babson and Newcomb 2004).

North Korean enterprises have been instructed that they are responsible for covering their own costs – that is, no more state subsidies. But at the same time, the state has administratively raised wage levels, with certain favoured groups (such as military personnel, party officials, scientists and coal miners) receiving supernormal increases (Gey 2004: Table 2). These adjustments of real wages across occupational groups could be interpreted as an attempt to enhance the role of material incentives in labour allocation, or alternatively simply an attempt to reward favoured constituencies. Likewise, the state continues to maintain an administered price structure, though by fiat, state prices are being brought in line with prices observed in the markets. The North Koreans have not announced any mechanism for periodically adjusting prices, however, so that over time disequilibria, possibly severe, will develop.

In essence, enterprise managers are being told to meet hard budget constraints, but they are being given little scope to manage. Managers have been authorized to make limited purchases of intermediate inputs and to make autonomous investments out of retained earnings. They are also permitted to engage in international trade. Yet it is unclear to what extent managers have been sanctioned to hire, fire and promote workers, or to what extent remuneration will be determined by the market. This is problematic (as it has been in other transitional economies): the state has told the enterprises that they must cover costs, yet it continues to administer prices and, in the absence of any formal bankruptcy or other 'exit' mechanism, there is no prescribed method for enterprises that cannot cover costs to cease operations, nor, in the absence of a social safety net, is it clear how workers from closed enterprises would survive.

Anecdotal evidence suggests that North Korean enterprises are exhibiting a variety of responses: some have set up side businesses, either as a legitimate coping mechanism or as a dodge to shed unwanted labour; some have cut wages (despite the official wage increase); some have kept afloat by procuring loans from the Central Bank (the North Koreans have sent officials to China to study the Chinese banking system, which, although it may well have virtues, is also the primary mechanism through which loss-making state-owned enterprises are kept alive); and some enterprises have closed. It is likely that some enterprises will be kept in operation, supported by implicit subsidies, either through national or local government budgets, or soon-to-be non-performing loans from the Central Bank. The expansion of domestic credit in the absence of any significant increase in domestic supply in turn contributes to domestic inflation. Some indication of this can be gleaned from the black market value of the North Korean *won*, which has depreciated steadily since the reforms were introduced, with one mid-2004 report putting it at 1,600 *won* to the US dollar.[20]

In the agricultural sector, the government has implemented a policy of increasing the procurement prices of grains to increase the volume of food entering the PDS, along with a dramatic increase in PDS prices to consumers, with the retail prices of grains rising by 40,000 to 60,000 per cent in the space of six months after July 2002. The increase in the procurement price for grain was motivated in part to counter the supply response of farmers, who, in the face of derisory procurement prices, were diverting acreage away from grain to tobacco, and using grain to produce liquor for sale.

The maintenance of the PDS as a mechanism for distributing food is presumably an attempt to maintain the social contract that everyone will be guaranteed a minimum survival ration, while narrowing the disequilibrium between the market and plan prices. Residents are still issued monthly ration cards; if they do not have sufficient funds to purchase the monthly allotment, it is automatically carried over to the next month. Wealthy households are not allowed to purchase quantities in excess of the monthly allotment through the PDS. The system is organized to prevent arbitrage in ration coupons between rich and poor households.[21]

Some have questioned the extent to which this is a real policy change and how much it is simply a ratification of system-fraying that has already occurred – there is considerable evidence that most food, for example, was already being distributed through markets, not the PDS. However, this may indeed be precisely the motivation behind the increases in producer prices – with little supply entering the PDS people increasingly obtained their food from non-state sources, and by bringing more supply into state-controlled channels the government can try to reduce the extent to which food is allocated purely on the basis of purchasing power. Yet another motivation may be to reduce the fiscal strain imposed by the implicit subsidy provided to urban consumers.

WFP reports that, after the July 2002 price changes, prices for grain in the farmers' markets rose 'significantly' while PDS prices remained largely unchanged (WFP 2003b). Anecdotal accounts suggest that as a consequence, despite the increase in procurement prices, the policy has not been successful in coaxing back domestic supply (as distinct from international aid) into the PDS system. Although daily rations through the PDS have been raised, the practical importance of this is unclear, other than perhaps to alter the maximum allocation per household when food is available. The system no longer appears to be the primary source of food, and indeed anecdotal reports indicate that the system is not operating in all areas of the country.

When China began its reforms in 1979, more than 70 per cent of the population was in the agricultural sector – as was the case in Vietnam when it initiated reforms the following decade. De-bureaucratization of agriculture under these conditions permits rapid increases in productivity and the release of labour into the nascent non-state-owned manufacturing sector. The key in this situation is that change is likely to produce few losers: farmers' incomes go up as marginal and average value product in the agricultural sector increase; the incomes of those leaving the farms rise as they receive higher-wage jobs in the manufacturing sector; and urban workers in the state-owned heavy industry sector benefit as their real wages rise as a result of lower food prices associated with expanded supply. The efficiency gains in agriculture essentially finance an economy-wide Pareto-improvement (i.e. nobody is made worse off). This dynamic was understood by Chinese policymakers, who used a combination of the dual-price system (allowing the market to surround the plan, to use a Maoist metaphor) and side payments to state-owned enterprises, their associated government ministries and allied local politicians, to suppress political opposition to the reforms. The existence of a large, labour-intensive agricultural sector is one of the few robust explanators of relative success in the transition from central planning to the market (Åslund *et al.* 1996).

In contrast, North Korea has perhaps half that share employed in agriculture. As a consequence, the absolute magnitude of the supply response is likely to be smaller and the population share directly benefiting from the increase in producer prices for agricultural goods is roughly half as large as in China and Vietnam. This means that reform in North Korea is less likely to be Pareto-improving than in the cases of China or Vietnam. Instead, reform in North Korea is more likely to create losers and, with them, the possibility of unrest, as discussed below.

In sum, there is little if any evidence of resurgence in industrial activity, and consensus among most outside observers is that, at the time of writing, marketization has not delivered as hoped. The main 2003 and 2004 harvests were fairly large, but it is unclear how much of this was due to favourable weather, to provision of fertilizer aid by South Korea, and/or to incentive changes.

At the same time that the government announced the marketization initiatives, it also announced tremendous increases in administered wages and prices. To get a grasp on the magnitude of these price changes, consider this: when China raised the price of grains at the start of its reforms in November 1979, the increase was in the order of 25 per cent. By comparison, North Korea has raised the prices of maize and rice by more than 40,000 per cent. In the absence of huge supply responses, the result has been an enormous jump in the price level and ongoing inflation.[22]

Unfortunately, macroeconomic stability at the time that reforms are initiated is the second robust predictor of relative success in transition from a planned economy to a market economy (Åslund *et al.* 1996). High rates of inflation do not portend well for North Korea.

Under these conditions, access to foreign currency may act as insurance against inflation, and in fact the black market value of the North Korean *won* has dropped steadily since the reforms were announced. Those with access to foreign exchange, such as senior party officials, will be relatively insulated from the effects of inflation. Agricultural workers may benefit from 'automatic' pay increases as the price of grain rises, but salaried workers without access to foreign exchange will fall behind. In other words, the process of marketization and inflation will contribute to the exacerbation of existing social differences in North Korea.

The third component of the North Korean economic policy change is the formation of various sorts of special economic zones (SEZs).[23] In September 2002, the North Korean Government announced the establishment of a special administrative region (SAR) at Sinuiju. In certain respects the location of the new zone was not surprising: the North Koreans had been talking about doing something in the Sinuiju area since 1998. Yet in other respects the announcement was extraordinary. The North Koreans announced that the zone would exist completely outside North Korea's usual legal structures, that it would have its own flag and issue its own passports, and that land could be leased for fifty years. To top it off, the SAR would not be run by a North Korean, but instead by a Chinese-born entrepreneur with Dutch citizenship named Yang Bin, who was promptly arrested by the Chinese authorities. Press reports over the next two years subsequently touted a Hong Kong businessman-philanthropist, Kim Jong-il's brother-in-law, and an ethnic Korean Republican mayor of a small town in California (!) to succeed Yang. In October 2004, it was reported that North Korea was abandoning the project.

Ultimately, the industrial park at Kaesong, oriented toward South Korea, may have a bigger impact on the economy than either the Rajin-Sonbong or Sinuiju zones. In the long run, South Korean SMEs (small and medium-sized enterprises) will be a natural source of investment and transfer of appropriate technology to the North. However, in the absence of physical or legal infrastructure, they are unlikely to invest. The eventual signing of four economic cooperation agreements between the North and South on issues such as taxation and foreign exchange transactions could be regarded as providing the legal infrastructure for economic activity by the SMEs. However, the North Koreans have inexplicably failed to open the necessary transportation links to South Korea on their side of the demilitarized zone (DMZ), though the park was scheduled to open in late 2004. Negotiations with the South on this issue continue.

The fourth component of the economic plan consisted of passing the hat. In September 2002, during the first-ever meeting between the Heads of Government of Japan and North Korea, Chairman Kim managed to extract from Prime Minister Koizumi a commitment to provide a large financial transfer to North Korea as part of the diplomatic normalization process to settle post-colonial claims, despite the shaky state of Japanese public finances.[24] Each of the leaders then expressed regrets for their countries' respective transgressions and agreed to pursue diplomatic normalization. However, Kim's bald admission that North Korean agents had indeed kidnapped twelve Japanese citizens and that most of the abductees were dead set off a political firestorm in Japan. This revelation, together with the April 2003 admission that North Korea possessed nuclear weapons in contravention of multiple international agreements, put the diplomatic rapprochement on hold, and with it the prospects of a large capital infusion from Japan, diminishing the already dim prospects of admission to international financial institutions such as the World Bank and Asian Development Bank. A second visit to Pyongyang by Prime Minister Koizumi in July 2004 generated a resumption of Japanese aid. However, after the first tranche had been delivered, the disclosure that the remains of one allegedly deceased Japanese abductee were not in fact her bones (indeed were probably the remains of several individuals) created such a political backlash that the Japanese Government suspended further aid deliveries and passed legislation making it easier to impose economic sanctions on the DPRK.

Conclusions

North Korea is into its second decade of food crisis. It experienced a famine in the 1990s that killed perhaps 3 to 5 per cent of the pre-famine population. Yet remarkably little has changed since then: grain production has not recovered, and inexpertly enacted policy changes, a deteriorating diplomatic environment, donor fatigue and an utterly ruthless government keep the country on the precipice of famine.

Unlike other Communist countries that have experienced famine, the case of North Korea represents less the introduction of misguided policies than the cumulative effect of two generations of economic mismanagement and social engineering. As a consequence, the policies are so embedded in the social and political fabric of the country that they may well prove more difficult to reverse than has been the case elsewhere. The country could improve food availability by freeing up resources currently devoted to the military, but as long as the government pursues 'military first' politics, this is unlikely.

Aid is not a viable long-term solution to the North Korean food crisis – the food gap is too large and the political sustainability of aid too precarious. And while incentive reforms could contribute to productivity increases in agriculture, given the economic fundamentals of the DPRK – a high ratio of population to arable land, relatively high northerly latitude and short growing season – it is doubtful whether a food security strategy based on domestic agricultural revitalization is advisable either.[25] Only industrial revitalization and a relaxation of the balance of payments constraint that would allow North Korea to import bulk grains on a commercial basis – like its neighbours South Korea, China and Japan do – are likely to meet human needs and obviate the need for concessional assistance.

It is not at all clear that the current leadership is willing to countenance the erosion of state control that would accompany the degree of marketization necessary to revitalize the economy. The leadership of the DPRK regards 'survival' as the first in a lexicographic set of preferences, and the regime has a history of confounding predictions of its demise. Moreover, for the last decade it has been enabled by neighbours who, for their own reasons, prefer its continued existence to its disappearance. The amount of external assistance necessary to keep it on 'survival rations' is not large (Michell 1998). In economic terms, the DPRK is a relatively small Chinese province – and it is likely that neither China nor South Korea will stand by idly while their neighbour implodes. Ironically, it is rival South Korea – which for economically self-interested reasons fears the North's collapse – that has emerged as its most reliable benefactor.

Considerable research suggests that in the absence of a firm ideological commitment to reform, the provision of aid impedes policy change by enabling governments to avoid difficult and painful policy choices (Noland 2004). If this interpretation is correct, then we should expect hesitancy in the implementation of reforms, and a strong reliance on the international social safety net supplied by the rest of the world – especially China and South Korea, which place less emphasis on transparency and non-discrimination in the provision of relief. The problem is that such an outcome in all likelihood implies the continuation of the North Korean food crisis.

Notes

1 This chapter has been produced by kind permission of the Institute for International Economics. I would like to thank Paul Karner for research assistance, and Stephen Devereux and Wing Lam for helpful comments on an earlier draft.
2 The issue of excess deaths is analysed in more detail below. On the difficulty of assessing North Korea's population statistics, see Eberstadt and Banister (1992) and Eberstadt (2001).
3 See Devereux (2000) for an overview.
4 See Foster-Carter (1994), Hunter (1999), Lankov (2003) and KINU (2004) on the classification system.
5 For detailed examinations of the prison camp system, see Hawk (2003) and KINU (2004). Kang (2002) is the memoir of one camp survivor.
6 Jonathon Watts, 'How North Korea is Embracing Capitalism,' *The Guardian*, 3 December 2003. See also Kim (2003), Amnesty International (2004), and Woo (2004) for analyses of food insecurity issues.

7 See Smith (1998) on the difficulties of estimating North Korean supply of, and demand for, grains, and a withering critique of the FAO and WFP's methodology for estimating these magnitudes.

8 These figures should be viewed with a degree of scepticism. In all probability, the import figures do not include food obtained through barter transactions on the Chinese border as well as food provided by Chinese provincial governments. Both became important in the late 1990s as the famine intensified and the North Korean control system began to fray. Nor do the aid figures include aid from China, which reportedly reached 500,000 tonnes in 1996. See Noland (2000) for more details.

9 For example, a UN survey concluded that the flooding displaced 500,000 people, not the 5.4 million the government initially claimed. See also Smith (1998). In Brunel's terms, this apparent attempt to exploit the situation to obtain aid would make North Korea an 'exposed' famine at the same time as it was a 'hidden' famine! North Korean Government control of information and access has been an ongoing issue throughout the whole emergency.

10 A notable exception in this regard was the Asia Regional Director of the WFP, John Powell, who observed correctly that 'the major problem facing the DPRK in food supply and food production is structural. It is not natural disasters' (Seoul, Reuters, 2 December 2001).

11 A careful analysis of trade 'mirror statistics' indicates that while commercial imports of bulk grains dropped considerably during the 1990s, North Korea continued to import small quantities of 'bread or biscuits', 'cakes or pastries' and even 'diet infant cereal preparation', presumably to be consumed by the political elite and their offspring (Eberstadt 1998).

12 Noland (2000: Table 5.2) provides nine examples of 'food for talks'. One example is the February 2003 US Government announcement, in the run-up to diplomatic talks over the North Korean nuclear weapons programme, that it would provide 40,000 tonnes of grain to North Korea, despite the fact that the North Koreans had not fulfilled the June 2002 aid transparency and monitoring conditions that had been reaffirmed the previous month, January 2003, by USAID Administrator Andrew Natsios. China implicitly linked its donations to political behaviour continuing in the diplomatic manoeuvring around the Six Party Talks over the North Korean nuclear programme in 2003 and 2004. Japan explicitly linked its support to diplomatic developments when cutting off aid in 2002, restoring it in 2004, then suspending it again later that year.

13 That said, it has frequently been alleged that the North Korean authorities have diverted aid intended for humanitarian uses for other purposes. In one such example, a Thai senate committee concluded that rice sold to North Korea on concessional terms had been diverted to West Africa (*Joongang Ilbo*, 22 May 2002). Another case was the discovery by Australian authorities of US food aid on the heroin-laden *Pong Su*, seized in April 2003.

14 There have been persistent rumours that data compiled on defecting North Korean soldiers record a decrease in their average size, implying that the onset of the food crisis was sometime in the 1980s. The Korean People's Army has reportedly lowered its minimum height requirement for male conscripts from 150 cm to 125 cm.

15 See Noland (2000), Natsios (2001), Kim (2003) and J. W. Lee (2003) for further details.

16 See Manyin and Jun (2003) and Snyder (2003b) for details. Korean-speaking South Korean officials are the obvious exception to this rule. However, the South Koreans have shown little enthusiasm for monitoring their aid contributions, making visits on only roughly a monthly basis to supervise the distribution of 400,000 tonnes of rice in 2003 and 2004.

17 These reports are not conclusive – it is plausible that the bags have simply been recycled. At the same time, the North Korean authorities go to great lengths to deny foreigners access to these markets. See Manyin and Jun (2003) for a more extensive discussion of aid diversion issues.

18 USAID Administrator Natsios, for example, explained that 'there are needs in other areas of the world. If I have a choice to make, it's going to provide the food aid where we can assure that it's going to those at risk' (Doug Struck, *Washington Post*, 5 December 2002).

19 See J. Lee (2002), Chung (2003), Frank (2003), Nam (2003), Newcomb (2003), Oh (2003) and Gey (2004).

20 Chosun Ilbo, July 27, 2004; translated as 'South Korea reports defections rising despite North efforts to tighten border', *BBC Worldwide Monitoring*, 29 July 2004.

21 Oh (2003) claims that the ration coupons have been abolished and, in theory, wealthy households can buy unlimited supplies through the PDS.

22 See Frank (2003), Noland (2003) and Oh (2003) for recitations of other, non-agricultural, price increases.

23 The first such zone was established in the Rajin-Sonbong region in the extreme north-east of the country in 1991. It has proved to be a failure for a variety of reasons, including its geographic isolation, poor infrastructure, onerous rules and interference in enterprise management by party officials. See Jung *et al.* (2003) for an appraisal of the North Korean SEZ policy.

24 Japanese officials did not deny formulas reported in the press that would put the total value of a multiyear package in the form of grants, subsidized loans, and trade credits at approximately $10 billion. This magnitude is consistent with the size of Japan's 1965 post-colonial settlement with South Korea, adjusted for population, inflation, exchange rate changes and interest foregone. Given the puny size of the North Korean economy, this is a gigantic sum. See Manyin (2003) for further discussion.

25 Some aid agencies have attempted to emphasize increasing agricultural efficiency as a means of alleviating the North Korean crisis. The North Koreans have played to this tendency, for example in 2000 announcing through the WFP that, with good weather and $250 million in additional assistance, it would be self-sufficient within two years. For the most sophisticated rendition of an 'agriculture-centric' strategy, see McCarthy (2001).

References

Amnesty International (2004) 'Starved of rights: human rights and the food crisis in the Democratic People's Republic of Korea (North Korea)' (available at www.web.amnesty.org/library/index/engasa240032004).

Åslund, A., Boone, P. and Johnson, S. (1996) 'How to stabilize: lessons from post-communist countries', *Brookings Papers on Economic Activity*, 1: 217–313.

Babson, B. and Newcomb, W. (2004) 'Economic perspectives on demise scenarios for DPRK', unpublished.

Central Bureau of Statistics (North Korea) (2002) 'Report on the DPRK nutrition assessment 2002', 20 November.

Chung, Y. (2003) 'The prospects of economic reform in North Korea and the direction of its economic development', *Vantage Point*, 26(5): 43–53.

de Waal, A. (2000) 'Democratic political process and the fight against famine', *IDS Working Paper* 107, Brighton: Institute of Development Studies.

Devereux, S. (2000) 'Famine in the twentieth century', *IDS Working Paper* 105, Brighton: Institute of Development Studies.

Eberstadt, N. (1998) 'North Korea's interlocked economic crises', *Asian Survey*, 38(3): 203–30.

Eberstadt, N. (2000) 'Our own-style statistics': availability and reliability of official quantitative data for the Democratic People's Republic of Korea', *The Economics of Korean Reunification*, 5(1): 68–93.

Eberstadt, N. and Banister, J. (1992) *The Population of North Korea*, Berkeley CA: Institute of East Asian Studies.

Eberstadt, N., Rubin, M. and Tretyakova, A. (1995) 'The collapse of Soviet and Russian trade with North Korea, 1989–1993: impact and implications', *The Korean Journal of National Unification*, 4: 87–104.

Flake, L. (2003) 'The experience of US NGOs in North Korea', in L. Flake and S. Snyder (eds), *Paved With Good Intentions: The NGO Experience in North Korea*, Westport, CT: Praeger.

Food and Agricultural Organization (FAO) (2003) *The State of Food Insecurity in the World 2003*, Rome: FAO.

Foster-Carter, A. (1994) 'Korea: sociopolitical realities of reuniting a divided nation', in T. Hendricksen and Kyong-soo Lho (eds), *One Korea?* Stanford, CA: Hoover Institute Press.

Frank, R. (2003) 'A socialist market economy in North Korea? Systemic restrictions and a quantitative analysis', unpublished paper, New York, NY: Columbia University.

Garenne, M. (2002) 'The political economy of an urban famine: Antananarivo 1985–1986', *IDS Bulletin*, 33(4): 55–62.

Gazdar, H. (2002) 'Pre-modern, modern, and postmodern famine in Iraq', *IDS Bulletin*, 33(4): 63–9.

Gey, P. (2004) 'North Korea: Soviet-style reform and the erosion of the state economy', *Internationale Politik und Geschellschaft*, Heft 1/2004: S. 115–33 (available at www.fes.de/ipg/online1_2004/artgey.htm, in German). English version Dialogue and Cooperation, Singapore, no. 1/2004.

Goodkind, D. and West, L. (2001) 'The North Korean famine and its demographic impact', *Population and Development Review*, 27(2): 219–38.

Hawk, D. (2003) *The Hidden Gulag*, Washington, DC: US Committee for Human Rights in North Korea.

Hunter, H.-L. (1999) *Kim Il-sung's North Korea*, Westport, CT: Praeger.

Jung, E., Kim, Y. and Kobayashi, T. (2003) 'North Korea's Special Economic Zones: obstacles and opportunities', in *Confrontation and Innovation on the Korean Peninsula*, Washington, DC: Korea Economic Institute.

Kang, C. (2002) *The Aquariums of Pyongyang*, New York, NY: Basic Books.

Kim, S. (2003). 'North Korea's unofficial market economy and its implications', *International Journal of Korean Studies*, 7(1): 147–64.

Kim, W., Lee H. and Summer, D. (1998) 'Assessing the food situation in North Korea', *Economic Development and Cultural Change*, 46(3): 519–34.

Korea Institute for National Unification (KINU) (2004) *White Paper on Human Rights in North Korea 2004*, Seoul: KINU.

Lankov, A. (2003) 'Pyongyang: rules of engagement', *Pacific Review*, 16(4): 617–26.

Lee, H. (2000) *North Korea: Strange Socialist Fortress*, Westport, CT: Praeger.

Lee, J. (2002) 'The implications of North Korea's reform program and its effects on state capacity', *Korea and World Affairs*, 26(3): 357–64.

Lee, J. W. (2003). 'Outlook for international agency assistance for North Korea', *Korea Focus*, 11(5): 77–93.

Lee, S. (2003) 'Food shortages and economic institutions in the Democratic People's Republic of Korea', unpublished doctoral dissertation, Department of Economics, University of Warwick, Coventry.

Manyin, M. (2003) 'Japan–North Korea relations: selected issues', Washington, DC: Library of Congress Congressional Research Service, 26 November.

Manyin, M. and Jun, R. (2003) 'US assistance to North Korea', Washington, DC: Library of Congress Congressional Research Service, 17 March.

McCarthy, T. (2001) 'Agriculture, cooperatives, and the Korean peace process: time matters', Paper presented at the North–South Institute Workshop 'The DPRK: Where From? Where To?', Ottawa, 9–10 April.

Michell, A. (1998) 'The current North Korean economy', in M. Noland (ed.), *Economic Integration of the Korean Peninsula*, Washington, DC: Institute for International Economics.

Nam, S. (2003) 'Moves toward economic reforms', *Vantage Point*, 26(10): 18–22.

Natsios, A. (2001) *The Great North Korean Famine*, Washington, DC: US Institute for Peace.

Natsios, A. (2003) 'Testimony', Committee on Foreign Relations, Subcommittee on East Asian and Pacific Affairs, United States Senate, 5 June.

Newcomb, W. (2003) 'Reflections on North Korea's economic reform', *Korea's Economy 2003*, vol. 19, Washington, DC: Korea Economic Institute of America.

Noland, M. (2000) *Avoiding the Apocalypse: The Future of the Two Koreas*, Washington, DC: Institute for International Economics.

Noland, M. (2003) 'Famine and reform in North Korea', *Working Paper* 03–5, Washington, DC: Institute for International Economics.

Noland, M. (2004) *Korea After Kim Jong-il*, Washington, DC: Institute for International Economics.

Noland, M., Robinson, S. and Wang, T. (2001) 'Famine in North Korea: causes and cures', *Economic Development and Cultural Change*, 49(4): 741–67.

Oh, S. (2003) 'Changes in the North Korean economy: new policies and limitations', *Korea's Economy 2003*, vol. 19, Washington, DC: Korea Economic Institute of America.

Powell, J. (2002) 'Testimony before the subcommittee on East Asia and the Pacific House International Relations Committee' (available at www.house.gov/international_relations/107/powe0502.htm).

Ravallion, M. (1987) *Markets and Famines*, Oxford: Clarendon Press.

Robinson, W., Lee, M., Hill, K. and Burnham, G. (1999) 'Mortality in North Korean migrant households: a retrospective study', *Lancet*, 354: 291–5.

Sen, A. (1981) *Poverty and Famines: An Essay on Entitlement and Deprivation*, Oxford: Clarendon Press.

Smith, H. (1998) 'The food economy: catalyst for collapse?', in M. Noland (ed.), *Economic Integration of the Korean Peninsula*, Washington, DC: Institute for International Economics.

Smith, H. and Huang, Y. (2003) 'Trade disruption, collectivisation and food crisis in North Korea', in P. Drysdale, Y. Huang, and M. Kawai (eds), *Achieving High Growth: Experience of Transitional Economies in East Asia*, London: Routledge.

Snyder, S. (2003a) 'The NGO experience in North Korea', in L. Flake and S. Snyder (eds), *Paved With Good Intentions: The NGO Experience in North Korea*, Westport, CT: Praeger.

Snyder, S. (2003b) 'Lessons of the NGO experience in North Korea', in L. Flake and S. Snyder (eds), *Paved With Good Intentions: The NGO Experience in North Korea*, Westport, CT: Praeger.

Terry, F. (2001) 'Feeding the dictator', *Guardian*, 6 August.

United States Department of State (2004) *Country Reports on Human Rights Practices, North Korea*, 25 February (available at www.state.gov/g/drl/rls/hrrpt/2003/27775.htm).

WFP (1998) 'Nutritional survey of the DPRK', November, Geneva.

WFP (2003a) 'Child nutrition survey shows improvements in DPRK but UN agencies concerned about holding onto gains', 20 February, Pyongyang/Geneva.

WFP (2003b) 'Public Distribution System (PDS) in DPRK', 21 May, DPR Korea Country Office.

Woo, S. (2004) 'North Korea's food crisis', *Korea Focus*, 12(3): 63–80.

10 Why do famines persist in the Horn of Africa?

Ethiopia, 1999–2003

Sue Lautze and Daniel Maxwell[1]

Introduction

In 1999–2000 and again in 2002–2003, Ethiopia suffered wide-scale humanitarian crises, triggered in part by drought but ultimately caused by a variety of factors, both domestic and international. Whether these crises constituted 'famines' or not was hotly debated by practitioners and policy-makers at the time. In retrospect there is little doubt that both these crises were famines, although the magnitude of human suffering or loss of life was not as extensive as during the famine of 1984–1985. Though the television images in 1999–2000 were more dramatic, the 2002–2003 crisis was more widespread.

While the international community was slow to respond in 1999–2000, the 2002–2003 crisis was met with a more timely response, particularly in terms of emergency food assistance from the Ethiopian and US Governments. The reasons for the improved humanitarian response in 2002–2003 are not simply that the lessons from 1999–2000 were well learned. Some of the lessons from emergency responses in Ethiopia and elsewhere have yet to be taken on board by the Government of Ethiopia (GoE), the donors or the operational agencies, especially with respect to basic emergency non-food interventions. The very differing responses to the two crises are better explained by relations between donors and the Ethiopian Government than they are by humanitarian response capacity at the times of the crises.

Despite a flurry of post-crisis activities, there is to date only a partial consensus about the steps necessary to prevent small- and large-scale famines from returning to Ethiopia in the short, medium or long term. As has happened in the aftermath of every crisis since 1985, the donor community and the GoE vowed in both 2001 and 2004 to deal with under-lying causes as a means of preventing similar crises in future. However, the politics and strategies of a major humanitarian response are very different from those entailed in the long-term poverty reduction efforts that remain urgently required to reduce Ethiopia's vulnerability to repeated crises. Some of the government's proposed strategies for addressing vulnerability are controversial (e.g. resettlement of farmers from drought-prone areas), and this is both dampening donor support for and delimiting the discourse about famine prevention strategies in Ethiopia. Regrettably, the conditions for famine in the Horn of Africa continue virtually unabated.

This chapter draws on recent experience in Ethiopia to add to the general understanding of famine in the twenty-first century. The chapter briefly reviews the history of famine in Ethiopia and discusses key lessons arising from the 1999–2000 and 2002–2003 crisis responses, before analysing the underlying processes that continue to cause these distressingly frequent events. The key constraints to addressing the causes of famine comprise the conclusions to the chapter.

The history of famine in Ethiopia[2]

Famine is not a new phenomenon in Ethiopia, or in the Horn of Africa. Historical accounts and records left by palace chroniclers, residents and travelling foreigners reflect that disasters such as famines and plagues were believed to be punishments from God for failing the true faith (Hussein 1976). Historical accounts dating from the medieval period and the better-documented accounts from the sixteenth and seventeenth centuries suggest that famine was a frequent occurrence through the ages. While drought is commonly regarded as the main cause of Ethiopian famines, Pankhurst notes that socio-economic factors played a significant role. These included natural phenomena (e.g. deforestation, soil erosion and exhaustion), technological constraints (primitive agricultural tools, inadequate grain storage) and social trends (e.g. fragmentation of land holdings, systems of land tenure, arbitrary taxation and civil wars) (Pankhurst 1984). Widespread public health impacts compounded the nutritional stress associated with food crises (Toole and Waldman 1990), the latest of which has been the HIV/AIDS epidemic.

While the central and northern highlands (primarily Wollo and Tigray) have long been considered Ethiopia's most famine-prone areas, historical accounts indicate that the pastoral areas of the east and south were vulnerable to intermittent crises as well. Sen (1981: 87) rightly analysed the 1972–1974 famine as 'really two Ethiopian famines', one affecting crop farmers in the northern highlands, the second afflicting pastoralists in the south-eastern lowlands. Traditionally, livelihoods in the pastoral areas were better adapted to cope with drought, but recurrent crises have undermined coping capacities over time. Studies in Borana Zone (southern Oromiya Region) indicate that the pattern since 1980 appears to be a 'herd crash' every six to eight years (Desta 1999). Elders in Shinille Zone (Somali Region) reported six major droughts between 1951 and 2000 – on average, one every eight years (Abdi 2001).

In the late twentieth century, major famines were a significant threat to government power. The Wollo famine of 1973 contributed to Haile

Selassie's overthrow in 1974. The 1984–1985 famine contributed in no small way to the mobilization of forces that eventually led to the overthrow of the Derg. In response to this historical pattern, key political actors within Ethiopia and beyond have focused their concerns on the acute phase of famine as a discrete event with clear political consequences, rather than understanding famine to be a long-term process of deepening risk and vulnerability with clear causal factors beyond the immediate triggers of an event. The two views have sharply differing implications for famine prevention and response strategies, with the former held by both the GoE and the donors – a point that can be noted in the nature of their short-term, food aid-dominated emergency response patterns and a marked absence of long-term effective strategies for reducing famine risks.

When the Ethiopian People's Revolutionary Defence Forces (EPRDF) took power in 1991, the Relief and Rehabilitation Commission (RRC) was recast as the Disaster Prevention and Preparedness Commission (DPPC) and given a broader mandate befitting its name. Significant resources were devoted to improved famine early warning systems, focused on the north-eastern highland agricultural areas (because vulnerability was believed to be the greatest in these areas and/or because it was the political heartland of the EPRDF). A strategic reserve, the Emergency Food Security Reserve (EFSR), was established to ensure that adequate food stocks were available to respond to 'outbreaks' of famine in the interim time it took to mobilize an international response. All of these measures were designed to prevent those types of acute famine events that cause regimes to fall. Against this criterion, these systems have worked remarkably well. The current government remains remarkably invulnerable to famine, in part due to the government's successful shifting of the political geography of famine in Ethiopia. This has been effected through relief and development food aid policies, among other measures, that protect the politically favoured central and northern highlands at the expense of the more marginalized communities of the nation's periphery (Clay et al. 1999).

The international response has also focused on the salient fact that famines have led to the overthrow of governments in Ethiopia. The nature of relations between the GoE and the international donor community has informed not only the response to acute famine events, but also the nature of efforts (or lack thereof) to deal with underlying causes of food and livelihood insecurity in between acute crises. In recent years, both GoE and donor policies and strategies have been aimed primarily at preventing famine 'events'. Efforts have largely focused on trying to predict and prepare better for acute crises and to mitigate their worst impacts more effectively, particularly on nutritional status, mortality and distress migration.

By contrast, there has been an inadequate focus on long-term development strategies to address directly the underlying processes that lead to the most obvious manifestations of acute crises. Indeed, several unusually good harvests in the mid- to late 1990s led many observers to think that conventional rural development strategies had overcome the famine threat in post-revolutionary Ethiopia (Masefield 1997). Poverty indicators improved and the numbers of people requiring food assistance dropped. The onset of the 1999–2000 crisis was as much a shock to this 'development optimism' as it was to the livelihoods of affected communities. However, the people of Ethiopia are likely to be more vulnerable to another acute crisis today than they were even in 1999.

The 1999–2000 and the 2002–2003 famines

The 1999–2000 crisis

The 1999–2000 crisis was the most far-reaching to hit Ethiopia since the catastrophic famines of the mid-1980s.[3] It was actually several events joined together (most of them triggered by drought or at least very erratic rainfall). With an early warning system (EWS) and emergency response agencies designed to detect and respond to rainfall and production anomalies in the agricultural highlands of Ethiopia, the EWS failed adequately to detect the escalating vulnerability in the pastoral areas, where the crisis struck hardest.

In both the agricultural and pastoral areas, the failure of the rains (and attendant failure of crops and pastures) contributed to a decline in food availability and access, and a collapse of livelihoods. The impact of the 1999–2000 crisis was made more substantial by a failure of rapid and/or appropriate responses. Even with the most immediately available resource – food aid – a major gap developed in the pipeline during late 1999 and early 2000 (Figure 10.1), while non-food responses (especially in health, water and sanitation) lagged throughout the crisis.

Simultaneously, the EFSR was only partially stocked at the outset of the crisis, and was not able to bridge the gap in the international response. Figure 10.1 shows substantial shortfalls in food available for distribution throughout the second half of 1999 and the first several months of 1999–2000. The EFSR held a stock of only about 75,000 tonnes of grain. This was about a quarter of its capacity of 307,000 tonnes, and much less than the 450,000 tonnes required to bridge the deficit in the first six months of the acute crisis (Hammond and Maxwell 2002).

Molla (2001), citing DPPC data, notes that the Somali Region received food aid equivalent to only 20 per cent of the assessed requirement during 1999. Given the lack of information about the nature and distribution of vulnerability among pastoralist communities in the region, the assessed requirement was lower than actual needs. Such shortfalls in deliveries in 1999 contributed to deepen the impact of the crisis in the Somali Region during 2000.

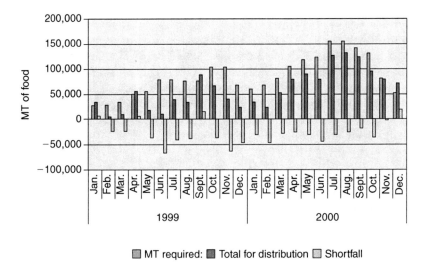

Figure 10.1 Shortfall in food distributions (MT) in Ethiopia in 1999–2000 (source: DPPC Fortnightly Bulletins, WFP; FEWSNET/CARE (2000)).

Note
Figures are combined from several sources; for any given month they might not be precisely correct due to differences in the way monthly totals were calculated by different sources. Overall, they do present an accurate picture.

By March 2000, when the crisis was 'discovered' by the international media, these cumulative response failures had resulted in widespread human malnutrition and mortality, while the drought had also led to widespread losses of livestock assets (Sandford and Habtu 2000). Although the emergency response had been increasing by the time the media spotlight turned on the Somali Region, the media portrayed the crisis as being widely ignored. Once again the media could claim that it was they who had brought it to the attention of the policymakers, as they had in 1984. By August 2000, over ten million people were on the food aid rolls. The hardest hit areas of the Somali Region had suffered human mortality estimated to be in the tens of thousands (Salama *et al.* 2001).

The crisis and the response were vastly complicated by a destructive and vicious war with Eritrea, fought between mid-1998 and June 2000 over a disputed border area with symbolic importance but no significant strategic value to either country. The war was not the cause of the humanitarian crisis in Ethiopia, but it provided the geo-political backdrop to the donor response. Most donor governments viewed it as a futile dispute between two belligerent, chronically impoverished and drought-affected countries, neither of which would compromise to find a peaceful solution. Both diverted substantial portions of their national resources to the fighting – and therefore away from the drought crisis affecting both countries.

After a two-year stalemate, Ethiopia mounted a major offensive against Eritrea in May 2000 (at the height of the famine), eventually breaking through Eritrean defences and effectively ending the war.[4]

The end of the war prompted increased donor support for responses to the humanitarian crisis in Ethiopia. By year's end, the humanitarian crisis was declared over. Post-crisis evaluations found that the response was characterized by the familiar problems of logistical and bureaucratic delays, and of information inadequacies and poor linkages with responses. More importantly, though, there were serious problems of mistrust between the GoE and donors. Initially mistrust was apparent over the means of assessing and reporting assistance needs, but this was substantially heightened by the GoE's determination to prosecute the war despite the humanitarian crisis in the country (Hammond and Maxwell 2002; White 2004). For the most part, the donor community focused resources on immediate responses to the crisis; adequate support for addressing underlying causes was lacking by both the Ethiopian and international communities. Perhaps people thought that there would be plenty of time to prepare for the next crisis, since a powerful – but inaccurate – narrative is that famine strikes Ethiopia only about once every ten years.

The 2002–2003 crisis

An even more widespread emergency became apparent in Ethiopia beginning in early 2002 in the Afar region, and by mid-2002 in other parts of the country. The story of this crisis is one of repeated underestimation of needs, due in part to inadequate analysis of the impact of cumulative stresses on a range of livelihoods systems throughout Ethiopia. Scepticism on the part of some in the international donor community, especially the European Commission, led to semantic quibbling over whether or not 'famine' had returned to Ethiopia. The US Government's food aid response was notably robust, but key non-food interventions lagged damagingly behind, as they had just three years earlier.

The crisis differed from the 1999–2000 famine in that a number of 'real-time' studies were conducted by external famine experts. Many in the donor and relief practitioner communities in Addis Ababa were particularly keen to avoid the acrimonious post-crisis public and academic criticisms of their responses that had followed the 1999–2000 crisis. At the end of the day, however, a familiar pattern emerged: a food aid-dominated relief response that was adequate to prevent regime change; a weak non-food aid response; lack of adequate support to livelihoods systems in the midst of crisis; a premature hastening by officials of all stripes within and beyond Ethiopia to declare the crisis over; and a lack of a coherent, post-crisis strategy to reduce the embedded vulnerabilities that characterize a wide range of Ethiopian livelihoods systems. What had changed were Ethiopia's relationships with some key donors. By 2002, Ethiopia's relationship with the West (especially the US) had been substantially transformed by the events in New York and Washington, DC on 11 September 2001. Famine in Ethiopia was no longer just a humanitarian concern – it was also a question of geo-political stability in a frontline state for the US-declared 'war on terror'.

The 2002–2003 crisis arrived so soon on the heels of the 1999–2000 drought that many affected households, communities and regions did not have sufficient respite for recovery before the latest crisis intensified. An emergency food aid response – eventually reaching a total of 1.8 million tonnes – was launched but, as in the previous crisis, the non-food aid response was lacking in both timeliness and appropriateness.[5] In addition, the overall response was hindered by dissonance in the donor community regarding the exact nature of the crisis, in particular on whether to classify the situation as a famine or not. The resulting delays in response as organizations quibbled prompted one observer to describe a new form of mortality in times of crisis in Ethiopia: 'Death by Definition'.

Although the scale of the crisis was repeatedly underestimated, many of the traditional early signals were detected in crop-dependent areas, and contingency plans and response scenarios were in place by mid- to late 2002 (Anderson and Choularton 2004). However, the systems failed to detect and adequately understand the cumulative, corrosive effects of multiple livelihoods shocks affecting a broad range of Ethiopian communities. Depressed global prices for coffee left farmers and wage labourers deeply vulnerable, even in the absence of further shocks. The collapse of domestic maize prices following a glut on the market in early 2002 resulted in a substantial reduction in acreage of maize planted that year. Traders working the informal trading routes between Ethiopia and Somalia were affected by border closures as the GoE clamped down on 'contraband' trade. Pastoralists were unable to market their livestock in Saudi Arabia, due to continued import bans on Ethiopian livestock following an outbreak of Rift Valley Fever. Lastly, government campaigns for water harvesting and resettlement coincided with these and other processes that deepened vulnerabilities.

Although the crisis was 'announced' in September 2002, warning signals preceded that date by a number of months. The pastoral areas of the Afar Region were hit as early as February. Poor livestock conditions and increased distress sales combined to depress returns to pastoralists at a time when grain prices increased considerably, often to unaffordable levels. With the exception of the Somali Region, where a newly instituted early warning system developed in the aftermath of the 1999–2000 crisis provided good information, localized systems of traditional early warning in pastoral areas failed to translate into timely warnings at the national or international level. Rainfall in the preceding season was also poor, leading to serious and widespread shortages of water and pasture, leaving livestock vulnerable to diseases and resulting in extensive livestock deaths in some zones. The drought seriously affected livestock populations in parts of Oromiya and the Somali region as well. Based on these developments, the DPPC revised its estimate in the July–December 2002 emergency assistance appeal to a maximum of 5.7 million people in need of assistance by August 2002. As the DPPC had done in the January food aid appeal, the government requested cereals only; no request for pulses, oil or supplementary food was made. The November 2002 multi-agency pre-harvest assessment, conducted by over twenty teams in fifty-three zones, confirmed that the lowland areas in the north, east, south and central parts of the country were severely affected, as were some central highland areas. Maize and sorghum production failure was estimated between 70 and 100 per cent. The Central Statistics Authority estimated that total production had fallen by 25.8 per cent compared to the previous year. A joint UN/Government Appeal, launched in December 2002, included $75 million for non-food sectors (particularly emergency water and public health-care requirements). This was later increased to $81 million, but the non-food assistance needs of the country remained seriously under-resourced throughout the crisis (Anderson and Choularton 2004).

Official estimates of vulnerable populations increased sharply starting in January 2003. The multi-agency pre-harvest assessment teams concluded that a total of 11.3 million people would require food aid beginning January 2003, while an additional 3.1 million people were categorized as needing 'close monitoring' – but the GoE was unable to declare a total of 14.4 million people in need of food aid in January 2003, having appealed for only 5.7 million in August 2002. By the 2003 rainy season, however, following additional assessments and appeals, 13.2 million people were officially identified by the government as needing emergency food assistance. This officially made the numbers of people affected by the 2002–2003 crisis nearly twice the number affected by the 1984–1985 famine. Unlike 1984–1985, however, population displacements to camps were minimized by both highly decentralized distributions of food and internal controls on population movement related to government policies of ethnic federalism.[6] These policies discouraged cross-regional migration, while prohibitions against providing relief in urban areas discouraged rural-urban migration.

Comparing 1999–2000 and 2002–2003

Several important themes emerge from a comparison of these two crises.

Early warning systems

Much effort has gone into the development of early warning systems in Ethiopia. To its credit, the GoE was quick to signal the crisis in 2002, although it did underestimate the magnitude of the problem. While there were problems with information in both 1999–2000 and 2002–2003, neither crisis was hidden (as the 1984–1985 crisis had been). In both 1999–2000 and 2002–2003, however, EWS failed to give adequate information about the nature and depth of the crisis in some key areas. The pastoral EWS notably failed in 1999–2000, and although it was improved in the Somali Region in 2002–2003 (the hardest hit area in 1999–2000) it failed to provide timely information about other pastoral areas. In 2002–2003, EWS information was a particular constraint in the SNNPR Region, where new 'hot spots' were continually 'discovered' by assessment teams throughout the course of the crisis. In large part, this was due to the dismantling of the region's EWS by the government in the 1990s.

Food/non-food response

In both 1999–2000 and 2002–2003, the response to the crisis was overwhelmingly focused on food and was notably deficient in other emergency interventions. As one example, in its 2003 budget the US donated nearly half a billion dollars worth of food aid but less than $20 million in other emergency assistance. While *ex post* evaluations highlighted the inadequacy of the non-food response in 1999–2000, real-time analyses highlighting this problem were conducted in 2003. There is little question that international food assistance – on a massive scale – was required to deal with the consequences of both the 2000 and the 2003 crises. While the food aid was quite late in 2000, and often did not amount to a full food basket to meet nutritional requirements in either year, the criticism here is not that food aid constituted a major part of the response. The criticism is rather that food alone was an insufficient response in either crisis – in fact, the lack of corollary inputs, especially emergency health care and water, seriously limited the effectiveness of the food aid response. Moreover, by focusing so much attention on meeting short-term consumption needs, donors and other humanitarian actors conceptualized the acute phase of famine as a discrete event rather than as the logical outcome of the underlying livelihoods crisis – a point that can be noted in the marked absence of longer-term strategies for reducing famine risks.

Crisis over; business as usual

The 2002–2003 crisis was rather arbitrarily declared over in early 2004, in no small part due to internal Ethiopian Government and external international donor pressure to reduce food aid recipient numbers, while also signalling that conditions had returned to 'normal' so that development activities could restart. Complacency following major relief efforts appears to follow historical patterns. A review of US Government Title II emergency food assistance to Ethiopia between 1983 and 2003 shows how emergency assistance tapers off dramatically following acute crises

(USAID nd). By 2001, much of the focus of USAID-Ethiopia had returned to the *status quo* of food security programming – at pre-crisis funding levels. Again, the criticism is not that programmes quickly began to focus on longer-term food security issues – this is exactly as it should be. However, the relatively meagre level of resources devoted to this task in comparison with the resources devoted to crisis response, and the lack of a coherent strategy that connected emergency response to long-term vulnerability reduction, rendered the emphasis on longer-term solutions ineffective.

What? Famine, again?

When the DPPC began to issue warnings about the crisis in 2002, many in the international humanitarian and diplomatic community felt that, surely, 'this cannot be happening again' – it was 'too soon' for another major crisis to evolve in Ethiopia. This was in part due to the widely accepted, popular narrative that major disasters in Ethiopia only happen about once a decade, notably in 1973–1974, 1984–1985, 1990–1992 and 1999–2000. The 'once a decade' narrative is also rooted in the ten-year cycle whereby severe droughts have coincided with changes in Ethiopia's political leadership or its governance systems (e.g. 1974 and the fall of the Imperial Regime; 1984 and the change from military dictatorship to a Communist party based system; 1991 and the fall of the Derg). The 'once a decade' narrative, while seductive, is nevertheless ahistorical. In addition to the recurrent crises affecting pastoralist communities, farming populations in Ethiopia have been vulnerable to frequent cycles of disasters that include droughts, usually followed by pests or floods and frequently exacerbated by conflict.

What triggers a response?

The lack of response in 1999 to an obvious, rapidly deteriorating situation appalled many in the humanitarian community. By contrast, the international community – especially the Americans – mounted a major food aid effort quickly in late 2002 in response to existing information and appeals. While the efforts of a few key individuals in donor agencies account for some of the difference, recent research (Darcy and Hofmann 2003; Olsen *et al.* 2003) indicates that humanitarian need alone and the strength of humanitarian networks are not particularly influential factors in stimulating a crisis response from donors. Early warning information, while necessary, is also far from sufficient. The same research showed that the media plays a clear role only when there is no vital strategic interest at stake. Vital strategic interests of donor countries are paramount in determining the level of a response. The single most salient difference between 1999–2000 and 2002–2003 is the fact that the GoE and donors were at loggerheads over the war with Eritrea in 2000, whereas Ethiopia was the major regional partner of the US in its global 'war against terrorism' in 2003. Ethiopia's quest for regional super-power status was the common denominator, but the donor response to this quest was radically different in 2002–2003.

The merging of international political and security issues with questions of humanitarian policy have been analysed elsewhere under the rubric of 'coherence' (Macrae and Leader 2000). Though no-one in the donor community would admit it publicly in 1999–2000, pressure on Ethiopia and Eritrea to settle their conflict peacefully contributed to at least the delay, if not denial, of humanitarian assistance. While a few committed individuals saw to it that the 2002–2003 crisis was quickly brought to the attention of US policymakers, there is little doubt that American strategic interests in ensuring the support of Ethiopia in the war against terrorism was a critical influential factor in determining the level and speed of the response. While this factor worked to the clear advantage of the GoE in 2002–2003, there is little to celebrate in this latest chapter of the politicization of humanitarian response. At the end of the day, essential non-food emergency assistance and support for the recovery of livelihood systems remain badly lacking for the people of Ethiopia. However, for vulnerable populations living in less strategically important areas elsewhere in the region (Burundi, Democratic Republic of Congo, etc.), woefully under-funded response to conflict-related crises remains the norm.

Addressing the underlying causes

In both 1999–2000 and 2002–2003, the trigger for EWS and humanitarian action was drought or erratic rainfall, but the factors underlying these crises were much more complex. Foremost among these factors is an increasing level of destitution, the decline of rural livelihoods and the lack of alternative urban-based or rural non-farm employment options. A lack of basic services and rural infrastructure; taxation and land policies that do not promote investment in agriculture but force smallholders to deplete scarce resource bases for short-term survival; and international economic shocks such as the collapse of coffee prices and restrictions on livestock exports to the Middle East are additional contributory factors. This combination of factors has been referred to by FEWS NET (2003) and Raven-Roberts et al. (2004) as 'inter-locking vulnerabilities'. These vulnerabilities are shown in Figure 10.2.

The major interlocking factors include:

- Rapid population growth in the order of 3 per cent per year, meaning that the total population of Ethiopia has increased by more than 50 per cent since the 1985 famine
- Declining average rainfall, with greater variability on a year-to-year

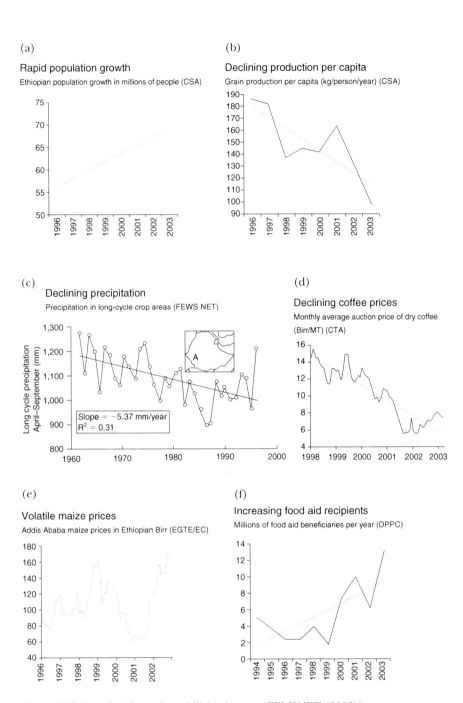

Figure 10.2 Inter-locking vulnerabilities (source: FEWSNET (2003)).

basis, which increases the prospects of both drought- and flood-
related emergencies

- Declining per capita food production, from an average of 180 kg of
grain per person per year in 1996 to 120 kg in 2002
- Declining coffee prices, with falling hard currency reserves for the
government and new vulnerabilities among previously wealthier
coffee farmers and other rural groups
- High volatility of basic food grain prices, e.g. maize prices fluctuated
between 60 and 180 Birr over a twelve-month period between late
2001 and late 2002, depressing commercial producer incentives for
grain in the midst of a major crisis
- Increasing numbers of destitute people and increasing numbers of
people requiring long-term social assistance as a form of welfare
support.

The trends presented in Figure 10.2 give little reason for optimism. These
combined pressures on the rural economy have rendered millions of
households nearly assetless and living close to the edge of survival. This
widespread condition of fragile existence partially explains why drought,
which is typically considered a 'slow-onset' crisis, appeared to erupt so suddenly and devastatingly in mid- to- late 2002.

Destitution, of course, is the result of the trends pictured in Figure
10.2, as well as the result of repeated exposures to shocks. The dynamics
of destitution go far beyond what can be depicted in Figure 10.2. A major
study of destitution in highland Ethiopia (Devereux *et al.* 2003) focused
not only on obviously measurable factors such as asset ownership and
income, or bio-physical well-being measures such as health and nutritional
status, but also on less easily measured elements such as social exclusion
and political marginalization (a finding echoed by Lautze *et al.* 2003).

The level of assistance for food-insecure households, even in non-crisis
years, is also problematic. As Figure 10.3 depicts, even in 'good' years
Ethiopia requires substantial levels of food aid. The proportion of food aid
pledged compared to food aid requirements is highly variable, and is typically higher in 'crisis' than in non-crisis years (see Hammond and Maxwell
2002). On average, about 70 per cent of assessed need is met on an annual
basis, but this figure ranges from a low of 50 per cent in some years to a high
of 100 per cent in 2003.[7] It can be inferred that vulnerable populations identified in food security assessments are more likely to receive assistance in
years of large-scale crisis than they are during more localized events.

The impact on livelihoods during years not labelled as national crises
includes the steady decline in asset ownership, either through forced sales
of physical assets or through the depletion of land and natural resource
assets by over-intensification. In the absence of coherent, generous and
widespread programmes of crisis recovery, more households end up on
the rolls of the 'chronically eligible' for long-term food aid receipts.

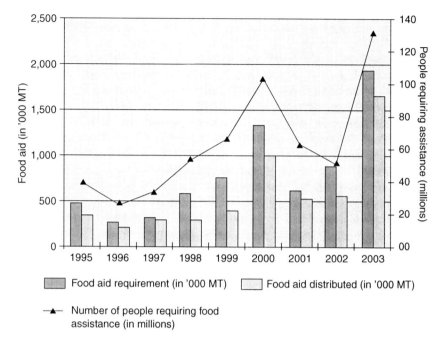

Figure 10.3 Food assistance requirements and levels of response (1995–2003) (source: FEWSNET).

A plethora of other factors have been highlighted as contributing to rural vulnerability and livelihood insecurity in Ethiopia. These include high degrees of land tenure insecurity; poor infrastructure and poorly functioning markets; inequitable taxation; skewed political representation that contributes to the marginalization of some groups, including those on the peripheral regions that have been strongly affected in the recent crisis (SNNPR, Afar, Somali); a nascent civil society that has yet to serve as an effective voice for marginalized groups; and government 'development' policies that have perverse effects on livelihood security, at least in the short term (over-emphasis on technical fixes like rainwater harvesting, or 'social engineering' interventions like population resettlement schemes). At the time of writing in late 2004, close to record numbers of people remain on the food aid rolls. In the medium term, any anti-famine strategy in Ethiopia will have to involve substantial safety nets and a sustained humanitarian response capacity, but it must also address critical underlying factors.

Components of a new strategy for promoting food security have been proposed by the 'New Coalition for Food Security in Ethiopia,' a group comprised primarily of government departments, donors and a few international NGOs, but not Ethiopian civil society. Anti-famine interventions remain heavily food-focused, even if the underlying analysis is broader. The main strategies proposed by the 'New Coalition' revolve around:

1   Developing a safety-net mechanism for annually recurrent 'predictable' food aid needs, so that assistance to chronically vulnerable groups can be facilitated more quickly than the current humanitarian response approach (which inevitably involves assessments, appeals, donor responses, etc. before assistance is made available for targeted groups). Safety nets are viewed by the GoE and key donors as a strategy for both famine prevention and poverty alleviation. They are expected to function alongside humanitarian response, with the former targeted to chronically food-insecure populations and the latter targeted to emergency-affected groups.

2   Increased investment in agriculture and rural infrastructure as the leading sector (called Agricultural Development-Led Industrialization, or ADLI). The main emphasis is on improving agricultural production through improved agricultural technology, soil and water conservation measures (with heavy emphasis on water harvesting techniques), improved livestock production support services, and diversification of production.

3   Diversifying rural household income sources through improved access to credit and diversified skill-sets.

4   Improved rural health-care systems.

5   Voluntary resettlement of substantial proportions of the rural population (in the first phase, 2.2 million people in three years) from currently chronically vulnerable areas to less populated areas elsewhere, but only within the settlers' administrative region of origin.

It remains to be seen whether donors will support these efforts to the degree required, or indeed if there is adequate consensus that these policy prescriptions will be effective in reducing medium- and long-term vulnerability among Ethiopia's poor and destitute. Of particular concern is the viability of the government's ambitious programme of resettlement. The GoE continues to proceed with resettlement programmes despite concerns that many settler communities are not viable. The drain on government resources that the resettlement programme represents, as well as the unfavourable history of resettlement in Ethiopia (especially during the crisis of 1984–1985), poses dilemmas for donors when they consider their support for other GoE development programmes.

The US, the European Union and the World Bank have committed themselves to supporting the development of safety nets, but safety nets are predicated on the assumption that they will only be needed for a relatively short period (three to five years) before recipients can be 'graduated' (i.e. achieve self-sufficiency). Donor contributions to agriculture, rural development and rural health have historically been underfunded, and to date there is little to indicate a sea change in donor attitudes towards rural development. However, for safety-net programmes to successfully 'graduate' recipients in a relatively short timeframe, substantial investment in rural development will be required alongside the safety-net interventions.

Donors, in the meantime, have pushed ahead to develop their own strategies for combating famine in Ethiopia, which overlap with, but do not completely conform to, the government's strategy. The US strategy tends to still highlight food assistance in the form of food for safety nets rather than emergency food aid. The donor community does not appear to have reached (or even sought) consensus on non-food strategies in emergencies, including the role for complementary cash-based relief strategies (Marchione and Novick 2003).

In Ethiopia today, donors are concerned about the impact of crises on poverty reduction strategies but not to such an extent that they have developed adequately aggressive long-term strategies for reducing famine vulnerability. The PRSP process has promoted a degree of harmony across donor strategies for Ethiopia, at least in terms of their development portfolios. The process has provided a forum for dialogue and engagement between the donors and the government. The PRSP's agenda:

> includes the ADLI strategy, reform of the civil service and the judiciary, decentralization and empowerment and capacity building ... to stimulate a poverty-reducing growth strategy by creating an enabling environment to support private sector development and provide more efficient delivery of public services.
>
> (European Food Security Network 2001)

Many donors have adopted elements of this strategy to mirror their own.

However, disasters generally still tend to be viewed by donors (and the GoE) as exogenous events, something that must be dealt with in order to return to the tasks of development (Duffield 2001). Notably missing from the PRSP analysis is any recognition that Ethiopia's disasters are endogenous, i.e. embedded in Ethiopia's ecological, economic, political and social systems. The historical view that disasters strike at the whim of nature remains powerful in contemporary Ethiopian development discourse. In short, while there is evidence of renewed effort to achieve a consensus on reducing food insecurity in Ethiopia, it is unclear if the programmes evolved thus far will substantially reduce – much less overcome – the threat of famine.

Conclusion: why do famines persist?

Recent famines in Ethiopia have been largely contained from a political viewpoint, but at increasing cost to poor, destitute and marginalized populations. Though popular discourse continues to characterize famines in the Horn of Africa as exogenous 'events' – and attributes the causation of these events largely to the whims of nature – clear reasons for the persistence of famine are built into Ethiopia's position in the international economy, the policy objectives of the GoE and its donor partners, and in the responses of humanitarian agencies. Famines persist in Ethiopia in no small part because of the forces of globalization. The livestock import bans that prevented Afar and Somali pastoralists from marketing their livestock to the Middle East, for example, cannot be ameliorated with a sack of food aid. The long-term collapse in the price of coffee has radically altered the distribution and manifestations of vulnerability in Ethiopia. A lack of integrated cereal markets continues to undermine financial returns to – and rational planning by – smallholder producers in the highlands and in western Ethiopia. Long-term efforts to combat famine must address these – and a plethora of other – policy issues.

The two crises that have already struck Ethiopia in the twenty-first century can be characterized as famines. In their 'famine scales' study, Howe and Devereux (Chapter 2, this volume) categorize the Ethiopia crisis of 1999–2000 as a 'level 3' or 'moderate' famine. However, the patterns of suffering were articulated in either a more diffuse manner or were concentrated in more local contexts than were the catastrophic crises of the mid-1980s. Localized or highly diffuse crises appear to provoke less dire political consequences than do crises involving concentrated and massive deaths in 'famine camps', as in 1984–1985. The implication of these differing manifestations of famine for the development and relief strategies before, during and after famines is enormous. For the classic famine image, there can be no room for debate: large numbers of starving people camped *en masse* in areas where foreign NGOs and the UN are present is a famine. The diffuse suffering caused by the creeping collapse of livelihood systems that characterized much of the 2003 crisis can be a famine to academics and front-line aid workers – or it can merely be 'a normal bad year for Ethiopia' for policymakers and headquarters officials.[8] The point is that the diffuse nature of the 2003 crisis neither drew the media attention nor aroused the public concern of earlier famines. The implication is that had there not been substantial geo-political interest in stability in the Horn of Africa, the crisis might have been much worse.

It is worth returning to the question of mortality estimates in the 1999–2000 crisis, in particular the US Centre for Disease Control and Prevention study (Salama *et al.* 2001). The article's mortality estimates were accompanied by a sharp critique of the non-food responses as well as the inadequacies of food aid alone in preventing disaster mortality. In particular, the juxtaposition of remarks by the head of WFP claiming that 'famine had been averted' with epidemiological evidence pointing to the contrary caused a flurry of debate in Addis Ababa. Two years after its publication, tempers in Ethiopia were still running high about the article. Unfortunately, as the subsequent response to the crisis of 2002–2003 was to prove, much of this was defensive posturing by agencies rather than effective soul-searching about lessons learned. This has led one of us to note elsewhere that famines in Ethiopia are neither declared nor averted, but rather are declared to be averted (Lautze and Raven-Roberts 2004).

Food aid as *the* instrument of containment of crises continues to demonstrate unshakable resilience in the face of criticism from a wide range of observers about the insufficiencies of food aid-dominated responses to humanitarian crises. Food availability decline models continue to inform both early warning and the character of disaster response in Ethiopia. Crises, therefore, are conflated with food production shortfalls, especially of highland crops, and crisis response is equated with food aid rations. 'Success', at least from one view, is measured in terms of the proportion of food aid contributions provided compared to the assessed requirement.[9] This dominant model of analysis and response continues to overshadow both the 'health crisis' and 'livelihood crisis' models of analysis and response. There is no question that food assistance is and should be an ingredient of humanitarian response – indeed, as one of us has argued elsewhere, the criteria for the deployment of food as one element of humanitarian response clearly existed in Ethiopia in both 1999–2000 and in 2002–2003.[10] The point is that famines continue to be viewed mainly as food crises, with food aid the main implied need. The issue at stake here in terms of humanitarian response is the 'what else?' question. The longer-term issues are manifold, and not particularly amenable to a food aid response, but the system precludes serious reflection on the use of the food aid.

Related to this is the dominant narrative about the distinctions between 'chronic' and 'acute' vulnerable populations. This debate is also couched largely in terms of food production and food aid needs. This crowds out the influence of other useful explanations of vulnerability arising from analysis of famines and complex emergencies. In particular, the predominant form of vulnerability in complex emergencies is known to arise from political marginalization rather than either technical deficiencies in production or the vagaries of weather (Keen 1994). By keeping the debate focused on technical questions, the critical but uncomfortable questions about the relationship between acute suffering and lack of political empowerment are avoided. While vulnerable populations in the politically more important highland areas are recognized as 'chronically vulnerable' and hence 'chronically eligible' for food aid (and now, safety net assistance), it is the chronically *ineligible* – the highly vulnerable populations on the periphery who have less history of food aid receipt, and much less institutionalized machinery to make assistance available – that have demonstrated the most acute suffering in recent crises. It is no accident that the distribution of recent vulnerabilities to famine in Ethiopia closely corresponds with the lowland pastoral and southern minority populations of Somali, Afar and the SNNPR. In brief, the real issues underlying the persistence of famine are about the lack of political inclusion, not the lack of technical interventions.

The humanitarian agencies are also 'doing well by doing good'. They are deeply integrated into the pattern of crisis identification, rapid expansion of massively expensive relief programmes, and return to 'development' post-haste, post-crisis. The humanitarian community needs to look closely at the lessons from recent crises in Ethiopia, especially the implications of the lack of large-scale population displacement, which was prevented in 2003 by decentralized food aid distribution. Given the poor state of the health system in Ethiopia, there was very little in terms of non-food emergency assistance that reached these numerous but scattered populations (although localized success by the Ministry of Water Resources is worth noting). Humanitarian organizations generally shied away from engagement with the Ministry of Health during the 2002–2003 crisis, in part because NGOs are particularly poor at fixing systems in times of crisis in general, and in part because the Ministry of Health had demonstrated a weak (at best) interest in responding to the crisis. The scholarship on famine, including Salama *et al.*'s (2001) article on Gode, has taught the humanitarian community about the dangers of large-scale population migration and concentration; what recent famines in Ethiopia need to teach us is the danger of vulnerable populations staying *in situ*. What, for example, are the primary causes and patterns of malnutrition, morbidity and mortality when vulnerable people stay at home but are unable to access public, private or international assistance?

Lessons from 2003 include the need for decentralized health surveillance (in addition to food security monitoring), more attention to basic health care and water – and the systems that provide both, whether in times of crisis or not. The humanitarian community must also articulate much more clearly that addressing the processes of destitution – not simply improving rapid response – is the most important component of famine prevention in Ethiopia. However, the fact that the humanitarian community was largely excluded from the 'New Coalition for Food Security' discussions reflects the bifurcated – rather than integrated – view of short-term and longer-term factors in the dominant famine analysis prevailing in Addis Ababa.

The media, for the most part, were kept at bay in 2003 because the classic image of famine – so strongly imprinted on the public eye in the starvation at Korem when broadcast by the BBC in 1984 – was prevented from materializing, again due to decentralized food aid distributions. The collapse of livelihoods and widespread but diffuse health crises are simply not as compelling an image as famine camps, competing for media attention with the more graphic images of war and displacement that dominate today's headlines. This is important, especially to powerful interests whose objectives are inevitably as much about political stability as about reducing humanitarian suffering.

With a host government and an international community in denial about the existence – and therefore the nature – of famine in Ethiopia, and with a clear lack of consensus about addressing the political causes of famine (as opposed to containing the political consequences thereof), it is not difficult to surmise the reasons for the persistence of famine in this part of the Horn of Africa. The interests that defy understanding of the famine process in Ethiopia exhibit what Mark Duffield terms 'functional ignorance' (Duffield 1996). From the point of view of powerful actors, perhaps especially the US, the responses to the recent famines can be considered a success for more reasons than simply the fact that they were not followed by the collapse or toppling of the government, although one could surmise that this is *the* lesson the GoE can take away from these crises. Meanwhile, the lack of publicity afforded by the diffuse nature of the crisis allows the UN and the humanitarian community the opportunity to resist calling crises 'famines'. The sensitivity surrounding the term 'famine' in Ethiopia is not a benign debate about semantics, but rather serves a highly functional purpose. To paraphrase the famous insight of David Keen by turning it on its head, there are benefits of non-famines.

The question of why famines persist in the Horn of Africa therefore hinges largely on the way in which the problem of famine is defined: in terms of political containment or in terms of political empowerment. Famines defined as 'events' have largely been proven to be containable – albeit at considerable (and increasing) effort and expense. Famines defined as the logical outcomes of longer-term processes have hardly even been dented by the efforts of the past two decades – as evidenced by the interlocking vulnerabilities graphically depicted earlier in this chapter. Donor concerns about political stability tend to preclude honest and constructive critiques of the GoE's long-term recovery programmes. Clearly, exposures to the vagaries of global politics and the world market have far surpassed the vagaries of weather as the driving force of vulnerability in Ethiopia. The question now remains whether there is adequate impetus from any of the key actors in Ethiopia – the government, donors, international organizations and affected populations – to effect the radical transformation in the systems of vulnerability identification and strategies required for alleviating risks and vulnerabilities across multiple time-frames.

Notes

1 This chapter reflects the personal views of the authors, and does not represent the official views of either Tufts University or CARE International.
2 Unless otherwise noted, this section draws heavily from Lautze *et al.* (2003).
3 The 1999–2000 crisis has been reviewed in depth by Hammond (2001),

Hammond and Maxwell (2002), Maxwell (2002), Molla (2001), Salama *et al.* (2001) and Sandford and Habtu (2000). This section draws on these reviews.

4 There was a substantial humanitarian crisis in Eritrea resulting from the invasion, but that is beyond the scope of this paper.

5 Like the 1999–2000 crisis, the 2003–2003 crisis has been evaluated by numerous authors, including Lautze *et al.* (2003), Anderson and Choularton (2004), OCHA (2004) and Raven-Roberts *et al.* (2004). This review draws on all of these evaluations.

6 This policy of the current government redrew regional boundaries to conform with broad ethnic groupings. The upshot for population movement, especially planned resettlement, is that people are discouraged from settling outside their region of origin.

7 Although not depicted in Figure 10.3, the food aid appeal for 2003 was eventually 100 per cent resourced.

8 An actual quotation to one of the authors from a donor agency official.

9 This view is moderated somewhat by the reliance on widespread monitoring of nutritional status and occasional mortality surveys, but it is nevertheless the main point of the introductory paragraph of the OCHA-led evaluation of the emergency response (OCHA 2004).

10 Barrett and Maxwell (2005) argue that food aid is an appropriate and necessary intervention in emergencies where there is both an underlying shortfall in food availability and market failures that require that food be provided in-kind – conditions that existed in parts of Ethiopia in both 2000 and 2003.

References

Abdi, M. (2001) 'A briefing note on the pastoral family in Shinile Zone of the Somali Region', mimeo, Addis Ababa.

Anderson, S. and Choularton, R. (2004) 'Retrospective analysis – 2002–2003 crisis in Ethiopia: Early warning and response', Nairobi: FEWS NET.

Barrett, C. and Maxwell D. (2005) *Food Aid After Fifty Years: Recasting its Role*, London: Routledge.

Clay, D., Molla, D. and Habtewold, D. (1999) 'Food aid targeting in Ethiopia. A study of who needs it and who gets it', *Food Policy*, 24(4): 391–409.

Darcy, J. and Hofmann, C. (2003) 'According to need? Needs assessment and decision-making in the humanitarian sector', *HPG Report* 15, London: Overseas Development Institute.

Desta, S. (1999) 'Diversification of livestock assets for risk management in the Borana pastoral system of Southern Ethiopia', unpublished PhD Dissertation, Logan: Utah State University.

Devereux, S., Sharp, K. and Yared Amare (2003) 'Destitution in Wollo, Ethiopia', *IDS Research Report* 55, Brighton: Institute of Development Studies.

Duffield, M. (1996) 'The symphony of the damned: racial discourse, complex political emergencies and humanitarian aid', *Disasters*, 20(3): 173–93.

Duffield, M. (2001) *Global Governance and the New Wars: The Merging of Development and Security*, New York, NY: Zed Books.

European Food Security Network (2001) 'Donors shifting to sector and budget support: final report', Brussels: EFSN.

FEWS NET (2003) 'The evolution of crisis: a chronology of food insecurity in Ethiopia', Addis Ababa: FEWS NET.

FEWS NET/CARE (2000) *Greater Horn of Africa Food Security Update*, 15 December, Nairobi: FEWS NET/CARE.

Hammond, L. (2001) 'Lessons learned study: Ethiopia drought emergency 1999–2000', Addis Ababa: USAID-Ethiopia.

Hammond, L. and Maxwell, D. (2002) 'The Ethiopian crisis of 1999–2000: lessons learned, questions unanswered', *Disasters*, 26(3): 262–79.

Hussein, A. M. (1976) *Rehab: Drought and Famine in Ethiopia*, London: International African Institute.

Keen, D. (1994) *The Benefits of Famine: A Political Economy of Famine and Relief in Southwestern Sudan 1983–1989*, Princeton, NJ: Princeton University Press.

Lautze, S. and Raven-Roberts, A. (2004) 'Famine (again) in Ethiopia?', *Humanitarian Exchange*, 27: 16–18.

Lautze, S., Aklilu, Y., Raven-Roberts, A., Young, H., Kebede, G. and Leaning, J. (2003) *Risk and Vulnerability in Ethiopia: Learning from the Past, Responding to the Present, Preparing for the Future*, Medford: Feinstein International Famine Center, Tufts University.

Macrae, J. and Leader, N. (2000) 'Shifting sands: the search for 'coherence' between political and humanitarian responses to complex emergencies', London: Overseas Development Institute.

Marchione, T. and Novick, P. (2003) 'Famine prevention framework for Ethiopia: decreasing vulnerability – building a resiliency safety net', Addis Ababa: USAID.

Masefield, A. (1997) 'Food security in Ethiopia: crossing the great divide?' Brighton: Institute of Development Studies.

Maxwell, D. (2002) 'Why do famines persist? A brief review of Ethiopia 1999–2000', *IDS Bulletin*, 33(4): 48–54.

Molla, D. (2001) 'When early warning fails to trigger early response: a case study from the 1999–2000 experience in the mainly pastoral Somali region of Ethiopia', Paper presented to the workshop on 'Pastoral Early Warning and Early Response Systems', Mombasa, Kenya, 13–15 November.

OCHA (2004) 'Evaluation of the response to the 2002–03 emergency in Ethiopia', Steering Committee for the Evaluation of the Joint Government and Humanitarian Partners Response to the 2002–03 Emergency in Ethiopia, Addis Ababa: OCHA.

Olsen, G., Carstensen, N. and Hoyen, K. (2003) 'Humanitarian crises: what determines the level of emergency assistance? Media coverage, donor interests and the aid business', *Disasters*, 27(2): 109–26.

Pankhurst, R. (1984) *The History of Famine & Epidemics in Ethiopia Prior to the 20th Century*, Addis Ababa: Relief and Rehabilitation Commission.

Raven-Roberts, A., Noor, A., Eshete, D., Sahlu, W., Kebede, G. and Gaudreau, M. (2004) 'Clinging to the hillsides: risk, vulnerability, and resilience in Southern Nations Nationalities and Peoples Region (SNNPR)', A report prepared for the United States Agency for International Development Office for Foreign Disaster Assistance (USAID/DCHA/OFDA), Washington DC: USAID.

Salama, P., Assefa, F., Talley, L., Spiegel, P., van der Veen, A. and Gotway, C. (2001) 'Malnutrition, measles, mortality, and the humanitarian response during a famine in Ethiopia', *Journal of the American Medical Association*, 286(5): 563–71.

Sandford, S. and Habtu, Y. (2000) 'Emergency response interventions in pastoral areas of Ethiopia', Addis Ababa: DFID.

Sen, A. (1981) *Poverty and Famines: An Essay on Entitlement and Deprivation*, Oxford: Clarendon Press.

Toole, M. J. and Waldman, R. J. (1990) 'Prevention of excess mortality in refugee and displaced populations in developing countries', *Journal of the American Medical Association*, 263(4): 3296–302.

USAID (nd) 'US Government food assistance to Ethiopia 1984–2002', Addis Ababa: USAID/Ethiopia.

White, P. (2004) 'Sovereignty and starvation: the food security dimensions of the Eritrea-Ethiopia war', in M. Plaut (ed.) *Unfinished Business – Ethiopia and Eritrea at War*, London: Red Sea Press.

11 Increased rural vulnerability in the era of globalization

Conflict and famine in Sudan during the 1990s

Luka Biong Deng

Introduction

The linkages between the persistence of famine and contemporary processes of globalization are rather blurred, not least because of the way globalization is perceived. Globalization is generally seen as an abstract concept, as 'out there' rather than being an integral part of our daily lives as individuals, communities or nations. This perception tends to mask the salience of the global dimension in understanding the determining circumstances of our livelihoods, and indeed our lives. In reality, globalization directly influences the life of the individual, whose own decisions equally affect the structures of globalization and the global forces – the mass media, multinational corporations, global economic trends, international trade relations, political alliances and institutions – that create and condition opportunities for individual choice (Sklair 2002: 2). It is the latter that has been championed by free market economists, whose thinking about globalization is dominated by impersonal forces and liberal market principles against which, paradoxically, the individual has little power. With the expansion and deepening of market competition worldwide, globalization is increasingly regarded as synonymous with the irresistible processes of economic, political, cultural and technological change that are apparently sweeping aside all national boundaries (Duffield 2000: 70).

Although the current wave of optimism regarding globalization is understandable in some respects, there is a need to recognize that the forces of globalization are equally producing certain undesirable outcomes. There is a growing consensus that globalization is creating and encouraging new and durable forms of disparity and instability in the South. Globalization has produced new actors at supranational, international and local levels, that are increasingly appropriating state authority from both 'above' and 'below' (Duffield 2000: 70). Very often the power of these actors, particularly international financial institutions, intergovernmental organizations, international NGOs and multinational corporations, supplants and overrules the social and development policies and priorities of poor countries in the South. Besides these external actors, local organizations together with newly privatized agencies and other commercial actors have taken on a wide range of roles formerly associated with the nation state and the public domain (Duffield 2000: 71). Although these new actors threaten to undermine national sovereignty, the state nonetheless tends to be held entirely accountable for any major crisis, such as a famine or civil war, while the new actors exonerate themselves from any responsibility.

Besides weakening the authority of the state in the South, the emergence of globalization has been accompanied by increasingly frequent civil conflicts and 'complex emergencies', particularly in Africa. Despite this apparent association, there is a tendency to analyse these wars in terms of internal (national or local level) causes and solutions. However, this chapter will provide evidence to show that global factors such as the colonial legacy, internationally sponsored 'development', the debt burden, the arms trade and activities of multinational corporations have also contributed greatly to the causation and sustenance of these wars. Specifically, in this atmosphere of liberalized global markets that are free from many regulatory requirements and in which minimum standards of human rights are often not observed, multinational corporations have become heavily engaged in the extraction of mineral resources in conflict-prone countries. The activities of these corporations – often backed by foreign governments – not only sustain and prolong civil wars, they also contribute to gross human rights abuses and increased vulnerability to famine, particularly in Africa. The case of Sudan attests to this collusion between humanitarianism and the ill-defined corporate responsibility of the multinational corporations. The new forms of political and economic advantage resulting from liberalized global markets have led Castells (1998) to argue that globalization has prompted the emergence of 'a globalized criminal economy'.

These global dynamics are crucially important in understanding famine causation and increased vulnerability in many parts of the world. This partly explains why we are seeing the emergence and persistence of 'new famines' that are not adequately captured by current theories and conceptual frameworks. It is this dimension of analysis that is the weakest link in our understanding of contemporary famines.

The main objective of this chapter is to analyse poverty in Sudan in the 1990s and, in particular, the famine of 1998, to unravel and widen our understanding of the global dynamics that are creating the conditions for heightened levels of vulnerability in many parts of the world. The next section discusses the theoretical linkages between complex emergencies and vulnerability. The level of vulnerability in terms of poverty and famines in Southern Sudan is analysed in the third section. The fourth section discusses causal factors, including how new global factors directly increased vulnerability in Sudan in the 1990s. General conclusions are presented in the final section.

The 'complex emergencies' approach and vulnerability

Various approaches offer complementary or competing analytical frameworks in an attempt to explain levels of vulnerability in rural areas of developing countries. These include the entitlement approach (Sen 1981), coping strategies (Davies 1993), food security (Devereux and Maxwell 2001), sustainable livelihoods (Scoones 1998), the asset-vulnerability framework (Moser 1998), social risk management (Siegel and Alwang 1999) and complex political emergencies (CPEs) (Cliffe and Luckham 1999).

Among these approaches, 'CPEs' or 'complex emergencies' provides an explanation for increased vulnerability during civil war, and offers an heuristic framework to help understand post-Cold War disasters (Cliffe and Luckham 1998, 1999; Goodhand and Hulme 1999). The new global interdependence that emerged after the Cold War ended in the late 1980s has been accompanied by an increasing frequency of complex, large-scale disasters that are highly politicized and have often eluded effective humanitarian intervention (Duffield 1993: 131). One characteristic aspect of these complex disasters is that national governments typically lack the capacity or the political will to reach and assist the needy, and may even resist external efforts to do so. This has resulted in international NGOs filling the gap by establishing parallel systems of service delivery, largely financed by international donors, that have gradually supplanted government structures (Duffield 1993: 132). South Sudan is a case in point, as successive regimes during the 1980s and 1990s denied access to needy citizens and obstructed emergency operations (Cater 1986; Deng 1999). In such a complex context, vulnerability to famine must be seen not as a natural disaster but as a socio-political crisis and a new post-Cold War phenomenon.

The roots of the 'complex emergencies' approach lie in the limitations of earlier approaches, such as entitlements and coping strategies. These approaches are inadequate to explain the phenomenon of political survival in the context of complex emergencies, as they neglect issues of power and consider only the victims of famine, ignoring the beneficiaries. Duffield (1993: 134) argues that, despite the fact that the literature on coping strategies has informed policy debates about the responses of people exposed to crises, it fails to recognize underlying power dynamics, as some coping strategies may involve the transfer of assets away from those in distress. Keen (1994: 213), on the basis of detailed accounts from Sudan, argues that the real roots of vulnerability to famine may lie less in a lack of purchasing power within the market than in a lack of people's access to the means of power – both political representation and lobbying capability. Interestingly, Keen observes a positive relationship between markets and violence, in the context of Sudan. With the development of a market-oriented economy which has created winners and losers, the losers resorted to violence in order to survive the harsh realities of uneven development and inherent inequities of the market.

Duffield (1993: 134) emphasizes that it is 'this political as opposed to economic construction of African famine, which has been argued to limit the usefulness of Sen's (1981) entitlement analysis'. Drawing heavily on the arguments of Rangasami (1985) and on their own work in conflict zones, particularly in the Horn of Africa, the 'complex emergencies' theorists (Mark Duffield, David Keen, Alex de Waal) developed an alternative framework for analysing vulnerability to starvation and famine. The main propositions of this framework include that all disasters have winners as well as losers, and that famines result from the conscious exercise of power in pursuit of gain or advantage. Accordingly, vulnerability to famine is perceived as an outcome of a process of impoverishment, resulting from the transfer of assets from the politically and economically weak to the politically and economically strong, and through sectarian and counter-insurgency warfare activities. Famines are therefore stratifying rather than levelling processes, which tend to increase economic and social inequalities. The complex emergencies approach also suggests that coping strategies are defective during civil war, as a result of conscious efforts by aggressors to undermine the ability to cope. It is in the light of this complexity of power relations and the political dimension that famine cannot be attributed to natural disasters or market failure, nor can it be characterized as a temporary shock if its continuation is advantageous to the powerful (Duffield 1993: 134).

There is no doubt that the complex emergencies approach has added a new and important dimension to vulnerability analysis. The drastic increase in the incidence of famine that is related to civil war and conflict attests to the importance of political vulnerability, rather than economic failures or natural disasters alone, in undermining or destroying rural livelihoods. This approach complements rather than negates the entitlement approach, which has the comparative advantage of unpacking the dynamic effects of generic shocks (political, economic, natural) on the household's livelihood. The complex emergencies approach provides a framework for understanding the macro- or meso-political context and the dynamics of power relations.

It is inappropriate to argue that the coping strategies and entitlement approaches are defective because they overlook the issue of power relations. After all, these approaches focus on the risk-related behaviours of households exposed to shocks; they do not claim to analyse the determinants of vulnerability. On the other hand, the analysis of power relations, particularly the strategies adopted by the winners and those in power, does describe the characteristics, intensity and severity of political vulnerability that unfolds differentially at a household level. Clearly, the 'complex emergencies' approach does not claim that political shocks affect all households in the same way, nor that households respond passively to such shocks. A holistic understanding of vulnerability requires both macro-level analysis in order to understand the context of vulnerability, as well as micro-level analysis to understand how such shocks unfold and are responded to by diverse households. Like other approaches, the complex emergencies approach limits its analysis of political vulnerability to the level of the state, and generally fails to consider the global dimensions.

Poverty and famine during civil war in Sudan

Sudan is geographically the largest country in Africa, covering an area of about one million square miles. It is also a land of extraordinary diversity, with an estimated population of about thirty-two million that is divided into fifty-six ethnic groups and more than 595 sub-ethnic groups, who speak more than 115 languages. Sudan is justifiably considered a microcosm of Africa because of its central location, reflecting within its borders all the racial, ethnic, religious and cultural diversity of the continent.

Tragically, since achieving independence in 1956 Sudan has been at war with itself, and thirty-eight of the past forty-eight years have been squandered in two protracted civil wars, the first lasting from 1955 to 1972, the second starting in 1983 and ending only with the signing of a peace agreement in January 2005. These conflicts have been perceived as reflecting a cleavage between the dominant Islamic and 'Arabized' north, comprising two-thirds of the land and population of the country, and the subordinated – but potentially richer – African south, which is predominantly 'traditional' in its religious beliefs.

Since the second civil war erupted in 1983, Sudan has experienced recurrent famines, most notably in 1984, 1988, 1991 and 1998. South Sudan, which did not experience famine either during the first civil war or in the period between the civil wars (1972–1982), experienced two major famines in 1988 and 1998. The increased vulnerability to famine of the war-affected population in recent decades highlights the need to understand better the new global factors that have contributed to the causation and sustenance of civil conflict in Sudan.

Dynamics of poverty: the curse of assets during civil war

The links between civil war and persistent vulnerability to famine can best be understood by examining the manner in which contemporary civil wars are conducted. In the context of Sudan, communities attach more significance to counter-insurgency warfare than to conventional warfare between the government and rebels, because counter-insurgency warfare has more direct impacts on their livelihoods. In order to unpack the dynamics of conflict and famine in South Sudan in the 1990s, Deng (2002a; 2003) classifies counter-insurgency into *exogenous* and *endogenous* warfare, where *endogenous* counter-insurgency emanates from within the community while *exogenous* counter-insurgency originates from outside. Deng (2002a) shows that *endogenous* counter-insurgency warfare has more profoundly negative effects on rural livelihoods and household asset management strategies than other forms of conflict.

It was found in the case of Sudan's civil war that the initial level of household asset-holdings was positively related to the occurrence of endogenous counter-insurgency warfare, with non-poor households being more susceptible than the poor, because their assets (especially livestock) were systematically targeted by the insurgents, who exploited their insider knowledge of local wealth distribution and asset management strategies. Conversely, exogenous counter-insurgency activities consisted mainly of random raids that affected community members more or less indiscriminately. As a consequence, the initially wealthy were more vulnerable to losing their assets, becoming destitute and even losing their lives – a reversal of the prediction of the entitlement approach, that vulnerability to famine is inversely correlated to incomes and asset-holdings.[1] A strong and significant positive correlation was found between famine mortality in 1998 and initial wealth, particularly among households exposed to endogenous counter-insurgency warfare, whereas a 'normal' inverse correlation prevailed among households exposed to drought elsewhere in South Sudan (Deng 2002a). Interestingly, social assets were affected in a similar way to physical assets: while social capital was found to erode in the context of endogenous counter-insurgency, social cohesion and community-based risk-sharing arrangements tend to strengthen during exogenous counter-insurgency.

The stratification of communities according to wealth is complex because the understanding of poverty varies considerably across cultures and disciplines. Despite recent shifts in the conceptualization of poverty toward multi-dimensional measures, it remains widely assumed that 'the poor' can be identified by using a single indicator (Ellis 2000). Most commonly used poverty measures are either 'subjective' (e.g. community wealth ranking) or 'objective' (e.g. income or consumption poverty headcounts derived from household budget surveys). The main problems noted by Bevan and Joireman (1997) concerning consumption poverty measurement in rural Africa are even more pronounced in a civil war situation, partly because people tend to rely increasingly on sources of food that are difficult to measure accurately – secondary crops like vegetables, wild foods, erratic deliveries of food aid – and to reduce their reliance on more easily recalled and quantifiable sources, such as market purchases. As a result of measurement difficulties during civil war, in fieldwork undertaken in South Sudan I opted to use the personal wealth ranking methodology to stratify the sample households into three wealth groups: poor, modal and non-poor (Deng 1999; 2002a).

Applying personal wealth ranking in two communities exposed to different types of counter-insurgency – endogenous (Gogrial) and exogenous (Abyei) – the results for the incidence and dynamics of poverty during the civil war are presented in Tables 11.1, 11.2 and 11.3. It is clear from Table 11.1 that there was a significant movement into the poor category during the 1990s, particularly among communities exposed to endogenous counter-insurgency warfare. This increased incidence of poverty is reinforced by the low immobility measure (I),[2] particularly among non-poor households. In order to quantify the dynamics of poverty, we adapt the proportional hazards model suggested by Cox (1972) and Baulch and McCulloch (1998) to calculate and compare the probability of entering or exiting poverty in the 1990s. It is clear from Table 11.2 that no household in our sample stood any chance of escaping poverty (0.00) during civil war, while households exposed to endogenous counter-insurgency were more likely to enter poverty (1.00) than those exposed to exogenous counter-insurgency warfare (0.8). Female-headed households and richer households were more likely to become poor during the civil war, as shown in Table 11.3.

The magnitude of famine in 1998

A community's nutritional status is generally assessed indirectly, through the nutritional status of children younger than five years. A nutrition survey conducted by UNICEF in June 1998 in Bahr el Ghazal region showed a considerable deterioration in nutrition status, particularly in areas exposed to counter-insurgency warfare (Awiel, Wau, Twic and Gogrial), as shown in Figure 11.1. While the level of severe acute malnutrition averaged about 20 per cent among the resident population, it reached as high as 40 per cent among the internally displaced population. The nutrition assessment also indicated a higher prevalence of malnutrition among boys than girls, though this difference eroded as the situation started improving. A review of the social profile of households with children in feeding programmes in Gogrial showed no significant differences between poor and non-poor households, suggesting that structural changes had occurred to the initial wealth status of households living in communities exposed to counter-insurgency warfare (Deng 1999: 12).

The size of the population in South Sudan is a highly politicized statistic, and is hotly debated by the local authorities and humanitarian agencies, as there are no commonly agreed population estimates. Even the results of national population censuses conducted in 1973 and 1983 were doubted by the people of South Sudan, who argued that both censuses under-enumerated the actual population. The long history of instability and civil war in South Sudan has also caused considerable distortions in the demography of the region, particularly in patterns of migration and

Table 11.1 Poverty dynamics: transition and movement during civil war in the 1990s

Research communities	Initial household wealth status	Level of household wealth status in the 1990s		
		Non-poor	Middle	Poor
Abyei	Non-poor	14 (6.6%)	44 (20.9%)	11 (5.2%)
	Middle	0 (0%)	81 (38.4%)	32 (15.2%)
Poor	0 (0%)	3 (1.4%)	26 (12.3%)	
	Chi-square =78.64	*Kendall's tau-b = 0.457*	*N = 211*	*I = 0.573*
Gogrial	Non-poor	0 (0%)	8 (3.9%)	59 (28.8%)
	Middle	0 (0%)	4 (2%)	96 (46.8%)
Poor	0 (0%)	2 (1%)	36 (17.5%)	
	Chi-square=4.15	*Kendall's tau-b= 0.111*	*N = 205*	*I = 0.195*

Source: Deng (2003)

Table 11.2 Simple poverty entry and exit probabilities during civil war in the 1990s

Research communities	Probability of entering poverty in the 1990s	Probability of escaping poverty	
		Poverty in the 1990s	Head count, 1990s (%)
Abyei	0.80	0.00	93.4
Gogrial	1.00	0.00	100.0

Source: Calculated from Table 11.1. If the middle households group is treated as non-poor households, then the results in Table 11.2 will be different. The probability of entering poverty will respectively be 0.236 and 0.928 in Abyei and Gogrial area, while the probability of escaping poverty will respectively be 0.103 and 0.053.

Table 11.3 Household characteristics and level of poverty during civil war in the 1990s

Characteristics of head of household	Correlation between characteristics of household and wealth status in the 1990s	
	Abyei community Pearson's R	Gogrial community Pearson's R
Initial Wealth	+*	+
Sex	–*	–*
Age	–	+
Marital Status	–*	–
Education	+	+

Source: Deng (2003).

Note
*Indicates significant at the 5% level

fertility, which makes any attempt to assess aggregate famine mortality necessarily subjective.

In assessing mortality during the 1998 famine, I used data from *Médecins Sans Frontières* (Belgium), Sudan Relief and Rehabilitation Association (SRRA) and a survey that I conducted in 1999. These sources revealed that the crude mortality rate (CMR) among the resident population in Bahr el Ghazal in 1998 was comparable to CMRs in other recent African famines, such as Ethiopia in 1973 and 1984–1985, Darfur (north Sudan) in 1984–1985 and Niger in 1974. However, among the displaced population and children under five, CMRs during the famine in Bahr el Ghazal were far higher than any other recent African famines, as shown in Figure 11.2. The CMR in July 1998 was as high as twenty-six per 10,000 people per day among the adult displaced population and forty-six per

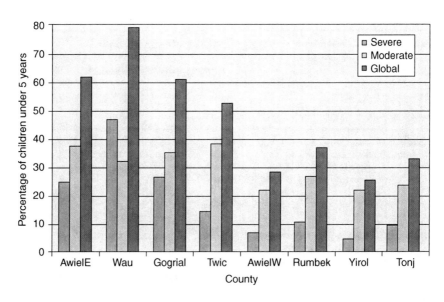

Figure 11.1 Prevalence of malnutrition in Bahr el Ghazal, 1998.

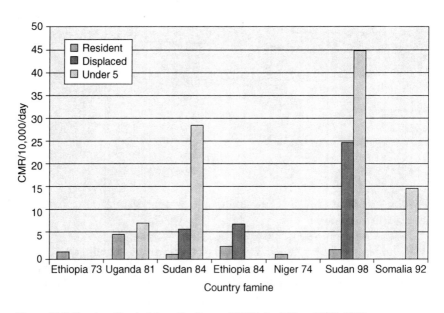

Figure 11.2 Famine Crude Mortality Rates (CMR) in Africa, 1973–1998.

10,000 among children under five. These mortality rates significantly exceed the normal CMRs for developing countries (Salama *et al.* 2001: 564).

As a baseline CMR was not available to assess excess mortality during the famine in 1998, I used the 1973 national census crude death rate of thirty-six per 1,000 persons during the census year (approximately 1/10,000 per day) as a proxy for baseline crude mortality. With actual CMR as provided by various sources, I estimated excess mortality to be around 70,000 people during the famine in 1998 (Deng 1999: 17). Alternatively, using the emergency CMR cut-off of 1/10,000 per day as a baseline,[3] together with the actual average CMR of 1.9 for the resident population of Bahr el Ghazal (721,529) and the CMR of 14.8/10,000 per day for the internally displaced population (141,505), calculated from various sources (Deng 1999: 16), the excess mortality during the period of the famine (April 1998 to January 1999) is estimated at approximately 78,000 persons.

Unfolding the global dimension of poverty and famine causation

The fundamental question is: Why were communities in South Sudan more prone to recurrent famines during the recent civil war (1983–2005) than during the first civil war (1955–1972)? Based on the experience of the famine in 1998 and the increased incidence of poverty during the 1990s in Sudan, the global dimension is discussed below to provide a more comprehensive explanation of the 'new famines' and increased poverty in the era of globalization. The aim is to contribute to both theoretical debates and the empirical analysis of famines.

Depressing though it is to be explaining the persistence of famine long after it ought to have been eradicated (Devereux 2000), understanding the causes of famine in the contemporary world remains an important ingredient of a new famine prevention policy agenda. Most theories attribute the causes of famine to local-level shocks or processes such as ecological disaster, excessive population growth, economic crisis or civil war. This conceptualization resulted in famine initially being perceived as an 'act of God' or 'law of nature', while it has more recently been regarded as an 'economic failure' at the household level and an 'act of man' at the national level (Devereux 2001: 120). As such, the global dimension has been overlooked. As discussed below in the context of South Sudan, global factors such as the colonial legacy and the roles of the World Bank, International Monetary Fund, Arab investment, multinational corporations and international humanitarian agencies, each contributed in different ways to the vulnerability that resulted in famine in 1998.

British colonial legacy: structural political vulnerability and exclusion

The first civil war that erupted in 1955, shortly before independence in 1956, was primarily caused by the British colonial authorities, who wrongly forged the present ('united') Sudan after pursuing a pattern of development which created social, economic and political inequalities that disadvantaged the South during the colonial period. For southerners, the independence that was reached between the British colonial authorities and the northern elite merely meant changing the face of colonial power from the British to the Arabized northerners (Deng 1995: 135).

Unsurprisingly for most southerners, successive post-independence central governments deliberately pursued policies that aimed to marginalize them socially, economically and politically. Immediately following independence, the army, police and administrative positions in southern Sudan were overwhelmingly filled by northerners, with southerners occupying less than 10 per cent (fourteen out of 152) of the total senior posts (Oduho and Deng 1963: 18). Also, by 1960 the South had less than an 8 per cent share in intermediate education, a 4 per cent share in secondary education and a 5 per cent share of university places (sixty out of 1,216 total students), despite constituting about 30 per cent of the national population (Oduho and Deng 1963: 46).

Even during the brief period of relative peace (1972–1982) after the Addis Ababa Agreement that granted self-government to South Sudan in 1972, the longstanding inequalities between North and South worsened further. The South, ravaged by seventeen years of civil war, failed to receive adequate revenue transfers from central government, and the average realized budget for the Southern Regional Government during the decade of peace barely covered 20 per cent of the planned budget (Deng 2002b: 14). As a result of inadequate resourcing, public services deteriorated and inter-regional inequalities in service provision widened. For example, the number of people per hospital bed in 1980 was about 800 in North Sudan, but 2,000 in the South. Inequality was more dramatic in terms of access to education, as about 2,000 northerners shared one primary school in 1980 compared to 8,000 southerners. Even more striking was admission to the national university, where about 3,500 northerners but almost 200,000 southerners were competing for one place in 1983. These profound horizontal inequalities generated a sense of frustration and feeling of injustice and exclusion that eventually led people in the south to resort again to armed struggle (Yongo-Bure 1993: 51). Garang (1987: 21) argued that 'under these circumstances the *marginal cost* of rebellion in the South became very small, zero or negative; that is, in the South it pays to rebel'.

During the second civil war, successive central governments in the north promoted fierce counter-insurgency warfare and invoked an Arab-Islamic paradigm to mobilize the North Sudan, Arab and Islamic world against the allegedly 'infidel' South, particularly in regions adjacent to North Sudan, such as Bahr el Ghazal. These policies, which were aimed at ruining people's livelihoods, transferring assets, extracting natural resources and enslaving the South, are rooted in the British colonial legacy, which handed over the south to northern domination. It is this colonial legacy that has created the structural vulnerability that continues to haunt and decimate the communities of South Sudan.

Crisis of subsistence: internationally-sponsored development and reform

The neo-Malthusian thesis attributes civil wars to environmental degradation leading to critical scarcities of natural resources and increasingly violent competition for these scarce resources (Homer-Dixon 1999). In the context of Sudan, some environmentalists have attributed the genesis of the second civil war to natural resource scarcity, particularly in North Sudan. Suliman (1999: 88) argues that the nature of conflict in Sudan has evolved from being a classic ethno-religious conflict to one that is mainly over resources. The economic and resources crisis in the North, which emerged as a driving force in the Sudan civil war, is primarily attributed to internationally sponsored development and policy reforms adopted in the 1970s.

In the early 1970s, the central government initiated policies, sponsored by the World Bank, that encouraged and subsidized shifts towards large-scale, commercial and export-oriented agriculture as a 'quick fix' towards rapid economic development. In 1970 the government passed the 'Unregistered Land Act', which effectively legitimized the state's control and ownership of virtually any piece of land in the country. This Act allowed the government to expropriate thousands of hectares of prime savannah from the farming and pastoral communities, and to lease this land to wealthy citizens and foreign investors for capital-intensive farming (Kebbede 1999: 115). It is estimated that during the 1970s, an average of 8,750 square kilometres of forest was destroyed annually to make way for mechanized farming (Berry and Geistfeld 1983: 69). The World Bank alone provided funding for the clearing of more than two million hectares of nomadic grazing land for large-scale farms (Bennett 1987: 57). In 1973, 84,388 hectares of the most fertile land in southern Kordofan were turned into publicly- and privately-operated mechanized farming schemes, with loans obtained from the World Bank (Ahmed 1983: 55). In southern Blue Nile, a wealthy Saudi Prince obtained a ninety-nine-year lease on 464,000 hectares of land 'to produce sorghum to feed animals in the oil-rich nations' (Prendergast 1990: 41). One consequence of the wholesale forest clearance in the 1970s was the rapid decline of the *Acacia Senegal*, an important tree for poor farmers as a source of both charcoal and gum (Cater 1986: 10).

As a result, many subsistence-oriented farmers, nomadic and semi-nomadic pastoralists in northern Sudan lost their farms and grazing lands during the 1970s. Pastoralist and agropastoralist communities in southern

Kordofan and Darfur were compelled to look southwards for new grazing lands or settlement areas, creating tensions and conflicts over scarce pastures and farming land. The expansion of mechanized farming accelerated the deforestation and exhaustion of the soil that contributed to recurrent droughts in the early 1980s. In western Sudan, peasants and pastoralists became increasingly vulnerable, and eventually succumbed to a drought-triggered famine in 1984–1985. These events (drought, subsistence crisis and famine) forced destitute former herders in western Sudan to seek to replenish their stock through raiding, and traders with squeezed profit margins to turn to financing cattle raiding in the South as a lucrative business (de Waal 1996: 8). The subsistence crisis in western Sudan also made it easy for successive central governments to recruit the destitute herders to fight the rebellion in the South through counter-insurgency warfare, which subsequently precipitated the famine of 1988. Keen (1994: 78) shows how famine and displacement in Bahr el Ghazal during the 1980s were strongly correlated, both geographically and chronologically, with militia raids.

Besides the crisis of subsistence in the rural communities of northern Sudan, the debt burden and structural adjustments prescribed by the International Monetary Fund (IMF) in the late 1970s crippled the national economy. While Sudan's foreign debt was about US$424 million in 1970, it reached US$6.1 billion in 1983. The debt/export ratio increased from 1.13 to 5.78 over the same period, with debt servicing alone consuming most of the country's export earnings. As a result of the second 'oil shock' in 1979–1980, coupled with deteriorating terms of trade, the cost of imports doubled between 1980 and 1983, while export earnings declined sharply. Consequently, the trade deficit reached US$626 million in 1983, compared with a trade surplus of $10.8 million in 1968. The level of foreign reserves had shrunk by 1983 to almost a quarter of their 1965 level. An IMF stabilization and austerity intervention in 1978, which aimed to control public spending, increase revenue and encourage exports, did not improve the situation, and Sudan's foreign debt was rescheduled in January 1983.

By the early 1980s, therefore, the Sudanese economy had imploded to the point of bankruptcy. In an attempt to divert attention from this 'financial crisis of unprecedented magnitude' (Daly 1993: 22), appease right-wing Islamist opponents and retain power, the vulnerable central government stepped up 'Islamization' and abrogated the Addis Ababa Peace Agreement in 1983, thereby reigniting civil war in South Sudan.

The curse of mineral resource abundance in the South: multinational corporations

The thesis attributing civil wars to natural resource scarcity has been challenged by evidence suggesting that, to the contrary, natural resource *abun-*

dance is actually the primary cause of many conflicts. Recently, some economists have provided both theoretical and empirical support for the proposition that natural resource deposits often motivate rebels' greed and fuel civil wars (Collier 2000). The case of Sudan, however, suggests that it was the greed of the ruling elite and multinational corporations, rather than of rebels, that generated grievances and rebellion in the south. The present South Sudan's first historical contacts with the outside world – Arabs, Turkey, Egypt, Britain – were characterized by brutal invasions by outsiders who were 'destitute of wealth' and searching for resources to plunder, such as gold, ivory, water and slaves (Churchill 1940: 2). This pattern of extraction of natural resources from South Sudan for the benefit of outsiders has continued with brutality on a massive scale, except that some of the key actors have changed as multinational corporations, in particular, have assumed an increasing role. The South, which is well-endowed with natural resources and wealth, has paradoxically become the victim of its own virtues, exposing it to increased vulnerability to recurrent famines.

The extraction of oil from South Sudan by multinational corporations triggered the second civil war in the early 1980s, and sustained it through the 1980s and 1990s. When commercial deposits of oil were discovered in South Sudan in 1979 by the Chevron Oil Company, information relating to the oilfield's location and the quantities of oil involved was deliberately concealed from the public for fear that the discovery of such a huge economic resource in the South would trigger a renewed desire among southerners to secede. Southerners, for their part, feared that the central government would expropriate their oil resources, which were desperately needed for economic rehabilitation after seventeen years of civil war. These fears about the intentions of the ruling northern elite crystallized in 1980, when the central government redrew the map of Sudan so that the northern areas of the south, where the oilfields were discovered, were shifted into North Sudan (Lesch 1998: 48). This action was followed by physically relocating the site of the oil refinery, from Bentiu in the South to Kosti and later to Port Sudan, in the North.

In an effort to create a stable operational environment for Chevron to extract oil without interference from the South, the central government unilaterally breached the Addis Ababa Peace Agreement in 1983, by dividing the South into three weaker regions and transferring southern soldiers (former rebel fighters) to the North. These actions further provoked and infuriated the southerners, and directly triggered the resumption of civil war. Immediately after the southern rebel movement was formed in 1983, it attacked and disrupted Chevron's oilfield developments, forcing the company to suspend its operations by mid-1984.

The idea of a 'militia strategy' in Sudan's civil war, which was originally linked to oil development, gained momentum in the late 1970s and early 1980s, when the central government failed to provide security around

Chevron's oilfield operations in the South. With the economic crisis at the same time, the central government sub-contracted impoverished Arab pastoralists in western Sudan as a local self-provisioning 'protection force' for the oilfields. This 'militia strategy' was later adopted by successive near-bankrupt central governments as an opportunistic way of waging counter-insurgency warfare in the South during the 1980s and 1990s.

In order to resume oilfield development in the South, the central government encouraged divisions within the rebel movement's ranks, and succeeded in creating a split in 1991. It then used the rebel splinter groups together with Arab militias to intensify counter-insurgency warfare during the 1990s. By 1992 oil production had resumed, and Sudan started exporting oil in 1997 – a year before the famine in Bahr el Ghazal. It is hardly surprising that this famine is closely correlated with the extraction of oil, as oil revenues generated the necessary resources to finance the central government's military expenditure. The Sudanese military budget was 80.6 billion Sudanese pounds in 1995–1996, a year before oil exports began, but it reached 932 billion Sudanese pounds in 2000, when oil accounted for about 75 per cent of Sudan's total export revenues (Figure 11.3). It is instructive to observe from Figure 11.3 that inflation in Sudan declined dramatically from 1997 onwards, principally as a result of oil extraction from the South, while the CMR among children under five reached as high as 46/10,000 per day during the famine in Bahr el Ghazal region in 1998.

The oil development has devastated the livelihoods of communities around the oilfields, as the government's military strategy was intensified and geographically focused to displace local inhabitants. Independent reports (Gagnon and Ryle 2001; Christian Aid 2001) show how oil funded

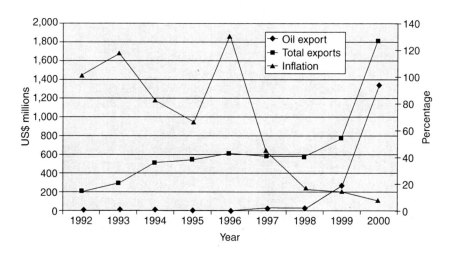

Figure 11.3 Sudan oil export and consumer price inflation, 1992–2000.

and sustained the civil war and how the government pursued a 'scorched earth' policy, violating human rights to clear the oilfield areas of civilians in order to make way for oil exploration by foreign international oil companies. There are about seventeen exploration and twenty-five development oil wells in South Sudan, managed by multinational corporations from Canada (Talisman), Sweden (Lundin), France (Elf), Italy (Agip), Austria (OMV-AG), Netherlands (Royal Dutch Shell), Belgium/France (TotalFina), the Gulf, Malaysia and China, with an estimated daily production of more than 250,000 barrels. These multinational corporations became complicit in the government's 'scorched earth' policy, because they effectively funded the war, exacerbating the suffering of inhabitants of the oilfield areas and derailing the prospects for peace in Sudan for many years (Gagnon and Ryle 2001: 33; ICG 2002: 132).

International aid policy: the normalization of crisis

The dilemma faced by humanitarian interventions during complex emergencies is encapsulated in the conventional wisdom among development agents that 'Africans do not starve, they cope' (Seaman 1993: 27). Davies (1993: 61) argued that this emphasis on 'coping' under stress may blind policymakers to the need for a radical reappraisal of the threats to people's livelihoods in marginal areas, and might require more radical interventions to address chronic vulnerability. Since the mid-1990s there has been increasing criticism of humanitarianism, particularly relief aid, which stands accused of addressing symptoms rather than causes, creating dependency, incapacitating social institutions and undermining the formation of efficient and competitive markets. These criticisms resulted in the idea of a 'relief-development continuum' (Maxwell and Buchanan-Smith 1994) gaining momentum, with an increasing emphasis on reducing emergency relief and working with communities to increase their capacities and thus ensure sustainability. One unfortunate consequence of this way of thinking was that dealing with emergencies became incorporated into normal development programming. This 'normalization of crisis', as described by Bradbury (1998), is characterized by a creeping acceptance of higher levels of vulnerability, malnutrition and morbidity. One indicator of this 'normalization' of emergencies has been a shift in donor funding away from relief aid, along with a global decline in aid transfers and persistent under-funding of UN operations in complex emergencies (Bradbury 1998: 334).

In South Sudan, relief food delivered by the WFP declined from 30,020 tonnes in 1993 to only 12,484 tonnes in 1997, just a year before the famine, with Bahr el Ghazal often receiving the least (Figure 11.4). This decline in relief food during the 1990s did not reflect the increasing vulnerability in Bahr el Ghazal region, where counter-insurgency warfare was intensifying and drastically eroding the basic means of livelihoods. During

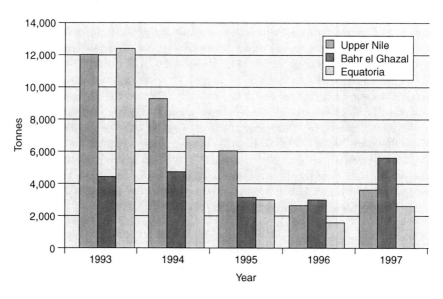

Figure 11.4 WFP food deliveries to South Sudan, 1993–1997.

1996 and 1997, relief food actually delivered by WFP to South Sudan constituted only 12 per cent and 38 per cent respectively of assessed needs
(Deng 1999: 70). For the same years, WFP received only 62 per cent
(US$25 million) and 50 per cent (US$22 million) respectively of its total
annual appeal for humanitarian operations in South Sudan. By June 1998,
when the famine reached its peak in Bahr el Ghazal, the UN and WFP had
only received 48 per cent and 54 per cent of their respective appeals
(US$109 million and US$32 million). As a result, the minimum food
requirement target was only met by WFP in November 1998, seven months
after the famine became apparent in April (Deng 1999: 72).

Instead of challenging the shifts in international aid policy that steadily
reduced relief entitlements, the leading aid agencies operating in South
Sudan appeared to become complacent and accommodating of crisis.
Even when the famine occurred in 1998, some aid agencies resisted recognizing it as a 'famine' and sought instead to 'normalize' it by describing it
as 'extreme distress' or 'crisis', or even as 'normal transitory food insecurity' (Deng 1999: 6). By the time crude mortality and malnutrition rates
reached unacceptable levels in April–May 1998, most British aid agencies,
which were among the few aid agencies operating in the Bahr el Ghazal
region, curiously decided that the crisis in the Sudan did not warrant a
national appeal. While the agencies were divided about the severity of the
situation, the media intervened and British press coverage of Sudan
peaked in May (Figure 11.5). It was this intense media and public interest
in the UK, paradoxically, that resulted in the belated announcement of a

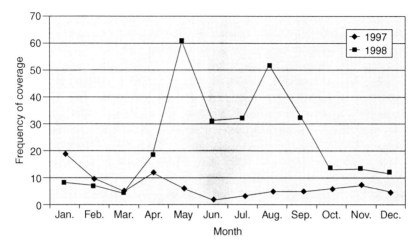

Figure 11.5 Selected coverage of Sudan in the British Press, 1997–1998.

national appeal for Sudanese famine victims by several British aid agencies on 21 May 1998.

It is not surprising that the food security monitoring systems implemented by these development-oriented aid agencies were insensitive to increasing vulnerability in the Bahr el Ghazal region in 1998. Most of these monitoring systems are implicitly designed under the doctrine of 'Africans do not starve, they cope', which tends to normalize any crisis. For example, 'food economy assessment' estimates of the vulnerable population in 1998 show not only a considerable *decline* in vulnerability in Bahr el Ghazal, but also show no significant difference in vulnerability among the regions of South Sudan (Deng 1999: 99).

Valuable time was wasted during the early stages of the famine in Bahr el Ghazal, partly because commonly accepted criteria for defining an emergency or famine were absent, and partly because influential stakeholders attempted to conceal the reality and to project the situation as normal. Some leading aid agencies feared that the declaration of a humanitarian emergency would jeopardize their ongoing programmes. As the famine was gaining momentum in March–April, for instance, the UN programme 'Operation Lifeline Sudan' (OLS) was preoccupied with meeting global targets in a polio eradication campaign (Deng 1999: 82). Certain agencies went so far as to conceal the facts about the famine from the media, and took measures designed to manage the press that were reminiscent of the Sudanese Government's restrictive attitude to press freedom (Alagiah 1998).

Conclusion

Although the Bahr el Ghazal famine of 1998 was primarily caused by civil war, it cannot be entirely attributed to internal factors. The analysis presented in this chapter has revealed how global factors translated into increasing household vulnerability in South Sudan, mainly by triggering a resumption of civil war but specifically by the intensification of counter-insurgency warfare. It is common for external observers to internalize the causes and blame for contemporary civil wars in Africa, and the famines that are often associated with them, and to insist that internal solutions are necessary and sufficient. This view, which absolves the international community of any responsibility for either causing or resolving such crises, needs to be revisited in the light of growing evidence that highlights the global dimension. While internal factors are predominant in analysing civil wars, they are insufficient unless contextualized in the bigger picture of global interconnectedness. Bearing this in mind, what lessons can be drawn from the Sudan famine of 1998?

First, analysis of Sudan's civil war reveals the role of global causes, which will require global solutions. International actors should accept that they are part and parcel of the 'permanent emergency' (Duffield 1993) in Sudan. While the British Government, among others, blames the Sudan Government or the rebels for the conduct of the civil war, it has a moral obligation to accept its own responsibility in the genesis of this crisis, which is rooted in its colonial legacy. The tendency for the international community to deny its own liability is paradoxical in a world characterized by a discourse of interconnectedness and globalization. As rightly argued by Macrae (1998: 315), 'this assertion of isolationism marks an increasing accommodation with and acceptance of catastrophe which is surely shameful'.

Second, Sudan's experience has shown how the extraction of mineral resources by multinational corporations, indirectly supported by internationally sponsored development programmes, has exacerbated and sustained counter-insurgency warfare in the South through a period of intensive exploitation of oil in the region. The commonly held view, that contemporary civil wars are a result of the criminal acquisitiveness of rebels, triggered by the lure of mineral resources, masks the global dimension – particularly the greed of multinational corporations that are becoming key players in such wars, in Sudan and in many other African countries. The case of Sudan presents a classic example of the complex and uneasy coalition between humanitarianism and multinational corporations, which requires a global analysis and global solutions. The apparent inability of the international community to protect communities that are subjected to gross human rights abuses and increasing vulnerability to famine, while at the same time multinational corporations are exploiting and extracting valuable natural resources in the vicinity, is a profound challenge to the global values that humanitarianism seeks to promote.

Third, the case of the Sudan famine in 1998 shows how humanitarian agencies operating in complex emergencies run the risk of compromising the criteria and standards for defining a famine or emergency, by normalizing crises for fear of jeopardizing their long-term programmes. This lack of standardized, globally accepted and explicit criteria or thresholds for defining an emergency or famine is one reason why humanitarian interventions are often late, and accountability is lacking (see Howe and Devereux, Chapter 2, this volume).

Finally, while there may be opportunities for pursuing rehabilitation and even development programmes during civil war, it must never be forgotten that communities in conflict-prone areas are constantly and acutely vulnerable to destitution, displacement and death (Deng 2002a). Until the underlying structural and global causes of this vulnerability are accepted and properly understood in each local context, the international community risks continuing to divert resources and attention away from complex emergencies and conflict-triggered food crises, and the real causes of – and responsibility for – these 'new famines' will remain unacknowledged and unaddressed.

Notes

1 Of course, the entitlement approach only explains 'legal famines'; it was not designed to explain famines that occur precisely because property rights – and basic human rights – are systematically and brutally violated (see Devereux, Chapter 4, this volume).
2 The 'immobility measure' (I) has been suggested by Scott and Litchfield (1994) to compare the persistence of different dimensions of poverty, and is calculated as the sum of the cell frequencies (trace (M)) along the leading diagonal of the square transition matrix (M) divided by the number of individuals in the panel (N). The value of the immobility measure varies between zero, when there is complete mobility, and one, when there is complete immobility (Baulch and Masset 2003).
3 The UN's Refugee Nutrition Information System (RNIS) defines a $CMR > 1/10,000$ per day as a 'serious situation' and a $CMR > 2/10,000$ per day as an 'emergency out of control' (WFP 2000: 39).

References

Ahmed, A. (1983) 'Traditional agriculture in northern district of southern Kordofan province', in M. H. Awad (ed.), *Socio-economic Change in the Sudan*, Khartoum: University of Khartoum Press.

Alagiah, G. (1998) 'Hungry for Truth', *Guardian*, 25 May 1998.

Baulch, B. and Masset, E. (2003) 'Do monetary and non-monetary indicators tell the same story about chronic poverty? A study of Vietnam in the 1990s', *World Development*, 31(3): 441–53.

Baulch, B. and McCulloch, N. (1998) 'Being poor and becoming poor: poverty status and poverty transitions in rural Pakistan', *IDS Working Paper* 79, Brighton: Institute of Development Studies.

Bennett, J. (1987) *The Hunger Machine*, Cambridge: Polity Press.

Berry, L., and Geistfeld, S. (1983) *Eastern African Country Profile*, Worcester, MA: Clark University.

Bevan, P. and Joireman, S. (1997) 'The perils of measuring poverty: identifying the 'poor' in rural Ethiopia', *Oxford Development Studies*, 25(3): 315–43.

Bradbury, M. (1998) 'Normalizing the crisis in Africa', *Disasters*, 22(4): 328–38.

Castells, M. (1998) 'End of millennium', in *The Information Age: Economy, Society and Culture*, Vol. III, Oxford: Blackwell.

Cater, N. (1986) *Sudan: The Roots of Famine*, Oxford: Oxfam.

Christian Aid (2001) *The Scorched Earth: Oil and War in Sudan*, London: Christian Aid.

Churchill, W. (1940) *The River War: An Account of the Conquest of the Sudan*, London: Eyre and Spottiswoode.

Cliffe, L. and Luckham, R. (1998) 'Complex political emergencies and the state: towards an understanding of recent experiences and an approach for future research', *COPE Working Paper* 2, Leeds: Centre for Development Studies, University of Leeds.

Cliffe, L. and Luckham, R. (eds) (1999) 'Complex political emergencies', *Third World Quarterly*, 20(1): 27–50.

Collier, P. (2000) 'Economic causes of civil conflict and their implications for policy', mimeo, Washington, DC: World Bank.

Cox, D. (1972) 'Regression models and life-tables', *Journal of the Royal Statistical Society*, B(34): 187–220.

Daly, M. (1993) 'Broken bridge and empty basket: the political and economic background of the Sudanese civil war', in M. Daly and A. Sikainga (eds), *Civil War in the Sudan*, London: British Academic Press.

Davies, S. (1993) 'Are coping strategies a cop out?', *IDS Bulletin*, 24(4): 60–72.

de Waal, A. (1996) 'Contemporary warfare in Africa: changing context, changing strategies', *IDS Bulletin*, 27(3): 6–16.

Deng, F. (1995) *War of Visions: Conflict of Identities in the Sudan*, Washington, DC: Brookings Institution.

Deng, L. (1999) 'Famine in the Sudan: causes, preparedness and response: a political, social and economic analysis of the 1998 Bahr el Ghazal famine', *IDS Discussion Paper* 369, Brighton: Institute of Development Studies.

Deng, L. (2002a) 'Confronting civil war: a comparative study of household assets management in Southern Sudan', *IDS Discussion Paper* 381, Brighton: Institute of Development Studies.

Deng, L. (2002b) 'The Curse of Mineral Resources: The Case of Revenue-Sharing Arrangements in the Sudan', *Consultation Report* 4, Sudan Peace-Building Programme, African Renaissance Institute (ARI) and Relationships Foundation International (RFI), UK

Deng, L. (2003) 'Confronting civil war: a comparative study of household livelihood strategies in Southern Sudan', unpublished PhD thesis, University of Sussex, Institute of Development Studies.

Devereux, S. (2000) 'Famine in the twentieth century', *IDS Working Paper* 105, Brighton: Institute of Development Studies.

Devereux, S. (2001) 'Famine in Africa', in S. Devereux and S. Maxwell (eds), *Food Security in Sub-Saharan Africa*, London: ITDG Publishing.

Devereux, S. and Maxwell, S. (eds) (2001) *Food Security in Sub-Saharan Africa*, London: ITDG Publishing.

Duffield, M. (1993) 'NGOs, disaster relief and asset transfer in the Horn: political survival in a permanent emergency', *Development and Change*, 24: 131–57.

Duffield, M. (2000) 'Globalization, transborder trade, and war economies', in M. Berdal and D. Malone (eds), *Greed and Grievances: Economic Agendas in Civil Wars*, London: Lynne Rienner Publishers Inc.

Ellis, F. (2000) *Rural Livelihoods and Diversity in Developing Countries*, Oxford: Oxford University Press.

Gagnon, G. and Ryle, J. (2001) *Report of an Investigation into Oil Development, Conflict and Displacement in Western Upper Nile, Sudan*, Ottawa: Sudan Interagency Reference Group of Canada.

Garang, J. (1987) *John Garang Speaks*, London: Kegan Paul International.

Goodhand, J. and Hulme, D. (1999) 'From wars to complex political emergencies: understanding conflict and peace-building in the new world disorder', *Third World Quarterly*, 20(1): 13–26.

Homer-Dixon, T. (1999) *Environment, Scarcity, and Violence*, Princeton, NJ: Princeton University Press.

International Crisis Group (2002) 'God, oil and country: changing the logic of war in Sudan', *ICG Africa Report* 39, Brussels: International Crisis Group.

Kebbede, G. (1999) 'Losing ground: land impoverishment in Sudan' in G. Kebbede (ed.), *Sudan's Predicament: Civil War, Displacement and Ecological Degradation*, Aldershot: Ashgate.

Keen, D. (1994) *The Benefits of Famine: A Political Economy of Famine in South-West Sudan, 1983–1989*, Princeton, NJ: Princeton University Press.

Lesch, A. (1998) *Sudan: Contested National Identities*, Oxford: James Currey.

Macrae, J. (1998) 'The death of humanitarianism: an anatomy of the attack', *Disasters*, 22(4): 309–17.

Maxwell, S. and Buchanan-Smith, M. (eds) (1994) 'Linking relief and development', *IDS Bulletin*, 25(4).

Moser, C. (1998) 'The asset vulnerability framework: reassessing urban poverty reduction strategies', *World Development*, 26(1): 1–19.

Oduho, J. and Deng, W. (1963) *The Problem of the Southern Sudan*, London: Oxford University Press.

Prendergast, J. (1990) *The Struggle for Sudan's Soul*, Washington, DC: Center of Concern.

Rangasami, A. (1985) ' "Failure of exchange entitlements" theory of famine: a response', *Economic and Political Weekly*, 20(41 and 42): 1747–52, 1797–1801.

Salama, P., Assefa, F., Talley, L., Spiegel, P., van der Veen, A. and Gotway, C. (2001) 'Malnutrition, measles, mortality, and the humanitarian response during a famine in Ethiopia', *Journal of the American Medical Association*, 286(5): 563–71.

Scott, C. and Litchfield, J. (1994) 'Inequality, mobility and the determinants of income among the rural poor in Chile, 1968–1986', *Discussion Paper* 53, London: Development Economics Research Programme, London School of Economics.

Scoones, I. (1998) 'Sustainable Rural Livelihoods: A framework for analysis', *IDS Working Paper* 72, Brighton: Institute of Development Studies.

Seaman, J. (1993) 'Famine mortality in Africa', *IDS Bulletin*, 24(4): 27–32.

Sen, A. (1981) *Poverty and Famines: An Essay on Entitlement and Deprivation*, Oxford: Oxford University Press.

Siegel, P. and Alwang, J. (1999) 'An Asset-Based Approach to Social Risk

Management: A conceptual framework', *Social Protection Discussion Paper* 9926, Washington, DC: World Bank

Sklair, L. (2002) *Globalization: Capitalism and Its Alternatives*, Oxford: Oxford University Press.

Suliman, M. (1999) 'Civil war in Sudan: the impact of ecological degradation', in G. Kebbede (ed.), *Sudan's Predicament: Civil War, Displacement and Ecological Degradation*, Aldershot: Ashgate.

World Food Programme (WFP) (2000) *Food and Nutrition Handbook*, Rome: WFP.

Yongo-Bure, B. (1993) 'The underdevelopment of the Southern Sudan since independence', in M. Daly and A. Sikainga (eds), *Civil War in the Sudan*, London: British Academic Press.

12 Why are there no longer 'war famines' in contemporary Europe?

Bosnia besieged, 1992–1995

Fiona Watson

Introduction

War and famine have a long history of association. Starving out the enemy has been a tactic deployed throughout the ages, epitomized by the siege, where a population is surrounded, effectively cut off from outside supplies and subjected to bombardment. One of the first recorded sieges was the ten-year siege of Troy during the twelfth century BC, as described in Homer's epic poem *The Iliad*. More than 3,000 years later the siege is still being used as a weapon of war, most recently during the war in the former Yugoslavia in the early 1990s. During this conflict, areas of Bosnia and Herzegovina[1] were successfully besieged by the Bosnian Serb army, they were heavily shelled and access to supplies was prevented.

The conflict which broke out in the former Yugoslavia in 1992 shook the world. It was the first full-scale war in Europe since the Second World War, and it was to last a bloody three and a half years. Bosnia suffered heavy losses and widespread destruction. Some 2.7 million Bosnians, out of an original population of 4.4 million, either fled the country as refugees or were internally displaced. Thousands of the displaced sought refuge in small, besieged pockets, living in overcrowded conditions without adequate water and power supplies. Food supplies were abruptly reduced, economic activity was severely disrupted and welfare services were seriously affected. The severe winters typical of Bosnia, with temperatures dropping to below minus 20°C, exacerbated the suffering.

The impact of the war on populations trapped in the besieged areas of Bosnia threatened a humanitarian disaster on an unprecedented scale, and historical experience suggested a potential for widespread starvation. Blockades and sieges, which had taken place in Europe during the First and Second World Wars, had resulted in thousands of people dying from starvation and disease. Nonetheless, a famine did not occur. This chapter asks the question: Why was there no famine in the besieged areas of Bosnia during the war?

The next section begins with a discussion of the links between war and famine, then reviews European experiences of 'siege famines' during the twentieth century. Next, predictions of famine in Bosnia in the early 1990s are presented, and the reasons for the failure of these predictions to materialize are examined under two categories of explanatory factors: pre-crisis conditions (which were generally favourable and buffered the population against the threat of famine) and the international response (which was disproportionately generous). The concluding section summarizes the crucial differences between the averted famine in Bosnia and famines that have occurred in Africa, where pre-famine conditions are typically less favourable and the international response is often inadequate or too late.

War and famine

War was the single most important precipitating factor for famines during the 1990s, and was the major trigger for the humanitarian emergency in Bosnia. The number of internal conflicts has increased dramatically since the end of the Cold War (Rupesinghe 1994). In 1992, the year that war broke out in Bosnia, four major armed conflicts were ongoing in Europe, five in the Middle East, thirteen in Asia, seven in Africa and three in the Americas (ICRC 1994).[2] UNDP estimated that between 1945 and 1994 more than twenty million people had died in wars and other conflicts, and that up to 90 per cent of casualties in contemporary wars are civilians (UNDP 1994). These civilian deaths are largely the result of the interaction between forced migration, lack of basic health services and malnutrition (Green 1994).

The 1977 Additional Protocols to the Geneva Convention, to which most states in the world have subscribed and which are intended to provide protection for those caught up in warfare, explicitly state that:

1   Starvation of civilians as a method of warfare is prohibited.
2   It is prohibited to attack, destroy, remove, or render useless objects indispensable to the agricultural areas of the production of foodstuffs, crops, livestock, drinking water installations and supplies, and irrigation works, for the specific purpose of denying them for the sustenance value to the civilian population or to the adverse Party, whatever the motive, whether in order to starve out civilians, to cause them to move away, or for any other motive.

(UN 1977)

Nevertheless, food plays a significant role in political, economic and military spheres during war, and is a powerful propaganda tool. Devereux (1993) lists six ways in which war causes or contributes to famine:

1   Disruption of agricultural production
2   Undermining of local economies

3   Interruption of food flows, both trade and aid
4   Creation of new patterns of demand for food (e.g. farmer-producers become soldier-consumers)
5   Undermining of people's ability to cope with adversity
6   Creation of refugees.

Macrae and Zwi (1994) categorize the use of food as a weapon under three headings: acts of *omission*, where governments fail to monitor adequately and plan for food security in all sections of a country; acts of *commission*, where attacks are made on the means of production and procuring food; and acts of *provision*, where food is selectively supplied to government supporters. They argue that:

> Deliberate interventions in food marketing, distribution and aid flows, and attacks on production during war have contributed to, and in some cases caused, successive famines in Ethiopia, Angola, Southern Sudan, Somalia and Mozambique.
>
> (Macrae and Zwi 1994)

Some observers saw the war in Bosnia as a war for food. In an article entitled 'Defeated by the battle for food', Haris Nezirovic, a Bosnian journalist who was in the enclave of Srebrenica during the spring of 1993, wrote:

> The year-old war in the east Bosnian Muslim enclave of Srebrenica has not been a conflict between organized military units, but a desperate struggle for food, waged with arms and motivated by an instinct for survival. As long as food could be found, the soldiers fought. When it vanished, the army became another group of refugees scavenging for nourishment. Food, one of the main weapons in the Serbian armoury in Bosnia, decided who won and lost.
>
> (Nezirovic 1993)

In addition to the adverse effects that war has upon food supply, it also has an adverse effect on public health. The World Health Organization (WHO) notes that war generates three kinds of public health problem (WHO Regional Office for Europe 1995): first, problems related to breakdown of existing health-care systems and normal preventive actions, 'for example, the lack of food, clean water, heating, electricity and systematic rubbish collection, plus the disruption of vaccination programmes, increases the risks of infectious diseases'; second, problems related to war-related physical injuries (lost limbs, spinal cord lesions, traumatic brain injuries, etc.); and third, mental health problems due to the traumatization of the population and violations of human rights committed in the war. The first public health problem is directly linked to the development of famine.

Perhaps the most extreme example of the association between war and famine is when a siege or blockade is used as a deliberate tactic for genocide. During the war in Bosnia, the Bosnian Serbs were accused of adopting 'siege and starvation tactics' (Traynor 1993) and UNHCR (United Nations High Commission for Refugees) reportedly referred to the situation in Srebrenica as 'ethnic cleansing by starvation' (cited in Silber and Little 1995). These accusations were not necessarily exaggerated when viewed in the light of previous experiences of famines that were deliberately induced by siege in twentieth-century Europe.

War and famine in twentieth-century Europe

Anyone who thinks of famine as a problem afflicting impoverished countries in Africa and Asia might be surprised to learn that Europe has suffered at least seven major famines within the past hundred years. Four of these resulted from sieges or blockades during the First and Second World Wars (the others occurred in the Soviet Union in peacetime), and they affected civilian populations more than military personnel. These four famines are briefly described below.

The allied blockade of Germany: March 1915 to 1918

The allied blockade of Germany was initiated by the British and French on 11 March 1915, shortly after the outbreak of the First World War, and was maintained until the war ended in 1918. Neutral ships bound for Germany were apprehended at sea, escorted into British or French ports and detained, effectively giving the Allies long-range control of German commerce. By September 1916, the British fleet was single-handedly intercepting an average of 135 merchant ships every week.

As a result of the blockade, conditions within Germany deteriorated. Unemployment stood at between 20 and 40 per cent, and although the Government provided 10.5 Deutsche Marks per week to a family of four in which no-one was employed, the real value of the payment was eroded by hyper-inflation. Food supplies declined, food prices soared and rationing was instituted. The diet in Germany was initially reduced to bread and potatoes. Failure of the potato crop in 1916 led, however, to turnips replacing potatoes as the main staple, and the particularly severe winter of 1916–1917 was dubbed the 'turnip winter'. The daily bread ration, established at 225 grams per person per day in 1915, fell to 160 grams in 1917, with dough made from 55 per cent rye flour, 35 per cent wheat flour and 10 per cent substitutes (Vincent 1985). As conditions worsened, rye flour was replaced by turnips. Only the very young, invalids, expectant mothers and the elderly were permitted milk.

As one observer noted: 'the daily bread was now a luxury' (cited in (Schrienier 1918). The collective weight of the German population plummeted sharply and micronutrient deficiency diseases spread rapidly. The incidence of actual starvation was reported to be particularly high in jails, asylums and other institutions where inmates only had access to an unsupplemented food ration (Vincent 1985). Cases of tuberculosis (TB), rickets, influenza, dysentery, scurvy, keratomalacia and hunger oedema became rife. TB was reported to be the major cause of death, but was initially limited largely to the elderly. As the disease spread, however, TB began to affect adults and young children, while deterioration of hygiene standards contributed to the spread of disease.

The human toll was enormous. The number of deaths in Germany increased from 88,235 in 1915 to 293,760 in 1918, despite a drop in the birth rate from 30/1,000 to 15/1,000 between 1914 and 1919. Mortality increases were particularly high among children and the elderly. The death rate of children between the ages of one and five years rose by 50 per cent, and among children from five to fifteen years by 55 per cent (Vincent 1985).

The Warsaw ghetto: November 1940 to July 1942

The Germans invaded Poland in September 1939. By October 1940, they had confined approximately 380,000 Jews in a 3.5-square-mile area of Warsaw that normally housed about 160,000. In March 1941 the population in the ghetto reached a peak of 445,000, representing about 30 per cent of the Warsaw population. The area was surrounded by a ten-foot high wall and was sealed off on 15 November 1940. Jews were forbidden to go outside the area without permission on penalty of being shot on sight, and no contact with the outside world was allowed. The Nazis calculated that they could destroy the population in the Warsaw ghetto in nine months through mass starvation and accompanying infectious diseases (Winick 1994).

Rationing in Poland began in December 1939. By 1941, the official ration provided 2,613 kcal per day for Germans in Poland, 699 kcal for Poles, and 184 kcal for Jews in the ghetto (Roland 1992). The Jewish rations were clearly not meant for survival. While severe food shortages affected the whole of Warsaw, those outside the ghetto were able to trade with farmers to supplement their official rations. Inside the ghetto, access to food was much worse. Poor hygiene conditions reignited typhus and an epidemic flared up. A further hardship was the cold. In December 1941, the Nazis requisitioned all furs for their soldiers at the Russian front. The electricity supply to the ghetto was cut off for extended periods, and the practice of sleeping in clothes facilitated the spread of typhus through lice.

Between November 1940 and June 1942, doctors working inside the ghetto recorded a total of 70,381 deaths, of which 18,237 were due to starvation, 2,509 to typhus and the remainder to 'unknown' causes, though this was usually believed to be starvation (Fliederbaum *et al.* 1994). This was equivalent to a crude mortality rate (CMR) of approximately 125 deaths per 1,000 of the population per year. There was a seasonal pattern, with higher death rates during the cold winter months than in the summer. One observer gave a harrowing account of the desperate conditions within the ghetto:

> People of all ages died in the streets, in shelters, in homes, and in hospitals. Wdowinski used to walk about one kilometre from his home to Czyste Hospital, and often saw six to ten bodies lying in the street each day ... Those found dead on the street usually had not died there. The family commonly removed a body from their home onto the street, after removing all evidence of identity. In that way, they might be able to use the extra ration card for a few days ... mothers hid dead children under beds for days in order to receive a larger food ration.
>
> (Roland 1992)

Although people inside the ghetto officially had no access to other sources, some black-market trading and smuggling of food did occur, which is why the Nazis were unable to starve all the inhabitants. Mass deportation of Jews in the ghetto to the gas chambers in the extermination camps of Treblinka and Auschwitz began on 22 July 1942, and in May 1943 the Warsaw ghetto was finally razed to the ground.

The siege of Leningrad: September 1941 to January 1944

In September 1941, Leningrad was surrounded by German forces and the order was issued to 'tighten up the blockade and level the city to the ground by shelling from the air' (cited in Jones 1994). During the 900 days of the siege, Leningrad suffered incessant aerial bombing and shelling from long-range guns. Moreover, the winter of 1941–1942 was particularly severe – the coldest in more than a century. Lack of fuel reduced the power supply, badly affecting heating and restricting cooking; water and sewerage systems were damaged by shelling, and there were increasing food shortages.

Supplies could not be airlifted in because of the activities of the Luftwaffe, though some provisions were brought in by lorry across the iced-over Lake Ladoga. The ration of bread, which was set at 500 grams for manual workers and 300 grams for 'mental' workers in September 1941, fell to an all-time low in December 1941, at 250 grams for manual workers and 125 grams for 'mental' workers (equivalent to a maximum of 875 kcal and 438 kcal per day respectively), supplemented with a meat ration of between seventy-five and 150 grams per month and small amounts of sugar, fat, potatoes and other vegetables. Not only were the rations small, but the nutritional value of the bread was also low, consisting of 'about one-half defective rye flour, the rest being substitutes such as cellulose, malt, and bran' (Smith 1947). The population grew some food in parks and gardens, but people were reportedly reduced to eating rats, glue from furniture joints and wallpaper (Whealey n.d.).

Lyudmila Anopova, who was a child during the siege, described her experience of the winter of 1941–1942 as follows:

> all the provisions in the town were burned – and with them all traces of the old life. Famine descended upon Leningrad ... I'm hungry every moment of the day. Provisions are sold on ration books. We have to stand in a long queue at the shop on Kirovsky Prospect. For our six ration books we get a little millet, some dry onion, now and again a piece of frozen meat. We stand there for hours. We are frozen but we wait and suffer in silence. In the morning, we do not have the strength to get up.
>
> (*St Petersburg Times* 1995)

Weight loss was estimated to be up to 33 per cent of pre-starvation weight, while scurvy, pellagra and night-blindness had all appeared by the end of the winter. Diseases such as dysentery, bronchopneumonia and tuberculosis were rampant, and a typhus epidemic started but was controlled. Estimates of deaths attributable to starvation during the siege range from 630,000 to one million out of a pre-war population of 2.5 million – equivalent to a CMR of between 112 and 178 per 1,000 population per year (Keys *et al.* 1950; Salisbury 1969).

The Dutch 'hunger winter': September 1944 to May 1945

Also during the Second World War, the Dutch 'hunger winter' of 1944–1945 had particularly adverse effects on the densely populated cities of western Holland: Amsterdam, Rotterdam and The Hague. The famine was provoked by a strike by Dutch railway workers, which was requested by the Dutch Government in exile in the expectation that this would bring speedy liberation by impeding the transport of German troops and supplies, thus undermining their strength in occupied Holland. The Germans retaliated by issuing a decree prohibiting the transport of food into those areas of the country still under German control. Roads and canals were guarded to prevent smuggled goods being brought in, and while country dwellers were able to live without much distress, urban populations only a few miles away suffered immense deprivation. After six weeks the decree was rescinded and food could once again be brought into the cities, but in their five years of occupation the Germans had so gutted the Dutch transport infrastructure that it was difficult to get food into the stricken cities.

The winter of 1944–1945 was one of the most severe in years, and barges were unable to make their way through the frozen canals to bring in food. There was no electricity, wood, coal or running water, and the sewerage system broke down. The war had already caused food shortages and rationing had been introduced in May 1940 (Stein *et al.* 1975). The blockade led to rations being successively cut, and by January 1945 the food situation had reached crisis level. In Amsterdam the daily ration amounted to just 450 kcal per day and the population was reduced to eating tulip bulbs and, in some cases, family pets. The distress is described by Anderson (1995):

> The authorities closed down the schools and the factory owners put their employees on indefinite leave. The factories were too cold and besides, they had no materials with which to make anything. Public transport had virtually ceased. People had long dug up streetcar tracks to get their hands on wood. And people began to die, particularly the very old and the very young. The elderly froze in their unheated apartments and the children succumbed to diseases unknown in modern Holland. Before the war, Holland had been one of the best fed and healthiest countries imaginable, now in five short years Holland was one of the most miserable places on earth.

Mortality from undernutrition was reported to be 104 deaths per week in The Hague (total population 500,000) and 136 per week in Rotterdam (total population 650,000), and a total of 2,351 deaths were recorded in Amsterdam over the period November 1944 to July 1945 (total population 700,000) (Smith 1947).

Common characteristics

The cases described above share a number of common features. First, urban civilian populations were the worst affected and, as access to food depended on food imports, the blockades caused massive food shortages. Ration systems were instigated, but ration levels failed to meet requirements and urban inhabitants were forced to seek alternative sources of food, which were inadequate. Second, a collapse in public services led to water and power shortages, and a breakdown in the public health system. In the Warsaw ghetto and Leningrad, this led in turn to the spread of epidemic diseases, particularly diarrhoeal diseases. Third, cold European winters exacerbated the situation. Despite relatively good pre-crisis nutritional and health status, extremely high levels of malnutrition and mortality were recorded. These were the consequence of lack of food, disease and freezing winters.

Predictions of famine in Bosnia

Many factors that precipitated localized siege famines in Europe during both World Wars were similar to those afflicting Bosnia in the early 1990s: a sudden disruption of the food supply; serious shortages of water, power and heating; inadequate shelter; overcrowding; disintegration of preventative and curative health services; and cold winters. Furthermore, humanitarian agencies were apparently unable to bring in enough food aid to Bosnia to meet the shortfall. During the first six months of the siege of Sarajevo, only 20–25 per cent of estimated food needs could be airlifted into the city (James 1992; Robertson 1992), while between January 1993 and March 1994 food aid needs were never fully met, averaging only 50 per cent for Central Bosnia (WFP 1994a).

The media and international humanitarian agencies alike predicted famine as winter approached in 1992 and again in 1993. In the autumn of 1992, newspapers reported that famine was 'expected to set in within two months' and that 'experts' anticipated up to '300,000 deaths from cold and starvation' in Bosnia during the coming winter (Pick and Traynor 1992; Pick and Fairhall 1993). There was particular concern about conditions in besieged Sarajevo. In September 1992, the World Health Organization (WHO) had sent a consultant to the region 'to predict the probability of malnutrition and death in Sarajevo, given current food supplies' (James 1992). The consultant's findings made grim reading. Food supplies being airlifted into Sarajevo were grossly inadequate (providing an intake of only 375 kcal per head per day), and children were likely to become 'profoundly wasted within one month'. By the third or fourth week of November children would begin to die, while adults would only survive into late December. The consultant further warned that micronutrient deficiency diseases including scurvy and pellagra would occur, as current food supplies were not nutritionally balanced (James 1992). A further WHO consultancy visit to Bosnia in October 1992 warned that:

> there has been a large and cumulative shortfall (of food) which is expected to lead to malnutrition in the most vulnerable within weeks . . . it is unlikely that there are sufficient (food) stocks to buffer the effects of the coming famine, signs of which have already appeared in Tuzla in vulnerable groups despite the fact that winter has not yet started.
>
> (Golden 1992)

By December 1992 the situation in Sarajevo was judged to be critical, with no electricity or fuel in the city, an extreme scarcity of food, and only one source of water – the brewery well. A WHO consultant stated that:

> The people are starving and in danger of freezing to death . . . The streets [are] filthy and piled with rubbish. The people are pale,

stressed and haggard. Some rummage through the rubbish. Dogs roam the streets and their carcasses lie beside the roads.

(Redmond 1992)

Despite these dire predictions and reports from such authoritative sources as the WHO, the expected famine failed to materialize and widespread malnutrition did not occur. In the latter part of 1993, however, a 'Bosnian winter of hunger' was feared, as money, food and fuel supplies were by now exhausted (Narayan 1993; Traynor 1993). The World Food Programme (WFP) was particularly concerned about the besieged enclaves of eastern Bosnia, where the situation was described as 'critical ... as reports of starvation are emerging' (WFP 1993). The UNHCR noted:

> While last year displaced people and refugees went through the winter reasonably well, there are well founded fears that this coming winter may be a humanitarian disaster of unprecedented proportions. Unlike last year, people have few stocks left at home, if any at all, and there is no commercial traffic in large areas of Bosnia. In addition, after a year of inappropriate diet, people are weaker. Local infrastructures have been further damaged by war and there is less water, sanitation and electricity available.
>
> (UNHCR 1993)

Fortunately, famine again failed to occur.

Exaggerated predictions of disaster are fairly common during emergencies. The media tend to want a 'good' story, governments want to draw attention to the plight of their people, while humanitarian agencies wish to maximize donations by emphasizing the potential human toll. Nevertheless, there was good reason to believe that the situation for populations in the besieged areas of Bosnia could easily deteriorate and result in widespread starvation and death. This had happened to previously healthy, well-nourished populations in Europe under blockade, as described above, and authorities, including United Nations (UN) organizations, were aware that a repeat of former European famines could all too easily occur.

Why was there no famine in Bosnia?

Although it is tempting to avoid yet another redefinition of the word 'famine', it is essential to adopt some definition for practical reasons: a famine has to be recognized in order to trigger an appropriate response. A more pertinent reason here is that it will not be possible to establish that there was no famine in Bosnia unless we know what a famine is. For present purposes, therefore, famine is used to refer to:

an extreme set of conditions, which affect a population and where a severe and exceptional reduction in access to food is characterized by elevated malnutrition rates, which together with a rise in disease prevalence is life-threatening.

While the besieged populations of Bosnia were subjected to horrifying conditions, including an abrupt and severe reduction in food *availability*, the decline in food *accessibility* did not become so critical as to be deemed a famine. The population retained access to a variety of alternative sources of food and people were able to adopt a series of coping strategies in order to obtain food (Watson and Vespa 1995). These are illustrated in Box 12.1. Furthermore, despite the collapse of the health-care system, disruption of water supplies, erosion of environmental sanitation services and a subsequent rise in infectious disease (e.g. a thirteen-fold increase in incidence of diarrhoeal diseases (Puvacic and Weinberg 1994)), epidemics of the big killers (cholera, dysentery, typhus) were avoided. Adults lost weight and wasting levels among the elderly rose (Vespa and Watson 1995), but there was no widespread malnutrition, nor were there raised mortality rates associated with malnutrition.

It is argued here that pre-crisis conditions and the huge humanitarian response to the crisis in Bosnia played crucial roles in averting famine. Comparisons are made with African countries that experienced famine during the 1990s, to establish the significant differences and identify which criteria led to elevated vulnerability in the African cases but reduced vulnerability to famine in Bosnia.

Box 12.1 Coping strategies employed in the besieged areas of Bosnia

Direct link with food	*Indirect link with food*
• Cultivation of gardens	• Paid employment:
• Food parcels from relatives abroad	– formal (e.g. army, police, trading)
• Reduction in intake of food	– informal (e.g. selling firewood, knitwear)
• Change in dietary patterns	• Private savings
• Barter (e.g. cigarettes for food)	• Sale of possessions
	• Cash gifts from relatives abroad
	• 'Illegal' activities (e.g. black-market, smuggling, stealing, prostitution, etc.)

Pre-crisis conditions

There were a number of crucial factors in pre-war Bosnia that protected the population against famine during the war. These include sound socio-economic conditions, good health and nutrition status, and a demographic profile with a majority of adults who were able to look after the vulnerable – children and the elderly (i.e. a low dependency ratio).[3]

The economy, standard of living and education levels in Bosnia were all relatively good before the war, while the physical and social infrastructure was well developed. Some basic indicators of well-being are presented in Table 12.1, and show that the former Yugoslavia was much better off compared to African countries which experienced famine during the 1990s. The underlying structural failures (chronic food insecurity, poverty, underdeveloped infrastructure), which have played crucial roles in causing famine in Africa and Asia, were not present in Bosnia before the war. Thus, although the war had devastating consequences, the population was better equipped to deal with the adverse environment.

Health indicators for the former Yugoslavia and for African countries which experienced emergencies during the 1990s are shown in Table 12.2, and illustrate the differences in pre-crisis health status and access to health services. Although many of the data are missing or unreliable, in general the population of the former Yugoslavia were less likely to die

Table 12.1 Economic and living standard indicators in selected countries, 1990

Countries	GDP per capita (PPP$)[a]	Life expectancy (years)	IMR[b] (per 1,000 live births)	Adult literacy (%)
Former Yugoslavia	3,060	72	20	93
Angola	840	46	128	42
Ethiopia	369	46	125	n/a
Liberia	857	54	131	40
Mozambique	1,072	48	149	33
Rwanda	657	50	112	50
Sierra Leone	1,086	42	146	21
Somalia	836	46	125	24
Sudan	949	51	102	27
Zaire	367	53	96	72

Source: UNDP 1993; WHO 1992; World Bank 1992.

Notes

n/a = not available.

a PPP = Purchasing Power Parity. The purchasing power of a country's currency is the number of units of that currency required to purchase the same representative (or similar) basket of goods and services that a US dollar (the reference currency) would buy in the United States (UNDP 1995)

b 1991 rates.

Table 12.2 Health indicators in selected countries

Countries	One-year-olds immunized		Maternal mortality rate (per 100,000 live births) 1988	Population per doctor 1984
	1990–92			
	polio	measles		
Former Yugoslavia	81	76	27	250
Angola	13	26	900	17,750
Ethiopia	13	10	900	78,780
Liberia	28	61	600	9,340
Mozambique	53	60	800	n/a
Rwanda	85	81	700	35,090
Sierra Leone	72	65	1,000	13,620
Somalia	18	30	900	19,950
Sudan	67	66	700	10,190
Zaire	31	31	700	13,540

Source: UNDP 1993; UNICEF 1993.

Note
n/a = not available.

prematurely, lived for longer, had better access to health services and received better quality health care than the African populations. Thus, the health of the Bosnian population was not stressed before the war. Rather, health status and standards of care were good and the population was better able to combat adverse health conditions compared to populations elsewhere who were already suffering from poor health. A further factor that protected the Bosnian population was the pre-crisis disease epidemiology. Before the war, rates of *chronic* diseases were on the rise in Bosnia, but there were low rates of *infectious* diseases (diarrhoea, acute respiratory infection, AIDS, malaria, etc.), which are associated with malnutrition and mortality in poorer countries. Furthermore, vaccination levels were high so that the majority of children were protected against potentially deadly childhood diseases. The deterioration of the public health system was therefore likely to have a less devastating and slower impact on health status.

Malnutrition, unassociated with specific disease syndromes, was rarely seen in Bosnia before the war. Obesity, on the other hand, was a problem. A study of non-manual workers in Sarajevo found that while only 4.3 per cent of adults were underweight (Body Mass Index (BMI) below 18.5), 8 per cent were obese (BMI above 30.5) (Zec *et al.* 1995). Although population level data on adult nutritional status are scarce, Figure 12.1 illustrates the different patterns of obesity and malnutrition in Europe and the USA compared to African and Asian countries for which data are available. Relatively good pre-crisis nutritional status was an important factor in protecting the Bosnian population against dangerous weight loss. The

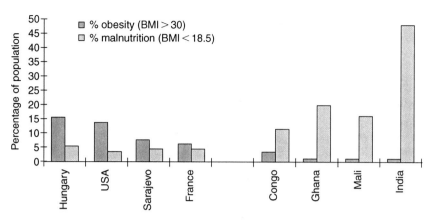

Figure 12.1 Obesity and malnutrition in selected countries (source: Shetty and
   James 1994; Zec *et al.* 1995).

Note
Only limited data from developing countries on obesity and malnutrition are available.
These data are from population surveys carried out between 1975 and 1990.

initial 'fat stocks' of the Bosnian population acted as a buffer against malnutrition, and it would have taken longer for malnutrition to develop in
this population compared to already nutritionally stressed populations.

Evidence from famines in developing countries shows that mortality
and malnutrition rates are highest among young children (Toole and
Waldman 1990, 1993) because of their vulnerability to food shortage and
infection. The demographic structure of developed countries, including
pre-war Bosnia, was very different from that in developing countries,
however. There were proportionally fewer young children and a greater
proportion of the elderly, as Figure 12.2 demonstrates. Overall, this meant
that in Bosnia the dependent population who are most vulnerable during
a crisis represented a lower percentage of the population than in developing countries. Thus, there were proportionally more able-bodied adults to
take care of vulnerable children and elderly people.

International response to the crisis

The war in the former Yugoslavia sent shock-waves throughout the world.
This was the first major war in Europe since the Second World War, and
the sight of European women and children fleeing from their villages
jolted the memories of those who had witnessed similar scenes fifty years
previously. Even before the war started in Bosnia, the UN Security Council
had passed its first resolution demanding an immediate cessation to hostilities in Croatia and ordering a complete arms embargo on Yugoslavia
(Resolution 713, September 1991). The fighting continued, however, and
in February 1992 the first peace-keeping forces were sent by the UN to

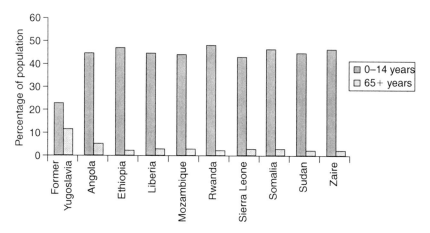

Figure 12.2 Age distribution in selected countries, 1990 (source: World Bank 1992).

maintain stability in the Serbian-held areas of Croatia (Glenny 1992; Kaplan 1994; Mercier 1994; Bennett 1995; Silber and Little 1995).

The war spread to Bosnia in the spring of 1992. As stories of ethnic cleansing and concentration camps in Bosnia began to filter out, the consciences of Western countries became increasingly uncomfortable and international diplomatic efforts to solve the crisis were intensified. A series of attempts to orchestrate a cease-fire and political agreement between the warring parties were made. Though many of the agreements were signed, each one was broken and the atrocities continued until the signing of the Dayton Peace Agreement in December 1995.

Decisive military action by the UN was not forthcoming throughout the war in Bosnia, and it was NATO who carried out the air strikes against key Bosnian Serb targets in September 1995, which were instrumental in bringing an end to the war. Instead the UN opted to respond to the crisis by sending humanitarian aid, and military action was restricted to a joint UN Protection Force whose specific mandate was to protect the safe delivery of humanitarian aid (UN 1993).

The worldwide attention paid to the crisis in the former Yugoslavia was reflected in the magnitude of the appeals made for aid and the subsequent donor response. As a result, the humanitarian assistance operation in the former Yugoslavia was one of the largest humanitarian initiatives ever undertaken by the international community (UNHCR and WFP 1998). Donations to the former Yugoslavia tended to be more generous than to African countries also facing crises during this period, leading to large disparities in per capita spending.

For example, in 1992, the year that war broke out in the former Yugoslavia, UNHCR, the lead UN agency, received a total of $294.4

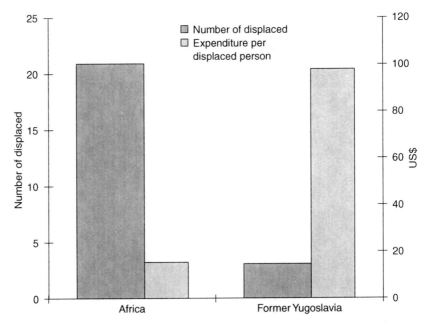

Figure 12.3 UNHCR expenditure for 1992 (source: UNHCR 1994).

million for the former Yugoslavia from specifically earmarked Special Programme money. Contributions for 1993 were expected to double to $447.6 million (UNHCR 1994). The large donations changed the proportion of world UNHCR expenditure completely, with Europe receiving more than Africa (see Figure 12.3). Thus, while Africa held about one-third of the world's refugee population in 1992, UNHCR expenditure per person on the fifteen million displaced and six million refugees in Africa was about $13.5, while in the former Yugoslavia, spending per person on the three million refugees and displaced was about $98.

Similarly, the European Community Humanitarian Office (ECHO) – currently the largest food aid donor in the world – spent ECU 1,221 million on humanitarian aid in the former Yugoslavia between 1992 and 1998 and only ECU 390 million between October 1993 and 1998 on the Great Lakes crisis, which affected Rwanda, Burundi and neighbouring countries (Disaster Management Unit n.d.). In 1993 alone ECHO's allocations to relief operations in the former Yugoslavia were 395 million ECU, which represented no less than 63 per cent of ECHO's total expenditure for the year (ECHO 1994).

Food aid contributed a significant proportion of humanitarian aid, and the cost of purchasing, transporting and distributing food in the former Yugoslavia was enormous. WFP estimated that the food aid operation cost $1.3 million per day at the beginning of 1993 (WFP 1993). In total, some

$710 million for over 1.14 million tons of food were provided to the former Yugoslavia between 1992 and 1997. The majority of this went to Bosnia.

The vast amounts of food aid going to the former Yugoslavia were reflected in patterns of expenditure. For example, WFP per capita spending (for relief and development projects) in sub-Saharan Africa was $1.80 compared to $5.43 in Europe and the Commonwealth of Independent States in 1993, largely due to increased food aid flows to the former Yugoslavia (WFP 1994b). In 1998, WFP expenditure on each returnee, displaced person and war victim in the former Yugoslavia was projected to be $13.55, while spending on each victim of conflict in the Rwanda/Burundi region was $6.14 and on each displaced person and refugee in Liberia was $1.78 (WFP 1998).

The differences in expenditure are, however, partly due to the different costs involved in transporting and distributing food in Europe compared to Africa. When the actual quantities of food aid distributed per person are compared, there is greater equity. For instance, during 1993, when the war in the former Yugoslavia was at its height, an estimated 343,772 tonnes of relief food aid was distributed to 3.78 million beneficiaries. This is equivalent to about 91 kg per beneficiary. In 1994, during the Great Lakes crisis, 359,612 tonnes were distributed in Burundi, Rwanda, Tanzania, Uganda and Zaire to approximately four million beneficiaries. This is equivalent to about 89 kg per beneficiary.

Nonetheless, a detailed study analysing food aid flows concluded that there was progressively greater diversion of US food aid from developing countries to eastern Europe and the former Soviet Republics during the early 1990s (Benson and Clay 1998). The authors estimate that, globally, between ten and twelve million tons of cereals food aid, or about 20 per cent of shipments, were diverted from developing countries to eastern Europe between 1989–1990 and 1993–1994.

Although enormous amounts of food aid were channelled into Bosnia, WFP food aid deliveries to Sarajevo and Central Bosnia, prior to the cease-fire in February 1994, fell short of estimated requirements. In the five months before the ceasefire, an average of 84 per cent of food aid requirements was delivered to Sarajevo and only 38 per cent to Central Bosnia. Furthermore, the ration distributed during this period was designed to meet minimum energy and protein requirements and was deficient in several essential micronutrients. The inadequate levels of vitamin A, vitamin C, niacin, riboflavin and iron were of particular concern, as outbreaks of deficiency diseases due to a lack of these micronutrients have occurred in recent emergencies (Toole 1994).

If estimated requirements for food aid had been accurate and there was a shortfall in food aid distributions, malnutrition including micronutrient deficiencies would have occurred during this period. Although the population of the besieged areas lost weight and may have suffered from sub-clinical micronutrient depletion, there were no clinical signs of mal-nutrition, and anthropometric status did not drop to a critical level. It is therefore concluded that food aid requirements were over-estimated in Bosnia. The dependency on food aid, though great, was not as large as estimated, and the populations in besieged areas were able to survive by accessing food from alternative sources. It can therefore be argued that the food aid response to the crisis in Bosnia was successful partly because there was an over-estimation of needs, which meant that failures in the distribution system (an almost inevitable occurrence in conflict situations) were not disastrous.

Conclusion: protection from famine

The preceding discussion allows a number of conclusions to be drawn about the factors that helped to protect the populations of the besieged areas of Bosnia against famine.

First, the relatively good socio-economic conditions in pre-war Bosnia meant that the population was better able to withstand the adversities of war. The underlying structural failures (chronic food insecurity, poverty, underdeveloped infrastructure), which have played crucial roles in causing famine in developing countries, were not present in pre-war Bosnia. Furthermore, the cumulative effects of repeated crises (e.g. successive years of drought, as in many African famines) are much worse than a single acute crisis (e.g. an atypical period of conflict and economic disruption, as in Bosnia). Household vulnerability increases through the progressive depletion of food stocks and capital assets as a result of repeated assaults.

Second, the initially good health and nutrition status of the Bosnian population was a significant protective buffer against health and nutrition stresses. Healthy people, whose immune systems have not been repeatedly compromised, are better able to combat an adverse health environment than unhealthy people. Fatter people take longer to become malnourished than thinner people.

Third, the disease epidemiology in pre-war Bosnia showed a pattern of low rates of infectious diseases and high rates of chronic disease. Vaccination levels were also relatively good. Epidemics of infectious disease are less likely to occur in such circumstances than in environments which already have high rates of infectious diseases, as in developing countries.

Fourth, the age distribution in pre-war Bosnia favoured able-bodied adults over children and the elderly. There were therefore proportionately fewer vulnerable children and elderly people per adult than in developing countries. Thus, the ability to care for and protect the vulnerable within the community was probably better.

Finally, the vast humanitarian response to the crisis in Bosnia helped to alleviate suffering. Although food aid was apparently inadequate to meet requirements during particularly critical periods of the war, the over-estimation of needs meant that failures in the distribution system were not disastrous, and besieged populations were able to resort to alternative sources of food.

Notes

1 For the sake of brevity, Bosnia and Herzegovina will be referred to as Bosnia.
2 A major armed conflict is defined as a conflict in which at least 1,000 battle-related deaths have been reported since the beginning of the conflict (ICRC 1994).
3 Dependency ratio is the ratio of the population defined as 'dependent' – children under fifteen and the elderly over sixty-four years – to the working-age population, aged fifteen to sixty-four (UNDP 1993).

References

Anderson, A. A (1995) 'Forgotten chapter: Holland under the Third Reich', transcript of lecture at The University of Southern California.

Bennett, C. (1995) *Yugoslavia's Bloody Collapse: Causes, Course and Consequences,* London: Hurst & Company.

Benson, C. and Clay, E. J. (1998) 'Additionality or diversion? Food aid to eastern Europe and the former Soviet Republics and the implications for developing countries', *World Development,* 26(1): 31–44.

Devereux, S. (1993) *Theories of Famine,* London: Harvester Wheatsheaf.

Disaster Management Unit (n.d.) 'European Community Humanitarian Office (ECHO)', UNDP Project VIE/93/031 (available at www.undp.org.vn/dmu/dmu/en/echo.htm, accessed 17 August 2005).

ECHO (1994) 'Humanitarian aid: annual report, 1993', Brussels: European Community Humanitarian Office.

Fliederbaum, J., Heller, A., Zweibaum, K. and Zarchi, J. (1994) 'Clinical aspects of hunger disease in adults', *Nutrition* 10: 366–71.

Glenny, M. (1992) *The Fall of Yugoslavia,* London: Penguin Books.

Golden, M. H. N. (1992) 'Nutrition in Bosnia during the current emergency', report on a visit to Bosnia, 4–15 October 1992.

Green, R. H. (1994) 'The course of the four horsemen: costs of war and its aftermath in sub-Saharan Africa', in J. Macrae and A. Zwi (eds), *War and Hunger: Rethinking International Responses to Complex Emergencies,* London: Zed Books.

ICRC (1994) *Children and War,* Geneva: ICRC.

James, W. P. T. (1992) 'Food supplies and nutritional surveillance in the Republic of Bosnia and Herzegovina', Report on a visit to Zagreb, 29 September to 6 October, WHO Regional Office for Europe.

Jones, L. (1994) 'Siege survivors pay their tributes', *St Petersburg Press,* 90.

Kaplan, R. D. (1994) *Balkan Ghosts: A Journey Through History,* London: Papermac.

Keys, A., Brozek, J., Henschel, A., Mickelson, O. and Taylor, H. L. (1950) *The Biology of Human Starvation,* Minneapolis, MN: The University of Minnesota Press.

Macrae, J. and Zwi, A. (1994) 'Famine, complex emergencies and international policy in Africa: an overview', in J. Macrae and A. Zwi (eds), *War and Hunger: Rethinking International Responses to Complex Emergencies*, London: Zed Books.

Mercier, M. (1994) *Crimes without Punishment: Humanitarian Action in Former Yugoslavia*, London: Pluto Press.

Narayan, N. (1993) 'Eyewitness: trickle of aid fails to lift the gloom in central Bosnia', *Guardian*, London.

Nezirovic, H. (1993) 'Defeated by the battle for food', *Guardian*, London.

Pick, H. and Fairhall, D. (1993) 'Clinton's plan for Bosnia aid gets a mixed reception', *Guardian*, London.

Pick, H. and Traynor, I. (1992) 'Britain relents over Bosnian refugees after Hurd wins day over Home Office', *Guardian*, London.

Puvacic, Z. and Weinberg, J. (1994) 'Impact of war on infectious disease in Bosnia-Herzegovina', *British Medical Journal*, 309: 1207–8.

Redmond, A. (1992) 'Report on visit to Sarajevo: 30 December 1992', Geneva: WHO.

Robertson, A. (1992) 'Overview of nutritional situation at 31st October 1992', Zagreb: WHO.

Roland, C. G. (1992) *Courage Under Siege: Disease, Starvation and Death in the Warsaw Ghetto*, New York, NY: Oxford University Press.

Rupesinghe, K. (1994) *Advancing Preventive Diplomacy in a Post-Cold War Era: Suggested Roles for Governments and NGOs*, London: Relief and Rehabilitation Network.

Salisbury, H. E. (1969) *The Siege of Leningrad*, London: Secker and Warburg.

Schrienier, G. E. (1918) *The Iron Ration: Economic and Social Effects of the Allied Blockade on Germany and the German People*, London: J. Murray.

Shetty, P. S. and James, W. P. T. (1994) 'Body mass index: a measure of chronic energy deficiency in adults', *FAO Food and Nutrition Paper* 56, Rome: FAO.

Silber, L. and Little, A. (1995) *The Death of Yugoslavia*, London: Penguin Group/BBC Worldwide Ltd.

Smith, C. A. (1947) 'Effects of maternal undernutrition upon the newborn infant in Holland (1944–1945)', *Journal of Pediatrics*, 30: 229–43.

Stein, Z., Susser, M., Saenger, G. and Marolla, F. (1975) *Famine and Human Development*, Oxford: Oxford University Press.

St Petersburg Times (1995) 'Siege Of Leningrad survivor relives her childhood terror', 31 January (available at www.archive.sptimes.ru/archive/sppress/91/siege.html).

Toole, M. J. (1994) 'Preventing micronutrient deficiency diseases', Paper presented at a workshop on the 'Improvement of the Nutrition of Refugees and Displaced People in Africa', Machakos, Kenya, Geneva: ACC/SCN.

Toole, M. J. and Waldman, R. J. (1990) 'Prevention of excess mortality in refugee and displaced populations in developing countries', *Journal of the American Medical Association*, 263(4): 3296–302.

Toole, M. J. and Waldman, R. J. (1993) 'Refugees and displaced persons: war, hunger, and public health', *Journal of the American Medical Association*, 270(5): 600–5.

Traynor, I. (1993) 'Bosnian winter of hunger feared', *Guardian*, London.

UN (1977) 'Protocol 1 Additional to the Geneva Conventions', Article 54, Protection of Objects Indispensable to the Survival of the Civilian Population, Geneva: UN.

UN (1993) *The United Nations and the Situation in the Former Yugoslavia*, New York, NY: United Nations Department of Public Information.

UNDP (1993) *Human Development Report 1993*, New York, NY: Oxford University Press.

UNDP (1994) *Human Development Report 1994*, New York, NY: Oxford University Press.

UNDP (1995) *Human Development Report 1995*, New York, NY: Oxford University Press.

UNHCR (1993) 'Report from the UNHCR Office of the Special Envoy for former Yugoslavia', Zagreb: UNHCR.

UNHCR (1994) 'UN Report of the UNHCR General Assembly: official records forty-eighth session', 12, New York, NY: UNHCR.

UNHCR and WFP (1998) 'UNHCR/WFP joint evaluation of emergency food assistance to returnees, refugees, displaced persons and other war-affected populations in Bosnia and Herzegovina', Rome: WFP.

UNICEF (1993) *The State of the World's Children 1993*, New York, NY: Oxford University Press.

Vespa, J. and Watson, F. (1995) 'Who is nutritionally vulnerable in Bosnia-Herzegovina?', *British Medical Journal*, 311: 652–4.

Vincent, C. P. (1985) *The Politics of Hunger: The Allied Blockade of Germany*, Athens, OH: Ohio University Press.

Watson, F. and Vespa, J. 1995 'The impact of a reduced and uncertain food supply in three besieged cities of Bosnia-Herzegovina', *Disasters*, 19(3): 216–34.

Whealey, K. (n.d.) 'Rescuing traditional food crops', *Seed Savers Exchange*.

WFP (1993) 'WFP in the former Yugoslavia', *Situation Report* 1, Rome: WFP.

WFP (1994a) 'WFP in the former Yugoslavia', *Situation Report* 8, Rome: WFP.

WFP (1994b) *Annual Report 1994*, Rome: WFP.

WFP (1998) 'Status of 1998 food needs, contributions and shortfalls for WFP-assisted emergency and protracted relief operations and projected 1998 resource availability for development', Rome: WFP.

WHO (1992) 'Highlights on health in Azerbaijan', Copenhagen: WHO.

WHO (1995) 'Annual report 1995: WHO humanitarian assistance to Bosnia and Herzegovina, Croatia and the Federal Republic of Yugoslavia (Serbia and Montenegro): war and health – crossing the bridge to peace', Copenhagen: WHO Regional Office for Europe.

Winick, M. (1994) 'Hunger disease: prospective overview', *Nutrition*, 10: 365–80.

World Bank (1992) *World Development Report 1992*, New York, NY: Oxford University Press.

Zec, S., Telebak, B., Sljepcevic, O. and Filipovic-Hadziomeragic, A. (1995) 'Nutrition in pre-war Sarajevo', *European Journal of Clinical Nutrition*, 49: 6–10.

13 Is democracy the answer?

Famine prevention in two Indian states

Dan Banik

Introduction

One of India's most creditable achievements in the past five decades has been the prevention of famine. The impressive progress in increasing food production and economic growth has enabled successive national governments to pursue a food security strategy consisting of direct anti-poverty programmes, public distribution of subsidized foodgrains, nutrition-based programmes and the provision of health facilities. While these efforts have successfully prevented famine, the food and nutritional security of a large portion of the Indian population, especially in rural and inaccessible areas, remains precarious. For example, despite a large food surplus in the past five years, millions of Indians suffer from malnutrition and chronic undernutrition which, on occasion, leads to 'starvation deaths' – a highly politicized issue in India.

This chapter starts by critically examining the relationship between democracy and famine prevention, taking as a starting point Amartya Sen's famous claim that no famine has ever occurred in a democratic country. Subsequently, I will take Sen's argument further and focus on the (in)ability of democratic institutions to combat chronic undernutrition and resulting 'starvation deaths' that lack the sensational characteristics of a famine. The political triggers of an independent media and active opposition parties that work successfully to prevent famine in India are notably ineffective with regard to chronic undernutrition and starvation. I will focus on why this is so. The empirical material is drawn from two states on India's east coast – Orissa and West Bengal. In particular, I will focus on reported instances of starvation deaths in the tribal-dominated and drought-prone Kalahandi district in western Orissa, which over the past few decades has achieved notoriety as the 'starvation capital' of India, despite regular press coverage and expressed political concern over severe drought-induced distress. I then compare the Kalahandi case with that of tribal-dominated and drought-prone Purulia district in neighbouring West Bengal state, where no starvation-related deaths have been reported despite recurrent food crises.

Amartya Sen on democracy and famine prevention

Sen claims that independent India has successfully prevented famines due to its democratic political structure (Sen 1984: 84).[1] Indeed, in spite of near-famine conditions in 1965–1967, 1970–1973, and during more recent droughts in the 1980s and 1990s, the last major famine in India occurred in 1943–1944 in Bengal, where an estimated 1.5 to three million people died. Interestingly, Sen (1983; 1984) argues that India's success is not primarily the result of raising food output per head, as is often thought. Famine has actually been prevented despite lower food production than in many countries in the Sahel, and a lower rate of economic growth than China. Drèze and Sen (1989; 1995) have gone on to argue that the prevention of famines in India has been a result of extensive 'entitlement protection' efforts that rely on the operation of two complementary forces: the *administrative system*, which intelligently aims at recreating lost entitlements caused by flood, drought or economic slump; and the *political system*, which is instrumental in getting the administrative system to work as and when required. Drèze and Sen are, however, careful to point out that the administrative structure for combating famines may be non-operational and ineffective in the absence of a 'political trigger'. By influencing government policy via 'public action' in the form of political activism, criticism and opposition, many actors in Indian society contribute to triggering government response for the prevention of famine. A similar political triggering mechanism did not (and still does not) exist in China, which was the main reason why the Chinese authorities, once they had initiated relief measures to combat the 'Great Leap Forward' famine of 1959–1961, were not held accountable for their failure to prevent mass starvation. Hence, the role of democracy is crucial.

In his book *Development as Freedom*, Sen (2000) argues that the promotion and strengthening of democracy is crucial for the process of development on three grounds. First, democracy has *intrinsic importance* as a value in itself and has direct relevance for the promotion of basic capabilities – including social and political participation. Sen (1999) has also argued in some detail for democracy as a 'universal value'. Second, democracy makes possible various *instrumental contributions* in ensuring that people are able to express their economic needs, and to claim and receive political attention in support of meeting these basic needs. Third, democracy has a *constructive* role in the very understanding and identification of what constitutes 'needs' in a social context. Civil and political rights enable public discussion, debates, participatory politics and criticism, which play a major role in the understanding and conceptualization of 'needs' and public responses to meet them. Each of these three features needs to be considered while evaluating a democratic system (Sen 2000: 157–8). Having established that democracy is crucial for economic development, Sen revisits his 'democracy and famine prevention' argument, but interestingly qualifies his earlier statements by using the term 'substantial famine' although he does not clarify what he means by 'substantial' (Sen 2000: 51–3):

> Indeed, no substantial famine has ever occurred in a democratic country – no matter how poor. This is because famines are extremely easy to prevent if the government tries to prevent them, and a government in a multiparty democracy with elections and free media has strong political incentives to undertake famine prevention. This would indicate that political freedom in the form of democratic arrangements helps to safeguard economic freedom (especially freedom from extreme starvation) and the freedom to survive (against famine mortality).

Sen (2000: 51–3) goes on to note that democracies have the potential to respond to large crises far better than non-democracies, and that this factor may not be much noticed in non-crisis times:

> The security provided by democracy may not be much missed when a country is lucky enough to be facing no serious calamity, when everything is running along smoothly. But the danger of insecurity, arising from changes in the economic or other circumstances or from uncorrected mistakes of policy, can lurk behind what looks like a healthy state.

In his work over the years, Sen has highlighted several features of public action that avert famine in democracies. These can be grouped under three main categories.

First, since widespread starvation does not occur simultaneously in all sectors and in all regions, an independent and critical media can provide a sensitive system for early warning and prediction of famines 'by making discriminating use of available information' (Sen 1987: 14). In this context, an active and vigorous newspaper system can usefully supplement the work of economic analysis 'by reporting early signs of distress with predictive significance'. More recently, Sen has emphasized the importance of freedom of speech and expression (Sen 2000: 152):

> We have reason to value liberty and freedom of expression and action in our lives, and it is not unreasonable for human beings – the social creatures that we are – to value unrestrained participation in political and social activities. Also, informed and unregimented *formation* of our values requires openness of communication and arguments, and political freedoms and civil rights can be central for this process. Furthermore, to express publicly what we value and to demand that attention be paid to it, we need free speech and democratic choice.

In particular, the role of a free press is crucial in providing early warning of impending food crises. Sen (2000: 180–1) believes that as long as the press is free, it will perform this task of providing information and early warning, thereby making it difficult for the authorities not to react with urgency:

> A free press and the practice of democracy contribute greatly to bringing out information that can have an enormous impact on policies for famine prevention (for example, information about the early effects of droughts and floods and about the nature and impact of unemployment). The most elementary source of basic information from distant areas about a threatening famine are enterprising news media, especially when there are incentives – provided by a democratic system – for bringing out facts that may be embarrassing to the government (facts that an authoritarian government would tend to censor out). Indeed, I would argue that a free press and an active political opposition constitute the best early-warning system a country threatened by famines can have.

Second, on the question of the agency best equipped to anticipate and tackle famine threats and ameliorate deprivation, Sen believes the responsibility should fall on 'those who provide relief and also take other steps for curing famine threats' and 'this role, naturally enough, falls primarily on the government of the country in question' (Sen 1987: 14). While the primary agency in this context is the state, Sen recognizes the importance of the role of the market and the role of various non-state actors – national and international voluntary agencies, the extended family, the community, etc. – that may usefully supplement state action.

Third, democracy allows citizens to make use of a range of opportunities available, but to what extent these are used, Sen argues, will depend on the existing functioning of multiparty politics and the nature of the dominant values in society (Sen 2000: 154–5). The role of political parties and organized opposition groups is therefore particularly important, as they can exert political pressure to prevent the government from abusing power and ignoring the interests of the deprived and those vulnerable to famine.[2] Thus, the nature of domestic politics determines the level of responsiveness shown by the political authorities.

Although newspapers may provide information and early warning, state action needs to be accountable if it is to serve its real purpose. This is where Sen highlights the importance of a democratic political culture and adversarial politics, although he cautions that these must not be seen as 'mechanical devices for development', since their 'use is conditioned by our values and priorities, and by the use we make of the available opportunities of articulation and participation' (Sen 2000: 158). The public needs to understand and be aware of issues and participate actively in shaping the course of state action. How citizens of a country make use of various opportunities available to them in order to voice their demands and claim remedial action – 'public enlightenment' – is vital in addition to democratic rules and procedures (Sen 1987: 15; Sen 2000: 154).

With regard to the Indian case, Sen argues that with independence from British rule, the newly elected rulers gave explicit priority to preventing famine, and this idea matured with political activism. Thus, public action in India has effectively ensured that successive governments must respond quickly and forcefully to actual or potential calamities. In contrast to highly visible forms of suffering like famine, Sen is, however, aware of the failures of democracies like India to combat less visible phenomena like those of regular undernutrition, gender inequality or persistently high levels of illiteracy. Political parties in India have been successful in ensuring that large-scale famines are not allowed to take place but they have done little to put the silent and less visible forms of suffering on the political agenda. Sen is very critical of the 'docility of the opposition' which has allowed the Indian government to 'get away with unconscionable neglect of these vital matters of public policy' (Sen 2000: 155):

> Democracy has been especially successful in preventing those disasters that are easy to understand and where sympathy can take a particularly immediate form. Many other problems are not quite so accessible ... While the plight of famine victims is easy to politicize, these other deprivations call for deeper analysis and more effective use of communication and political participation – in short, a fuller practice of democracy.

A major attraction of Sen's liberal rights hypothesis, as de Waal (1996) has rightly pointed out, lies in the fact that it gives a human rights *raison d'être* for international media and aid organizations, and a suggestion of wider relevance to socio-economic issues for human rights campaigners. In the following sections, I will critically discuss the relationship between democracy and famine prevention by focusing on three sets of issues. These correspond primarily to the ways in which the terms 'famine', 'democracy' and 'public action' are understood.

The need to operationalize 'famine'

At present, national governments, voluntary organizations, international aid agencies, academics and the media use a variety of terms to describe and define an imminent or ongoing food-related crisis affecting large groups of people. These include 'hunger', 'acute food insecurity', 'starvation', 'food emergency', 'food crisis' and 'near-famine situation', which in turn are sometimes used interchangeably with 'famine'. This leads to confusion and disagreement with regard to the detection and response of an observed phenomenon. For example, 'famine' is sometimes used as a form of early warning of an impending crisis by the local and international media, while on other occasions the term is used to describe an event where mass deaths are already taking place.[3] While the declaration of a famine can mobilize world attention, unrestricted usage can backfire when it is subsequently proved that the observed phenomenon, although a crisis, was not a famine. Thus, the credibility of the term 'famine' is at stake, and its frequent usage results in the loss of the sense of urgency associated with the term. Aware of such pitfalls, there is often caution and reluctance on the part of governments and agencies to declare a famine, even when they are convinced that the situation warrants such a declaration.

Like many authors, Sen too fails to operationalize famine and related terms. Indeed, Sen is generally inattentive to famine definitions, although he did make a significant observation on the distinction between famine, starvation and poverty when he wrote: 'Famines imply starvation, but not vice versa. And starvation implies poverty, but not vice versa' (Sen 1981: 39). In recent years, Sen (2000) has also used the word 'substantial' together with 'famine', perhaps in an effort to qualify his earlier assertions. However, within Sen's framework, it is particularly difficult to place the phenomenon of 'starvation deaths' – where people die from starvation but the situation cannot be described as one of 'mass starvation' that characterizes a 'famine'. Sen operates with a dualistic distinction between chronic hunger on the one hand and famine on the other. In reality, numerous levels or phases between these two extremes must be recognized. I have therefore argued elsewhere (Banik 2003) that a clear separation and subsequent operationalization of 'famine' and related terms like 'malnutrition', 'severe undernutrition', 'starvation' and 'famine threat' is needed in order to avoid ambiguity and confusion.[4] I argue that 'famine' is not the same as 'severe undernutrition', and that occasional 'starvation deaths' do not constitute 'famine'.

By differentiating between famine and related terms, it is also possible to strengthen Sen's argument and demonstrate that it can be applied well primarily to famine countries like Ethiopia, Sudan and North Korea. This is important, as authors like Rangasami (1985), de Waal (1989, 2000) and Edkins (2000) have criticized Sen's approach for identifying famine with an extraordinary 'event' of starvation instead of a lengthy drawn-out process which also includes death due to disease. The question that needs to be addressed is: should a famine be understood as an exceptional 'event' with a given timeframe, or should it be seen as a continuous 'process' of malnutrition and undernutrition resulting in mass starvation, disease and finally full-blown famine? This question is relevant precisely because if one applies a definition of famine that requires a large number of deaths or equates famines with extraordinary catastrophes of the kind witnessed in Ethiopia in the 1970s and 1980s, then Sen is correct in his observation that democratic India has never had a famine since independence. If, on the other hand, one operates with a famine definition that allows for a lesser number of casualties within an extended time period, then Sen's observation of India's success in preventing famine may appear more problematic, given the frequency with which starvation deaths are reported in the local, regional and national press.

Democracy and freedom

A controversial aspect of the relationship between democracy and famine prevention relates to whether certain countries like Bangladesh (1974) and Sudan (1985–1986) should be considered democracies during recent famines. Conversely, there are several cases, like Nigeria (1974), Kenya (1984) and Zimbabwe (1982–1984), where non-democratic regimes have successfully prevented the escalation of major food crises into famine. Sen himself has been surprisingly reluctant to elaborate on how exactly democratic processes work in promoting a person's entitlement to food. His understanding of democracy is essentially a liberal one, and he assumes that opposition parties and a free press are consistently interested in promoting the interests of the poor and vulnerable. In a study of the role of the Indian press in anti-hunger strategies, Ram (1990: 187) is generally supportive of Sen's ideas and finds 'a highly positive correlation on the role of an independent press' and the prevention of famine. However, he observes that although the overall role and concerns of the Indian press are valuable, 'habits of impression, exaggeration, and oversimplification might detract from this role', and that 'there is a tendency to dramatize and sensationalize the coverage of poverty and hunger on a mass scale while missing out deeper structural features and processes' (Sen 1990: 187). These factors contribute to a loss of press credibility. In a study of the role of the press in covering drought and starvation in India, I found that many newspapers are unable to influence public policy due to ownership structures – especially when newspapers are owned by politicians from opposition parties. The quality of news reports is a further barrier, as most journalists and 'stringers' are poorly paid and often lack training in journalism (Banik 2003).

Echoing Sen, de Waal (1997: 7–8) suggests that India's success in averting famine since gaining independence is due to the 'vigilance of its political achievement'. However, he goes on to argue that it is important to locate human rights within political processes, and identifies 'a specific 'political contract'[5] that has ensured an enforceable freedom from famine in India.' For de Waal, this 'political contract' is 'the result of a popular movement successfully articulating a right, and forcing a reluctant government to comply with its claims' (de Waal 1997: 11). In contrast to India, most of Africa has not implemented a similar political contract between the state and its citizens and this, according to de Waal (1996: 28), explains Africa's poor record at famine prevention:

... there has been little or no opportunity for famine prevention to emerge as a right in Africa. The only exceptions may be among certain urban populations, where the right to relatively cheap food has become deeply entrenched. The central reason for this is that famine never became the politicized issue in the same way that it was in India.

De Waal accepts there has been a handful of exceptions and 'partial exceptions' to this argument, for instance when the Wollo famine in Ethiopia (1973) was used by revolutionaries to remove Emperor Haile Selassie. While combating famine was a major priority of the revolution, it was 'quickly hijacked by a military dictatorship which in due course went on to inflict an even more severe famine on the Ethiopian people' (de Waal 1996: 28). In a similar fashion, during the height of the civil war in Ethiopia in the 1980s the Tigrayan People's Liberation Front (TPLF) expressed a clear anti-famine commitment and was able to gain considerable popular support among the people. However, and ironically, after the TPLF came to power in 1991, its anti-famine contract weakened considerably, and there have been several 'minor famines' in Ethiopia since the early 1990s.[6] Further, the 1984–1985 famine in Sudan weakened the Nimeiri Government, and the opposition allied to remove the government by citing its failure to prevent famine. However, once they removed Nimeiri, these so-called 'democratic forces' abandoned the famine issue. These instances lend support to de Waal's assertion that an anti-famine contract has never really materialized properly in Africa, and that this explains recurrent famines in the continent.

While this is an attractive argument, de Waal appears to overstate the existence of a 'political contract' in preventing famine in India. In certain states, there may be a form of political demand for protective social security. Particularly in Kerala and West Bengal, the generally high level of political awareness among the population (particularly in rural areas) has meant that local issues, including the politics of food, are highly politicized. The cadre-based Communist Party of India, Marxist (CPIM) and its Left Front allies in both states have a strong rural support base and are generally active in raising local issues, since local party workers provide information and are generally held accountable by the local population.[7] Similarly, starting in the late 1980s, Tamil Nadu was one of the first states in India to initiate a comprehensive set of social security programmes covering pensions (for the elderly, widows and deserted wives), maternity assistance, subsidized food for Below Poverty Line (BPL) households, nutritional and health programmes under the Integrated Child Development Services (ICDS), etc. Thus, Kerala, West Bengal and Tamil Nadu appear to stand out from the rest of India and, according to Harriss (2000: 18–19), this is largely explained by the historical fragmentation of caste/class structures and the comparatively 'stronger representation of lower castes/classes' in local politics in these states. In addition, one can argue that in all three states, state action has been usefully supplemented by active participation from civil society organizations and actors.[8]

My argument so far is that there are certain states in India that have managed to provide some form of basic social security to large portions of their populations. It is also possible that in these states, signals of imminent food crises and starvation will be quickly communicated to the authorities by local party workers, thus preventing major loss of life. However, in terms of India's general success at preventing famine, I would argue that there is little evidence of what de Waal calls a 'political contract'. Instead, the key issue appears to be whether government is willing to acknowledge and declare a 'crisis'. Indian public administration usually manages to respond to crises in an impressive manner, and Drèze and Sen (1989; 1995) are correct to observe that politicians trigger bureaucratic response. However, in order to activate this trigger, politicians must first publicly declare a crisis and risk being criticized for failing to prevent it in the first place. Being very visible and involving large-scale suffering, famines are easy to combat, since not being seen to do something to tackle the situation is unthinkable in India. By contrast, the quiet persistence of malnutrition, chronic undernutrition and recurrent episodes of small-scale starvation-related deaths in isolated areas are less visible and do not receive the same kind of attention as a famine. These silent forms of suffering require that political authorities admit and declare a 'chronic crisis' and then take appropriate steps to combat it, which may involve very different public responses than those adopted to prevent high-profile famines.

Rubin (2001) provides an interesting viewpoint when he argues that Sen's argument can be divided into two distinct interpretations – 'strict' and 'weak'. According to a strict interpretation, 'a famine would never be able to occur in a democratic society with a free press', while a weak interpretation entails merely 'hypothesizing that democracy and free press increase the government's responsiveness thus not excluding the possibility of a famine in a democratic society altogether' (Rubin 2001: 78). I largely agree with Rubin, and believe that Sen's argument works best in terms of a broad ('weak') interpretation, whereby democracy and free press increase government responsiveness to famines. This means that it remains possible for famine to occur in weak, transitional and unstable electoral democracies. Transitional democracies where electoral procedures have recently been introduced can witness famines simply because democracy has not taken root properly and the society lacks a sustainable political culture and political stability. For example, the experiment with a parliamentary system in Sudan in 1986–1989, while important from the electoral point of view, was not able to guarantee and safeguard basic freedoms to the Sudanese. Similarly, the Bangladesh famine in 1974 took place despite the presence of an elected government in Dhaka. Bangladesh had recently become independent from Pakistan, and the government, elected in 1973, was not able to put in place an effective system of governance to tackle natural disasters and resulting food shortages. Thus, famine in both Sudan and Bangladesh can be explained with regard to a broad interpretation of Sen's argument – democracy increases government responsiveness, but this function is limited if the democratic process is not yet stable or fully institutionalized.

In contrast, non-democracies may enjoy considerable success in preventing famine as long as certain freedoms (although not extensively political in nature) are guaranteed – including freedom of speech and expression, together with the freedom to organize – even though regular free and fair elections are not held. Take the case of the successful effort of the military regime in Nigeria to prevent famine in its northern states during the major drought in 1972–1973. Reddy (1988) has documented the active role played by Nigerian newspapers in highlighting drought and deprivation and influencing the regime to launch an impressive and effective response.

The point here is that a focus on certain basic freedoms is indeed relevant and important to capture the complex web of processes by which victims of, and those vulnerable to, starvation and famine articulate their problems – directly or indirectly through prominent citizens and organizations – and seek redress from the ruling authority. Many definitions of 'democracy' attach considerable if not exclusive attention to the role of elections. Sen himself has recently pointed out that democracy has two related features: the voting aspect and the open public deliberation aspect. He cites the example of Pakistan under General Musharraf and, while agreeing that free and fair elections need to be held as soon as possible, simultaneously argues that it is important to remember that public deliberation in Pakistan under Musharraf has been much more open and free than in previous democratically-elected governments.[9]

Thus, while elections are important, they do not guarantee successful public deliberation in preventing starvation and famine. In this sense, a democratic system provides necessary but not sufficient conditions for famine prevention. While democracies guarantee certain basic freedoms, there is no guarantee that citizens are actually in a position to utilize these freedoms properly. Hence, Sen's argument functions best when not rigorously interpreted.

Public action and its limits

If we take a broad or 'weak' interpretation of Sen's argument – that democracy and free press increase government responsiveness – as a starting point, the next challenge is to tackle the issue of why the same democratic freedoms and public action are not able to combat less sensational forms of suffering, like chronic malnutrition, that often result in starvation and death.

To Sen 'public action' entails concern for – and the motivation to do something to improve – the lives of others. It involves 'what people can do by demanding remedial action and through making governments accountable' (Sen 1990). 'Public action' involves public delivery of goods and services by both state and non-state (e.g. market) actors. However, this is only part of the picture. What is crucial is that the public, heterogeneous as it is, participates in the process of social change in both 'collaborative' and 'adversarial' ways. The public needs to be collaborative in aspects of government policy – literacy drives, health campaigns, land reform, famine relief measures – that require such cooperation for successful implementation. In addition, the public needs to influence government initiatives and demand proper government response by performing an adversarial and critical role. This is achieved by political activism, hard-hitting investigative journalism and informed public criticism (Drèze and Sen 1995: 88–9). In this context, it is also 'essential to see the public not merely as 'the patient' whose well-being commands attention, but also as 'the agent' whose actions can transform society' (Drèze and Sen 1989: 279). Public action in combating hunger thus needs to take note of this dual understanding of the public as both passive (a 'patient' in need of care) and active (an 'agent' of change).

A focus on public action, according to Sen, helps not only to assess the nutritional needs of the vulnerable but also to acknowledge the importance of access to complementary services like health care, clean drinking water, sanitation, etc. Sen goes on to argue that the importance of public action lies in its potential for enhancing the ability of people to undertake valuable elementary capabilities, such as the ability to avoid undernourishment and related morbidity and mortality, as well as more sophisticated social capabilities such as taking part in the life of the community and achieving self-respect.

While Sen has repeatedly argued that despite success at preventing famines, India has failed to address the problem of regular hunger, he does not take the argument further to explain why this is so. According to Currie (2000), Drèze and Sen's (1989) understanding of 'public action' is vague and they fail to identify the sets of conditions under which public action can be successful or unsuccessful in promoting government commitment to combat starvation and famine. One major difficulty with the concept is who precisely constitutes the 'public'. This is particularly relevant in a country like India, where the distinction between the public and private spheres is often blurred. Further, Currie (2000: 24) argues that the 'range of political actions adopted by citizens to put pressure on government, and the range of responses adopted by office-holders, is too narrowly defined' in Sen's model of public action. Currie suggests that any analysis of public action should take into account not just formal articulation within the system of democratic politics, but also articulation using 'alternative channels' where a range of strategies are adopted by both administrators and citizens whenever 'the democratic political process fails to meet the needs and expectations of citizens' (Currie 2000). He therefore asserts that the Drèze and Sen model can only offer a partial explanation of the role of democratic governments in combating starvation.

While Sen (1986: 41) admits that the Indian political system cannot afford a famine 'both because it would be too acute and because it cannot take place quietly', there is nonetheless a pressing need to understand why regular cases of severe malnutrition and starvation deaths, in various parts of India, are not viewed as important enough to warrant immediate remedial action. The focus of the next section of this chapter is therefore to explore the conditions under which democracy and public action in India succeed in preventing sensational famines but generally fail in combating low-profile malnutrition and starvation.

Two case studies: Kalahandi (Orissa) and Purulia (West Bengal)

A study of the states of Orissa and West Bengal, situated on the eastern coast of India, provides a useful insight into anti-famine policies pursued in India since the country became independent in 1947. With a population of 31.7 million in 2001, Orissa is regarded as a so-called 'backward state', with one of the highest poverty levels in India. It also has a long history of underdevelopment and low political mobilization. West Bengal, with a population of seventy million, is India's most densely populated state, and is almost as poor as Orissa, with nearly three-fifths of the population living below the poverty line. Both states also experienced comparable rates of growth in gross foodgrain production in the decade between 1981 and 1991 – 6.6 per cent in West Bengal and 4 per cent in Orissa.

The two states differ, however, on one crucial front, namely the prevalence of and responses to starvation. Kalahandi district[10] in Orissa is widely regarded as the 'starvation capital' of India. Historically, Kalahandi faced numerous drought-induced famines, and even since 1947 the district has endured recurrent droughts and ensuing food crises. The drought that plagued Orissa in 1966–1967 was particularly severe on Kalahandi, and several thousand people were reported in the media to have perished from starvation and disease. Much of Kalahandi's notoriety, however, developed in the mid-1980s, when a string of press reports on child sale and starvation deaths forced Prime Minister Rajiv Gandhi to visit the district in 1985. This was also when the whole nation began hearing of Kalahandi on a daily basis as media interest, especially in the national English language press, increased manifold. With severe droughts in 1986–1987, the situation in the district was grim, and a few concerned individuals and organizations petitioned the courts, alleging hundreds of starvation deaths and a general neglect of the district by the state government in

Orissa. Subsequent inquiries conducted by the judiciary concluded that starvation deaths had indeed taken place, and the Government of Orissa and several high-ranking bureaucrats in the state were indicted for failing to take preventive action. These petitions and the subsequent court rulings further increased media interest in the Kalahandi story in the 1990s (Banik 2003). Kalahandi was back in the national limelight in 1993, when newspaper reports indicated that thousands of people in the district were severely affected by a drought and that almost 500 people had starved to death. Similar stories on Kalahandi appeared on a regular basis in the press in the period 1996–2000. In December 1996, the central government formally identified Kalahandi as one of forty-one districts in India 'prone to starvation'.[11]

Purulia, in west-central West Bengal, is one of the poorest and most backward of the state's eighteen districts.[12] Almost half of its 2.5 million population were classified in the BPL category in 2000. Interestingly, Purulia shares many of the characteristics of Kalahandi, starting with a high percentage of Scheduled Caste (19.4 per cent) and Scheduled Tribe (19.2 per cent) in the population.[13] The literacy rate is low (45.6 per cent), and even lower among women (13.3 per cent). Over 90 per cent of the population live in rural areas, with agriculture being the main source of livelihood. Purulia has rich but fast-depleting natural resources, a low intensity of cultivation, and over two-thirds of those involved in agriculture are marginal farmers. The average size of operational landholdings in the district in 1991 was 0.99 hectares – far less than the 1.94 hectares in Kalahandi. While only six of thirteen administrative blocks in Kalahandi are classified as drought-prone, all twenty blocks of Purulia fall into this category.[14]

Apart from the district capital, Purulia town, most of the villages suffer from food shortages and water scarcity during years when the monsoon rains are erratic and unevenly distributed. However, despite recurrent drought episodes, high population density, undeveloped agricultural potential, stagnation in industry and high levels of malnutrition, no starvation deaths have ever been reported in Purulia. What explains Purulia's success in preventing starvation deaths in comparison to Kalahandi? What lessons can be learnt from the two cases? Most importantly, is it possible to identify certain conditions under which democracy and public action work better to prevent starvation deaths in Purulia than in Kalahandi?

Administrative procedures and response

Bureaucrats at all levels in Orissa readily admit widespread malnutrition in Kalahandi, although they are reluctant to admit openly to cases of starvation death. This is partly due to their understanding of a 'starvation death' in very strict terms (e.g. 'a person must go without food and water for ten consecutive days') but also because they fear the wrath of their political masters if they openly make such politically explosive admissions. Therefore, from the bureaucratic point of view, all deaths in Kalahandi occur from natural causes and disease. Indeed, the entire administrative response is geared towards denying press reports instead of actively investigating long-term vulnerabilities that can cause starvation.

Many senior district officials are also demotivated, due to the high frequency and arbitrariness with which they are transferred from one post to another throughout various districts of the state. These rapid transfers adversely affect the implementation of development programmes, especially in chronically poor and drought-prone districts like Kalahandi.[15] Demotivation also arises from the thankless nature of being posted to a remote and 'difficult' district like Kalahandi, as officials are seldom praised for their efforts under difficult circumstances, and critical press reports on starvation deaths ruin any attempts to 'develop' the district. Related to the problem of frequent transfers is the acute shortage of qualified personnel in many departments. Doctors, nurses, teachers and other professionals from coastal districts of Orissa refuse to be posted to Kalahandi, and large numbers of posts in the district administration remain vacant. This puts additional pressure on those already overburdened with numerous responsibilities.

In contrast to Kalahandi, no starvation deaths are reported from Purulia district. While there is widespread malnutrition in Purulia, the district administration has excelled at providing an immediate response to instances of acute distress and destitution. An important characteristic feature of Purulia is the generally high level of political consciousness of villagers in the district, which means that if an individual or group were facing starvation, the district administration would hear of it relatively quickly. In addition to information from block-level officers, ruling-party workers and Panchayat[16] representatives provide an alternative source of early warning of distress.[17]

In West Bengal, the dominance of the ruling Left Front Government for the past twenty-five years has provided political stability. Frequent and arbitrary transfers of bureaucrats do not take place, and there is a practice of continuity in the district administration in Purulia. The stability of tenure gives district officials ample time and motivation to supervise the implementation of specific development programmes, as well as being better prepared to tackle drought-related emergencies. Officials, however, complain that the strong political influence exercised on the bureaucracy by political parties in the ruling coalition has dampened bureaucratic morale, as there is little room for individual creativity and initiative. Indeed, the bureaucrat–politician relationship in West Bengal is very different from that in Orissa. The Panchayat system has been a major success in West Bengal, and elected Panchayat representatives enjoy considerable power vis-à-vis local bureaucrats – thus they are accustomed to frequently 'interfering' in administrative matters in order to exercise political control over decision-making. This very factor – active inputs provided by political parties at the grassroots level to administrators – is responsible for triggering a successful administrative crisis response to combating starvation deaths in Purulia.

The effectiveness of the 'political trigger'

In spite of the presence of widespread deprivation in districts like Kalahandi, the formal trappings of democracy are in place and working in Orissa. Interestingly, the average voter seems to have exercised his or her franchise with some aplomb. The two main political parties that have dominated Orissa politics in the past few decades – Congress (I) and the Janata Dal (subsequently, Biju Janata Dal) – have each formed governments in Orissa state after the other has been voted out of power amidst allegations of starvation deaths, poor government response to natural disasters and other administrative bunglings.

Importantly, the political opposition in Orissa, although traditionally fragmented, manages to unite on the issue of starvation deaths. In addition to being highly critical of the government's policies in the national Parliament and the Orissa Legislative Assembly, opposition parties also manage, on some occasions, to launch joint campaigns aimed at ousting the ruling party from power on issues related to drought and starvation deaths. It is interesting to note that, although a recurrent feature in Orissa, drought alone does not trigger political activity to the same extent as when it is combined with reports of starvation deaths. In this sense there is considerable politicization of the issue, and political parties use it to demonstrate the incompetence and callousness of the sitting government. Although publicity generated from such political activity is useful for purposes of drawing attention to the plight of the poor in Kalahandi, unsubstantiated allegations of starvation deaths can also prove to be a liability which diminishes the credibility of similar allegations in the future. This factor strengthens the argument made above, about the usefulness of applying clearly operationalized understandings of famine and related terms.

While there has been a change in government every five years in Orissa since the mid-1980s, the political situation in West Bengal is a picture of stability, with more than twenty-five years of Left Front rule under the leadership of the CPIM. The political opposition is fragmented, and does not enjoy the kind of mass support as the ruling coalition.[18] In Purulia district, the Left Front and its allies thoroughly dominate the political landscape and the opposition has little support except in a handful of small areas.

A major difference between the two cases is that the rural population of Purulia generally displays a higher level of political consciousness than their Kalahandi counterparts. This is reflected not only in terms of high voter turnout during elections, but also in the continued support that the CPIM and its allies have received from rural areas. The high level of voter mobilization results in frequent complaints by villagers to local party workers whenever something goes wrong or when drought-related distress conditions appear in the villages. In this context, the local organization and presence of CPIM cadres in virtually all villages of Purulia is invaluable. Party workers routinely provide early warning information on drought, food shortage and major epidemics directly to the district administration and the CPIM leadership at district level. Two issues that local party workers in Purulia argue are of particular importance concern monitoring of drinking water (keeping a close watch on conditions of tubewells and ponds) and monitoring of food access (keeping a close eye on changes in local prices of foodgrains). Once information of a potential crisis in the offing is passed on to local officials, the district administration and the CPIM party unit in Purulia then pass it on to government ministers and senior bureaucrats in Kolkata, the state capital. Under such circumstances, requests for additional personnel and financial assistance are made.

Press coverage of food crises and starvation

Starvation deaths are politically so controversial that few newspapers avoid reporting on it if their reporters find evidence of destitution and starvation. However, the credibility of news reports alleging starvation deaths is particularly undermined when politicians own and control newspapers, and when terms like 'malnutrition', 'starvation' and 'famine' are used interchangeably by various actors, particularly journalists. In Orissa, every important newspaper is either owned and/or managed by a politician (Jeffrey 1997). Thus, in the Kalahandi case, when an opposition party-controlled daily highlights cases of starvation deaths, the ruling party-controlled daily may avoid the issue totally. Consequently, successive ruling parties in Orissa have traditionally not taken the press seriously and newspaper reports on starvation in Kalahandi, more often than not, tend to be dismissed by the government as being 'politically biased'.

Further, local journalists often use the term 'famine' to describe the situation in Kalahandi. In reality, what they are reporting is short-term and seasonal starvation that sometimes leads to death when accentuated by disease. While the use of 'famine' is sensational and guarantees a front-page article, it simultaneously undermines the credibility of news reports when policymakers dismiss these as 'baseless', 'unbelievable', 'totally false' and 'politically motivated'. Using such excuses, the government does not act to combat a crisis, as the only official response regarding starvation deaths is to deny that such deaths take place. In fact, most district officials in Orissa appear to be under government instructions never to admit to the occurrence of starvation deaths within their administrative areas.

The national, state-level and local press have on occasion been able to perform an early warning function in highlighting drought-related distress and starvation. For example, in the period September–November 1996, dailies like *The Hindu*, *The Indian Express* and *Prajatantra* repeatedly warned the Orissa Government of an imminent food crisis and the alarming level of food insecurity in drought-hit areas. Most reports, however, usually deal with an event that has already taken place. One reason for this inability to provide adequate and timely early warning can be traced to the fact that local correspondents are poorly paid and sometimes not paid at all. Stringers and journalists get roughly 15 per cent of all advertising revenue they can generate for their papers. However, despite low incomes from the profession, local journalists feel it is advantageous to have a 'press card', which is useful for making new contacts and receiving favours. Kalahandi journalists seldom have their travel expenses covered, unless something truly big and sensational comes up. This means that they cannot travel to distant (often inaccessible by road) areas of Kalahandi facing food scarcity and extreme deprivation. In most instances, the local journalist relies on hearsay and guesswork instead of investigative reporting. Similarly, journalists based in the major cities of Orissa like Bhubaneswar and Cuttack have little incentive to visit far-flung areas hardest hit by drought and starvation. An occasional visit to Kalahandi may be undertaken if the news content is sensational enough. As one correspondent put it: 'People must die in large numbers in order for my editor to sanction money for me to visit the area'.

There are two important differences between the state-level press in Orissa and West Bengal, relating to the pattern of newspaper ownership and the influence of the state capital city. First, in contrast to Orissa, where politicians own and edit most newspapers, in West Bengal major businesses own and run the influential dailies, and the print media largely enjoy freedom from political control. Second, in comparison to Orissa, which has several small cities spread over the state, West Bengal has only one major city, Kolkata, where all major dailies are traditionally based. Consequently, the main readership of the major dailies consists of the large urban middle-class residing in Kolkata and the surrounding areas. In contrast to Orissa, which has several cities of similar size (and where local editions of various regional newspapers are published), rural news does not sell newspapers in Kolkata. This has led to news reports being mostly Kolkata-centric, catering to the interests of the urban readership.

Several Bengali-language dailies and periodicals are published from the districts of West Bengal, but their readership and influence are limited. In Purulia, for instance, those who are literate read Kolkata-based dailies, and local newspapers are virtually non-existent. The few weeklies that are published occasionally (many of them have an unstable financial basis) are not professional in character and are seldom taken seriously by the authorities. The local press in Purulia is similar to that of Kalahandi, being characterized by low circulation rates, unstable finances and irregular publication. It was surprising that during the height of a severe drought in West Bengal in 1998–1999, the local press in Purulia largely ignored drought-related distress. In general, most newspapers prefer covering crime, corruption in local government, visits by prominent district-level and state-level political leaders, and local cultural activities. Consequently, news from Purulia seldom makes it to Kolkata newspapers unless it contains sensational material. Similarly, few correspondents from Kolkata make regular trips to the district.

In a comparative perspective, reporting on Kalahandi in the national and state-level dailies has been far more frequent and investigative in character than reporting on Purulia. Therefore, in terms of the total volume of reports, Kalahandi fares far better. This is explained partly by the fact that there are no sensational starvation deaths to report in Purulia, and partly by the relative indifference of Purulia-based and Kolkata-based newspapers to stories from rural areas. It is also important to reiterate that, in contrast to Orissa, political parties and influential leaders in West Bengal do not own and/or edit major dailies. This means that the press in West Bengal enjoys far more credibility than in Orissa.[19] It is therefore not possible for opposition parties and their leaders to publish sensational reports in order to malign the government. In this sense, the Government of West Bengal cannot easily dismiss press reports as being politically biased.

Conclusion

Despite unprecedented technological progress in the twentieth century, the threat of famine continues to loom over many countries, including India. In this chapter I have discussed the role of democracy and public action in preventing famine, taking a starting point in Amartya Sen's work. The topic warrants increased attention as new definitions and understandings of famine are resulting in situations where events that were not previously counted as famines are increasingly viewed as such. Similarly, depending on how one understands and defines 'democracy', one could argue that famines also take place in democratic societies. In this context India provides an instructive example, where over 200 million men, women and children suffer from a combination of chronic malnutrition and severe undernutrition, and more than 2.5 million children in India die every year before reaching the age of five. This is clearly a major problem that needs to be seen in parallel with Sen's claim that democratic India has successfully avoided famine. The country has in the past witnessed, and will continue to experience in the future, numerous situations that can best be described as 'famine threats'. Thus far India has managed to prevent such famine threats from escalating into major famines, and there is reason to believe that India will continue to enjoy success on this issue. In this respect, Sen is correct: democracy and public action do work well towards preventing famine in India.

A more mixed picture emerges on India's ability to prevent cases of starvation death. The phenomenon is difficult to define, and most of these deaths take place in rural, often remote, areas – far removed from the seats of power. Given this relative invisibility, chronic malnutrition and severe undernutrition causing starvation deaths is not recognized as a major crisis warranting the same kind of response that is reserved for famine. Hence, India's record so far has been most impressive whenever 'crisis' has been clearly defined and when there is an unambiguous understanding and consensus on the seriousness of the situation.

The comparison between Kalahandi and Purulia shows that there are differences even within India's democratic political system in terms of the ability to prevent starvation deaths. In Purulia there appears to be a consensus that, despite widespread malnutrition, starvation deaths must never be allowed to take place. The presence of political party workers and institutions of local self-government at the village level and their active role in providing information to administrative and political authorities appear to explain Purulia's success at preventing starvation deaths. Thus the role of local politics and presence of effective structures of decentralized government is crucial. In contrast, public action to prevent people from falling below the 'starvation line' is not forthcoming in Kalahandi. Instead of complementing each other, institutional interactions here are often characterized by mutual suspicion and lack of cooperation among bureaucrats, politicians, voluntary organizations and the press. Political opposition is thus not in itself a guarantee for preventing starvation deaths, especially when politicians are preoccupied with politicizing the issue – hurling accusations, which the ruling party conveniently denies – rather than being concerned with deteriorating health and nutritional status which cause death.

There appears to be a general consensus among successive ruling parties in India that the term 'starvation', like 'famine', must be avoided at all cost. Conversely, 'malnutrition' is a relatively safe term to use, given that it is widespread not just in India but throughout the world, and ruling parties in India are confident that they will not be held politically accountable for failing to tackle malnutrition. Therefore, Indian democracy excels at emergency-type responses, and this explains its success in avoiding famine. While this is a creditable achievement, there is a need for a concerted effort directed at preventing starvation deaths in non-emergency contexts as well. Governments, whether democratic or non-democratic, must recognize the goal of saving lives as a major concern. In this task, long-term efforts at preventing famine will be strengthened when chronic malnutrition, severe undernutrition and starvation deaths are treated with the high priority they deserve.

Notes

1 Coromandel lecture (1981), published as Sen (1984).
2 Sen also argues that even 'fairly authoritarian political leaders have, to a great extent, to accept the discipline of public criticism and social opposition' (Drèze and Sen 1989: 19). He points to the examples of South Korea and Pinochet's Chile, and argues that 'Many of the social programs that served these countries well were at least partly aimed at reducing the appeal of the opposition, and in this way, the opposition had some effectiveness even before coming to office' (Sen 2000: 154).
3 For a useful framework which places famine theories into the three broad categories of food availability decline theories, economic theories, and socio-political theories, see Devereux (1993).
4 A similar task has been undertaken by a group of academics at the Institute of Development Studies, University of Sussex. For further details, see Devereux (2002) and Howe and Devereux (2004, also Chapter 2, this volume).
5 Elsewhere, de Waal (1996) refers to this as a 'social contract'.
6 See Lautze and Maxwell, Chapter 10, this volume.
7 In the case of Kerala, successive Congress party governments have generally upheld social security provisions put in place by the Left Front Government. Thus, there has been a formal institutionalization of social security (i.e. especially in the bureaucracy in terms of redistributive policies) which makes it difficult for non-Communist parties like the Congress to abandon such schemes, given the high level of public demand (personal communication, Olle Törnquist, University of Oslo). In the case of West Bengal, the Left Front has been in power since 1977 without losing a single election. As such, it is difficult to comment on whether other ruling parties would have continued the system put in place by the Left Front Government.
8 Personal communication, Olle Törnquist, University of Oslo.
9 Interview: Amartya Sen, Oslo, December 2001 and March 2002, Oslo; Sen's talk on globalization in, 'A Closing Conversation on Globalization with President Lawrence Summers and Amartya Sen', Harvard University, 13 April 2002.
10 In April 1993, the Nawapara sub-division of the district was declared as a separate 'Nuapada' district and separated from Kalahandi. It is still common to refer to 'undivided' Kalahandi district as comprising present-day Kalahandi and the recently established Nuapada district. However, here the focus is only on what currently constitutes Kalahandi district.
11 The Central Planning Committee identified in total forty-one districts in India, spread across twelve states, prone to starvation deaths ('41 districts prone to starvation deaths', *The Times of India*, 2 December 1996).
12 For an overview of key statistics for the district, see Government of West Bengal (1999a, 1999b, 1999c).
13 'Scheduled Caste' (SC) is an administrative term introduced by the British to denote communities (castes) outside the *Varna* system. 'Scheduled Tribes' (ST) is an administrative term that denotes 255 ethnic communities that were among the earliest inhabitants of India. For the past couple of centuries, these groups have been seen to be economically and socially backward. Tribal communities are traditionally self-contained, and in many respects distinct culturally and ethnically from mainstream communities.
14 Of the thirty-four blocks that are covered under the Drought Prone Areas Programme (DPAP) in West Bengal, Purulia alone has twenty of these blocks.
15 For a detailed study on the relationship between frequent transfers of civil servants and the effects on the implementation of development programmes in India, see Banik (2001).

16 Panchayati Raj is a three-tier system (district, block, village levels) of decentralized government in India.
17 Field visits confirmed the overwhelming support enjoyed by the CPIM in rural areas of Purulia. Almost every village had a few mud walls painted with the symbols of the CPIM party, and in larger villages there was usually a very visible 'party office'.
18 The main opposition party for a considerable time was the Congress. However, internal feuds between various factions and subsequent splits have weakened the party. The main opposition party in the state in recent years has been the Trinamul Congress, a breakaway faction of the Congress party.
19 In a recent study, Besley and Burgess (2002) rank sixteen Indian states in terms of government responsiveness to media coverage. West Bengal ranks third, far higher than Orissa, which finds itself in twelfth place.

References

Banik, D. (2001) 'The transfer Raj: Indian civil servants on the move', *European Journal of Development Research*, 13(1): 104–32.
Banik, D. (2003) 'Democracy, drought and starvation in India: testing Sen in theory and practice', unpublished Doctoral thesis, University of Oslo, Department of Political Science.
Besley, T. and Burgess, R. (2002) 'The political economy of government responsiveness: theory and evidence from India', *Quarterly Journal of Economics*, 117(4): 1415–51.
Currie, B. (2000) *The Politics of Hunger in India: A Study of Democracy, Governance and Kalahandi's Poverty*, Basingstoke: Macmillan.
de Waal, A. (1989) *Famine That Kills: Darfur, Sudan, 1984–85*, Oxford: Clarendon Press.
de Waal, A. (1996) 'Social contract and deterring famine: first thoughts', *Disasters*, 20(3): 194–205.
de Waal, A. (1997) *Famine Crimes: Politics & the Disaster Relief Industry in Africa*, Oxford: James Currey.
de Waal, A. (2000) 'Democratic political process and the fight against famine', *IDS Working Paper* 107, Brighton: Institute for Development Studies.
Devereux, S. (1993) *Theories of Famine*, London: Harvester Wheatsheaf.
Devereux, S. (ed.) (2002) 'The new famines', *IDS Bulletin*, 33(4).
Drèze, J. and Sen, A. (1989) *Hunger and Public Action*, Oxford: Clarendon Press.
Drèze, J. and Sen, A. (1995) *India: Economic Development and Social Opportunity*. Delhi: Oxford University Press.
Edkins, J. (2000) *Whose Hunger? Concepts of Famine, Practices of Aid*, Minneapolis, MN: University of Minnesota Press.
Government of West Bengal (1999a) *District Statistical Handbook 1998 – Purulia*, Calcutta: Bureau of Applied Economics and Statistics.
Government of West Bengal (1999b) *Statistical Abstract, 1997–1998*, Calcutta: Bureau of Applied Economics and Statistics.
Government of West Bengal (1999c) *Key Statistics – Purulia 1998*, Purulia: Bureau of Applied Economics and Statistics.
Harriss, J. (2000) 'How much difference does politics make? Regime differences across Indian States and rural poverty reduction', *LSE Development Studies Institute Working Papers* 00–01, London: LSE.

Howe, P. and Devereux, S. (2004) 'Famine intensity and magnitude scales: a proposal for an instrumental definition of famine', *Disasters*, 28(4): 353–72.

Jeffrey, R. (1997) 'Oriya: "identifying . . . with newspapers": Indian language newspapers 3', *Economic and Political Weekly*, 32(11): 511–14.

Ram, N. (1990) 'An independent press and anti-hunger strategies: the Indian experience', in J. Drèze and A. Sen (eds), *The Political Economy of Hunger. 1: Entitlement and Well-Being*. Oxford: Clarendon Press.

Rangasami, A. (1985) ' "Failure of exchange entitlements" theory of famine: a response', *Economic and Political Weekly*, 20(41 and 42): 1747–52, 1797–801.

Reddy, S. (1988) 'An independent press working against famine: the Nigerian experience', *The Journal of Modern African Studies*, 26(2): 337–45.

Rubin, O. (2001) 'Entitlements, employment programmes and democracy: an assessment of Amartya Sen's famine contributions', unpublished MA thesis, Copenhagen: Department of Political Science, University of Copenhagen.

Sen, A. (1981) *Poverty and Famines: An Essay on Entitlement and Deprivation*, Oxford: Clarendon Press.

Sen, A. (1983) 'Development: which way now?', *The Economic Journal*, 93(372): 745–62.

Sen, A. (1984) 'Food battles: conflicts in the access to food', *Food and Nutrition*, 10(1): 81–9.

Sen, A. (1986) 'How is India doing?' in D. Basu and R. Sisson (eds), *Social and Economic Development in India: A Reassessment*, New Delhi: Sage Publications.

Sen, A. (1987) *Hunger and Entitlements*, Helsinki: World Institute for Development Economics Research (WIDER), United Nations University.

Sen, A. (1990) 'Public action to remedy hunger', *The Arturo Tanco Memorial Lecture*, August 1990, London, arranged by The Hunger Project and CAB International, in association with The Commonwealth Trust and The Royal Institute of International Affairs (available at www.thp.org/reports/sen/sen890.htm).

Sen, A. (1999) 'Democracy as a universal value', *Journal of Democracy*, 10(3): 3–17.

Sen, A. (2000) *Development as Freedom*, New York, NY: Anchor Books.

14 Can GM crops prevent famine in Africa?

Ian Scoones

Introduction

A recent book – *Seeds of Contention: World Hunger and the Global Controversy over GM crops* – by the former Director-General of the International Food Policy Research Institute (IFPRI) and World Food Prize winner, Per Pinstrup-Andersen, opens with a story. The story concerns a 'skinny three year old girl' who 'lay dying on a mat, surrounded by crying relatives' in a village in south-western Zimbabwe during the summer of 1999 (Pinstrup-Andersen and Schioler 2001: 1). The imagery is powerful, the story is familiar from media reports of famine in Africa, and the conclusion presented is unambiguous: well-harnessed, agricultural biotechnology can solve the problems of famine and hunger in the developing world.

The argument of that book, and a growing array of publications from reputable, well networked organizations – including CGIAR (Consultative Group on International Agricultural Research) centres like the IFPRI, national science academies, the OECD, the Rockefeller Foundation and the World Bank[1] – is simple. With growing populations and declines in yield growth of basic food crops in the post-Green Revolution era, increasing yield growth is essential to avoid famine. New biotechnological applications, and in particular transgenics (GM crops),[2] are an important part of the way forward. This is portrayed by some as perhaps the only feasible – and ethical – standpoint for the international community. Pinstrup-Andersen again states:

> If technological development by-passes poor people, opportunities for reducing poverty, food insecurity, child malnutrition and natural resource degradation will be missed, and the productivity gap between developing and developed country agriculture will widen. Such an outcome would be unethical indeed.
>
> (Pinstrup-Andersen and Cohen 2000: 22)

This storyline is seen as particularly pertinent to Africa, where the potential gains of the Green Revolution have not been achieved, and trends in per capita agricultural productivity are, it seems, endlessly downwards. Poverty is rising, and all indicators of food insecurity point to a doomsday scenario. Everyone agrees that something must be done. Enthusiasts for GM crops in Africa offer a neat and hopeful scenario. Thus Florence Wambugu argues in her book *Modifying Africa: How Biotechnology can Benefit the Poor and Hungry* (Wambugu 2001: 70):

> Having missed the Green Revolution, African countries know they cannot afford to pass up another opportunity to stimulate overall economic development by developing their agriculture. Biotechnology gives us that opportunity – and we are determined to grasp it.

Professor Jennifer Thompson from the University of Cape Town in South Africa is similarly strident in her book *Genes for Africa* (Thompson 2002: 170):

> Africa needs GM crops as part of its quest for sustainable agriculture and in order to feed its population ... Europe has enough food and may not want GM technology, but this does not mean that the developing world should be forced to do without it.

Both are honest, heartfelt pleas; both appear to be based on logic and common sense. But do they stand up to scrutiny? Can the famines that continue to plague Africa – both 'new' and 'old' – be banished to history forever, with the application of science and the promotion of technology? This chapter grapples with this question by asking some searching questions about the assumptions underlying the hopeful storylines told by the GM enthusiasts. This analysis seeks to situate the debate about technology – and GM crops in particular – in a wider understanding, looking at what types of technology are likely to be available, who will own and control them, and what consequences these will have for poor, marginal people, particularly in Africa. In critiquing the optimistic technology-driven scenario, the chapter also puts the counter-arguments under the microscope. To what degree are alternatives available? Are these realistic, given the scope and scale of the challenge?

The chapter is, however, necessarily speculative in character. There are very few GM crops available in Africa, most of them under test. The only GM crop being legally grown by smallholder farmers in Africa is insect-resistant GM cotton (using the *Bacillus thuringensis* (Bt) gene) in South Africa[3]. So, can GM crops help prevent famine? This chapter outlines the contours of the debate, offering some tentative conclusions about how the debate needs to be reframed, if technologies such as GM are to play a part in famine prevention strategies in Africa.

The chapter is organized as follows. The next section looks at the framing of the problem and how a GM solution arises from this. The following section examines the data and models that support such an assessment, and their limits. The next section questions the assumptions used by pro-GM advocates for the African context. It also examines the alternative scenarios offered for a non-GM future, and highlights the limitations of these arguments too. The conclusion returns to the question posed in this chapter's title, and suggests that the answer is complex, context-dependent and uncertain. Rather than brave statements of faith for or against GM crops – as offered by Pinstrup-Andersen, Wambugu, Thompson and those who oppose their stances – what is needed is a more informed debate about the relationships between livelihood pathways and technology demands, located in particular settings – especially those where food insecurity and vulnerability are high – and, crucially, involving those likely to be the users of technologies, rather than their self-appointed spokespersons.

The pro-GM narrative: food supply is the problem, technology is the solution

The core justification for the increasingly influential pro-GM position is essentially neo-Malthusian in character. Production (and to some extent nutrition improvement) is the key, the argument goes, while redistribution to improve access to food, while important, is infeasible to implement. For example, the highly influential Nuffield Council reports (Nuffield 1999, 2004) reject the option of redistribution, and argue for a focused technological solution to create a pro-poor biotechnology:

> Political difficulties of redistribution within, let alone among, countries are huge. Logistical problems and costs of food distribution also militate against sole reliance on redistributing income (i.e. demand for food) to meet present, let alone future, needs arising from increasing populations in less developed countries. Hence we must stress the importance of any new options that will secure higher direct and indirect employment and cheap food in labour-surplus developing countries ... What is required is a major increase in support for GM crop research and outreach directed at employment-intensive production of food staples within developing countries.
>
> (Nuffield 1999)

Similarly, the Hunger Task Force report (HTF 2005), prepared for the Millennium Project, is extraordinarily silent on issues of access and distribution. Instead, it again focuses on an essentially technology-driven route to tackling hunger and meeting the Millennium Development Goal (MDG) targets.

For the biotechnology advocates, population pressure is the core factor and the Green Revolution is the model solution, while a focused biotech

'Gene Revolution' is the ideal future. The FAO's biotech policy statement – echoed in the much criticized 2004 State of Food and Agriculture report (FAO 2004)[4] – follows this often repeated line:

> Agriculture is expected to feed an increasing human population, fore-cast to reach 8,000 million by 2020, of whom 6,700 million will be in the developing countries. Although the rate of population growth is steadily decreasing, the increase in absolute numbers of people to be fed may be such that the carrying capacity of agricultural lands could soon be reached given current technology. New technologies, such as biotechnologies, if properly focused, offer a responsible way to enhance agricultural productivity for now and the future . . .
>
> (FAO 2000: para 1)

This argument is taken further by some, with analyses highlighting future prospects of scarcity-induced famines leading to political instability, conflict and resource-based wars (cf. Homer-Dixon 1994).[5] Thus, encompassing this argument, boosts in agricultural yield and overall production are the solution not only to the 'old' famines, but also 'new' ones too.

The echoes and promise of the Asian Green Revolution remain remarkably potent in these narratives. The banishing of famine in India, for example, is put down in large part to the widespread uptake of Green Revolution high-yielding rice and wheat varieties. From the late 1960s, these resulted in phenomenal yield growth, initially in the irrigated areas and then more broadly (Lipton and Longhurst 1989), with the consequence that today India has significant stockpiles of food held at national level. The massive growth in production and productivity of course has not, however, prevented hunger in Asia. The 'paradox of plenty' (Sharma 2002) – with large central food surpluses yet localized pockets of dearth – is today's scenario in India.

This is different to the situation in large parts of Africa. Here national, sometimes regional, food supply deficits are faced, prompted by drought, war and conflict, political instability and a host of other factors discussed at length in other chapters of this book. Declining per capita agricultural productivity – created by the deadly combination of growth in crop yields being insufficient to offset increasing demand due to population growth – seems the obvious justification for a technology-led agricultural growth path, with new biotechnologies coming to the rescue just in time. But how rigorous is this justification? Where does it apply and where doesn't it? The following sections explore these questions in more depth.

Justifying a position: data, models and scenarios

The 'feeding a hungry world' narrative is reflected in the justification for most policy positions on GM crops of mainstream international organizations, and in much biotechnology industry publicity material. These arguments are based on more than hunches. Increasingly sophisticated – but inevitably assumption-laden – models have been developed to make the case. For example, an influential IFPRI report on 'World food prospects' (Pinstrup-Andersen *et al.* 1999) argues that demand for cereals will escalate by 40 per cent by 2020, due to increasing populations, growing urbanization and rising incomes. Rising demand for meat is resulting in a 'livestock revolution' which will require increasing volumes of grain for fodder. In order to meet this demand, yield increases are essential, as cultivated areas are only expected to rise by 20 per cent. With trends in yield growth predicted to continue downwards, this will require a doubling of imports of grains to the developing world. Projected population increases are concentrated in Asia, with India and China accounting for one-third of the estimated growth to 2020. In the model, China accounts for one-quarter of global increases in demand for cereals, and two-fifths of the increased demand for meat. Although population growth is not as significant in Africa (especially given the HIV/AIDS pandemic), and there remain opportunities for increasing production through expansion of cultivated area, sub-Saharan Africa is the region least able to deal with the consequences, according to the model. This is exacerbated by declines in yield growth, world food prices and availability of food aid.

Drawing on FAO data, and as an input to the MDG debate, another recent IFPRI report focused on Africa, where 200 million people are estimated to be undernourished (160 million as a result of chronic conditions) and around forty million suffering acute food insecurity each year (Benson 2004). A third of pre-school children are stunted, over 40 per cent of these being in Nigeria, Ethiopia and the Democratic Republic of Congo (DRC). Many Africans, especially women and children, have specific nutrient deficiencies due to poor diets and other factors. Globally, iron-deficiency anaemia affects an estimated 1.5 to 2.1 billion, primarily women and children; over 200 million people are vitamin A deficient; and iodine deficiency disorder affects between 740 and 1,500 million (Smith and Haddad 2000; Graham *et al.* 2001).

The trends in these statistics are particularly worrying. According to FAO measures, undernourishment has almost doubled in Africa, from around 110 million in 1970 to 200 million by 2000. Overall population growth in Africa between 1990 and 2001 was 2.4 per cent per annum, outstripping growth in the value of agricultural production. Poor agricultural growth is linked to low fertilizer use, which averages only 13 kg/ha in Africa compared to around 80 kg/ha in India, combined with low levels of irrigation coverage (4 per cent compared to around 40 per cent in South Asia)[6] and a lack of response to new varieties, including poor uptake of hybrids. But, as the IFPRI report points out, these patterns are highly differentiated. Major increases in food insecurity during the last decade have been concentrated in Burundi, the DRC, Madagascar, Somalia, Tanzania and Zambia. Only three countries saw decreases in undernourishment figures in this period, including Ghana and Nigeria. The highest concentrations of undernourished people, according to these measures, are found in the rural areas of southern and northern Nigeria, southern and central Malawi, the Ethiopian highlands, and Burundi, Rwanda and southern Uganda.

In terms of agricultural productivity, again, patterns are far from uniform. Declines in continent-wide agricultural productivity occurred particularly between 1973 and 1985, coinciding with major upheavals in a number of countries, but then stabilized, admittedly at a low level, into the 1990s (Masters *et al.* 1998). However, not everything is doom and gloom in African agriculture. Since 1984 significant output increases in cereals have been recorded in certain places, due to both yield growth and area expansion. This has been particularly dramatic in the Sahelian region, where good rainfall encouraged returning migrants and others to open up new areas of land, and to invest in soil- and water-conservation measures and new varieties (Gueye and Toulmin 2003). Successes in maize production also occurred in east and southern Africa, in particular periods when the conditions were right. The well-documented, small-holder-led post-independence maize boom in Zimbabwe was mirrored to some extent in Zambia (from 1970–1989), Malawi (1983–1993) and Kenya (1965–1980) (Smale and Jayne 2003). Declines since 1990 have, however, been evident across the region: not because the technology was absent, but for an array of other reasons, notably the withdrawal of state support for agricultural research, extension, input delivery and output marketing under liberalization reforms (see articles in Scoones *et al.* 2005). The growth of cassava production (prompted in part by the availability of Tropical Manioc Selection (TMS) cultivars) in west Africa, but also in east and southern Africa where it was not traditionally grown as a staple food crop, is another example of an unheralded success (Nweke 2004). Although these more discrete successes have not been on the scale of the Asian Green Revolution, they should not be dismissed through a sole focus on gloomy aggregate statistics.

Disaggregating the generalized statistics that drive the debate is a key challenge if a more nuanced picture is to emerge and responses to famines, new and old, are to become more focused, targeted and ultimately effective. Disaggregation encourages a focus on patterns of causation, and prompts thinking about contextual, historical and political economy factors as part of the picture. Thus, for example, the causal factors resulting in undernourishment in southern Africa are hugely different to those in the conflict-torn parts of central and western regions of the continent, and different again to those in the Horn. This may seem obvious to those who know the complexities and differences on the continent, but to those who engage in policy debates at global and continental levels these complexities get too regularly passed over in sweeping generalizations that mean little on the ground.

In the same way, the explicit and implicit parallels with Asia and the earlier Green Revolution need interrogating. The key agricultural production challenges in Africa are unlikely to be met simply by new high-yielding varieties, of the sort delivered by the breeding efforts of the 1960s. African agronomic challenges are much more difficult. Soil moisture and nutrient deficits are a key issue, due to lack of irrigation and large expanses of poor, ancient soils. However, these challenges are highly variable – between uplands and lowlands, between gardens and outfields, between heavy soil patches and sandy areas, and so on (cf. Scoones 2001; Fairhead and Scoones 2005). Simple technological solutions with wide spill-over benefits are unfortunately unlikely in Africa. The Green Revolution in Africa must take a very different form, requiring a very different type of research effort and set of technological solutions (Conway 1997). The question is, can GM crops be part of this?

In coming to an assessment, though, we should be wary of the statistics (even when disaggregated) that guide so much policy and inform the current debate. Most of the generalized prognoses that food security and famine policy rely on come from FAO national statistics, including the widely-used indicators of average household food energy availability. These figures are notoriously unreliable, particularly where national data collecting capacities are weak, as in most African countries (Smith 1998; FAO 2003). When particular indicators are tested against comparable data from household expenditure surveys, both the ranking of incidence and the magnitude of estimates are found to differ wildly (IFPRI 2004). When several data points over time from different surveys are used – for example, to look at stunting rates (Benson 2004) – the trends are highly variable and often contradict those derived from standard statistical sources. Household expenditure surveys suggest that the FAO data significantly underestimate levels of undernourishment (IFPRI 2004), while other observations suggest the opposite is true. For example, as discussed above, cassava accounts for a substantial proportion of food intake in Africa. Yet cassava, like other root crops and staples like *enset* (false banana) – which is central to food security in Ethiopia's southern highlands – is systematically under-reported in many food assessment surveys.[7] Wild foods – again, highly significant to the nutrition of the poor – are a 'hidden harvest' and are not measured at all (Scoones *et al.* 1992; Campbell and Luckert 2003). By taking the data at face value, an overall negative pattern may obscure stories of success and survival which require a more complex understanding of what is going on in particular places for particular people.

There is little doubt, however, that across large parts of Africa for large numbers of people, undernourishment, whether of calories or nutrients – often both – is a major problem requiring urgent action. The scale of this problem, though, where it occurs, to whom and for what causes are far from certain. The neat maps identifying problem areas and 'hot spots' for action are based on levels of uncertainty and conjecture that do not pass the test of close scrutiny. As a spur to action they may serve a useful political purpose, but as scientific data they are far from perfect. Should such data be used as the basis for designing ambitious action plans and committing significant investments in new technology? Or should we be more circumspect, and bring our analysis to a more location-specific level, where guesswork and assumption-laden modelling is less the driver?

I will return to this dilemma later in the chapter, but for now let us accept the main, and unquestioned, argument that food insecurity and famine vulnerability are major problems in Africa. The question I want to turn to now is whether GM crops are the answer and, if so, what assumptions are required to justify this. Will technological solutions deliver real benefits to the poor, and so eliminate hunger and famine? Is the science up to it? Are the political and economic conditions right? Are enough public resources available? Will the private sector play ball? Are there any other solutions that might deliver similar – or even better – returns to the undeniably important issue of raising agricultural production, if given the support? These are some of the questions that are considered in the next section.

Testing assumptions: evidence from Africa

What are the advocates of a pro-poor biotechnology assuming when they argue for agricultural biotechnology as the solution to African famine vulnerability? We need to identify the assumptions and interrogate them, testing them against our knowledge of particular places, contexts and economic and policy trajectories. This section identifies a series of key assumptions.

Food and nutrient supply is the issue

As already discussed, one of the core arguments for GM crops is that yield growth declines – or at least stagnation in major staple crops – are such that demand, especially with growing populations, is outstripping supply. Technological innovation can help to increase yields, and these increases need to occur in magnitudes larger than available through conventional breeding techniques and agronomic management. GM crops, it is argued, are the solution to this dilemma (Lipton 2001). In addition, it is argued, GM crops can also help in meeting the 'hidden hunger' of nutritional insecurity by providing a supply of key nutrients through biotech-assisted 'biofortification' of crops (Bouis 2004).

Available data certainly indicate a stagnation of yield levels in key staples in Africa, and population growth rates, despite rising mortality levels due to AIDS, remain high. But this must be qualified. As discussed in the previous section, the reasons for food scarcity are highly variable across space and time. Failures of agricultural production and food supply are certainly part of the picture, but the simplistic neo-Malthusian scenario is an insufficient explanation. According to various data sources – including the standard FAO indicators – the places in Africa where food insecurity has grown in the past decade have been locations of ongoing political instability and conflict. This has undermined production, market opportunities and institutions supporting agriculture and rural livelihoods. Such conflict areas include the DRC, Burundi and Somalia in particular, but also Liberia and Sierra Leone. Other areas that have seen major increases in food insecurity are those where economic reform programmes have undermined the rural economy and increased vulnerabilities, such as Malawi, Tanzania and Zambia. In these areas, it is not food supply *per se* that is the cause of undernourishment, but a host of other factors combining to undermine safe and secure food supplies to households.

The major concentrations of food insecurity in Africa also include countries which have been relatively peaceful in the last decade, but have large populations. In Nigeria, for example, food supply is not the principal issue. Nigeria, of course, is a resource-rich country thanks to its significant oil resources, but poor governance and lack of investment in agriculture have meant that its economy has failed to take off since the oil-boom years of the 1970s. Despite this general picture of agricultural decline, there are well-documented cases within Nigeria where intensification of agriculture has resulted in major boosts in output. These include dryland areas like the Kano Close Settled Zone (Mortimore and Adams 1999; Mortimore and Harris 2005) and areas of the middle belt in the higher potential areas of the country.

Cases where food supply issues are more immediate include central and southern Malawi, and the Ethiopian highlands. Here, high population densities, farm subdivision and low levels of productivity mean that farmers are unable to produce enough food to meet their needs. This, though, has been the pattern for a long time, so why have food insecurity and livelihood vulnerability become more acute? Again, a huge array of factors comes into the picture. In Malawi, the transition from a state-dominated agricultural system to a liberalized one has not been smooth; declining wage labour opportunities on the commercial farms has hit hard; and restrictions on regional labour migration to Zimbabwe, South Africa and Zambia have undermined Malawian livelihoods (see Carr 1997; Devereux 2002; Dorward and Kydd 2002). In Ethiopia, conflict has plagued parts of the country over a long period; the decline in trading and migration opportunities, both cross-border and within the country, has impacted negatively on rural livelihoods; as has the collapse of state farms as a source of seasonal employment (Carswell *et al.* 2000; Devereux, *et al.* 2003).

Some parts of Ethiopia and Malawi can perhaps be seen as classic Malthusian cases, where a supply-oriented, technology-driven response is the most likely way out of the bind. Certainly, technology-oriented innovations have already had some impact. In Malawi, investment in integrated soil fertility management techniques for maize growing have shown some success (Mekuria and Waddington 2002; Snapp *et al.* 2002; Place *et al.* 2003), while in Ethiopia there have been positive impacts from maize-fertilizer-credit packages in higher productivity highland areas, through the government and SG 2000 programmes (Howard *et al.* 2003). In lower-input, more marginal areas, indigenous soil and water conservation efforts have seen significant returns – for instance, in dryland Tigray (Mitiku Haile *et al.* 2001). However, such responses, while important, have had impacts only at the margins. A radical reappraisal of options for rural livelihoods may be necessary, recognizing that agriculture, and its associated technologies, will only have an increasingly small part to play.[8]

So where in Africa has technological investment in crop-yield improvement had an impact on any scale? A number of cases have already been mentioned. These include the growth of cereal production in the Sahel (although much of this can be attributed to area expansion and improvements in rainfall); smallholder cotton production in both the Sahel and parts of southern Africa (Tefft 2004); cassava production in west and central Africa (Nweke 2004); disease-free banana planting in east Africa (DeVries and Toenniessen 2001); new rice varieties in West Africa (WARDA 2004); and open-pollinated and, to a lesser extent, hybrid maize production in east and southern Africa (Smale and Jayne 2003). All of these boosts in supply have been a result of a combination of factors, not just the crop technology. Agronomic management – of soils and water in particular – has been especially important, as well as the institutional context – markets, input supply, extension support, and so on (Haggblade 2004; Dorward *et al.* 2005; Wiggins 2005).

Therefore, technologies that can generate yield growth, especially in staples, and which also absorb labour and respond to the particular constraints faced by smallholder farmers, are clearly in demand. The right ones will – as the examples listed above demonstrate – be taken up eagerly by millions of farmers. However, all the technologies in these success stories have been fairly basic – including elementary breeding, work on pest resistance and management, and allied investments in soil and water management. None has resulted in the imagined – and perhaps needed – quantum jumps in productivity. Are transgenics then the answer?

GM technologies are the answer

Those promoting biotechnology as a solution therefore argue that the powerful new techniques of transgenics, combined with the data processing and analysis of genomics and bioinformatics, can deliver the type of solutions to the key agricultural constraints affecting poor people, including resistance to pests and diseases, salt and drought tolerance, and yield improvements in crops that have not responded to conventional breed-ing. These techniques in the longer term – with patience and the right type of support – will deliver the type of quantum leap returns that are needed to generate broad-based technology-led agricultural growth in Africa, along the lines seen before in Asia, so the argument goes.

Most recognize, however, that it has to be public research efforts that deliver these types of gains, as the research and development (R & D) effort must be focused on those crops and traits that the private sector will not touch. But is this pie-in-the-sky dreaming conjured up by public sector research scientists in need of big injections of funding? Biotechnology sci-entists themselves (at least in private) are divided on the issue.[9] Many agree that a single 'magic bullet' breakthrough, on a par with the Green Revolution dwarf-wheat varieties of the 1960s, is not likely. Others believe that the 'difficult' traits – like drought resistance and nutrient-use effi-ciency – are exceptionally difficult to engineer. Many agree that transgen-ics will be only part of the picture, and that the genomics techniques combined with such approaches as Marker Assisted Selection (MAS) may in fact be more powerful.

Most early GM research, and all the currently available products, are based on easy, single-gene traits where resistance to a certain pest or disease is conferred, at least temporarily. Thus the transgenic products being planted today include the Bt-related products (insect resistance) now being produced by Monsanto, as well as a number of other com-panies, and Monsanto's Round-up Ready herbicide-resistant trait. How useful are these first-generation products?

Bt cotton, for example, is now being planted in South Africa and is being tested widely elsewhere. Early results from South Africa suggest that the returns were good, exceeding those of conventional cotton (Thirtle *et al.* 2003; although see also Pschorn-Strauss 2005). The reduc-tion of pesticide use in cotton farming has many advantages. These chemicals are highly polluting and dangerous to humans who apply them without proper precautions. However, again, while early results on Bt cotton look promising, these are largely from sites where there is con-siderable back-up support, and farmers involved in experimenting with Bt cotton have more skills and are able to take the risk of higher seed costs. With only a few years of experience, pest-resistance issues have yet to be faced, although everyone agrees that these will arise – particularly as Bt use spreads from the controlled settings of early experimental areas where appropriate precautions (such as refugia) are applied. Also, the Bt product is only effective against certain pests – notably the cotton bollworm. In some years other pests – such as jassids and aphids – may be more important, requiring continued spraying, even of Bt plants. A key factor in the success of Bt cotton, then, is the background variety that the Bt gene is inserted into. This has not always been the optimal one, and in some places non-Bt cotton outperforms Bt, not because the

Bt does not have an effect but rather because its background variety is poor or inappropriate.

The other much-hyped transgenic product that has been tested extensively in Kenya is virus-resistant sweet potato (Wambugu 2001). This has seen less success, in part because sweet potato is a very different type of crop to cotton. Grown in small plots and gardens, it is often a 'women's crop', where the expectation of significant input costs is low. Cotton, in contrast, is often grown in settings with vertical integration of production and marketing and significant support from a parastatal or private company. The type of virus-free planting material that the transgenic product offers can also be gained through cheap alternative means. In Uganda, many farmers already use and have access to virus-free cuttings as well as virus-resistant varieties, both local and formally bred (deGrassi 2003).

The type of complex trait products that can respond to drought or nutrient deficiencies are, however, some way off. These are very taxing genetic engineering tasks, beyond the scope of most public research laboratories. As the scientist who helped build up Monsanto's biotechnology capacity in the 1980s commented, in relation to nitrogen fixation: 'if I could put all the genes needed to create a nitrogen fixing plant in corn, I would probably end up with a plant that resembled soya' (quoted by Hodgson 2000: 30). In other words, soya, as a nitrogen-fixing plant, is designed in a way to fix nitrogen, but maize (corn) is not.

Cheaper and more robust responses to these types of constraints may be available in the existing repertoires of African farmers. Soil-moisture and nutrient stress is hardly a new phenomenon for African agriculture. Well-documented responses to these constraints include various gardening techniques (mounding, digging, etc.); manuring and mulching; micro-spot application of fertilizers; digging of infiltration pits, small tanks and ponds; the building of soil or rock bunds, lines and mini-dams; and the use and enhancement of natural wetland patches (Reij and Waters-Bayer 2001; Scoones 2001). They are widely used, and where they are not, there are usually very good reasons. In places where soil- and water-conservation techniques have really taken off – for example in parts of the Sahel – the concomitant growth in agricultural output has been significant, far outstripping any gain that could be expected from breeding or genetic engineering.

The experience with GM crops so far suggests that GM technology is only going to be a partial answer to the problems besetting African agriculture. It certainly has something to offer for simple trait problems (e.g. insect/disease resistance), but with some major provisos. What is probably more generally applicable is the suite of broader non-GM biotechnological techniques. Thus tissue culture can help with the generation of clean planting materials in vegetative propagated crops (e.g. banana, cassava, potato, sweet potato and yams), and MAS work is improving identification and back-crossing of genes with local cultivars (e.g. for resistance to maize streak virus, yellow mottle virus in rice and cassava mosaic virus) (DeVries and Toenniessen 2001).

Some would argue that a non-GM strategy is not ambitious enough: the sky's the limit with GM technology, they would argue. There are, after all, a range of exciting experiments going on in laboratories around the world, particularly in the private sector (many of which are not yet publicly known, or are just rumours). There are some pipeline products that have real promise and could revolutionize agriculture, including dealing with the challenges of recalcitrant crops and difficult traits. Overcoming these challenges requires vision and commitment and, above all, resources, the argument goes (cf. Cohen 2005). Complaining doesn't help: the Green Revolution happened in a welter of (social scientists') scepticism, but it delivered beyond even its architects' wildest dreams. Surely, proponents argue, the GM revolution should be left to run its course, and be given the appropriate support.

Public research will deliver in partnership with the private sector

In the ideal world, a multi-tracked strategy – high-tech and low-tech, GM and non-GM and all variations in between – would of course be optimal. Try all avenues, and see what works where. However, GM research is high cost. Equipping a laboratory for drought-resistance GM research, say, and keeping it going over twenty years is not a small undertaking. The CGIAR system has US$400 million at its disposal for global public goods agricultural research annually, and African national agricultural research systems are notoriously under-resourced (Jones 2005). Does it make sense to allocate a significant portion of this limited public money (or even new money, which surely is required) to GM research? The way out of this dilemma is often seen as creating partnerships with the private sector, whose resources far outstrip those of the public sector.[10] But what are the prospects of this sort of arrangement delivering?

Public–private partnerships are the flavour of the month. These allow both funds and intellectual property to be shared for the public good, permitting the public and private sectors each to do what it does best. Thus, for example, intellectual property issues can be dealt with through arrangements modelled on the vitamin A rice deal brokered by the Rockefeller Foundation.[11] Private companies with proprietary rights over key genes or processes could in future give these up for public good research and development on 'orphan' crops and 'difficult' traits, with no strings attached. The African Agricultural Technology Foundation (AATF), for example, was set up by a consortium of government donor agencies, philanthropic organizations and private companies with the aim of facilitating such a process in Africa.[12]

In parallel, GM optimists hope that the private sector will independently deliver GM solutions to developing countries, suited to local needs in areas where returns are guaranteed, as they have done in other markets (such as hybrid seeds, or fertilizers). This might include high-value crops (e.g. horticulture), cash crops (e.g. cotton) and crops where hybrids are well established (e.g. maize). Indeed, the aggressive support for GM crops by Monsanto in the main developing world markets – notably China, India, Brazil and, to a lesser extent, South Africa – is witness to this dynamic already underway. Others will follow (and are doing so, whether from China or from the US/European multinationals) and producers will benefit, it is argued. Studies on Bt cotton, for example, show (with some fairly heroic assumptions) that producers take a significant share of the benefits of the new biotech product, with the company taking only a minority share (Pingali and Traxler 2002; Pray and Naseem 2003). The argument runs that the liberalized, competitive global markets that a rules-based trading system is supposed to facilitate will encourage low prices and delivery of the best technology. An urgent necessity is therefore that African producers engage successfully with these markets. This, it is argued, is as much a solution to food security as dealing with 'subsistence' crops. The associated technology fees applied will not prevent smaller farmers reaping the benefits of the new globalized agri-food system, it is argued. Indeed they must, if they are to remain farmers at all.

How realistic is this scenario of a private sector-led agricultural transformation in the food-insecure regions of Africa that are the focus of this chapter? In certain sectors in certain places – such as in horticulture, floriculture, cotton, cocoa and some oil seeds – it may be that, under some conditions, the global market beckons for the small-scale African producer. Low cost (in the face of Asian or subsidized European/US competition) and high quality (for demanding export markets and global standards) products are essential. Yet, implicitly or explicitly in such analyses, a very different type of farming future is envisaged. The economics of production for such markets often dictates large, consolidated units, or at least contract farming; vertical input/output support systems often run by a corporate entity; and strong, contracted links to agri-food value chains (Vorley 2003).

This may indeed be the future for some areas and commodities. For example, the cotton successes in Mali can be in part attributed to the effectiveness of the parastatal CMDT (Compagnie Malienne des Textiles), and in Zimbabwe to the now privatized Cottco. With the struggle to meet global market requirements, Bt cotton is increasingly likely to be part of the picture (GRAIN 2004). In the horticulture sector, quality and the meeting of standards are essential, given the importance of supermarket supply chains (Barrientos and Dolan 2003; Humphrey and Dolan 2004), and GM varieties may help in creating uniformity and extending shelf life. In such settings R & D investment in GM crops by cotton or horticulture companies pays for itself. The problems and crops are more amenable to genetic engineering (pests/diseases in cotton; shelf-life, size/quality in vegetables/fruits), and the similarity of enterprise (in terms of agronomic management, levels of inputs, scale economies) means too that spill-over technology is more likely from other commercial production systems in Europe, North America or Asia. These farmers may be 'smallholders' in the strict sense (having small farms), but in other respects are different to other smallholder producers, whose livelihoods are more diverse and complex. These are of course niche-specific enterprises, with variable consequences for poverty reduction (whether labour conditions for women on horticulture enterprises or contract farming conditions).

However, in the areas where undernourishment is growing or highly prevalent these conditions do not pertain, either now or in the medium term. There are few if any nascent commercial or contract farming arrangements for cotton or export horticulture in the DRC, Burundi, or even large parts of Zambia, Tanzania, Nigeria or Ethiopia. Here, non-export, largely locally-consumed staple crops remain most significant. It is here that low-cost, labour-absorbing (although qualified by HIV/AIDS) crop technologies are required, which can produce on poor quality marginal, water-deficit land with limited purchased inputs. These too are the areas where private sector returns are unlikely. There are not going to be large investments in these problems by the private sector now or in near-term future, and spill-over benefits are unlikely too. These are very different agricultural and livelihood systems, meaning different priorities and needs, and so different technologies.

It is here that the much-touted public–private partnerships, and the reinvigorated public sector, are supposed to deliver. However, the track record to date is not encouraging. International – and national – public research has not made a massive impact on these marginal areas. Returns to public agricultural research efforts have generally been highest in the well-resourced endowed areas, and among relatively richer farmers (Renkow 2000; Pardey *et al.* 2003). Although it can be argued that the potential marginal returns from such investments are higher in lower resource endowed areas (cf. Fan and Hazell 2001 for India), with some exceptions this potential has not been realized. Most research has been focused on irrigated areas, higher-value crops and richer farmers. It is too early to tell whether the new public–private partnership initiatives will follow the same trend. The vitamin A showcase example has yet to see wide application, and there may well be easier and cheaper ways of getting vitamin A to poor people. Other initiatives discussed above have largely made use of high-end technology in the hope that they may become widely applicable. But other questions arise. Does the private sector have appropriate technology and processes to share? Or is the fixation on the technology distorting our perspective on both the problem and potential solutions, which may lie in less glamorous and cheaper alternatives (cf. Scoones 2005)?

Regulatory issues will be dealt with

The regulation of GM crops has generated considerable controversy around the world, and is a significant part of the high real costs of GM crops. The Cartagena protocol on biosafety requires governments to set up national biosafety regulations, and develop the capacity to monitor and assess imports, trials and commercial plantings of GM crops (MacKenzie 2003). GM proponents assumed, at least in the early days, that food and biosafety issues would not be a major issue in the promotion of GM technology. It was assumed that transgenic products would be 'substantially equivalent' to other products, and in many cases the introduction of new crops would be a familiar process, not significantly different from traditional plant breeding. Regulatory issues would therefore be dealt with by the transfer of regulations from the US or Europe, requiring often only adaptation of existing legislative provisions. International 'capacity building' efforts in developing standardized, harmonized regulations for the agricultural biotechnology sector would smooth this process, it was assumed, and the new regulations would in turn be enforced consistently and effectively throughout the developing world.[13]

This, of course, has not come to pass. The advent of GM crops – for both good and bad reasons – has resulted in a storm of controversy and protest. Regulations have taken a long time to set in place, and the capacity of national governments in the developing world is typically limited. The imported regulations have equally proven inappropriate to local circumstances, and regulators, the public and scientists alike have been reluctant to take approvals in the US as an indicator that a product is safe in their own country. In Africa, only Zimbabwe and South Africa have biosafety legislation in place to date, with Kenya and Malawi having developed draft regulations. Other countries have been involved in discussions, but do not have the capacity to implement even rudimentary regulatory control.

Studies carried out in Kenya (Odame *et al.* 2003), South Africa (Mayet 2001) and Zimbabwe (Keeley and Scoones 2003) have looked at the implementation of biosafety regulations in Africa in practice. Many problems have been identified, issues increasingly highlighted by well-networked activist groups. For example, the regulatory frameworks offered by international organizations as templates have in each case had to be adapted significantly; the boards set up to oversee the regulations have in most cases not had the requisite resources to fulfil their mandate; regulators have not generated trust and legitimacy among a sceptical public, particularly in the face of protests by activist groups; illegal planting of GM crops has been suspected (via cross-border trade and illicit planting by companies) but not investigated and detected; and trade restrictions have been very difficult to implement. The importing of GM maize into southern Africa as food aid during 2002 highlighted many of these problems at a regional level. In particular, the negotiations around import restrictions emphasized the intensely political nature of GM crops. The political pressure exerted by the US Government in particular to accept GM food aid was construed by many as an attempt to bypass regulatory oversight by national governments and introduce GM maize into the region as a *fait accompli*, using the spectre of famine and the weapon of food aid as the route to override regulatory controls and impose new technologies, thereby creating new markets for US corporations (GRAIN 2002).

Given the huge stakes at play, GM crops are far from a neutral technology. While in the right hands, used for the right purposes and regulated through an effective, fair and transparent system, they may contribute to a multi-faceted response to famine and food insecurity in Africa, they are clearly only part of a more complex solution. The final section of this chapter asks under what conditions GM crops might help prevent famine, and what processes are required to come to a sensible policy position on this issue?

Conclusion

In 1999, the Nuffield Council highlighted some of the constraints of a GM future:

> As GM crop research is organized at present, the following worst case scenario is all too likely: slow progress in those GM crops that enable poor countries to be self-sufficient in food; advances directed at crop quality or management rather than drought tolerance or yield enhancement; emphasis on innovations that save labour costs (for example, herbicide tolerance), rather than those which create productive employment; major yield-enhancing progress in developed countries to produce, or substitute for GM crops now imported (in conventional non-GM form) from poor countries.
>
> (Nuffield 1999: 4.23)

This assessment applies as much today as it did then. The examination of the African context in this chapter echoes many of these concerns. Even if the science were up to it, a variety of other constraining factors are indicated. Among these are the limited availability of public funds (and the low likelihood of a sudden flood arriving soon); the complications of intellectual property arrangements (Byerlee and Fischer 2001), the aggressive insistence of the private-sector majors in holding on to their proprietary rights; and constraints associated with the way the agri-food industry is increasingly organized around a limited number of multinational companies. On current evidence, it seems likely that the limited publicly supported, pro-poor GM technologies will largely be cast-offs and will not make significant impacts on the problems of famine and food and nutrition insecurity in Africa, given where such problems are concentrated and the causes underlying these.

What is needed above all are some fundamental debates about these issues and trade-offs – not just assertions. Regarding the assumptions identified above, the answers are not clear for Africa, or anywhere else for that matter. Unfortunately the GM debate has become exceptionally polarized, with positions becoming entrenched around global and national struggles for positions (Stone 2002). This scenario – provoked and reinforced by fierce controversy, particularly in Europe, and the advocacy positions of corporates, governments and NGOs – has undermined the quality and depth of the debate about what type of agricultural future is wanted in different (highly context-specific) parts of the world, what type of agriculture improves livelihoods and reduces vulnerabilities, and what form of regulation responds to both scientific uncertainties and public disquiet.

There are, however, some experiments that offer insights as to how a different type of policy deliberation might occur, where alternative perspectives and different framings of the debate have a place. In the few examples that have been convened in the developing world around biotechnology, there has been concerted and often heated debate about the assumptions listed above. For example, in citizen juries and participatory scenario workshops, poor rural producers have asked – drawing on their own experience and their own worldviews – many searching questions about the impacts of a GM revolution, as currently conceived, on livelihood choices and options (Pimbert and Wakeford 2002; Rusike 2005). While inevitably imperfect and only experimental at this stage, such deliberative policy processes offer one route for encouraging a challenging of assumptions by those who are currently excluded from mainstream policy debates.

By moving the debate about what to do about food insecurity and famine to the particular contexts where it is faced, and involving those directly affected, there is a possibility of moving away from the generalized prognoses based on incomplete, sometimes inaccurate, data and assumption-laden models that dominate the debate today. Instead of constructing aggregate demand and supply models at regional, continental and even global levels, different questions might be asked about interacting livelihood and technology scenarios for real settings. Such analyses must encompass the contextual complexity and multi-faceted causalities that underlie conditions of famine and food insecurity. While such approaches are less amenable to the target-oriented audit culture of our times, they are perhaps more realistic and recognize that contexts do matter, and that technology design and promotion cannot be dissociated from social, economic and ecological settings. So can GM crops help prevent famine? Well, of course, it depends. In some specific places, for some particular people, perhaps yes; in other places, for other people, no. The challenge is to find out more about these settings and contexts, and avoid the inappropriate grandstanding that has dominated the debate so far.

Notes

1 See for example: World Bank (Kendall *et al.* 1997); CGIAR (1999); OECD (2000); Royal Society *et al.* (2000); Conway (1999).
2 Biotechnology as a term covers a whole range of applications. Some first-generation applications, such as tissue culture, are not controversial at all. Others, such as MAS, use genomics techniques (sequencing, screening, etc.) to speed up conventional breeding approaches. This chapter concentrates on the more recent transgenic applications (where genes from one species are moved to another), which have raised a range of regulatory concerns over environmental issues (impacts on biodiversity) and health issues (allergenic and toxicity effects).
3 In addition, field trials have taken place on Bt cotton in Zimbabwe (Keeley and Scoones 2003), and insect-resistant maize and virus-resistant sweet potato are under trial in Kenya (see Science and Development Network 2005).
4 This report was criticized by NGOs and others for taking a pro-GM stance. This prompted a response from the Director-General of FAO (see Diouf 2004).
5 This is now a highly influential argument, picked up by many media commentaries on Africa. However it has also been subjected to extensive critiques (see Hartmann 1998, among others).
6 Figures are derived from FAOSTAT (www.faostat.fao.org), with due qualifications (see below).
7 Although, in advance of the Malawi famine of 2000, cassava production was over-estimated (Devereux 2002).
8 This argument is, of course, recognized in the 'deagrarianization' (Bryceson and Jamal 1997) and 'livelihood diversification' debates (Ellis 1998; Ellis and Freeman 2004). The big, usually unanswered, question, however, is in what way – even when livelihoods are diversified (which they usually are) – will agriculture contribute, and what sort of agriculture – with what technology requirements – will this be (cf. Devereux *et al.* (2005) for Ethiopia)?
9 Based on research interviews with scientists in India, Zimbabwe, Brazil, UK and the US.
10 The top ten life science companies have R & D resources in excess of $3 billion per annum. The largest national agricultural research systems are all outside Africa (Brazil, India and China), and amount to less than $500 million per annum each (Pingali and Traxler 2002).
11 See Toenniessen (2000).
12 Eight problem areas have been determined as priority targets for AATF intervention: Striga control in cereals; insect resistance in maize; nutritional quality enhancement in maize and rice; cowpea productivity improvement; bananas and plantain productivity; mycotoxins in food grains; drought-tolerance in cereals; and cassava productivity increase (see www.aftechfound.org).
13 See, for example, early discussions associated with the major Global Environment Fund/UN Environment Programme effort www.unep.ch/biosafety/

References

Barrientos, S. and Dolan, C. (2003) 'A gendered value chain approach to codes of conduct in African horticulture', *World Development*, 31(9): 1511–26.

Benson, T. (2004) 'Africa's food and nutrition situation: where are we and how did we get there?', *2020 Discussion Paper* 37, Washington, DC: IFPRI.

Bouis, H. (2004) 'Hidden hunger: the role of nutrition, fortification and biofortification', Paper presented at the 2004 World Food Prize International Symposium, 'From Asia to Africa: rice, biofortification and enhanced nutrition', 14–15 October, Des Moines, Iowa.

Bryceson, D. and Jamal, V. (eds) (1997) 'Farewell to farms: deagrarianisation and employment in Africa', *Research Series*, 1997/10, Leiden: African Studies Centre.

Byerlee, D. and Fischer, K. (2001) 'Accessing modern science: policy and institutional options for agricultural biotechnology in developing countries', *IP Strategy Today* (available at www.biodevelopments.org/ip/ipst1.pdf).

Campbell, B. and Luckert, M. (2003) *Valuing the Hidden Harvest*, London: Earthscan.

Carr, S. (1997) 'A green revolution frustrated: lessons from the Malawi experience', *African Crop Science Journal*, 51(1): 93–8.

Carswell, G., de Haan, A., Dea, D., *et al.* (2000) 'Sustainable livelihoods in Southern Ethiopia', *IDS Research Report* 44, Brighton: Institute of Development Studies.

CGIAR (1999) 'Ensuring food security, protecting the environment, reducing poverty in developing countries: can biotechnology help?', CGIAR/National Academy of Science Conference, 21–22 October, Washington, DC.

Cohen, J. (2005) 'Poorer nations turn to publicly developed crops', *Nature Biotechnology*, 23(1): 27–33.

Conway, G. (1997) *The Doubly Green Revolution: Food for All in the Twenty-first Century*, Harmondsworth: Penguin Books.

Conway, G. (1999) 'GM foods can benefit the developing countries' (available at www.biotechknowledge.com/showlib_us.php3?1667).

deGrassi, A. (2003) 'Genetically modified crops and sustainable poverty alleviation in Sub-Saharan Africa: an assessment of current evidence', Accra: Third World Network – Africa.

Devereux, S. (2002) 'The Malawi famine of 2002', *IDS Bulletin*, 33(4): 70–8.

Devereux, S., Sharp, K. and Yared Amare (2003) 'Destitution in Wollo, Ethiopia', *IDS Research Report* 55, Brighton: Institute of Development Studies.

Devereux, S., Amdissa Teshome and Sabates-Wheeler, R. (2005) 'Too much inequality or too little? Inequality and stagnation in Ethiopian agriculture', *IDS Bulletin*, 36(2): 121–6.

DeVries, J. and Toenniessen, G. (2001) *Securing the Harvest: Biotechnology, Breeding and Seed Systems for African Crops*, Wallingford: CABI.

Diouf, J. (2004) 'Biotechnology: FAO response to open letter from NGOs' (available at www.fao.org/newsroom/en/news/2004/46429/index.html).

Dorward, A. and Kydd, J. (2002) 'The Malawi 2002 food crisis: the rural development challenge', *Journal of Modern African Studies*, 42(3): 343–61.

Dorward, A., Kydd, J. and Poulton, C. (2005) 'Beyond liberalisation: "developmental coordination" policies for smallholder agriculture', *IDS Bulletin*, 36(2): 80–5.

Ellis, F. (1998) 'Household strategies and rural livelihood diversification', *Journal of Development Studies*, 35(1): 1–38.

Ellis, F. and Freeman, A. (2004) 'Rural livelihoods and poverty reduction strategies in four African countries', *Journal of Development Studies*, 40(4): 1–30.

Fairhead, J. and Scoones, I. (2005) 'Local knowledge and the social shaping of soil investments: critical perspectives on the assessment of soil degradation in Africa', *Land Use Policy*, 22: 33–41.

Fan, S. and Hazell, P. (2001) 'Return to public investment in less-favored areas of India and China', *American Journal of Agricultural Economics*, 83(5): 1217–22.

FAO (2000) 'FAO statement on biotechnology' (available at www.fao.org./ biotech/state.htm: para 1).

FAO (2003) 'Measurement and assessment of food deprivation and undernutrition', Proceedings of an International Scientific Symposium, Rome: FAO.

FAO (2004) *The State of Food and Agriculture, 2003–2004: Agricultural Biotechnology. Meeting the Needs of the Poor?*, FAO: Rome.

Graham, R. D., Welch, R. M. and Bouis, H. E. (2001), 'Addressing micronutrient malnutrition through enhancing the nutritional quality of staple foods: principles, perspectives and knowledge gaps', *Advances in Agronomy*, 70: 77–142.

GRAIN (2002) 'Better dead than GM fed', *Seedling*, October, Barcelona: Genetic Resources Action International.

GRAIN (2004) 'GM cotton to invade West Africa' (available at www.corpwatch. org/article.php?id=9872).

Gueye, B. and Toulmin, C. (2003) 'Transformations in West African agriculture and the role of family farms', *Drylands Issue Paper* 123, London: IIED.

Haggblade, S. (ed.) (2004) 'Building on success: African agriculture', *2020 Focus* 12, Washington, DC: IFPRI.

Hartmann, B. (1998) 'Population, environment and security: a new trinity', *Environment and Urbanization*, 10(2): 113–28.

Hodgson, J. (2000) 'Crystal gazing the new biotechnologies', *Nature Biotechnology*, 18(1): 29–31.

Homer-Dixon, T. (1994) 'Environmental scarcities and violent conflict: evidence from cases', *International Security*, 19(1): 5–40.

Howard, J., Crawford, E., Kelly, V., Demeke, M. and Jeje, J. (2003) 'Promoting high-input maize technologies in Africa: the Sasakawa-Global 2000 experience in Ethiopia and Mozambique', *Food Policy*, 28(4): 335–48.

HTF (Hunger Task Force) (2005) *Halving Hunger: It can be done*, London: Earthscan.

Humphrey, J. and Dolan, C. (2004), 'The governance and trade in fresh vegetables: the impact of UK supermarkets on the African horticulture industry', *Journal of Development Studies*, 37(2): 147–76.

IFPRI (2004) 'Food insecurity in sub-Saharan Africa. New estimates from household expenditure surveys', Washington, DC: IFPRI.

Jones, M. (2005) 'Key challenges for technology development and agricultural research in Africa', *IDS Bulletin*, 36(2): 46–51.

Keeley, J. and Scoones, I. (2003) 'Contexts for regulation: GMOs in Zimbabwe', *IDS Working Paper* 190, Brighton: Institute of Development Studies:.

Kendall, H. W., Beachy, R., Eisner, T., *et al.* (1997) *The Bioengineering of Crops. Report of the World Bank Panel on Transgenic Crops*, Washington, DC: World Bank.

Lipton, M. (2001) 'Challenges to meet. Food and nutrition security in the new millennium', *Proceedings of the Nutrition Society*, 60: 203–14.

Lipton, M. and Longhurst, R. (1989) *New Seeds and Poor People*, London: Unwin Hyman.

MacKenzie, R. (2003) 'Globalisation and the international governance of biotechnology' (available at www.gapresearch.org/governance/RMregulationfinal.pdf).

Masters, W., Bedingar, T. and Oehnke, J. (1998) 'The impact of agricultural research in Africa: aggregate and case study evidence', *Agricultural Economics*, 19(1–2): 81–6.

Mayet, M. (2001) 'Critical analysis of pertinent legislation regulating genetic modification in food and agriculture in South Africa', Cape Town: Biowatch (available at www.biowatch.org.za/docs/gmo_act.pdf).

Mekuria, M. and Waddington, S. (2002) 'Initiatives to encourage farmer adoption of soil fertility technologies for maize-based cropping systems in southern Africa', in C. Barrett, F. Place and A. A. Aboud (eds), *Natural Resource Management in African Agriculture: Understanding and Improving Current Practices*, Wallingford: CABI.

Mitiku Haile, Fetien Abay and Waters-Bayer, A. (2001) 'Joining forces to discover and celebrate local innovation in land husbandry in Tigray, Ethiopia', in C. Reij and A. Waters-Bayer (eds), *Farmer Innovation in Africa: A Source of Inspiration for Agricultural Development*, London: Earthscan.

Mortimore, M. and Adams, W. (1999) *Working the Sahel: Environment and Society in Northern Nigeria*, London: Routledge.

Mortimore, M. and Harris, F. (2005) 'Do small farmers' achievements contradict nutrient depletion scenarios for Africa', *Land Use Policy*, 22: 43–56.

Nuffield Council on Bioethics (1999) *Genetically Modified Crops: The Ethical and Social Issues*, London: Nuffield.

Nuffield Council (2004) 'Independent Science Panel Report on Genetically Modified Food and Crops', London: Nuffield Council (available at www.foodfirst.org/progs/global/ge/isp/ispreport.pdf).

Nweke, F. (2004) 'New challenges in the cassava transformation in Nigeria and Ghana. Successes in African Agriculture Conference: background paper', *EPTD Discussion Paper* 118, Washington, DC: IFPRI.

Odame, H., Kameri-Mbote, P. and Wafula, D. (2003) 'Globalisation and the international governance of modern biotechnology: the implications for food security in Kenya', Final Report prepared for the FIELD/IDS Project on Globalisation and the International Governance of Modern Biotechnology funded by DFID, *IELRC Working Paper* 2003–2002, Geneva: IELRC.

OECD (2000) 'GM food safety: facts, uncertainties, and assessment', Conference on the Scientific and Health Aspects of Genetically Modified Foods, 28 February–1 March, Edinburgh.

Pardey, P., Wood, S. and Wood-Sichra, U. (2003) 'A review of agricultural productivity trends, technological changes and returns to research in sub-Saharan Africa', Washington, DC: IFPRI.

Pimbert, M. and Wakeford, T. (2002) 'Prajateerpu: a citizens' jury/scenario workshop on food and farming futures for AP, India', London: IIED and Brighton: Institute of Development Studies.

Pingali, P. and Traxler, G. (2002) 'Changing the locus of agricultural research: will the poor benefit from biotechnology and privatization trends?', *Food Policy*, 27(3): 223–38.

Pinstrup-Andersen, P. and Cohen, J. (2000) 'Biotechnology and the CGIAR', Paper for Conference on Sustainable Agriculture in the Millennium – Impact of Modern Biotechnology on Developing Countries, 28–31 May, Brussels.

Pinstrup-Andersen, P. and Schioler, E. (2001) *Seeds of Contention. World Hunger and the Global Controversy over GM Crops*, An International Food Policy Research Institute Book, Baltimore, MA: Johns Hopkins University Press.

Pinstrup-Andersen, P., Pandya-Lorch, R. and Rosegrant, M. W. (1999) 'World food prospects: critical issues for the early 21st century', *IFPRI Food Policy Report*, Washington, DC: IFPRI.

Place, F., Barrett, C., Freeman, A., Ramsich, J. and Vanlauwe, B. (2003) 'Prospects for integrated soil fertility management using organic and inorganic inputs: evidence from smallholder African agricultural systems', *Food Policy*, 28(4): 365–78.

Pray, C. and Naseem, A. 2003. 'Biotechnology R & D: policy options to ensure access and benefits for the poor', *ESA Working Paper* 03–08, Rome: Agriculture and Economic Development Analysis Division, FAO.

Pschorn-Strauss, E. (2005) 'Bt Cotton in South Africa: the Makhatini farmers', *Seedling*, April, Barcelona: GRAIN (available at www.grain.org/seedling_files/seed-05-04-3.pdf).

Reij, C. and Waters-Bayer, A. (eds) (2001) *Farmer Innovation in Africa: A Source of Inspiration for Agricultural Development*, London: Earthscan.

Renkow, M. (2000) 'Poverty, productivity and production environment: a review of evidence', *Food Policy*, 25(4): 463–78.

Royal Society, US National Academy of Sciences, Brazilian Academy of Science, Chinese Academy of Sciences, Indian National Science Academy, Mexican Academy of Sciences and the Third World Academy of Sciences (2000) *Transgenic Plants and World Agriculture*, London: Royal Society.

Rusike, E. (2005) 'Exploring food and farming futures in Zimbabwe. A citizens' jury and scenario workshop experiment', in M. Leach, I. Scoones and B. Wynne (eds), *Science and Citizens: Globalization and the Challenge of Engagement*, London: Zed Press.

Science and Development Network (2005) 'Kenya begins first open field trials of GM maize' (available at www.scidev.net, accessed 31 May 2005).

Scoones, I. (ed.) (2001) *Dynamics and Diversity: Soil Fertility and Farming Livelihoods in Africa*, London: Earthscan.

Scoones, I. (2005) 'Governing technology development: challenges for agricultural research in Africa', *IDS Bulletin*, 36(2): 109–14.

Scoones, I., Melnyk, M. and Pretty, J. (1992) *The Hidden Harvest. An Annotated Bibliography*, London: IIED.

Scoones, I., deGrassi, A., Devereux, S. and Haddad, L. (eds) (2005) 'New directions for African agriculture', *IDS Bulletin*, 36(2).

Sharma, D. (2002) 'The Kalahandi syndrome: starvation in spite of plenty' (available at www.dsharma.org/hunger/kalahandi.htm).

Smale, M and Jayne, T. (2003) 'Maize in eastern and southern Africa: 'Seeds' of success in retrospect', *EPTD Discussion Paper* 97, Washington, DC: IFPRI.

Smith, L. (1998) 'Can FAO's measure of chronic undernourishment be strengthened?', *Food Policy*, 23(5): 425–45.

Smith, L. C. and Haddad, L. (2000) 'Explaining child malnutrition in developing countries: a cross-country analysis', *IFPRI Research Report* 111, Washington, DC: IFPRI.

Snapp, S., Kanyama-Phiri, G., Kamanga, B., Gilbert, R. and Wellard, K. (2002) 'Farmer and researcher partnerships in Malawi: developing soil fertility technologies for the near-term and far-term', *Experimental Agriculture*, 38: 411–31.

Stone, G. D. (2002) 'Both sides now. Fallacies in the genetic modification wars, implications for developing countries and anthropological perspectives', *Current Anthropology*, 43(5): 611–30.

Tefft, J. (2004) 'Mali's white revolution: smallholder cotton from 1960 to 2003', *2020 Vision Focus 12* Brief 5, Washington, DC: IFPRI.

Thirtle, C., Beyers, L., Ismael, Y. and Piesse, J. (2003) 'Can GM technologies help the poor? The impact of Bt cotton in Makhatini Flats, KwaZulu Natal', *World Development*, 31(4): 717–32.

Thompson, J. (2002) *Genes for Africa*, Cape Town: Cape Town University Press.

Toenniessen (2000) 'Vitamin A deficiency and golden rice. The role of the Rockefeller Foundation' (available at www.mindfully.org/GE/Golden-Rice-Justify-Rockefeller.htm).

Vorley, B. (2003) 'Food Inc. Corporate concentration from farm to consumer', London: UK Food Group.

Wambugu, F. (2001) *Modifying Africa. How Biotechnology can Benefit the Poor and Hungry, A Case from Kenya*, Nairobi: Florence Wambugu.

WARDA (2004) 'Nerica rices' (available at www.warda.cgiar.org/publications/NERICA8.pdf).

Wiggins, S. (2005) 'Success stories from African agriculture: what are the key elements of success?', *IDS Bulletin*, 36(2): 17–22.

15 Priority regimes and famine

Paul Howe[1]

Introduction

Over fifteen years ago, in the aftermath of a major Ethiopian famine, Curtis *et al.* (1988) described the paradox posed by the continued existence of famine in a globalizing world. Observing that the twentieth century had seen more people die from famine than any earlier one, they pointed out that:

> [y]et in no previous era has famine been more preventable than the present; through unexcelled communication and transport possibilities and world grain reserves, the international capability exists to detect and remedy food shortages anywhere before famine results.
>
> (Curtis *et al.* 1988: 3)

This sentiment has subsequently been echoed in academic works (Millman and Kates 1990; Action Against Hunger 2001; Devereux *et al.* 2002), international conferences (cf. Institute of Development Studies 2002) and other global fora.

During the last decade, famines have occurred in Malawi in 2002 (cf. Devereux 2002; King 2002; International Development Committee 2003), Ethiopia in 1999–2000 (cf. Maxwell 2002), Sudan in 1998 (cf. Deng 1999), North Korea between 1995 and 1998 (cf. Lautze 1997; Natsios 2001), and Iraq during the 1990s (cf. Gazdar 2002). Yet these new famines involve issues – such as economic and political liberalization, international sanctions, HIV/AIDS, donor-government relations, genetically modified crops and human rights – that are not adequately captured by traditional approaches to famine analysis, since they link local conditions to the broader trends of globalization that are shaping our age (Devereux *et al.* 2002; Howe 2002).

This chapter proposes a new analytical approach to famines that may help to resolve the 'paradox of persistence'.[2] In so doing, it focuses on the concept of priorities. The use of the term 'priority' explicitly recognizes that choices and trade-offs are an integral part of decision-making. Since famine prevention (or creation) is only one of many priorities that exist in the globalizing world, it is necessary to untangle its relationship with others that simultaneously have claims (depending on the perspective) to immediacy and importance. By placing famine in the context of the wider competing choices in which decisions are made, it becomes possible to highlight the differences that exist among priorities from the global to the household levels and to trace more clearly the dynamics of famine causation over time.

Following this introduction, the next section situates the priority regime approach in the context of other recent analyses of famine. The third section outlines the basic concepts of this approach, explains how different priority regimes influence famine and identifies possible points of leverage in these situations. The next section illustrates how these concepts can be applied to the analysis of several recent famine situations, while the fifth section identifies some possible longer-term implications of this analysis. The final section provides some concluding thoughts on the priority regime approach.

Theoretical context

Famine literature

Over the past thirty years, there have been numerous attempts to develop frameworks for understanding and analysing famines. Several continue to have widespread influence, including neo-Malthusianism, the entitlement approach, complex political emergencies and anti-famine contracts. To a certain extent, they all reflected the concerns of their period and the changing context in which famines were perceived to be occurring, but none adequately addresses all the relevant aspects and complexities of contemporary famines.

In the 1960s and 1970s, in the midst of several drought-triggered famines, neo-Malthusians drew attention to a projected gap (that never actually materialized) between the world's ability to produce food and its growing population. Some writers posited dire scenarios (cf. *Famine – 1975! America's Decision: Who Will Survive?*, Paddock and Paddock 1967) in which richer countries would have to choose whom to save in poorer countries through the selective provision of food aid. This view (or at least its application on a global scale) was discredited, in part because it appeared to have exaggerated the magnitude of the problem and failed (as Malthus had in an earlier age) to foresee the agricultural production increases associated with the Green Revolution and other developments. It also lost favour because of its association with a set of uneasy moral assumptions about how such decisions should be made (cf. 'Lifeboat ethics', Hardin 1974).

Perhaps the most definitive critique of this approach was made with the publication of Amartya Sen's *Poverty and Famines* (1981). Examining four famines in the Sahel and the Indian sub-continent, Sen suggested that it was not lack of food *per se* but the inability to access it that lay at the root of many famines. His radical analysis shifted the emphasis from supply failures, or the unavailability of food, to demand failures, or the inability to command it. He identified four types of food entitlements available to an individual: production, labour, exchange and gift. He argued that it was a breakdown of the ability of groups of people to access food through any of these entitlements that created the conditions for mass starvation.

While the originality and importance of Sen's approach were widely acknowledged, several authors have also identified weaknesses in his framework. One limitation is its essentially 'atomistic' focus or 'methodological individualism' (cf. Fine 1997; Devereux, Chapter 4, this volume) – that is, the approach provides an analytical framework for identifying an individual's entitlement to food, but it provides less insight into the larger communal, national and international processes that contribute to a starving individual's inability to acquire adequate food. Fine (1997: 621) has argued that: 'As the entitlement approach has its roots at the micro level of the *individual* incidence of starvation ... it can at best point to the directions to be taken by macro analysis'. Because of this focus, the entitlement approach is somewhat limited in its usefulness for analysing the roles of local, national and global actors in famine situations.

In the 1990s, in the aftermath of the Cold War, there was a growing recognition of the role of conflict in famine causation. Sen's economics-based approach, however, could not adequately accommodate an analysis of civil strife, because it does not allow for 'extra-legal' entitlement transfers (Edkins 1996). This limitation, as well as the widespread feeling that researchers, aid workers and others were witnessing a fundamentally new phenomenon, led to the elaboration of a theory of 'complex political emergencies' (CPEs). This approach demonstrated that certain people actually benefit from the occurrence of famine (Duffield 1994a, 1994b; Keen 1994a, 1994b). It was associated with a wealth of new analytical insights, including asset transfers, and winner and loser stakeholder analysis. Mark Duffield's analysis showed how in southern Sudan, the systematic seizure of assets, which benefited certain groups, contributed to food crises among dispossessed groups. Similarly, David Keen demonstrated that the creation and perpetuation of famine conditions produced gains for some people, such as traders and militia. Luka Deng (2002) showed how wealthier groups – despite by definition having higher entitlements to food – are in fact more vulnerable to conflict-induced famine, as their assets are deliberately targeted by raiders and counter-insurgents.

However, by identifying civil conflict or war as a principal cause of contemporary famines, the CPE approach views these crises primarily as a dysfunction of the state. The global context has a role only to the extent that it helps create the broad conditions for civil strife. For example, in Macrae and Zwi (1994) the international distribution of economic wealth is identified as an underlying cause of war in Africa. The approach, therefore, does not focus on or fully explore a range of potentially relevant actors (e.g. the international media, donors, scientists and corporations) and processes (e.g. geo-political strategies and considerations, or climate change). More recent contributions to the literature on conflict do recognize the role of multinationals and foreign interests in creating and prolonging civil war (Collier and Hoeffler 2002; Deng 2002; Collier *et al.* 2003; see also discussion of 'New Wars' below).

A related approach emerged from Sen's observation (cf. Sen 1999) that famines do not appear to occur in stable democratic states with free presses. De Waal (1997, 2000) refined this argument by suggesting that it was not democracy *per se*, but the existence of an explicit or implicit 'anti-famine contract' between the people and the government that ensured effective famine prevention policies. India is often held up as an example of a country with a functioning and largely successful anti-famine contract – though its success is qualified by a recognition that it prevents famine, but not numerous deaths from malnutrition (Drèze and Sen 1989; Singh 1993; see also Banik, Chaper 13, this volume). This focus on the state and its relation to its citizens ignores a range of other interactions not based on those parties. For instance, in some countries, or parts of countries, selected international NGOs and donors take greater responsibility than governments for the food security of the populations to which they are delivering aid.

Despite being landmarks in the understanding of famine causation, all these approaches share three tendencies that limit their usefulness in grappling with the implications of the changing global context. First, to a certain extent each of these approaches *externalizes* the famine process, that is, they locate famine in a 'remote' area and delimit the relevant actors (at least in the onset and perpetuation of the crisis) to citizens of the countries in which they are occurring. Other international stakeholders are peripheral: sometimes attempting to ameliorate a situation, sometimes inadvertently exacerbating the crisis, but always dealing with a problem diagnosed and developing elsewhere.

Second, the approaches tend to *isolate* the famine process, by analysing it independently of other geo-political priorities and concerns. Famine vulnerability is often an inadvertent – or intentional – outcome of other, more highly prioritized goals. Moreover, it is not often recognized that individual famines have to compete for resources and international attention with other humanitarian crises in the region and the world.

Third, in attempting to understand famine causation, analysts have a tendency to *'negativize'* crises – that is, to examine almost exclusively the negative factors contributing to them (an important exception is Swift 1989). Typically, analysts highlight triggers such as drought or the outbreak of conflict, but in doing so they overlook the interaction of positive and negative factors. In fact, the reality is more complex. In many famine-prone countries, there exists an ongoing aid programme. In some cases, emergency relief is provided on an annual basis. Famines arise not when there is a series of negative shocks, but rather when a series of negative shocks is not adequately offset by positive ones.

When analysts integrate a range of global decision-makers, consider crises in the context of other priorities and understand both the positive as well as the negative processes involved, more dynamic and accurate representations of these crises begin to emerge. The international dimensions of famine have long been recognized in analyses. Numerous studies have identified a range of relationships of international actors and processes to famine (cf. Johnson (2003) on colonial influences on famine in the Sudan; Devereux (1993) on the United States' role in the Bangladesh famine in 1974; Watson (Chapter 12, this volume) on siege famines in Europe; among many others). Action Against Hunger (2001) has explored numerous case studies that implicate both national and international actors in the creation of famine.

Recently, attention has focused on the inequitable distribution of aid among crises around the world (Olsen *et al.* 2002; Darcy and Hofmann 2003). Darcy and Hofmann's study 'According to need?' (2003: 5) argues that 'international humanitarian financing is not equitable, and amounts allocated across various contexts do not reflect comparative levels of need'. Olsen *et al.* (2002) suggest that donor interests most often determine whether or not a humanitarian crisis is 'forgotten'. Watson (2002) notes that aid expenditure per person in response to crises in Europe often far exceeds that for similar situations in sub-Saharan Africa, though she clarifies that some of the difference is due to the higher transport and distribution costs in Europe.

What has been missing to date is an analytical framework for understanding famine in a globalizing world.

Other relevant literatures

In attempting to develop such a framework, several additional literatures can be drawn upon to provide insights into these issues – including the 'new wars', policy processes, participation and rights.

The literature on the 'new wars' in many ways offers a parallel attempt to integrate global dimensions into contemporary analyses, in order to understand the kinds of crises that are emerging today. Several authors (for example, Kaldor 1998; Duffield 2001) have shown how conflicts in places as diverse as the former Soviet Republics and the Sudan arise, in large part, from interactions among global, non-state networks. In so doing, these analyses subvert the traditional models of inter-state wars and civil conflicts. Duffield (2001), in particular, emphasizes the importance of taking a comprehensive view of the complex systems and processes that lead to crises. While drawing on these insights about the complexity and global nature of conflicts, this chapter takes a different approach to the problem of famine, by trying to identify the underlying patterns that guide the dynamics of these crises on the basis of 'priority regimes'.

The literature on policy processes is extensive and continues to grow (see Keeley and Scoones 1999 for a concise overview). At least since Clay and Schaffer (1984), authors have taken an increasingly nuanced view of development policy processes, highlighting the complex interactions of interests, actors and discourses that can lead to certain policies being formed, as well as to inadvertent and unexpected outcomes from their implementation. These insights will be important in the development of the priority regime approach, both in recognizing the complexities of policy formulation and implementation and in identifying possible ways to effect changes to them. However, it may also be helpful to highlight the different focuses of these approaches: while the policy process literature seeks to understand the formation of policy, a priority regimes approach looks at how different policies (and other factors) interact to produce famines.

The fields of participation, accountability and rights have gained considerable importance in development studies in the past thirty years. In the late 1970s and early 1980s participatory approaches were seen as a counter to the top-down style associated with previous development efforts (Chambers 1983), by recognizing the wealth of knowledge possessed by rural villagers and inviting them to have a say in the structuring of projects. However, there was frustration with a reliance on participatory approaches alone, because of their inability to create genuinely reciprocal relationships between villagers and 'experts', and because they could serve as a device to 'legitimize' the agendas of powerful external stakeholders while failing to address local inequalities (IDS 2000). Moreover, they often did not adequately consider their impact on community tensions (Shah and Shah 1995). Accountability of institutions has been identified as a necessary complement to participatory approaches. Recent work has tried to identify ways in which the poor and marginalized *claim* their rights through both participation and accountability (cf. Gaventa *et al.* 2002). These insights will resonate with some of the implications of a priority regime approach.

Priority regime approach: basic concepts

This section outlines some of the key concepts associated with the priority regime approach, as introduced in this chapter. It begins by defining priority regimes and providing examples of them. It then clarifies the relationships between priority regimes and famine, before exploring the differences among the priority regimes of various decision-makers, from the global to the household levels.

Priority regimes

Priority regimes can be defined as the set of concerns that are privileged in the decision-making and actions of institutions and individuals. They can be both formal (i.e. set out in mission statements, policy papers, project proposals or speeches) and informal (i.e. not explicitly documented). Examples of formal priority regimes include the Millennium Development Goals (MDGs), national poverty reduction strategies, organizational strategic plans, NGO project proposals and policy speeches. The MDGs, for instance, set out eight goals – related to poverty and hunger, education, gender, child mortality, maternal health, disease, environment and partnership – for UN member states to achieve by 2015 (United Nations 2004). These goals have framed the agenda for the UN and other humanitarian and development agencies, and are referenced in numerous policy documents and programmes.

According to the World Bank, 'Poverty Reduction Strategy Papers (PRSP) describe a country's macro-economic, structural and social policies and programs to promote growth and reduce poverty, as well as associated external financing needs' (World Bank 2004). Sierra Leone's Interim Poverty Reduction Strategy Paper has four emphases for the 'Transitional Phase' after its conflict: national security and good governance; re-launching the economy; social programmes; and ongoing poverty interventions (Republic of Sierra Leone 2001). The WFP has a *Strategic Plan 2004–2007* that sets out its priority areas (saving lives, livelihoods, nutrition, education, and capacity-building) for the four-year period (WFP 2003). As of June 2005, CARE USA had thirteen funded projects in Malawi, covering areas such as food aid, livelihoods, HIV/AIDS and capacity building (CARE USA 2005).

Formal priority regimes can also appear in the statements of a country's leaders. President Lula of Brazil has made ending hunger a major priority of his administration. In his inaugural address, he stated: 'If, by the end of my mandate, every Brazilian has food to eat three times a day, I shall have fulfilled my mission in life' (Embassy of Brazil 2004). In accordance with this priority, he established the Zero Hunger Programme (FAO 2003). While discrepancies may occur between stated aims and actual outcomes (cf. Clay and Schaffer 1984), the relevance of formal priority regimes is that they provide a framework for decision-making, actions and the allocation of resources – they set directions towards certain goals.

Informal priority regimes are not formulated in explicit statements or legally binding agreements (and in fact often subvert these). They may range from a household's goals for the family to a government's unspoken political aims. Informal regimes may coexist with formal ones, with the formal regime sometimes being used as a 'cover' for an informal one. The actions of decision-makers often reveal their informal or unstated priorities. For instance, a government may skew the allocation of humanitarian resources towards communities from its political power base, in accordance with an informal (and certainly unstated) priority regime to strengthen this power base through dispensing patronage. An awareness of both formal and informal priority regimes is critical to the analysis.

Priority regimes (as elucidated here) have three basic components – spatial, temporal and effectual – that determine their impact on famine causation. The *spatial* component refers to the geographic area targeted by a priority regime. An NGO conducting a primary health-care project may have a single district as its spatial locale, while a UNICEF/Ministry of Health polio vaccination programme may focus on the entire country. The spatial dimensions of priority regimes can be clearly seen in maps of NGO activities, which in some locations can be described as a 'scramble' to divide up the territory between international NGOs (cf. Devereux and Palmero (1999) on Mozambique; a similar phenomenon occurs in Northern Sudan). (Note, however, that often a government or NGO programme is not directed at the entire population living in a given area, but rather is targeted at a particular segment of the national or local population, such as poor farmers, pregnant women or schoolchildren).

The *temporal* component refers to the duration of the priority regime, which may vary greatly. For instance, an NGO development project may have funding for three years, while national poverty reduction strategies may set out a plan for a five-year period. Likewise, the 'vigilance' against famines that often characterizes post-crisis situations (among governments, donors, media and NGO representatives) may be short term, if it does not translate into more durable systems for prevention. The 'anti-famine contract' (de Waal 1997, 2000) for famine prevention, such as the one embodied in the Indian Famine Codes, is an example of a durable, long-term regime, since it has functioned with some success for over 100 years (cf. Drèze 1990; Singh 1993). The regimes that affect a given population may vary and change over time.

The third component of priority regimes is their *effect* on the food security of a population, which can be positive, negative, both or neither. Examples of regimes that are 'positive', in the sense that they directly support the food security and livelihoods of a population, include investment in agricultural development, or the provision of social safety nets. On the other hand, the Government of Sudan, using starvation as a weapon of war through proxy militia attacks on the civilian population of an area (Keen 1999), has had a directly negative, destructive effect on the food security and livelihoods of the population. These positive and negative effects can sometimes be unexpected and unintended. For example, a feeding centre established during a famine may attract large numbers of hungry people to the site, overwhelming its capacity and inadvertently creating a public health problem that increases mortality (see de Waal, 1989, on the 1984–1985 famine in Darfur, Sudan; or Lautze and Maxwell, Chaper 10, this volume, on the 1999–2000 famine in Ethiopia).

Unlike priority regimes, 'undirected occurrences' refer to processes or events over which people have limited or no control. Such occurrences that contribute to famine include natural disasters, epidemics and market fluctuations. They also have these three dimensions: spatial, temporal and effectual. A drought or a typhoon, for instance, will affect only a certain spatial area for a given duration of time. An HIV/AIDS epidemic in a country will have very different spatial and temporal patterns, but the same basic elements apply. Fluctuations in international markets can affect, for instance, coffee growers in a certain region for a season or more. The occurrences can also have positive and negative impacts. Floods in a country may have both: while wiping out crops and livestock, flooding may also create fishing opportunities and improve the soil for the next few years. While these factors contribute to crises, their negative effects can usually be offset by positive responses if the political will – or 'positive priority regime' – exists.

Populations are exposed to multiple, overlapping undirected occurrences and priority regimes, since governments, the UN, NGOs and corporations may all have relevant concerns in a given location. As a result, the regimes that affect a population vary and change over time. The application or removal of priority regimes represents a positive or negative shock to a system. Famines result among populations where a series of negative shocks are not sufficiently offset by positive ones to prevent a self-reinforcing dynamic leading to destitution and death.

Relationships between priority regimes and famine

A crucial insight is that the priority regimes that affect the famine process are often not formed around the specific topic of famine. Many (though certainly not all) policies that create vulnerability to famine have their origins in other objectives. Examples include the 'War on Terror', the investments of international oil companies, and structural adjustment policies. This insight permits us to identify a range of relationships between the priority regime and famine, including 'neglect', 'by-product', 'trade-off', 'means', 'famicide' and 'response'.

Neglect refers to situations where famine is not considered in the goals set by a given decision-maker. When governments do not bother to invest in certain marginalized population areas, or when the international community ignores a developing food crisis because they are focusing on completely different concerns, they are practising neglect. (It should be noted that neglect does not necessarily imply malicious intent.) The priority regimes do not impact the population with a direct positive or negative effect; rather they affect the population by their absence, by failing to produce a positive shock that compensates for the negative ones that are inducing famine. In this respect, priority regimes are often as important for what they exclude as for what they include.

By-product occurs when famine is a consequence of the actions related to a priority regime that privilege other goals above famine prevention. In this scenario, famine is not an important consideration in decision-making processes, but the pursuit of the higher goals may induce famine, either intentionally or unintentionally. Examples include situations where a war fought between governments raises famine vulnerability among civilian populations. In Afghanistan in 2002, for example, there was widespread concern that the US-led invasion, combined with several years of drought, could create famine conditions. Hunger can also arise from the implementation of ideological programmes (e.g. collectivization in the Soviet Union in the 1930s, or 'Great Leap Forward' policies in China in the 1950s). In such cases, famine vulnerability is a consequence of priority regimes that had other objectives but produced catastrophic outcomes.

Trade-off refers to situations where famine prevention is weighed as an explicit option but is not selected because of other policy goals that enjoy higher priority at the time. This situation may occur when, for example, governments cut agricultural subsidy programmes in order to meet the conditionalities for loans from the International Monetary Fund or bilateral lenders. Once the media are aware of a famine as a possible story, they make a trade-off if they decide not to cover this, giving preference to a different story instead. Trade-offs also arise when the government protects urban areas at the expense of rural ones in the event of a crisis, or when international donors allocate resources to one crisis situation at the expense of others (e.g. it was feared that the US-led intervention in Iraq in 2003 would divert humanitarian assistance from crises in Africa). Often trade-offs occur along a temporal dimension, with short-term goals sacrificed for long-term objectives, or *vice versa*. For instance, in famine situations villagers invariably reduce their immediate consumption of food, in order to preserve livelihood assets which would have to be sold to purchase the food (de Waal 1989).

Means refers to situations where famine is viewed as a necessary step to the achievement of a higher priority. An example is UN sanctions in Iraq, which, despite contributing to increased hardship and famine vulnerability among the Iraqi population, were viewed as a necessary means to force the regime into compliance with Security Council resolutions (see Gazdar, Chapter 6, this volume). In other situations, famine may be explicitly deployed as a means to an end. For instance, in many cases of siege (cf. Watson, Chapter 12, this volume), the starvation of the besieged population is viewed as an integral part of the strategy for achieving the surrender of a city and victory in the larger war. During the Dutch Hunger winter in 1944, the German army used famine as a means of undermining the Dutch resistance.

Famicide occurs when famine is an actively sought end in itself. It is closely related to means, but differs in that a final goal of the priority regime is the annihilation of the population. In this way, it has more affinities with genocide (hence the coinage in this chapter of the term 'famicide'). From a legal perspective, famicide might correspond to 'first degree faminogenic activity', as defined by Marcus 2003 (cf. Edkins, Chapter 13, this volume). Some of the government-backed militia attacks in southern Sudan during the 1980s and 1990s may be categorized in this manner (Human Rights Watch 1999; Keen 1999).[3]

Response refers to priority regimes where the goal is to contribute directly to the prevention or mitigation of famine situations. The interventions resulting from the priority regimes are therefore intended to represent 'positive shocks' that build the resilience of communities or offset the negative shocks associated with a famine event. These include government and NGO programmes that are designed to improve rural agriculture in famine-prone countries, as well as many humanitarian relief operations, from Biafra to Darfur.

Of course, in actuality the decisions are more nuanced, and it may not be a matter of an absolute choice between two options but rather one of degree. Moreover, priority regimes rarely lead in a linear manner to the achievement of the goals. Policy processes have unexpected and unintended outcomes. (Indeed, the 'by-product' outcome makes this explicit.) Nevertheless, the basic relationships described above capture some of the principal ways that priority regimes interact with famine, as summarized in Table 15.1 and Figure 15.1.

Relationships among the priority regimes of different decision-makers

The preceding discussion of scenarios has focused on the range of relationships that priority regimes can have to famine outcomes. It is also necessary to clarify the relationships among the priority regimes of various decision-makers in different situations in the globalizing world. These relationships can be examined through a discussion of the 'relativism of external factors'.

Table 15.1 Relationships of priority regimes to famine

Relationship	Description
Neglect	Famine is not considered in the decision-making process
By-product	Famine is an inadvertent by-product of another higher priority
Trade-off	An explicit decision is made to prioritize other goals instead of famine prevention
Means	Famine is a necessary means to a larger priority
Famicide	Famine is prioritized as an actively sought occurrence
Response	Famine is prioritized as an actively fought against occurrence

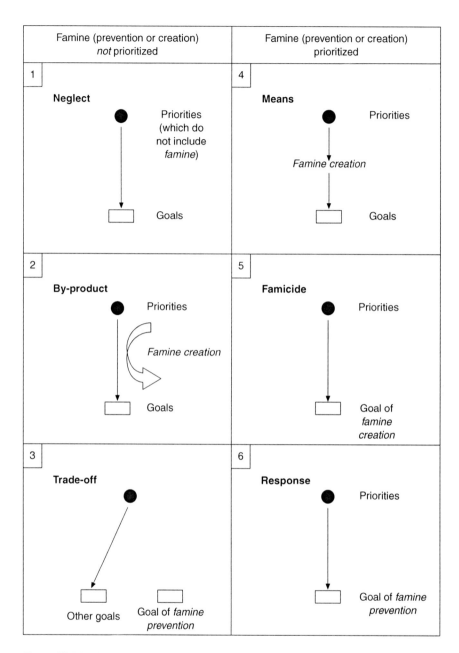

Figure 15.1 Basic relationships of priority regimes to famine.

An external factor is something over which a decision-maker has limited control. External factors can take the form of either the priority regimes of other decision-makers (e.g. the USA's 'War on Terror') or 'undirected occurrences' (e.g. floods, hurricanes, market fluctuations). External factors are 'relative' in at least two respects. First, they are relative to a given decision-maker. If an NGO sets up a primary health centre in a village, the NGO and the villagers may view this rather differently. For the NGO, the health centre reflects their priority regime: it is part of a larger primary health-care programme that draws on the NGO's expertise and experience, and it reflects their judgement about what they prioritize as being in the community's best interest. For the villagers, however, the health programme, over which they typically have little influence, will seem an external factor, a potentially positive intervention that nevertheless is not directly under their control. In this instance, the relative position of those involved in the intervention determines whether it is part of a priority regime or is an external factor (see Figure 15.2).

Although this example has focused on an NGO programme, the removal of agricultural subsidies, the imposition of international sanctions or an international conflict in their region also represent external factors for the affected villagers, but are priority regimes for other, more powerful decision-makers elsewhere.

External factors are also 'relative' in the degree of influence a decision-maker has over a factor. If the NGO has been inclusive and participatory in its formulation of the project, then the villagers may have had some influence on its design and implementation. This allows the priority regimes of the NGO to better reflect the priority regimes of the villagers, thus creating a priority regime that is shared by both sets of decision-makers. This relationship is illustrated in Figure 15.3.

A key point is that the relationships are not static and can be changed by interactions among decision-makers. This is true even in cases of subsidy removals, international sanctions, conflict and structural adjustment programmes. If a coalition – for example, of aid workers, journalists and affected populations – can be mobilized, awareness about a situation can be raised and the influence of more powerful decision-makers can sometimes be brought to bear in more appropriate and effective ways (see the section on 'Understanding and applying leverage').

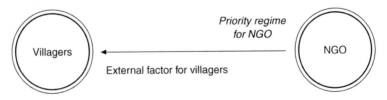

Figure 15.2 Relationship of priority regime to famine.

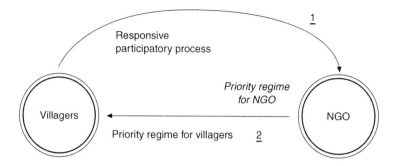

Figure 15.3 Priority regime and external factors.

To illustrate these points in relation to 'undirected occurrences', the climate is external for most decision-makers, producing shocks like droughts over which they have almost no control. However, even the weather is external to different decision-makers to different degrees. For instance, the President of the United States, through his decisions, arguably has a greater impact on global warming than does a villager in southern Sudan. On the other hand, many villagers in southern Sudan believe in rain-makers, who claim to have the power to control the weather. To the extent that these decisions and activities actually affect rainfall patterns, the climate is a relative, rather than an absolute, external factor.

The degree of influence is also not static in relation to external 'undirected occurrences'. For example, as our understanding of human influences on global warming improves over time, so policies such as control of greenhouse emissions might move higher up the priority agenda, and this in turn could affect the climate in drought-prone areas. HIV/AIDS demonstrates the contingency of 'undirected occurrences' in a different way. Among populations that have limited knowledge about the disease and its transmission, the virus is an external shock, with long temporal dimensions and extremely adverse consequences for food security (and lives). However, as knowledge is gained about the virus and more Global Fund and other resources are devoted to the prevention, treatment and mitigation of HIV/AIDS, so the external factor becomes susceptible to a degree of control.

Understanding and applying leverage

The relativism of external factors suggests that situations leading to famine can be altered if appropriate leverage can be found (see Table 15.2). The different relationships of priority regimes to famine have different points of leverage. For instance, when famine is a *by-product* of a higher priority, it may be possible to have the relevant decision-maker enlarge and accommodate famine prevention or response within its regime, without sacrificing the larger goal. In Afghanistan in 2001, there was widespread concern that the US-led invasion, combined with the drought, could create a famine. International NGOs advocated for the humanitarian cause and expanded the US's priority regime to include response efforts more fully. Where famine is an unwanted *means*, other approaches can be identified that allow the objective to be achieved without the unwanted effects. The introduction of 'smart sanctions' in Iraq was an attempt to alleviate the unwanted effects without preventing the achievement of the overarching priority (see Gazdar, Chapter 6, this volume).

Neglect can often be transformed by drawing attention to a crisis. A classic example is Michael Buerk and Mohammed Amin's BBC report on the Ethiopian famine in 1984, which immediately galvanized world interest. Sometimes, *trade-offs* are made under pressure. For instance, some of the IMF's loan conditionalities forced cuts in agricultural subsidies. In such situations, leverage can be found in removing some of the pressure, by finding solutions that satisfy multilateral agencies without creating famine vulnerability. In other instances, the government favours one region over another, and a difficult process of achieving a realignment of priorities must be initiated. Perhaps the most intransigent situation is *famicide*. Here, leverage will have to be found in priorities that the decision-maker places even higher than the creation of famine. For example, in Darfur in 2004, the threat of further economic sanctions on the Government of Sudan, followed by a UN Resolution in March 2005 that referred the situation in Darfur to the International Criminal Court, were intended to achieve compliance with the international community's demand that the government disarm the raiding militias.

In all these situations, awareness through information is part of the leverage. Decision-makers' access to and use of information is important in setting and altering priorities. The credibility of information has been an issue in a number of recent crises, including Malawi (Devereux 2002), Ethiopia (Maxwell 2002) and Sudan (Deng 1999).

Applying priority regime analysis

To clarify the use of these concepts, it may be helpful to apply them to the analysis of several recent famines or near famines. The priority regimes approach can be used to analyse the global and local dimensions of the process leading to famine as well as the famine itself. The three case studies below illustrate the use of priority regime analysis, by focusing on a key aspect of each of the crises.

Afghanistan, 2001–2002: by-product and response

In his first State of the Union address following the attacks on New York and Washington, DC on 11 September 2001, President Bush of the US

Table 15.2 Leverage in relationships of priority regimes and famine

Relationship	Description	Immediate leverage
Neglect	Famine is not considered in the decision-making process.	Drawing attention to the issue through coalitions of the media, NGOs, etc.
By-product	Famine is an inadvertent by-product of another higher priority.	Demonstrating how the decision-maker can accommodate famine prevention in its priority regime, without sacrificing its larger goal
Trade-off	An explicit decision is made to prioritize other goals instead of famine prevention.	Removing external pressure for trade-off, or working towards a realignment of priorities
Means	Famine is a necessary means to a larger priority.	If unwanted, finding ways that priority can be achieved without famine, while highlighting discrepancies between stated moral position and use of famine. If wanted, threatening even higher priorities of the decision-maker
Famicide	Famine prioritized as an actively sought occurrence.	Threatening even higher priorities of the decision-maker
Response	Famine prioritized as an actively fought against occurrence.	No change required

identified the 'War on Terror' as the primary aim of American foreign policy in the coming years:

> Our war on terror is well begun, but it is only begun. This campaign may not be finished on our watch – yet it must be and it will be waged on our watch … Our first priority must always be the security of our nation, and that will be reflected in the budget I send to Congress. My budget supports three great goals for America: we will win this war; we'll protect our homeland; and we will revive our economy.
>
> (Bush 2002)

By the time of this speech, a US-led military campaign, principally using proxy forces, had ousted the Taliban regime from power in Afghanistan. The regime had been accused of providing a safe haven for Osama Bin Laden, believed to be the mastermind of the terrorist attacks in America. The high priority that the US placed on the 'War on Terror', with its specific *spatial* and *temporal* focus on Afghanistan at the end of 2001, had led many in the humanitarian community to fear that famine would be a *by-product* of the invasion. The actual outcome of the situation shows the complexities of achieving leverage in such a crisis.

Even before the attacks in September 2001 a number of humanitarian agencies had warned of a possible famine in Afghanistan, due to repeated negative shocks of droughts in the region. In July 2001, a FAO/WFP Assessment Mission concluded that 'A third successive year of drought has left Afghanistan teetering on the brink of widespread famine and placed the lives of millions of people at risk', with five million people requiring assistance to fill a cereal deficit of one million tonnes (WFP 2001). The concern after 11 September was that the imminent US invasion would lead to massive displacement, creating an additional negative shock and at the same time preventing humanitarian aid – an offsetting positive shock – from reaching those in need.

The leverage in the situation lay in highlighting the threat to the population and identifying ways for the combatants to allow sufficient humanitarian assistance to reach those in need. Different approaches were taken. On the one hand, some humanitarian advocates, like Mary Robinson, the United Nations Human Rights Commissioner, argued for a pause in the bombing campaign: 'There's been three years of famine in Afghanistan, there's been military conflict internally, now there's this military assault and I understand the reasons, but we have to have as a priority the civilian population and their need to be secured for the coming winter' (BBC 2001). Her position nevertheless attempted to reconcile the objectives of the campaign with the humanitarian needs of those who might be affected.

On the other hand, Clare Short, the United Kingdom's Minister for International Development, argued that the goals of winning the war and assisting those in need could be achieved simultaneously (Spillius 2001). Indeed, it appears that the American administration believed that the provision of aid (in addition to being humane) could be an effective tactic in achieving victory. President Bush, in announcing $320 million in aid to Afghanistan, stated: 'This is our way of saying that while we firmly and strongly oppose the Taliban regime, we are friends of the Afghan people' (Online NewsHour 2001). The political calculation seems to have been that aid would help secure the support of the Afghan population for the goals of the intervention.

In practice, it proved difficult to balance the military intervention with relief efforts. Writing in the midst of the bombing campaign, Ford and Davis (2001) indicate that 'Getting aid into the country is difficult at best, and in some locations impossible. Almost all aid agencies have withdrawn from Afghanistan to neighbouring countries.' In another incident, Oxfam stopped a convoy of wheat from heading to Hazajarat to aid 400,000 people in the mountainous central area after a bomb exploded near its food depot in Kabul (Spillius 2001).

Much-publicized US military air-drops of relief were also heavily criti-

cized by aid agencies. They argued that air-drops were particularly ineffective, because they were not targeted and therefore unlikely to reach those
most in need. They also warned of the dangers of blurring the distinction
between military operations and humanitarian aid, arguing that the ability
to access those in need depended upon aid agencies being viewed as
neutral to the conflict (Ford and Davis 2001). In fact, the military air-
drops only amounted to one-quarter to one-half of 1 per cent of the
required aid, according to Andrew Natsios, Administrator of USAID (US
Embassy 2001).

By December 2001, circumstances on the ground had changed rapidly
with the sudden collapse of the Taliban regime. The unexpectedness of
these events was recorded by an Australian aid worker: 'I arrived at a time
when no one really imagined the war against the Taliban would finish so
quickly but the towns in Afghanistan fell one after the other in a ten-day
period and it was like a house of cards' (AusAID 2002). Aid shipments
rapidly increased, from 75,000 tonnes of wheat in the previous three
months to 118,000 tonnes in December (Oxfam 2002). By January 2002,
when the President made his speech, Catherine Bertini, Executive Director of the World Food Programme, could claim that 'There will be no
famine in Afghanistan this winter' (Feminist Daily News Wire 2002).

The war had not caused the anticipated famine, in part because it had
been unexpectedly brief. However, in addition, the pressure from humanitarian advocates had ensured that sufficient aid was delivered once conditions on the ground permitted. It is not clear, though, that in the
absence of a rapid victory the humanitarian needs of the population
would have been adequately accommodated with the military objectives.
In that case, humanitarian advocates would have been forced to explore
new and even more difficult tactics.

Sudan, 1998: Famicide and neglect

In the 1990s, the Government of Sudan conducted what might be termed
famicide in the Northern Bahr el Ghazal region of southern Sudan
(Human Rights Watch 1999; Keen 1999) while the international community, by and large, neglected the situation (though not necessarily with malicious intent). Engaged in a prolonged civil war with southern rebel
factions, the government supported a number of raids on civilians in the
area. Since the mid-1980s, the government-backed militias had attacked
villages along the train route from Barbanusa in the north to the garrison
town of Wau in the south. In 1994, the former rebel commander Kerubino Bol, who had defected to the government, began a series of additional raids in the same areas. By 1997, almost the entire population
(600,000) in the spatial area of Gogrial, Abyei and Twic counties in Northern Bahr el Ghazal had been forced to flee their homes up to three times
a year (Deng 1999).

Suffering the effects of both an *El Niño* drought and these raids, the villagers in the spatial area experienced a series of negative shocks, inadequately compensated for by aid from the international community. WFP food aid deliveries in 1996 and 1997 had only been 12 and 38 per cent respectively of the assessed need (Deng 1999), due to limited funding. Although the 1997 Annual Needs Assessment had indicated that affected populations were comparing the situation to the severe crisis in the late 1980s (WFP 1997), the UN Consolidated Appeal Process (CAP) for the Sudan requested less funding than in the previous year, because it was felt that sceptical donors would react negatively to greater demands (UN 1998; Danida 1999).

As the situation deteriorated, the government imposed a flight ban in January 1998, which effectively blocked the aid response for a critical two-month period. Moreover, after Kerubino switched sides again, a joint attack by Kerubino and the Sudanese People's Liberation Movement (SPLM) on the government stronghold of Wau early in the year led to the displacement of 130,000 people. Nevertheless, most international NGOs and UN agencies did not make adequate preparations for providing aid once the ban was lifted (Task Force 1998; Danida 1999). Donors were also not forthcoming with assistance. By April 1998, when conditions were already severe, only 20 per cent of the requested funds had been provided; by June 1998, only 40 per cent had been received and urgent appeals were still being made (Danida 1999).

The leverage in this situation involved getting the attention of the international community (to counter the neglect), then applying sufficient pressure on the Government of Sudan to halt the attacks (to counter the famicide). A coalition of activist NGOs and the Sudanese Relief and Rehabilitation Association (SRRA), the humanitarian wing of the SPLM, recognized the neglect of the international community and began working to draw attention to the severity of the situation through reports and video. A SRRA report on the situation in March 1998 used dramatic language:

> With the present level of humanitarian intervention in the region, it is imminent that thousands of women, children and elderly people will simply starve to death within the coming weeks because of inadequate food intake and poor health services.
>
> (SRRA 1998)

An SRRA video of conditions in the region was passed to the media through a contact in Norwegian People's Aid (Deng, pers. comm. 2001). A screening of the video was organized for international journalists and, as a result, a trip for over thirty people to see the conditions on the ground was organized for April 1998.

Although some NGOs and UN agencies took a different view of the emerging information, disputing the severity of the situation and questioning the motivations of these efforts, at a certain point international attention turned to the situation. According to one evaluation (Danida 1999), the 'agenda had changed overnight' with one aid worker quoted as saying 'we were suddenly being urged to prepare multi-million dollar proposals within days'. Relief efforts were stepped up in a full-out response. Aid deliveries exceeded targets by August 1998. International embarrassment and pressure forced the Government of Sudan to reduce the areas affected by the flight bans and to rein in some of the attacks.[4] By that time, however, over 70,000 people had lost their lives (Deng 1999). The combination of famicide plus relative neglect, exacerbated by natural occurrences, had led to a major famine in the spatial location of Bahr el Ghazal in southern Sudan during the temporal period of 1998.

Tragically, a scenario with some parallels was repeated in the Darfur region in western Sudan in 2003 and 2004.

North Korea, 1995–1998: means versus trade-off

While a variety of factors influenced the process leading to famine in North Korea in the mid- to late 1990s, the rural communities' vulnerability was caused primarily by the rapid decline of subsidies after the collapse of the Soviet Union, a series of floods in 1995 and 1996 and government mismanagement (see Noland, Chapter 9, this volume). Despite the increasing seriousness of the situation, these negative shocks were not adequately offset by positive aid flows due to a deadlock of the priority regimes of the US and the DPRK Governments.

For the US and many of its allies, famine (through the withholding of food aid) appears to have been seen as a means to achieving the larger priority of having the DPRK Government participate in negotiations (though there was some debate within the administration). By 1996, it had become US policy to use aid as a carrot for the DPRK Government's participation in four-party talks with South Korea, China and the US, which aimed to defuse the tension between the two Koreas, achieve concessions on nuclear proliferation and open the closed North Korean society to the rest of the world (Natsios 2001).

At times, the administration seemed to go further and to be intent on the collapse of the DPRK Government. On 8 May 1997, US State Department spokesperson, Nicholas Burns indicated the US Government's position:

> We do not favour the current economic system of North Korea … that has failed the North Korean people and has led to the starvation and deprivation that millions of North Koreans are now experiencing … We are not going to spend billions of dollars of American money to prop up a decrepit, ancient oxymoron, which is communist economics.
>
> (quoted in Lautze 1997)

The US allies of Japan and South Korea made inconsistent contributions to the relief efforts, reflecting their complex and changing relationships with the North Korean Government. At one point, when North Korea made initial overtures to Japan for assistance, South Korea warned the Japanese Government that the provision of humanitarian aid could seriously jeopardize the future of their relationship (Noland *et al.* 1999). The South Korean Government subsequently took other positions (Natsios 2001).

The DPRK Government made several trade-offs in relation to the famine. Unconditional requests for aid were traded off against its need to save face by not asking for assistance and its refusal to give way on key strategic issues without prior compensation. It also traded off the welfare of rural populations in favour of the urban elites and the military (Lautze 1997). In effect, it undertook a 'triage' policy, withdrawing resources from the politically marginalized and severely affected north-east of the country and concentrating them among the military and political elites in other regions (Natsios 2001). The deadlock represented a blockage that prevented the positive shocks of aid flows from compensating for the negative shocks in rural areas.

The leverage in this blockage lay in different places. Since the US Government appeared to be using famine as a *means*, the potential existed to highlight the moral dissonance between the American values and its infliction of famine for political gain. Indeed, this strategy appears to have been pursued by a diverse coalition of NGOs, rallying around a campaign called 'Stop the Famine'. They ran television advertisements on CNN and the *Today* show arguing for the need for greater US leadership (Hsiao 1997). Andrew Natsios, then Vice-President of World Vision, wrote an op-ed article in the Washington Post, criticizing the Clinton administration for politicizing famine relief, arguing that it undermined a longstanding policy of previous administrations:

> The government's inaction ... eviscerates the policy put in place by Ronald Reagan during the Ethiopia famine when he overruled his advisers and ordered food shipments: 'A hungry child knows no politics,' Reagan said, declaring that we would not use food as a weapon.
>
> (Natsios 1997)

Sue Lautze, a senior researcher at the Feinstein Famine Center, had conducted a USAID assessment in North Korea, and argued that the policy was not only immoral but also unlikely to be effective, given the historical experience with using famine as a means to achieve a change in government (Lautze 1997).

For the North Korean Government, the leverage lay in de-linking the aid from political concessions and providing face-saving manoeuvres to allow the government to accept aid, thereby removing a source of their trade-offs. However, it would also mean applying pressure on the government to ensure that aid was directed at those most in need and not allocated only to the political elites and the military (Natsios 2001).

Temporally, the deadlock lasted approximately two years before the decision to increase US aid to North Korea was made in August 1997. Spatially, the blockage affected the entire country, but particularly the northeast regions. The negative effects, uncompensated for by positive shocks, created a famine in which nearly 2.5 million people are estimated to have lost their lives (Natsios 2001).[5]

In many respects, the North Korean case has parallels with the famine or near famine in Iraq, where sanctions were used by the UN to force an autocratic government into compliance with Security Council Resolutions. In Malawi a similar stalemate occurred, with donors apparently withholding food aid as a means and the government making trade-offs at the expense of vulnerable populations (see Devereux and Tiba, Chapter 7, this volume).

Possible longer-term implications

These case studies have largely focused on how leverage can be gained in different situations in the short term. However, one of the implications of this analysis is that, in the longer term, structures and attitudes would need to be changed in ways that alter the priority regimes of decision-makers. Two approaches might be considered. The 'relativism of external factors' suggests that it might be possible, as a first approach, to increase the degree to which famine-affected populations can influence external factors. It argues for measures that empower individuals and local communities to claim greater influence over external priorities. NGOs would ensure that their programmes were more driven by the priorities of beneficiaries. It would also be important to support democratic processes, creating where possible an anti-famine contract with the government for famine prevention. The possibility of establishing a UN ombudsperson for food security should be considered in order to permit affected populations to have their voices heard in international institutions (cf. Mitchell and Doane 1999; Howe 2004).

However, such measures, on their own, may not be sufficient. It would also be necessary to take steps to ensure that governments and the international community make famine prevention a priority by creating adequate means of accountability (IDS 2002). Edkins (Chapter 3, this volume) proposes the criminalization of mass starvation, with the possibility of cases being heard at the International Criminal Court. Howe and Devereux (2002; 2004; also Chapter 2, this volume) have argued for the value of a widely accepted definition of famine – based on 'intensity and magnitude scales' – as a way to achieve greater accountability among national governments and the international community for famine causation. The criminalization of famine and the application of a clear definition linked to political accountability might force decision-makers to take famine creation and famine prevention (and hence early warnings) much more seriously.

Conclusion

In a famous book title with biblical allusions, Chambers (1983) emphasized the importance of 'putting the last first'. In many ways, the international development community over the past twenty years – through participation, rights and governance agendas – has sought to create a greater alignment of the priorities of humanitarian and global decision-makers with the needs of marginalized populations. The continued persistence of famine suggests that these efforts are incomplete.

This chapter has focused on how the interactions of various priority regimes and 'undirected occurrences' create famine conditions. It has described some of the combinations of the priority regimes – by-product and response, famicide and neglect, means versus trade-off – that seem to recur in the contemporary world. However, it has also identified possible points of leverage for addressing them. It shows how actions can be taken by coalitions of aid agencies, the media, donors and affected populations to improve the situation. By helping to create a language for analysing and discussing famine situations in a globalizing world, the priority regime approach may contribute towards more effective action.

Famine prevention is not and probably never will be the highest priority of the international community, except in specific places for particular reasons and for very brief periods of time. This chapter has identified ways to minimize the impacts of other priorities on famine creation in the short term, but the analysis also suggests that it will take concerted longer-term measures to realign priorities if 'famine in a globalizing world' is no longer to be viewed as a paradox but as an unacceptable contradiction.

Notes

1   The author would like to thank Stephen Devereux and Patrick Webb for helpful comments on earlier versions of this chapter. The interpretations and conclusions expressed are solely those of the author. They do not necessarily reflect the views of the United Nations World Food Programme or the United Nations' member states.

2   Several authors have used similar wording to describe this situation. Kates and Millman (1990: 389), for instance, speak of 'the persistence of hunger in a world of plenty' as a 'deeply troubling paradox of our time'.

3   Obviously, there are different views on this matter, and any final determination of culpability would require a decision from an international court.

4   A more fundamental change in the priorities of the Government of Sudan did not come until the United States took a renewed interest in the Sudan some years later after the 11 September 2001 attacks on New York and Washington,

DC. The US put pressure on both sides in the conflict to enter meaningful peace talks. Higher priorities, including the possibility of normalized economic relations with the US, created incentives for the Government of Sudan to stop the attacks in Bahr el Ghazal.

5 Note that other estimates are much lower. Noland (Chapter 9, this volume) puts the excess mortality in North Korea in the range of 600,000 to one million.

References

Action Against Hunger (AAH) (2001) *The Geopolitics of Hunger, 2000–2001: Hunger and Power*, London: Boulder.

AusAID (2002) 'Afghanistan: famine on an immense scale', 17 July 2002 (available at www.ausaid.gov.au, accessed 24 October 2004).

British Broadcasting Corporation (BBC) (2001) 'Millions at risk in Afghan crisis', 14 October 2001 (available at www.bbc.co.uk, accessed 24 October 2004).

Bush, G. (2002) 'The President's State of the Union Address 2002' (speech) (available at www.whitehouse.gov/news, accessed 24 October 2004).

CARE USA (2005) 'CARE's work' (available at www.careusa.org/careswork/projects/cindex_77.asp, accessed 5 June 2005).

Chambers, R. (1983) *Rural Development: Putting the Last First*, London: Longman.

Clay, E. and Schaffer, B. (eds) (1984) *Room for Manoeuvre: An Exploration of Public Policy in Agriculture and Rural Development*, London: Heinemann Educational Books.

Collier, P. and Hoeffler, A. (2002) 'Greed and Grievance in Civil War', *CSAE WPS* 2002–2001, Oxford: Centre for the Study of African Economies.

Collier, P., Elliot, V., Hegre, H., Hoeffler, A., Reynal-Querol, M. and Sambanis, N. (2003) *Breaking the Conflict Trap: Civil War and Development Policy*, Washington, DC: World Bank and Oxford University Press.

Curtis, D., Hubbard, M. and Shepherd, A. (1988) *Preventing Famine: Policies and Prospects for Africa*, London: Routledge.

Danida (Royal Danish Ministry of Foreign Affairs) (1999) 'Evaluation of Danish humanitarian assistance to Sudan 1992–98' (available at www.um.dk/danida, accessed 6 October 2003).

Darcy, J. and Hofmann, C. A. (2003) 'According to need? Needs assessment and decision-making in the humanitarian sector', *HPG Report* 15, London: Overseas Development Institute.

de Waal, A. (1989) *Famine That Kills: Darfur, Sudan, 1984–1985*, Oxford: Clarendon Press.

de Waal, A. (1997) *Famine Crimes: Politics and the Disaster Relief Industry in Africa*, Oxford: James Currey.

de Waal, A. (2000) 'Democratic political process and the fight against famine', *IDS Working Paper* 107, Brighton: Institute of Development Studies.

Deng, L. B. (1999) 'Famine in the Sudan: causes, preparedness, and response', *IDS Discussion Paper* 369, Brighton: Institute of Development Studies.

Deng, L. B. (2002) 'Confronting civil war: a comparative study of household assets management in Southern Sudan', *IDS Discussion Paper 381*, Brighton: Institute of Development Studies.

Devereux, S. (1993) *Theories of Famine*, London: Harvester Wheatsheaf.

Devereux, S. (2002) 'The Malawi famine of 2002', *IDS Bulletin*, 33(4): 70–78.

Devereux, S. and Palmero, A. (1999) 'Creating a framework for reducing poverty: institutional and process issues in national poverty policy: Mozambique country report', *A report for the Special Programme on Africa*, Brighton: Institute of Development Studies.

Devereux, S., Howe, P. and Deng, L. B. (2002) 'Introduction: the 'New Famines', *IDS Bulletin*, 33(4): 1–11.

Drèze, J. (1990) 'Famine prevention in India', in J. Drèze and A. Sen (eds), *The Political Economy of Hunger, Volume 2: Famine Prevention*, Oxford: Clarendon Press.

Drèze, J. and Sen, A. (1989) *Hunger and Public Action*, Oxford: Clarendon Press.

Duffield, M. (1994a) 'The political economy of internal war: asset transfer, complex emergencies and international aid', in J. Macrae and A. Zwi (eds), *War and Hunger*, London: Zed Books.

Duffield, M. (1994b) 'Complex emergencies and the crisis of developmentalism', *IDS Bulletin*, 25(4): 37–45.

Duffield, M. (2001) *Global Governance and the New Wars: the Merging of Development and Security*, London: Zed Books.

Edkins, J. (1996) '"Legality with a vengeance": famines and humanitarian relief in "complex emergencies"', *Millennium: Journal of International Studies*, 25(3): 547–75.

Embassy of Brazil in UK (2004) 'Zero Hunger Programme overview' (available at www.brazil.org.uk, accessed 9 November 2004).

Feminist Daily News Wire (2002) 'Humanitarian relief prevents famine in Afghanistan', 2 January 2002 (available at www.feminist.org/news, accessed 24 October 2004).

Fine, B. (1997) 'Entitlement failure?', *Development and Change*, 28(4): 617–47.

Food and Agricultural Organization (FAO) (2003) *The State of Food Insecurity in the World 2003*, Rome: FAO.

Ford, N. and Davis, A. (2001) 'Chaos in Afghanistan: famine, aid, and bombs', 11 November 2001 (available at www.msf.org, accessed 24 October 2004).

Gazdar, H. (2002) 'Pre-modern, modern, and post-modern famine in Iraq', *IDS Bulletin*, 33(4): 63–9.

Gaventa, J., Shankland, A. and Howard, J. (eds) (2002) 'Making rights real: exploring citizenship, participation and accountability', *IDS Bulletin* 33(2).

Hardin, G. (1974) 'Lifeboat ethics: the case against helping the poor', *Psychology Today*, September (reprinted in W. Aiken and H. LaFollette (eds), *World Hunger and Morality*, 2nd edn, 1995, Saddle River: Prentice Hall).

Howe, P. (2002) 'Through the looking-glass: 'hidden' famines, 'unexpected' famines, and the changing global context', mimeo, Brighton: Institute of Development Studies.

Howe, P. (2004) 'Contesting "famine": a study of definitional ambiguities and their implications for response and accountability in Southern Sudan', DPhil thesis, Brighton: Institute of Development Studies.

Howe, P. and Devereux, S. (2002) 'Towards an operational definition of famine', mimeo, Brighton: Institute of Development Studies.

Howe, P. and Devereux, S. (2004) 'Famine intensity and magnitude scales: a proposal for an instrumental definition of famine', *Disasters*, 28(4): 353–72.

Hsiao, S. (1997) 'NGOs, relief organizations, nonprofits join forces for television advocacy campaign on North Korea famine', 6 May 1997 (available at www.worldvision.org, accessed 1 November 2004).

Human Rights Watch (1999) *Famine in Sudan, 1998: The Human Rights Causes*, London: Human Rights Watch.

Institute of Development Studies (IDS) (2000) 'Theories, critiques and ideals of participation' (available at www.ids.ac.uk/ids/particip/research/critiques, accessed 4 April 2005).

Institute of Development Studies (IDS) (2002) *Learning the Lessons? Famine in Ethiopia, 1999–2000*, video, London: Rockhopper Productions.

International Development Committee, House of Commons (2003) *The Humanitarian Crisis in Southern Africa: Third Report of Session 2002–2003, Volume I*, London: The Stationery Office Ltd.

Johnson, D. (2003) *The Root Causes of Sudan's Civil Wars*, Oxford: James Currey and The International African Institute.

Kaldor, M. (1998) *New and Old Wars: Organized Violence in a Global Era*, Cambridge: Polity Press.

Kates, R. and Millman, S., 1990, 'On ending hunger: the lessons of history', in L. Newman (ed.), *Hunger in History: Food Shortage, Poverty, and Deprivation*, Oxford: Basil Blackwell.

Keeley, J. and Scoones, I. (1999) 'Understanding environmental policy processes: a review', *IDS Working Paper* 89, Brighton: Institute of Development Studies.

Keen, D. (1994a) *The Benefits of Famine: A Political Economy of Famine and Relief in Southwestern Sudan, 1983–1989*, Princeton, NJ: Princeton University Press.

Keen, D. (1994b) 'The functions of famine in Southwestern Sudan: implications for relief' in J. Macrae and A. Zwi (eds), *War and Hunger*, London: Zed Books.

Keen, D. (1999) 'Making famine in Sudan', *Field Exchange*, 6: 6–7.

King, S. (2002) 'Malawi food shortage: how did it happen and how could it have been prevented?', *Field Exchange*, 16: 21–2.

Lautze, S. (1997) *The famine in North Korea: Humanitarian Responses in Communist Nations*, Medford: Feinstein International Famine Center.

Macrae, J. and Zwi, A. (eds) (1994) *War and Hunger: Rethinking International Responses to Complex Emergencies*, London: Zed Books.

Marcus, D. (2003) 'Famine crimes in international law', *American Journal of International Law*, 97(2): 245–81.

Maxwell, D. (2002) 'Why do famines persist? A brief review of Ethiopia 1999–2000', *IDS Bulletin*, 33(4): 48–54.

Millman, S. and Kates, R. (1990) 'Toward understanding hunger', in L. Newman (ed.), *Hunger in History: Food Shortage, Poverty, and Deprivation*, Oxford: Basil Blackwell.

Mitchell, J. and Doane, D. (1999) 'An ombudsman for humanitarian assistance?', *Disasters*, 23(2): 115–24.

Natsios, A. (1997) 'Feed North Korea: don't play politics with hunger', *Washington Post*, 7 February.

Natsios, A. (2001) *The Great North Korean Famine: Famine, Politics, and Foreign Policy*, Washington, DC: United States Institute for Peace Press.

Noland, M., Robinson, S. and Wang, T. (1999) 'Famine in North Korea: causes and cures', *Institute for International Economics (IIE) Working Paper* 99–2. Washington, DC (available at www.iie.com/publications/wp/1999/99-2.pdf, accessed 9 November 2004).

Olsen, G. R., Carstensen, N. and Hoyen, K. (2002) 'Humanitarian crises: what determines the level of emergency assistance? Media coverage, donor interests, and the aid business', Paper presented at 'Forgotten Humanitarian Crises: Conference on the Role of the Media, Decision-makers and Humanitarian Agencies', 23 October, Copenhagen.

Online NewsHour (2001) 'Aiding Afghanistan', 5 October 2001 (available at www.pbs.org/newshour, accessed 24 October 2004).

Oxfam (2002) 'Update on Afghanistan', 14 January 2002 (available at www.oxfam.ca/news/Afghanistan, accessed 24 October 2004).

Paddock, W. and P. Paddock (1967) *Famine – 1975! America's Decision: Who Will Survive?* Boston: Little, Brown and Co.

Republic of Sierra Leone (2001) *Interim Poverty Reduction Strategy Paper,* June 2001 (available at www.poverty.worldbank.org/files/Sierra_Leone_IPRSP, accessed 4 April 2005).

Sen, A. (1981) *Poverty and Famines: An Essay on Entitlement and Deprivation*, Oxford: Clarendon Press.

Sen, A. (1999) *Development as Freedom*, New York, NY: Alfred A. Knopf.

Shah, P. and Shah, M. K. (1995) 'Participatory methods: precipitating or avoiding conflict?', *PLA Notes*, 24: 48–59.

Singh, K. S. (1993) 'The famine code: the context and continuity', in J. Floud and A. Rangasami (eds), *Famine and Society*, New Delhi: Indian Law Institute.

Spillius, A. (2001) 'Agencies round on Short over her 'publicity seeking' jibe', 19 October 2001, *Telegraph* (available at www.telegraph.co.uk/news, accessed 9 November 2004).

SRRA Database and Monitoring Office (1998) 'Report on a looming human tragedy in Bahr el Ghazal region', mimeo, Nairobi: SRRA.

Swift, J. (1989) 'Why are rural people vulnerable to famine?', *IDS Bulletin*, 20: 8–15.

Task Force (1998) 'SPLM/SRRA-OLS joint targeting and vulnerabilities task force final report', mimeo, Nairobi: Operation Lifeline Sudan.

UN (1998) *United Nations Consolidated Inter-Agency Appeal for Sudan, January – December 1998*, Geneva: UN.

UN (2004) 'UN Millennium Development Goals (MDG)' (available at www.un.org/millenniumgoals, accessed 9 November 2004).

US Embassy, Tokyo, Japan (2001) 'USAID Head stresses urgency of aid delivery to Afghanistan' (available at www.japan.usembassy.gov, accessed 24 October 2004).

Watson, F. (2002) 'Why are there no longer "war famines" in contemporary Europe? The case of the besieged areas of Bosnia 1992–5', *IDS Bulletin*, 33(4): 39–47.

WFP (1997) *1997 Annual Needs Assessment*, Lokichoggio: WFP.

WFP (2001) 'Afghanistan facing famine, millions of lives at risk', 3 July 2001 (available at www.wfp.org/newsroom, accessed 24 October 2004).

WFP (2003) *Strategic Plan (2004–2007)* (available at www.wfp.org/eb, accessed 4 November 2004).

World Bank (2004) 'Poverty reduction strategies and PRSPs: PRSP document library' (available at www.Poverty.worldbank.org/prsp, accessed 9 November 2004).

Index

Page numbers in *italics* refer to illustrations.